To Alex, Kath & Grace –

for allowing me to stay with you during my recent visit! I trust this book will serve you for many years to come!

Lew
25 Nov 2011

DOCUMENTS THAT SHAPED AUSTRALIA

Published in 2010 by Pier 9, an imprint of Murdoch Books Pty Limited

Murdoch Books Australia
Pier 8/9
23 Hickson Road
Millers Point NSW 2000
Phone: +61 (0) 2 8220 2000
Fax: +61 (0) 2 8220 2558
www.murdochbooks.com.au

Murdoch Books UK Limited
Erico House, 6th Floor
93–99 Upper Richmond Road
Putney, London SW15 2TG
Phone: +44 (0) 20 8785 5995
Fax: +44 (0) 20 8785 5985
www.murdochbooks.co.uk

Publisher: Diana Hill
Project Editor: Sophia Oravecz
Copy Editor and Indexer: Meryl Potter
Designer: Emilia Toia
Picture Researcher: Amanda McKittrick

Commissioned text copyright © John Thompson
Design copyright © Murdoch Books Pty Limited 2010

Every reasonable effort has been made to trace the owners of copyright materials in this book, but in some instances this has proven impossible. The author and publisher will be glad to receive information leading to more complete acknowledgements in subsequent printings of the book and in the meantime extend their apologies for any omissions.

All rights reserved. No part of this publication may be reproduced, stored in a retrieval system or transmitted in any form or by any means, electronic, mechanical, photocopying, recording or otherwise, without the prior written permission of the publisher.

National Library of Australia Cataloguing-in-Publication Data
Author: Thompson, John (John Robert), 1947–
Title: Documents that shaped Australia : records of a nation's
                heritage / John Thompson.
ISBN: 9781741965421 (hbk.)
Notes: Includes index. Bibliography.
Subjects: Australia—History—Sources
Dewey Number: 994

A catalogue record for this book is available from the British Library.

PRINTED IN CHINA. Reprinted 2011.

Warning: This book may contain the names and images of Aboriginal and Torres Strait Islander people now deceased.
Cover map: Australia, according to proposed divisions of 1838. *Journal of the Royal Geographical Society*, vol. 8, 1838.

DOCUMENTS THAT SHAPED AUSTRALIA

Records of a Nation's Heritage

JOHN THOMPSON

Contents

Introduction viii

1516	First report of the Southern Cross	2
1768	The secret instructions for James Cook	5
1770	Joseph Banks at Botany Bay	9
1770	James Cook claims New South Wales for the British Crown	13
1779	Joseph Banks promotes the idea of a settlement in New South Wales	17
1783	James Matra's proposal for a settlement	20
1786	Governor Phillip's first commission	25
1787	Arthur Phillip on the treatment of convicts in the new colony	27
1787	Governor Phillip's second commission	31
1787	Phillip's instructions	36
1787	New South Wales Courts Act	44
1787	Charter of Justice	47
1788	The arrival of the First Fleet	52
1796	A trio of theatre performances in Sydney	56
1813	Matthew Flinders writes to Sir Joseph Banks	58
1814	First crossing of the Blue Mountains	61
1817	A charter for banking in Australia	64
1819	The Bigge Report	67
1823	William Charles Wentworth's poem *Australasia*	70
1824	Wentworth and Wardell create the *Australian* newspaper	74
1828	Instructions to take possession of Western Australia	78
1828	A declaration of martial law in Van Diemen's Land	81
1829	An Act for the government of His Majesty's settlements in Western Australia	85
1835	John Batman's Melbourne deed	88
1835	John Batman and the founding of Melbourne	92
1835	Governor Richard Bourke's proclamation	95
1836	The *Church Act*	98
1836	Proclaiming the province of South Australia	101
1839	Thomas Mitchell describes the country of Victoria	103
1840	Ending the transportation of convicts to New South Wales	106
1846	A petition of the free Aborigines of Van Diemen's Land	109
1850	An Act to incorporate and endow the University of Sydney	112
1852	William Howitt's advice to emigrants and gold seekers	116
1852	The Diggers' Ten Commandments	120
1853	The Bendigo Goldfields Petition	124
1859	Rules of the Melbourne Football Club	128
1860	John McDouall Stuart plants the British flag	132
1860	Robert O'Hara Burke's speech and the last letter of William John Wills	134
1872	Joining the Overland Telegraph Line between Adelaide and Port Darwin	138
1878	A new anthem: 'Advance Australia Fair'	140
1879	Ned Kelly's Jerilderie Letter	143
1882	The legend of the Ashes	148
1888	A newspaper for women	150
1889	The 9 × 5 Impression Exhibition in Melbourne	152
1890	Sir Henry Parkes addresses the Federation Conference	156
1890	Andrew Barton 'Banjo' Paterson's 'The Man from Snowy River'	160
1891	Bushmen's Official Proclamation	165
1891	The Monster Petition in Victoria	170
1895	'Waltzing Matilda'	173
1895	Female suffrage in South Australia	177
1899	Creating the Mitchell Library	180
1900	*Commonwealth of Australia Constitution Act*	182

1900	Instructions for the inauguration of the Commonwealth of Australia 186
1900	The office of Governor-General and Commander-in-Chief of the Commonwealth of Australia 190
1900	Edmund Barton's speech on a new Australian Commonwealth 194
1901	A national flag for Australia 199
1901	Miles Franklin's *My Brilliant Career* 202
1901	*Immigration Restriction Act* 204
1904	Alfred Felton's bequest 206
1907	The Harvester judgment 209
1908	Dorothea Mackellar's Australia 212
1908	An Act to determine the Seat of Government of the Commonwealth 215
1911	Douglas Mawson's ambitions for the Antarctic expedition of 1911–14 218
1915	The first published account of the Anzac landing 220
1915	Keith Murdoch's letter to Prime Minister Andrew Fisher 224
1916	John Monash describes the first Anzac Day 231
1931	The Premiers' Plan 233
1933	The Bodyline Tests 236
1938	Australia Day conference of Australian Aboriginal people 238
1939	Royal Commission into the Victorian bushfires 242
1939	Robert Menzies declares war against Germany 246
1941	John Curtin declares war against Japan 251
1941	John Curtin's New Year message 254
1942	Robert Menzies' appeal to the middle class 258
1943	Enid Lyons delivers her maiden speech in federal Parliament 265
1945	Ben Chifley's radio address 269
1949	Ben Chifley's address to the Labor Party 272
1951	The ANZUS Treaty 274
1954	The Miles Franklin Award for Australian literature 279
1954	Premier J.J. Cahill plans an opera house for Australia 281
1959	The Antipodean Manifesto 284
1963	The bark petition of the Yolngu people 287
1964	Rupert Murdoch launches the *Australian* 290
1965	Australia enters the war in Vietnam 293
1967	The case of Ronald Ryan 295
1967	The referendum on altering the Australian Constitution 299
1972	Gough Whitlam launches the ALP election campaign 302
1972	A letter to the *Age* 304
1975	The Australia Council Charter 306
1975	Gough Whitlam and Vincent Lingiari meet at Daguragu 308
1975	*Racial Discrimination Act* 311
1975	The dismissal of Gough Whitlam's Labor government 314
1985	Lindy Chamberlain pleads for justice 318
1986	*Australia Act* 321
1991	A charter for the Special Broadcasting Service (SBS) 325
1992	*Terra nullius*, land rights and *Mabo* 327
1997	*Bringing Them Home* report 330
2001	John Howard's election policy speech 334
2006	A charter of human rights and responsibilities 336
2008	A national apology to the Stolen Generations 338

Acknowledgments 350

Picture credits 351

Sources 352

Note on texts 359

Index 360

ABOVE *General chart from 1814 of Terra Australis showing the parts explored between 1798 and 1803 by Matthew Flinders.*

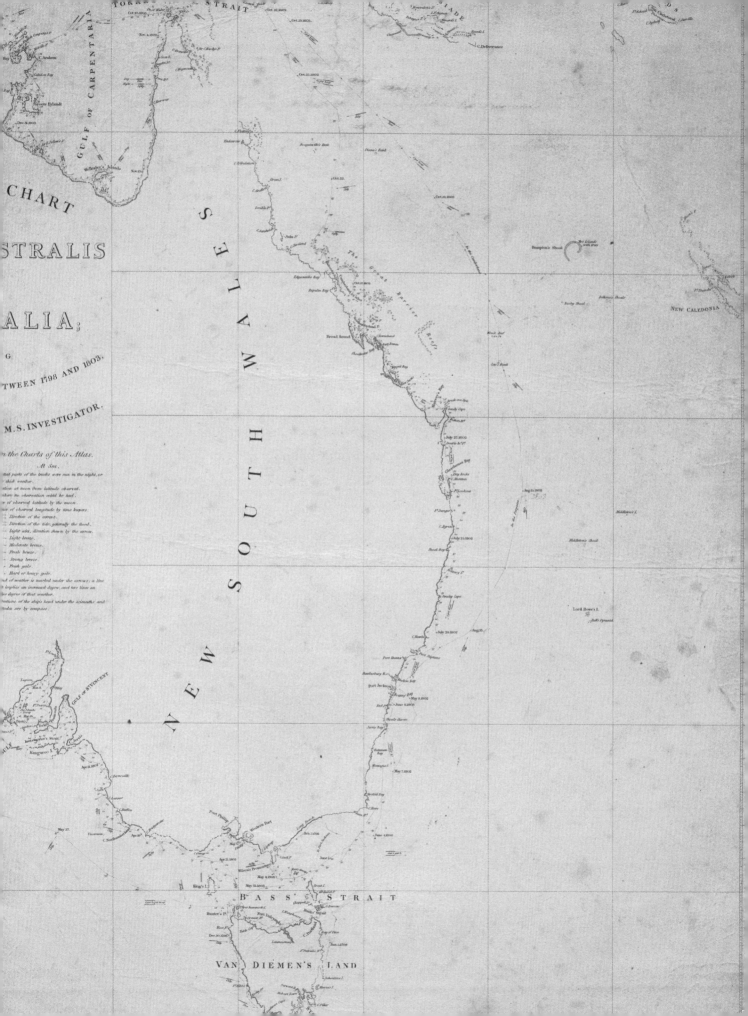

Introduction

In the year of grace 1788, in the heat of an Australian summer, two official ceremonies marked the beginnings of European settlement in Australia. The first took place on 26 January. It was little more than the modest hoisting of the British flag in the raw camp at Sydney Cove, selected by Governor Arthur Phillip only days after the safe arrival of his convict flotilla at Botany Bay. Generations of Australians in summer holiday mode have continued to commemorate that first flag raising: officially, 26 January is designated as Australia Day. Others know it differently: for them it is remembered as Invasion Day or the Aboriginal Day of Mourning.

A second and more elaborate ceremony was held on 7 February. It marked 'the memorable day which established a regular form of Government on the coast of New South Wales'. Strangely, this day of high purpose and stern resolve is not especially remembered in Australia, and no act of public observance recalls the occasion. But it is the day when the new authority of British power was asserted with some fitting pomp and ceremony. Martial music was played on fifes and drums and the judge-advocate read out two important official documents. One was the commission conferring on the new governor an extraordinary range of powers over the lives of those committed to his charge. The other document was the commission to constitute the courts of civil, military and criminal jurisdiction in the new territory. The governor then addressed his convict audience. Phillip's words that day do not survive—there is no document though, in the words of the young Watkin Tench, a member of the marine corps, we are told that '[the governor's] pointed and judicious speech' promised a regime of discipline and order where 'the rigour of the law [would] take its course against such as might dare to transgress the bounds prescribed'.

The ceremonial day of 7 February 1788 was not only about beginnings. Like the flag raising of 26 January, it marked what historian Grace Karskens has described as the almost instantaneous dispossession of the Aboriginal people from their country: 'the fatal turning point, where black "prehistory" is neatly sheared off so that the white "history" of city-making can begin'. Those who gathered on that February day were unknowing and probably indifferent to that fate as they contemplated their own survival in the isolation of a strange new land. But an understanding of sorts has come with time and with it there has evolved a national impulse to seek a just reconciliation between peoples, officially acknowledged some 220 years later in a formal national apology.

While the events of that distant February day have found no special place in the national memory, the documents read to the gathering of convicts, officers and men survive in the printed record. Their interest is such that they deserve to be better known and to be read as part of a spectrum of other historical documents that contribute to an understanding of some key moments in the nation's history. It is that idea that informs the choices made in this anthology of what has evolved as a collection of a hundred *Documents that Shaped Australia*.

The two documents surviving from the foundation year of 1788 are not the first Australian documents. Many others precede them, some reflecting the preparations for Captain James Cook's journey of exploration up the east coast of the continent in 1770, and others providing an insight into the preparations for settling Australia. Some of those early documents set the scene for the establishment of European settlement and offer some insight into the disruption that settlement caused to those already living in the country. If a single theme emerges in this book, it is the reminder that the dispossession of 1788 has cast a long shadow over the Australian polity.

This anthology was conceived in response to a perception that Australians lack a reverence for, or even an awareness of, some of the key historical documents signposting the evolution of our country from a remote convict settlement to a fully fledged nation. We envisaged a book that might look at the Australian past through a selection of documents that defined some of the key moments of the nation's history or that might touch in some memorable way on issues of particular historical significance or sensitivity. Were there any documents in Australia's historical tradition that might be compared with some of the great examples offered by the United States: the Declaration of Independence of 1776; or Abraham Lincoln's Emancipation Proclamation of January 1863, freeing the American slaves; or yet again Lincoln's brief address delivered at the dedication of America's first national military cemetery at Gettysburg?

But, unlike the United States, there is no national consensus that enshrines a canon of historical documents or their words as part of the collective Australian memory. Indeed it is only since the centenary of Federation in 2001 that the National Archives of Australia in Canberra has made a special feature of Australia's constitutional history in its specially named Federation Gallery. There, a selection of the nation's principal constitutional documents, including the *Commonwealth of Australia Constitution Act* and its Royal Commission of Assent and the Letters Patent establishing the office of governor-general, is now on permanent view. While this innovation has given a welcome prominence to documents that charted Australia's journey towards the founding ideal of the Australian Commonwealth—and with others marking later constitutional developments—the awareness of a broader Australian documentary heritage is limited.

Laconic, irreverent—and shy—Australians have seemed reluctant to set much store by grand statement or gesture: even the nation's Constitution, arguably the supreme 'shaping' document, is bereft of any uplifting preamble or any statement of civilising principle of the kind that confers distinction on its American counterpart. And while in Washington, DC entire passages drawn from some of the nation's most inspirational documents have been incised in stone or lettered in bronze to be read as an integral part of the capital's monuments and to reinforce the American nation's most noble ideas and aspirations, Canberra walls and public spaces, save for the intensely poignant Roll of Honour at the Australian War Memorial, are largely mute and bare.

It is only on Anzac Day, Australia's single occasion of supreme introspection, that texts have been accorded a special place in the rituals of remembrance held around the country, from the national observance in Canberra to more intimate services held at country war memorials and at Australian war cemeteries abroad. For these occasions, large and small, wherever they take place, two texts share a place of honour. But only one of these, the 'Anzac Requiem' or more simply 'The Requiem' as it is now called, has its roots directly in Australian experience. The other is a borrowing from England—the fourth stanza from Laurence Binyon's poem 'For the Fallen', which famously offers both consolation and a paradox:

> They shall not grow old, as we that are left grow old.
> Age shall not weary them, nor the years condemn.
> At the going down of the sun and in the morning
> We will remember them.

When it was first published in *The Times* in London in September 1914, Binyon's poem won immediate popularity both in England and in the wider British

Empire. In time, when memorials began to be raised to honour the fallen of the Great War, lines and phrases from Binyon's most inspired and felicitous stanza found an enduring place in inscriptions throughout the empire, including Australia, where it remains an unusually honoured and widely loved text, though its origins as part of Binyon's longer poem are little known.

The original words of the 'Anzac Requiem' were composed by the Australian war historian, C.E.W. Bean, and delivered for the first time at the national Anzac Day services in Canberra in 1944. Like Binyon's poem in 1914, the Requiem was an immediate success, and soon after it began to be incorporated into the Anzac Day liturgy in other parts of Australia. Bean himself had been a war correspondent and present at the original landing at Gallipoli on 25 April 1915. There was both an austere beauty and a particularity in his remembrance of 'those who still sleep where they were left—amid the holly scrub in the valleys and on the ridges of Gallipoli—on the rocky and terraced hills of Palestine—and in the lovely cemeteries of France'. But in time Bean's words were modified and adapted to acknowledge Australian military sacrifices in other wars and other places, and to embrace Australia's participation in the wider and more generalised mission of international peacekeeping. It is true that in the later refashioning of Bean's noble Requiem to the Anzac dead and those who served with them, a necessary recognition has been given to those who fought in other conflicts, but there is no single time-honoured Australian document that belongs to the ages. In the several revisions and adjustments that have been made to Bean's version of the Requiem, much of its original grace and beauty has been lost. So too is the direct connection to Gallipoli established in the person of Bean himself. His felicitous authorship created a document that existed briefly as a national statement of loss and mourning, and as one man's personal witness to a determination in battle that has come to define some of the best attributes of the nation's character.

As I commenced my journey of selection, it quickly became clear that the task involved some particular challenges. The most obviously pressing was to decide just how I might work with the rather vague term 'document'. While its meaning is immediately clear to historians, it is perhaps less so to general readers. But from the outset, I chose to give the term a wide meaning and to draw on a diverse range of historical texts: journal and diary entries; official commissions; charters and proclamations; speeches of various kinds; letters and cables; newspaper editorials, press announcements and despatches written by journalists; petitions; acts of Parliament; court judgements; and manifestos. The selection as it was finally made includes words from the will of author Miles Franklin, establishing her prize for Australian literature, and the text of the well-known ANZUS Treaty that joins the United States and Australia in a strategic alliance.

And there are other less conventional choices. These range from the national anthem 'Advance Australia Fair', presented in its original self-conscious nineteenth-century form as an almost instantly popular patriotic song, to a single lapidary inscription—the words incised on the monument built to honour the pioneers of the Overland Telegraph Line. An early inclusion was an extract from W.C. Wentworth's poem 'Australasia', published in 1823 and significant as one of the earliest literary expressions of national pride and a young man's prophecy of future Australian greatness. In similar mode, it seemed important to include an early version of the greatly loved words of Dorothea Mackellar's poem 'My Country' (written originally as 'Core of my Heart'), with its assertion of love for Australia's demanding and challenging geography and seasons in clear preference to

England's 'ordered woods and gardens'. Once known by heart by generations of Australians, this poem seemed to me to have been in its time every bit as powerful a 'shaping' document of Australian experience and sensibility as, say, the declarations of war and peace made in succession by prime ministers R.G. Menzies, John Curtin and Ben Chifley in 1939–1945—documents that stand in the traditional form and command attention by virtue of the historical circumstances that brought them into being.

But how to make readable and appealing choices from the plethora of possibilities, many of them documents written in archaic English and many of them dependent for comprehension on a specialist understanding of law or history? In this I was both helped and hindered by the work of two previous and distinguished anthologists. My own introduction to Australian history had been enlivened by the use of two collections of Australian documents. The first and most exciting—because it broke new ground and offered a vision of something greater—was Manning Clark's pioneering two-volume *Select Documents in Australian History* (1950–1955), which presented an abundant range of material illustrating the period 1788–1900. During the 1950s and 1960s, especially, Clark's two volumes, together with his *Sources of Australian History* (1957), had opened up to a more critical reading the then little-explored world of Australian history. Clark later built on the groundwork he had laid in his anthologies to construct his own original and powerful *A History of Australia*, published in six volumes between 1962 and 1987, which contributed significantly to building an audience for Australian history not only in schools and universities but also with the wider reading public.

Clark's documents were followed in 1973 by the work of historian F.K. Crowley, whose *Modern Australia in Documents*, published in five volumes, offered a dense portrait of Australia for the years from Federation in 1901 to 1970. Both Clark's and Crowley's compilations assembled hundreds of documents of many different sorts, some of them complete and others presented as extracts. Both too had been constructed principally with the interests of students in mind. My task was to distil and focus, to select a smaller range of material that might yet speak to larger themes or point the way to some sort of understanding of Australia's past as well as its evolution to its present state.

As a manuscripts curator in Melbourne and Canberra, I had contributed my own small part towards building and maintaining the nation's diverse documentary heritage. It is no exaggeration to say that the public accumulation of Australia's documentary heritage is vast and difficult to quantify. It is represented in a range of specialist research archives and collections in Australia and overseas, principally in Britain. The Australian repositories are wide-ranging and specialised, and their collections are abundant. They include imposing national institutions such as the National Archives of Australia, the National Library of Australia and the Australian War Memorial, together with the various state libraries, including the supremely important Mitchell Library collection in the State Library of New South Wales and the Australian Manuscripts Collection in the State Library of Victoria. Collections also reside in specialist repositories, such as those of the National Film and Sound Archive, the Australian Institute of Aboriginal and Torres Strait Islander Studies in Canberra and a number of university archival collections. Also important are the rich archival holdings relating to Australian art in the Research Library of the Art Gallery of New South Wales and the extensive collections of the Performing Arts Museum in Melbourne.

Almost from the outset I decided to frame the choices for this anthology with two singular symbolic statements.

The first was from a time long before the European settlement of Australia, but, other than by association, it was not an Australian document at all. It is the letter of 1515 written by the Italian sailor Andrea Corsali to his patron Guiliano de Medici, offering the first European depiction of the constellation of stars Australians call the Southern Cross. This link to what Corsali lyrically described as 'a marveylous order of starres' made the inclusion of this document irresistible, recognising the later enthusiastic adoption of the Southern Cross as the national symbol of Australia. That symbol is honoured equally on the national flag and the old Eureka flag of 1854, which still has a following of its own as an assertion of Australian independence and as a statement of protest.

Even as I began my work, the final choice of framing document was the national apology, which was then newly minted. It was perhaps not yet so much a 'shaping' document as one that looked back over Australia's difficult compact with its Indigenous peoples, but it seemed to be an essential inclusion, even though some have objected that the speech was high in rhetoric while offering nothing to Aboriginal Australians by way of material compensation for their collective pain and suffering since European settlement. But symbols too are important. A national apology had long been sought and in some quarters (largely for conscientious reasons) it had been fiercely resisted. For many Australians—and especially for Aboriginal Australians—it was received and understood as an essential but overdue expression of national sorrow and contrition both for the specific pain experienced by the so-called Stolen Generations, to whom it was principally addressed, and—by implication—for the larger pain of the original dispossession. It was seen by many to be the necessary prerequisite for the negotiation of a reconciliation between Black and White Australia.

If the apology inevitably looked back at the past, it also held out the idealistic hope for a better, richer and more productive future for all Australians.

In between these two 'bookend' documents, the selection ranges from the eighteenth century to the late twentieth century. The choices are arranged in a strict chronological sequence, but with no attempt made to deal comprehensively or substantively with particular thematic treatments of Australian history of the kind offered previously by Manning Clark and F.K. Crowley, or in Sally Warhaft's more recent and richly absorbing anthology of Australian speechmaking *Well May we Say ... The Speeches That Made Australia* of 2004. While debts are owed to each of these writers for particular ideas and choices of material, the selection made here is different and frankly eclectic, though it has always been made with an eye to the major strands of Australian history and to the inclusion of material from all of the Australian states and territories. By and large each choice stands alone, though there are occasional loose groupings, such as the body of documents that touch on the first European discovery and subsequent settlement of the east coast of Australia, or those that relate to the federation of Australia towards the end of the nineteenth century and in the early years of the new millennium. Some of the choices will be well known but others are more subtle—indicators or pointers to some larger movement of history rather than standing as landmarks themselves.

While many of these documents are linked to certain major historical events—the landing of the Anzacs at Gallipoli or the Australian declaration of war against Germany in 1939—others are of a more modest and personal kind, or are offered to present a tangential view of some larger issue or event. For example, William Howitt's letter from the Victorian goldfields in 1852 is not an intrinsically significant historical document. It was one of many such letters deliberately written to provide advice to those at home in England who were tempted to try their luck in Australia, but it is a lively narrative with interesting insights and opinions, and it survives as something of a curiosity. Sitting as it does with the humorous prescriptions for social order of the Diggers' Ten Commandments, or the petition of demands for reform of the goldfields administration issued by the miners at Bendigo not long before the Eureka rebellion, it provides a personal and intimate view of the transforming social upheaval of the Australian gold rushes of the mid-nineteenth century.

In a similar way, the letter written by the young Miles Franklin to *Bulletin* editor J.F. Archibald in 1901 is at once a proud personal announcement of the publication of her precocious novel *My Brilliant Career* and an assertion of a keen sense of national identity that was in flower in newly federated Australia. This private letter did not shape events or set a new course, but it is compelling evidence that something new was stirring in Australia and that the native-born Miles was a distinctive voice of the new Australia. From the same period, Edmund Barton's speech delivered shortly before the formal inauguration of the new Australian Commonwealth is not itself a landmark. The speech is an expressive public articulation, by the man who was soon to become our first prime minister, of what historian Marilyn Lake in 1994 called the 'goal of White Australia' as the founding principle of the country's nationhood. Its inclusion here acknowledges that historical truth, while in the later extract from the *Racial Discrimination Act 1975* there is the recognition that Australians in the later twentieth century eventually found it in themselves to repudiate the country's long tradition of officially sanctioned racism.

In no sense should this diverse and eclectic selection of documents be viewed as a canon. Nor is the selection offered as the 'best' or most significant hundred of the nation's historical documents. The notion that Australia's diverse national history can be distilled into a definitive selection of any set number of documents is as absurd as it is misleading. That history is too dense, complex and interconnected to be reduced to any process that singles out certain individual moments or events, and privileges them with a golden number. While centenaries of various kinds are properly celebrated as milestones—as impressive markers of the accumulated years of an individual's life, of a town or community or of a country—the number 100 is in the end simply that, a number, a convenience, a neat and symmetrical way of ordering experience, of marking time or, in this case, of arranging and presenting material.

Nor is there any proposition advanced here that privileges this selection of documents as being the definitive 'shapers' of Australian experience or identity. But as historians Martin Crotty and David Andrew Roberts have commented recently, 'turning points and crucial moments remain intrinsic to any reflection on the national story'. That unifying logic underpins this selection of documents and suggests a reading of this material, not as hallowed choices, but rather as examples taken across a range of Australian events and historical circumstances—some of crucial national importance but others more intimate and personal—and which represents a diversity of subjects and experience. In the choices made and in the chronological presentation of these documents, readers are invited to share in what Crotty and Roberts have termed a 'critical reflection on the Australian story as a pathway to active citizenship and national maturity'.

In the late 1930s the Australian writer Nettie Palmer worried that there might be some essential lack in the national character: was there, she wondered, 'something missing' in this country—too little interest in the past, no reverence for those who have shown outstanding qualities of mind and spirit? 'When we look back,' she mused in her diary, 'it is on great empty spaces; the significant dead have no memorials; the few statues in our parks are mainly of forgotten grandees and kings.' Palmer thought bleakly that the explanation for all this was that Australians 'have no sense of ourselves as a people, with a yesterday and tomorrow'. But as historian Ken Inglis has shown in *Sacred Places: War Memorials in the Australian Landscape*, his great survey history of Australia's sacred places, even in Palmer's day there was a richer and more complex tradition of national and local memorialising than perhaps she realised or allowed. So it is too with the nation's heritage of the written and spoken word: the documents that are the markers and the expression of this country's history and development, its moments of darkness and its times of shame, its mighty triumphs and its hopes for a richer and better future for the land and its peoples. These exist in a rich and complex abundance. They are the touchstones of the past and the best of them point the way to the future. It is that tradition of memorialising that is honoured and brought into the light in these snapshots of the Australian nation sampled across time and space.

John Thompson

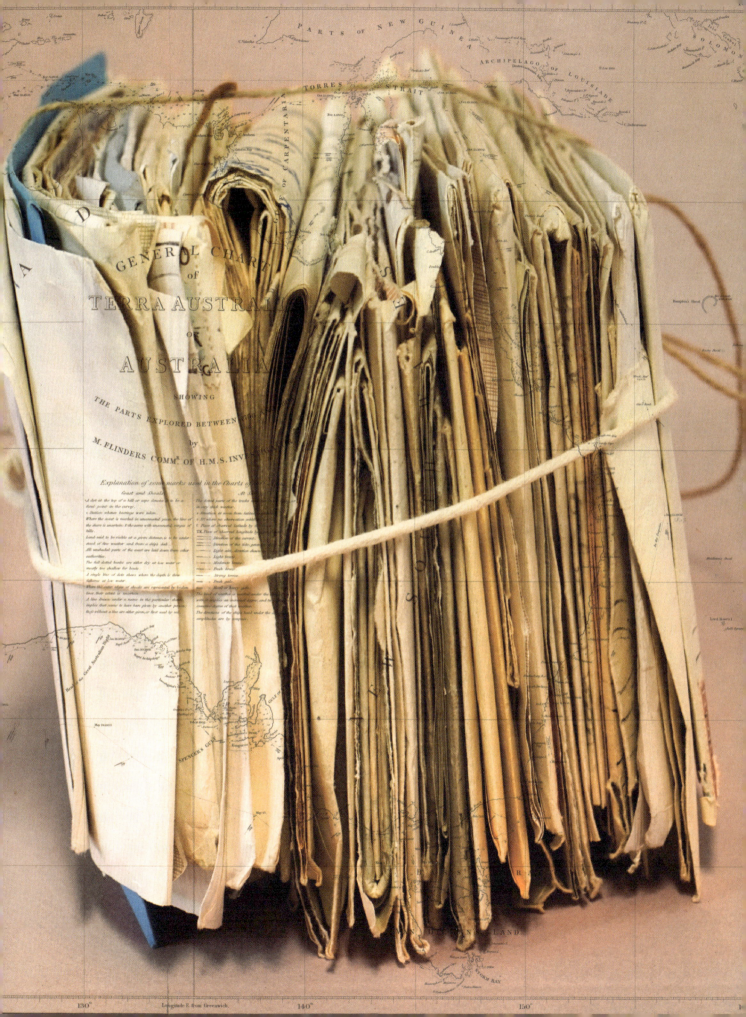

¶ Copia de la litera p. Andrea Corsali mandata alo Serenissimo
Prencipe Duca Juliano de Medici uenuta Dellindia del mese di
Octobre nel X.D.xvj.

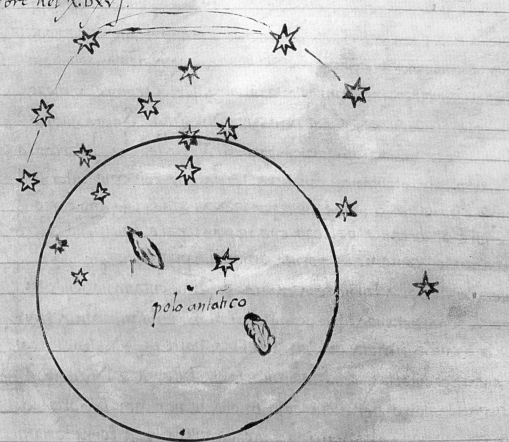

polo antatico

Illustrissimo Signore Unico S. mio Sal. et Racomandatione, &c.

Per obseruare quanto ad V. I. S. ad mia partita promessi di dare
a quella notitia de loci aquali in questo uiaggio mi occorressi perue
nire: Anchora che poco tempo e sono inla India non saranno come è mio
desiderio pigliando V.S. la buona uolunta mia si contentera depsa co
me lasia.

Dapoi nostra partita di clisbona sempre con prospero uento uscendo da
scirocco et libeccio passado lalinea equinoctiale fumo in altura di xxxvij
gradi in laltro hemisphero atrauerso di capo di bona speranza Clima uentoso
et freddo che inquel tepo andaua el sole ne segni septentrionali et troua

'a marveylous order of starres'

FIRST REPORT OF THE SOUTHERN CROSS

In 1515 a young Italian adventurer named Andrea Corsali (b. 1487) accompanied a Portuguese voyage down the African coast, around the Cape of Good Hope, and into the Southern and Indian oceans. After rounding the Cape, Corsali observed the constellation of stars now known as the Southern Cross. At Cochin in southern India he wrote to his patron, Giuliano de Medici, in Florence. His *Lettera*, first published in 1516, was translated into English by Richard Eden in 1555. A fine manuscript copy of the letter, written on vellum by Andrea Gritti, a Venetian scribe, is owned in Australia by the Bruce and Joy Reid Foundation and is on loan to the State Library of New South Wales.

Corsali was not the first person to have sighted what he called 'a marveylous order of starres', but he was the first to describe its distinctive form of a cross and to depict it in a drawing.

In its identification of the Southern Cross, Corsali's description is a document of high importance to Australia, where the constellation has assumed the status of a national symbol. A key marker for navigators, the distinctive pattern of the stars later appealed to the new settlers in Australia. By adoption, the Southern Cross became one of the foundations of Australian nationalism, a symbol of both unity and resistance: it appears on the Australian flag and it was adopted as a symbol of protest and defiance by the Eureka rebels at Ballarat in 1854. In his pioneering history

The Eureka Stockade (1854), Raffaello Carboni described the rebel flag as 'silk, blue ground, with a large silver cross, similar to the one in our southern firmament; no device of arms, but all exceedingly chaste and natural'.

ABOVE *Late fifteenth century portrait of Giuliano de Medici by Sandro Botticelli.*

OPPOSITE *Lettera of Andrea Corsali, sent to his patron Giuliano de Medici in 1516.*

After that we departed from Lisbona, wee sayled ever with prosperous wynde, not passynge owt of the Southeast and Southwest. And passyng beyonde the Equinoctial line, we were in the heyght of 37 degrees of the other halfe circle of the earth. And traversynge the cape of Bona Speranza a coulde and wyndy clime bycause at that tyme the soonne was in the north signes, we founde the nyght of xiii houres. Here we sawe a marveylous order of starres, so that in the parte of heaven contrary to owre northe pole, to knowe in what place and degree the south pole was, we tooke the day with the soonne, and observed the nyght with the Astrolabie, and saw manifestly twoo clowdes of reasonable bygnesse movynge abowt the place of the pole continually nowe rysynge and nowe faulynge, so keepynge theyr continuall course in circular movynge, with a starre ever in the myddest which is turned abowt with them abowte xi degrees frome the pole. Above these appeareth a marveylous crosse in the myddest of fyve notable starres which compasse it abowt (as doth charles wayne the northe pole) with other starres whiche move with them abowt xxx degrees distant from the pole, and make their course in xxiii houres. This crosse is so fayre and bewtiful, that none other hevenly signe may be compared to it as may appeare by this fygure.

Search for the great south land

THE SECRET INSTRUCTIONS FOR JAMES COOK

When James Cook sailed from Plymouth on the afternoon of 26 July 1768, he carried two sets of instructions. His first and public purpose, on behalf of the Royal Society, was to travel south to King Georges Island, modern-day Tahiti, to 'observe the Passage of the Planet Venus over the Disk of the Sun on 3rd June 1769'. The observations were needed to help establish the distance of the sun from the earth. But Cook was also secretly charged with a larger commission to search for *Terra Australis Incognita*, the great southern continent, thought to lie between the Cape of Good Hope and the Straits of Magellan. Dreams of that discovery had long inspired European interest in the Pacific. By the middle of the eighteenth century, Britain had set its sights firmly on the quest to unravel the mysteries of antipodean geography and with, of course, the aim of gaining control of new territory for both trade and strategic use.

Cook arrived in Tahiti on 13 April 1769, seven weeks before the transit was due. Despite some difficulty owing to poor weather, the observations were accurately made.

Cook then turned to his second set of instructions, making his way first to New Zealand, where he mapped the entire coast of the two islands, thus establishing that its northern tip was not in fact 'a part of the imaginary southern continent'. Having failed to locate the supposed great southern landmass, Cook then made what would prove to be the momentous decision to sail home along the unknown eastern coast of New Holland, the name which had been given to the Australian continent by the Dutch explorers in the seventeenth century. He charted the coast and named many landmarks. He made several landings, including at Botany Bay, and he had the first English encounters with the Indigenous inhabitants. The botanical discoveries made by Joseph Banks and Daniel Solander increased the tally of the world's known plant species by 10 per cent. On 22 August 1770, Cook claimed the East Coast of New Holland in the name of King George III and gave it the name New South Wales (see page 13). With Cook's *Endeavour Journal, 1768–1771*, the Additional Instructions is one of Australia's most significant foundation documents.

ABOVE *James Cook depicted in a lithograph by Josef Selb from the 1820s.*

Secret

By the Commissioners for executing the office of Lord High Admiral of Great Britain &c.

Additional Instructions for L^t. James Cook, Appointed to Command His Majesty's Bark the Endeavour.

Whereas the making Discoverys of Countries hitherto unknown, and the Attaining a Knowledge of distant Parts which though formerly discover'd have yet been but imperfectly explored, will redound greatly to the Honour of this Nation as a Maritime Power, as well as to the Dignity of the Crown of Great Britain, and may tend greatly to the advancement of the Trade and Navigation thereof; and Whereas there is reason to imagine that a Continent or Land of great extent, may be found to the Southward of the Tract lately made by Captn Wallis in His Majesty's Ship the Dolphin (of which you will herewith receive a Copy) or of the Tract of any former Navigators in Pursuits of the like kind; You are therefore in Pursuance of His Majesty's Pleasure hereby requir'd and directed to put to Sea with the Bark you Command so soon as the Observation of the Transit of the Planet Venus shall be finished and observe the following Instructions.

You are to proceed to the southward in order to make discovery of the Continent above-mentioned until you arrive in the Latitude 40 degrees, unless you sooner fall in with it. But not having discover'd it or any Evident signs of it in that Run, you are to proceed in search of it to the Westward between the Latitude before mentioned and the Latitude of 35 degrees until you discover it, or fall in with the Eastern side of the Land discover'd by Tasman and now called New Zeland.

If you discover the Continent above-mentioned either in your Run to the Southward or to the Westward as above directed, You are to employ yourself diligently in exploring as great an Extent of the Coast as you can; carefully observing the true situation thereof both in Latitude and Longitude, the Variation of the Needle, bearings of Head Lands, Height, direction and Course of the Tides and Currents, Depths and Soundings of the Sea, Shoals, Rocks &c and also surveying and making Charts, and taking Views of such Bays, Harbours and Parts of the Coast as may be useful to Navigation.

You are also carefully to observe the Nature of the Soil, and the Products thereof; the Beasts and Fowls that inhabit or frequent it; the fishes that are to be found in the Rivers or upon the Coast and in what Plenty; and in case you find any Mines, Minerals or valuable stones you are to bring home Specimens of each, as also such Specimens of the Seeds of the Trees, Fruits and Grains as you may be able to collect, and Transmit them to our Secretary that We may cause proper Examination and Experiments to be made of them.

You are likewise to observe the Genius, Temper, Disposition and Number of the Natives, if there be any, and endeavour by all proper means to cultivate a Friendship and Alliance with them, making them presents of such Trifles as they may Value, inviting them to Traffick, and Shewing them every kind of Civility and Regard; taking Care however not to suffer yourself to be surprised by them, but to be always upon your guard against any Accident.

Secret

By the Comm.rs for executing the Office of Lord High Admiral of G.t Britain &c.

Additional Instructions for Lt James Cook, appointed to command His Maj.ts Bark the Endeavour.

Whereas the making Discoverys of Countries hitherto unknown, & the Attaining a Knowledge of distant Parts which though formerly discover'd have yet been but imperfectly explored, will redound greatly to the Honour of this Nation as a Maritime Power, as well as to the Dignity of the Crown of Great Britain, & may tend greatly to the advancement of the Trade & Navigation thereof; & Whereas there is reason to imagine that a Continent or Land of great extent, may be found to the Southward of the Tract lately made by Cap.tn Wallis in His Maj.ts Ship the Dolphin (of which you will herewith receive a Copy) or of the Track of any former Navigators in Pursuits of the like kind; You are therefore in Pursuance of His Maj.ts Pleasure hereby requir'd & directed to put to Sea with the Bark you Command so soon as the Observation of the Transit of the Planet Venus shall be finished & observe the following Instructions. You are to proceed to the Southward in order to make discovery of the Continent abovementioned until you arrive in the Lat.de of 40°, unless you sooner fall in with it. But not having discover'd it or any Evident signs of it in that Run, you are to proceed in search of it to the Westw.d between the Lat.de beforementioned & the Lat.de of 35° until you discover it, or fall in with the Eastern side of the Land discover'd by Tasman & now called New Zeland.

If you discover the Continent abovementioned either in your Run to the Southw.d or to the Westw.d as above directed, You are to employ yourself diligently in exploring as great an Extent of the Coast as you can; carefully observing the true situation thereof both in Lat.d & Long, the Variation of the Needle, bearings of Head Lands, Height direction & course of the Tides & Currents, Depths & Soundings of the Sea, Shoals, Rocks &c. & also surveying & making Charts, & taking Views of such Bays, Harbours & Parts of the Coast as may be useful to Navigation. You are also carefully to observe the Nature of the Soil, & the Products thereof; the Beasts & Fowls that inhabit or frequent it, the Fishes that are to be found in the Rivers or upon the Coast & in what Plenty; & in case you find any Mines, Minerals, or valuable Stones you are to bring home Specimens of each, as also such Specimens of the Seeds of the Trees, Fruits &

The secret instructions for James Cook.

ABOVE *The first page of the secret instructions issued to James Cook.*

You are also with the Consent of the Natives to take possession of Convenient Situations in the Country in the Name of the King of Great Britain; or, if you find the Country uninhabited take Possession for His Majesty by setting up Proper Marks and Inscriptions, as first discoverers and possessors.

But if you should fail of discovering the Continent before-mention'd, you will upon falling in with New Zeland carefully observe the Latitude and Longitude in which that Land is situated, and explore as much of the Coast as the Condition of the Bark, the health of her Crew, and the State of your Provisions will admit of, having always great Attention to reserve as much of the latter as will enable you to reach some known Port where you may procure a Sufficiency to carry you to England, either around the Cape of Good Hope, or Cape Horn, as from Circumstances you may judge the Most Eligible way of returning home.

You will also observe with accuracy the Situation of such Islands as you may discover in the Course of your Voyage that have not hitherto been discover'd by any Europeans, and take possession for His Majesty and make Surveys and Draughts of such of them as may appear to be of Consequence, without Suffering yourself however to be thereby diverted from the Object which you are always to have in View, the Discovery of the Southern Continent so often Mentioned.

But for as much as in an undertaking of this nature several Emergencies may Arise not to be foreseen, and therefore not particularly to be provided for by Instruction before hand, you are in all such Cases, to proceed, as upon advice with your Officers you shall judge most advantageous to the Service on which you are employed.

You are to send all proper Conveyances to the Secretary of the Royal Society Copys of the Observations you shall have made of the Transit of Venus; and you are at the same time to send to our Secretary, for our information, accounts of your Proceedings, and Copys of the Surveys and drawings you shall have made. And upon your Arrival in England you are immediately to repair to this Office in order to lay before us a full account of your Proceedings in the whole Course of your Voyage, taking care before you leave the Vessel to demand from the Officers and Petty Officers the Log Books and Journals they may have Kept, and to seal them up for our inspection, and enjoyning them, and the whole Crew, not to divulge where they have been until they shall have Permission so to do.

Given under our hands the 30th July 1768

E^d Hawke
Piercy Brett
C. Spencer

By Command of their Lordships
Ph^p Stephens

On a voyage of scientific discovery

JOSEPH BANKS AT BOTANY BAY

Joseph Banks (1743–1820), naturalist and later a distinguished patron of science, left England in 1768 on board the *Endeavour* with Lieutenant James Cook. He had joined the voyage of scientific investigation and discovery at the instigation of the Royal Society, the sponsor of the expedition to observe the transit of Venus. The wealthy Banks was accompanied by a staff of eight, including the naturalists Daniel Solander and H.D. Spöring, and botanical artist Sydney Parkinson. The party made collections and observations throughout the voyage, including during the various landings made on the east coast of Australia.

Despite his first, rather lukewarm, impressions of Botany Bay, Banks later encouraged use of the site as a penal colony, becoming in time the acknowledged authority in England on New South Wales. Over the years he maintained a correspondence with all the governors of the colony from Phillip to Macquarie and received letters from some prominent early colonial personalities, including Ensign Barrallier, Gregory Blaxland, David Collins and Samuel Marsden.

In their respective journals, Cook and Banks provided detailed accounts of their first Australian landing at the place Cook eventually named Botany Bay. Curiously, there is a mismatch between the dating of events described in the two journals. The events described by Banks as taking place on 27–29 April 1770 are dated by Cook to 28–30 April 1770. But otherwise the accounts are similar in detail, though with clear differences of style and emphasis. Both offer factual and essentially descriptive accounts of the crucial first encounter with the Aboriginal people, an event marked from the outset by tension, suspicion and misunderstanding. Shots were fired; gifts were offered but ignored; and the Aborigines were retiring but also constantly alert and watchful. Of one thing Cook was in no doubt: 'all they seem'd to want was for us to be gone'. While Banks' descriptions are less emphatic, they nevertheless point to a fundamental failure in communication that would continue to mark relations between black and white in Australia.

ABOVE *Joseph Banks around the time of his departure for Botany Bay. Engraving by William Dickinson, 1774.*

APRIL 1770

28. The land this morn appeard Cliffy and barren without wood. An opening appearing like a harbour was seen and we stood directly in for it. A small smoak arising from a very barren place directed our glasses that way and we soon saw about 10 people, who on our approach left the fire and retird to a little emminence where they could conveniently see the ship; soon after this two Canoes carrying 2 men each landed on the beach under them, the men hauld up their boats and went to their fellows upon the hill. Our boat which had been sent ahead to sound now approachd the place and they all retird higher up on the hill; we saw however that at the beach or landing place one man at least was hid among some rocks who never that we could see left that place. Our boat proceeded along shore and the Indians followd her at a distance. When she came back the officer who was in her told me that in a cove a little within the harbour they came down to the beach and invited our people to land by many signs and word[s] which he did not at all understand; all however were armd with long pikes and a wooden weapon made something like a short scymetar. During this time a few of the Indians who had not followd the boat remain on the rocks opposite the ship, threatening and menacing with their pikes and swords—two in particular who were painted with white, their faces seemingly only dusted over with it, their bodies painted with broad strokes drawn over their breasts and backs resembling much a soldiers cross belts, and their legs and thighs also with such like broad strokes drawn round them which imitated broad garters or bracelets. Each of these held in his hand a wooden weapon about 2½ feet long, in a shape much resembling a scymeter; the blades of these looked whitish and some though[t] shining insomuch that they were almost of opinion that they were made of some kind of metal, but myself thought they were no more than wood smeard over with the same white pigment with which they paint their bodies. These two seemd to talk earnestly together, at times brandishing their crooked weapons at us in token of defiance. By noon we were within the mouth of the inlet which appeard to be very good. Under the South head of it were four small canoes; in each of these was one man who held in his hand a long pole with which he struck fish, venturing with his little imbarkation almost into the surf. These people seemd to be totaly engag'd in what they were about: the ship passd within a quarter of a mile of them and yet they scarce lifted their eyes from their employment; I was almost inclined to think that attentive to their business and deafned by the noise of the surf they neither saw nor heard her go past them. At 1 we came to an anchor abreast of a small village consisting of about 6 or 8 houses. Soon after this an old woman followd by three children came out of the wood; she carried several peice[s] of stick and the children also had their little burthens; when she came to the houses 3 more younger children came out of one of them to meet her. She often looked at the ship but expressd neither surprize nor concern. Soon after this she lighted a fire and the four Canoes came in from fishing; the people landed, hauld up their boats and began to dress their dinner to all appearance totally unmovd at us, tho we were within a little more than ½ a mile of them. Of all these people we had seen so distinctly through our glasses we had not been able to observe

the least signs of Cloathing: myself to the best of my judgement plainly discernd that the woman did not copy our mother Eve even in the fig leaf.

After dinner the boats were mann'd and we set out from the ship intending to land at the place where we saw these people, hoping that as they regarded the ships coming in to the bay so little they would as little regard our landing. We were is this however mistaken, for as soon as we approachd the rocks two of the men came down upon them, each armd with a lance of about 10 feet long and a short stick which he seemd to handle as if it was a machine to throw the lance. They calld to us very loud in a harsh sounding Language of which neither of us or Tupia [Tupaia, who was a Tahitian who had joined the *Endeavour* during the stopover in Tahiti; he later died of dysentery in Batavia] understood a word, shaking their lances and menacing, in all appearance resolvd to dispute our landing to the utmost tho they were but two and we 30 or 40 at least. In this manner we parleyed with them for about a quarter of an hour, they waving us to be gone, we again signing that we wanted water and that we meant them no harm. They remaind resolute so a musquet was fird over them, the Effect of which was that the Youngest of the two dropd a bundle of lances on the rock at the instant in which he heard the report; he however snatchd them up again and both renewd their threats and opposition. A Musquet loaded with a small shot was now fird at the Eldest of the two who was about 40 yards from the boat; it struck him on the legs but he minded it very little so another was immediately fird at him; on this he ran up to the house about 100 yards distant and soon returned with a sheild. In the mean time we had landed on the rock. He immediately threw a lance at us and the young man another which fell among the thickest of us but hurt nobody; 2 more musquets with small shot were then fird at them on which the Eldest threw one more lance and then ran away as did the other. We went up to the houses, in one of which we found the children hid behind the shield and a peice of bark in one of the houses. We were conscious from the distance the people had been from us when we fird that the shot could have done them no material harm; we therefore resolvd to leave the children on the spot without even opening their shelter. We therefore threw into the house to them some beads, ribbands, cloths &c. as presents and went away. We however thought it no improper measure to take away with us all the lances which we could find about the houses, amounting in number to forty or fifty. They were of various lengths, from 15 to 6 feet in length; both of those which were thrown at us and all we found except one had 4 prongs headed with very sharp fish bones, which were besmeard with a greenish colourd gum that at first gave me some suspicions of Poison. The people were blacker than any we have seen in the Voyage tho by no means negroes; their beards were thick and bushy and they seemed to have a redundancy of hair upon those parts of the body where it commonly grows; the hair of their heads was bushy and thick but by no means wooley like that of a Negro; they were of common size, lean and seemd active and nimble; their voices were coarse and strong. Upon examining the lances we had taken from them we found that the very most of them had been usd in striking fish, at least we concluded so from sea weed which was found stuck in among the four prongs.—Having taken the resolution before mentiond we returnd to the ship in order to get rid of our load of lances, and having done that went to that place at the mouth of the harbour where we had seen the people in the morn; here however we found nobody.—At night many moving lights were seen in different parts of the bay such as we had been usd to see at the Islands; from hence we supposed that the people here strike fish in the same manner.

29. The fires (fishing fires as we supposd) were seen during the greatest part of the night. In the morn we went ashore at the houses, but found not the least good effect from our present yesterday: No signs of people were to be seen; in the house in which the children were yesterday was left every individual thing which we had thrown to them; Dr Solander and myself went a little way into the woods and found many plants, but saw nothing like people. At noon all hands came on board to dinner. The Indians, about 12 in number, as soon as they saw our boat put off Came down to the houses. Close by these was our watering place at which stood our cask: they lookd at them but did not touch them, their business was merely to take away two of four boats which they had left at the houses; this they did, and hauld the other two above high water mark, and then went away as they came. In the Evening 15 of them armd came towards our waterers; they sent two before the rest, our people did the same; they however did not wait for a meeting but gently retird. Our boat was about this time loaded so every body went off in her, and at the same time the Indians went away. Myself with the Cap^tn &c. were in a sandy cove on the Northern side of the harbour, where we hauld the seine and caught many very fine fish, more than all hands could Eat.

'I now ... took possession of the whole Eastern Coast'

JAMES COOK CLAIMS NEW SOUTH WALES FOR THE BRITISH CROWN

Accounts of James Cook's three great voyages of maritime exploration were published immediately after the conclusion of each one, and all of them reached a wide audience in both England itself and Europe. But it was not until the middle years of the twentieth century that the text of Cook's own manuscript journals became available to the reading public. For Australians, the journal of the voyage of the *Endeavour* (1768–1771) is of particular significance, given Cook's momentous landing at the place he called Botany Bay and at several other points along the east coast, including the beaching of the badly damaged vessel at Endeavour River.

The other high point of the journey up the east coast of the Australian mainland is its symbolic (and contentious) culmination in the small ceremony Cook held on 22 August 1770, at a modest outlook on the place he was to call Possession Island. There, at about 6.00 pm, shortly before sunset, Cook 'hoisted English Coulers and in the Name of His Majesty King George the Third took possession of the whole Eastern Coast ... by the name of *New South Wales*'. The landing party fired three volleys of small arms, which were answered by a volley from the *Endeavour*, and so the ceremony concluded. Although Cook and his party could see smoke from numerous cooking fires and had in fact earlier that day witnessed 'a number of People upon this island', the naming ceremony assumed incorrectly that the east coast was a *terra nullius*—literally, unoccupied land. The ramifications of that assumption would be felt in difficult and complex ways by black and white Australians down through the years until its critical scrutiny by the High Court of Australia in its landmark *Mabo* judgment of 1992 (see page 327).

The manuscript of Cook's *Endeavour* journal is held by the National Library of Australia in Canberra, where it has an honoured place as one of the nation's most potent historical documents.

was never seen or visited by any European before us and ~~and therefore by the same title belongs to great~~ Notwithstand I had in the name of His Majesty taken posession of several places upon this coast I now once more hoisted English Colours and in the name of His Majesty King George the Third took posession of the whole Eastern Coast from the above Latitude down to this place by the name of New South Wales together with all the Bays, Harbours Rivers and Islands situate upon the said coast after which we fired three Volleys of small Arms which were Answerd by the like number from the Ship this done we set out for the Ship but were some time in getting on board on account of a very rappid Ebb Tide which set NE out of the Passage ever since we came in among the Shoals this last time. We have found a moderate Tide the flood setting to the NW and Ebb to the SE, at this place it is High-water at the Full and Change of the Moon about 1 or 2 oClock and rises and falls upon a perpendicular about 10 or 12 feet. We saw on all the adjacent Lands and Islands a great number of smookes a certain sign that they are Inhabited and we have dayly seen smookes on every part of the coast we have lately been upon.

Between

ABOVE *James Cook's journal entry for 22 August 1770.*

WEDNESDAY 22*d*. Gentle breezes at EBS and clear weather. We had not stood above 3 or 4 Miles along shore to the westward before we discoverd the Land ahead to be Islands detach'd by several channells from the Main land; upon this we brought too to wait for the yawl and called the other boats on board, and after giving them proper Instructions sent them away again to lead us through the Channell next the Main, and as soon as the yawl was on board made sail with the Ship after them; soon after we discoverd Rocks & shoals in this Channell, upon which I made the Signal for the boats to lead through the next Channell to the Northward laying between the Islands, which they accordingly did we following with the Ship, and had not less than 5 fathom water and this in the narrowest part of the Channell which was about a Mile and a half broad from Island to Island, At 4 oClock we anchor'd about a Mile and a half or 2 Miles within the entrance in 6½ fathom clear ground, distant from the Islands on each side of us one mile, the Main land extending away to the SW, the farthest point of which that we could see bore from us S 48° West and the South-wester-most point of the Islands on the NW side of the Passage bore S 76° West. Between these two points we could see no land so that we were in great hopes that we had at last found a Passage into the Indian Seas, but in order to be better informd I landed with a party of Men accompan'd by Mͬ Banks and Dͬ Solander upon the Island which lies at the SE point of the Passage. Before and after we Anchor'd we saw a number of People upon this Island arm'd in the same manner as all the others we have seen, except one man who had a bow and a bundle of Arrows, the first we have seen on this coast. From the appearance of these People we expected that they would have opposed our landing but as we approachd the Shore they all made off and left us in peaceable posession of as much of the Island as served our purpose. After landing I went upon the highest hill which however was of no great height, yet not less than twice or thrice the height of the Ships Mast heads, but I could see from it no land between SW and WSW so that I did not doubt but what there was a passage. I could see plainly that the Lands laying to the NW of this passage were composed of a number of Islands of various extent both for height and circuit, rainged one behind another as far to the Northward and Westward as I could see, which could not be less than 12 or 14 Leagues. Having satisfied my self of the great Probability of a Passage, thro' which I intend going with the Ship, and therefore may land no more upon this Eastern coast of *New Holland*, and on the Western side I can make no new discovery the honour of which belongs to the Dutch Navigators; but the Eastern Coast from the Latitude of 38° South down to this place I am confident was never seen or visited by any European before us, and Notwithstand[ing] I had in the Name of His Majesty taken posession of several places upon this coast, I now once more hoisted English Coulers and in the Name of His Majesty King George the Third took posession of the whole Eastern Coast from the above Latitude down to this place by the name of *New South Wales* together with all the Bays, Harbours Rivers and Islands situate upon the said coast, after which we fired three Volleys of small Arms which were Answerd by the like number from the Ship. This done we set out for the Ship but some time in getting on board an account of a very rapid Ebb Tide which set NE out of the Passage. Ever since we came in among the Shoals this last time we have found a Moderate Tide the Flood seting to the NW and Ebb to the SE. At this place it is High-water at the Full and Change of the Moon about 1 or 2 o'Clock and riseth and falls upon a perpendicular about 10 or 12 feet. We saw on all the Adjacent Lands and Islands a great number of smooks, a certain sign that they are Inhabited, and we have dayly seen smooks on every part of the coast we have lately been upon.

Between 7 and 8 oClock in the Morning we saw several naked people, all or most of them women, down upon the beach picking up Shells &c, they had not a single rag of any kind of Cloathing upon them and both these and those we saw yesterday were in every respect the Same sort of people we have seen every where upon the Coast; two or three of the Men we saw Yesterday had on pretty large breast plates which we supposed were made of Pearl Oyster Shells, this was a thing as well as the Bow and Arrows we had not seen before.

At Low-water which happened about 10 oClock we got under sail and stood to the SW with a light breeze at East which afterwards veered to NBE, having the Pinnace a head, depth of water from 6 to 10 fathom except in one place where we pass'd over a bank of 5 fathom. At Noon *Posession Island* at the SE entrance of the Passage bore N 53° East distant 4 Leagues, the western extreme of the Main land in sight bore S 43° West distant 4 or 5 Leagues, being all exceeding low. The SW point of the largest Island on the NW side of the Passage bore N 71 degrees West distant 8 miles, this point I named *Cape Cornwell* (Lat. 10°43' S, Longd 219°0') and some Low Islands laying about the Middle of the Passage which I call'd *Wallice's* Isles bore WBS½ S distant about 2 Leagues, our Latitude by Observation was 10° 46' South.

'the Climate is healthy and the Means of Support attainable'

JOSEPH BANKS PROMOTES THE IDEA OF A SETTLEMENT IN NEW SOUTH WALES

While he had delighted in the botanical discoveries made in Australia in 1770, Joseph Banks had not been notably impressed with Botany Bay. Yet nine years later on 1 April 1779, in the persuasive evidence he gave to a Select Committee of the House of Commons, Banks warmly commended it as a place that might sustain and eventually nourish a settlement, albeit one made up of young convicts. There were other proponents of such a settlement in Australia, but particular weight was attached to Banks' views, because he had known the country at first hand in the company of the great navigator James Cook, and his scientific prestige in England was immense. Over the years Banks became an especially keen advocate of matters to do with Australia and for the rest of his life he continued to take an interest in the country and its prospects. Some have called him 'the Father of Australia'.

The advice offered by Banks in 1779 was made in the context of the severe overcrowding of England's prisons and hulks following the loss of the American colonies and the end of transportation to North America. In turn, England's high crime rate and prison overcrowding were the result of a wider economic and social upheaval in the second half of the eighteenth century as the country began the transition from a rural and agricultural economy to an industrial one. The Committee's task was to determine 'how far Transportation [of Felons] might be practicable to other Parts of the World'. Australia's remote location, its healthy climate and the apparently tenuous occupation of the country by a thin peopling of indigenous inhabitants seemed to offer what historian Harold Carter called 'a small white light of hope' to a Committee that had weighed the prospects of such diverse and problematic locations as Senegal, the Gambia and Gibraltar.

For all the larger significance to Australia's future of Joseph Banks' testimony, it is a brief document of 500 words or so. It survives in condensed form in a transcription made from his oral evidence in the *Journal of the House of Commons,* 1779.

Your Committee thought proper, therefore, to examine how far Transportation might be practicable to other Parts of the World:

And

Joseph Banks, Esquire, being requested, in case it should be thought expedient to establish a Colony of convicted Felons in any distant Parts of the Globe, from whence their Escape might be difficult, and where, from the Fertility of the Soil, they might be enabled to maintain themselves, after the First Year, with little or no Aid from the Mother Country, to give his Opinion what Place would be most eligible for such Settlement? Informed your Committee, That the Place which appeared to him best adapted for such a Purpose, was *Botany Bay*, on the coast of *New Holland*, in the *Indian* Ocean, which was about Seven Months Voyage from *England*; that he apprehended there would be little Probability of any Opposition from the Natives, as, during his Stay there, in the Year 1770, he saw very few, and did not think there were above Fifty in all the Neighbourhood, and had Reason to believe the Country was very thinly peopled; those he saw were naked, treacherous, and armed with Lances, but extremely cowardly, and constantly retired from our People when they made the least Appearance of Resistance: He was in this Bay in the End of APRIL and Beginning of MAY 1770, when the Weather was mild and moderate; that the Climate, he apprehended, was similar to that of TOULOUSE, in the South of FRANCE, having found the Southern Hemisphere colder than the Northern, in such Proportion, that any given Climate in the Southern answered to one in the Northern about Ten Degrees nearer to the Pole; the Proportion of rich Soil was small in Comparison to the barren, but sufficient to support a very large Number of People; there were no tame Animals, and he saw no wild Ones during his Stay of Ten Days, but he observed the Dung of what were called KANGOUROUS, which were almost the Size of a middling Sheep, but very swift, and difficult to catch; some of those Animals he saw in another Part of the Bay, upon the same Continent; there were no Beasts of Prey, and he did not doubt but our Oxen and Sheep, if carried there, would thrive and increase; there was great Plenty of Fish, he took a large Quantity by hauling the Seine, and struck several Stingrays, a kind of Skate, all very large; one weighed 336 Pounds. The Grass was long and luxuriant, and there was some eatable Vegetables, particularly a Sort of wild Spinage; the Country was well supplied with Water; there was Abundance of Timber and Fuel, sufficient for any Number of Buildings, which might be found necessary. Being asked How a Colony of that Nature could be subsisted in the Beginning of their Establishment? He answered, They must certainly be furnished at landing, with a full Year's Allowance of Victuals, Raiment, and Drink; with all Kinds of Tools for labouring the Earth, and building Houses; with Black Cattle, Sheep, Hogs, and Poultry; with Seeds of all Kinds of EUROPEAN Corn and Pulse; with Garden Seeds; with Arms and Ammunition for their Defence; and they should likewise have small Boats, Nets, and Fishing-tackle; all of which, except Arms and Ammunition, might be purchased at the CAPE OF GOOD HOPE; and that afterwards, with a moderate Portion of Industry, they might, undoubtedly, maintain themselves without any Assistance from *England*. He recommended sending a large Number of Persons, Two or Three hundred at least; their

Escape would be difficult, as the Country was far distant from any Part of the Globe inhabited by EUROPEANS ... And being asked, Whether he conceived the Mother Country was likely to reap any Benefit from a Colony established in BOTANY BAY? He replied, If the People formed among themselves a Civil Government, they would necessarily increase and find Occasion for many EUROPEAN Commodities; and it was not to be doubted, that a Tract of Land such as *New Holland*, which was larger than the Whole of EUROPE, would furnish Matter of advantageous Return.

[Committee's Recommendations]

That the plan of establishing a Colony or Colonies of young convicts in some distant Part of the Globe, and in new-discovered Countries, where the Climate is healthy, and the Means of Support attainable, is equally agreeable to the Dictates of Humanity and sound Policy, and might prove in the Result advantageous both to Navigation and Commerce.

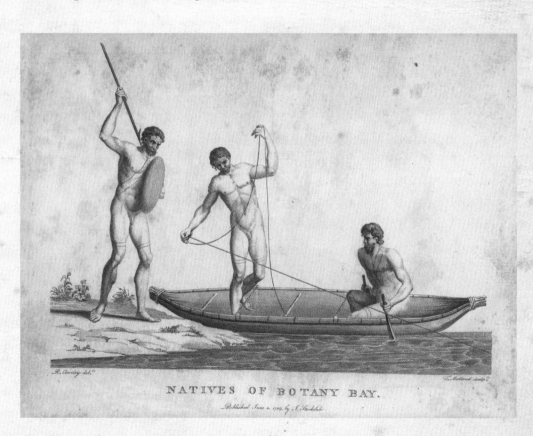

ABOVE *Aboriginal Australians at Botany Bay in an engraving from 4 June 1789.*

1783

'None are more inviting than New South Wales'

JAMES MATRA'S PROPOSAL FOR A SETTLEMENT

James Maria Matra (1746?–1806), sailor and diplomat, had served as a midshipman on board *Endeavour* in Cook's first voyage of 1769–1771. During the journey up the Australian east coast he had incurred Cook's displeasure and a suspension from duty for a shipboard delinquency. Cook noted that Matra was 'one of those gentlemen, frequently found on board Kings Ships, that can very well be spared, or to speake more planer good for nothing'. But during the voyage, Matra became acquainted with Joseph Banks. The two men formed a lasting friendship, united in part by their continuing interest in Australia. That interest would see the two travellers assume a role in informing the considerations that would lead to the founding of European settlement in Australia.

In England, Matra became a leading proponent of the idea of establishing a convict colony at Botany Bay, and his views were sought and noted at the highest levels of government and offered in testimony to a House of Commons Select Committee enquiring into the resumption of transportation (1785). While Matra's proposal certainly reflected the known views and interests of Joseph Banks, his scheme was well considered and clearly argued. Indeed, its guiding spirit was entrepreneurial. American born himself, Matra initially was less interested in the convict question than in providing an opportunity for the settlement of loyalists from the American colonies. He offered an optimistic account of the resources of the new country, its strategic significance and its proximity to New Zealand, with its supplies of flax and timber. With these elements, Matra's proposal emphasised the economic benefits that might be offered by Britain's new antipodean possession. As one of the few Europeans who had actually visited New South Wales, his testimony carried some weight. Certainly his views have been of interest to those Australian historians (most prominently Geoffrey Blainey) who have argued that Britain was not simply solving the convict problem when in 1786 it finally committed itself to a settlement in New South Wales.

A Proposal for Establishing a Settlement in New South Wales.

I am going to offer an object to the consideration of our Government what [that] may in time atone for the loss of our American colonies.

By the discoveries and enterprise of our officers, many new countries have been found which know no sovereign, and that hold out the most enticing allurements to European adventurers. None are more inviting than New South Wales.

Capt. Cook first coasted and surveyed the eastern side of that fine country, form the 38th degree of south latitude 'down to the 10th, where he found everything to induce him to give the most favourable account of it. In this immense tract of more than 2,000 miles there was every variety of soil, and great parts of it were extremely fertile, peopled only by a few black inhabitants, who, in the rudest state of society, knew no other arts than such as were necessary to their mere animal existence, and which was almost entirely sustained by catching fish.

The climate and soil are so happily adapted to produce every various and valuable production of Europe, and of both the Indies, that with good management, and a few settlers, in twenty or thirty years they might cause a revolution in the whole system of European commerce, and secure to England a monopoly of some part of it, and a very large share in the whole.

Part of it lies in a climate parallel to the Spice Islands, and is fitted for the production of that valuable commodity, as well as the sugar-cane, tea, coffee, silk, cotton, indigo, tobacco, and the other articles of commerce that have been so advantageous to the maritime powers of Europe.

I must not omit the mention of a very important article, which may be obtained in any quantity, if this settlement be made the proper use of, which would be of very considerable consequence, both among the necessaries and conveniences of life. I mean the New Zealand hemp or flax-plant, an object equally of curiosity and utility. By proper operations it would serve the various purposes of hemp, flax, and silk, and it is more easily manufactured than any one of them. In naval equipments it would be of the greatest importance; a cable of the circumference of ten inches would be equal in strength to one of eighteen inches made of European hemp. Our manufacturers are of the opinion that canvas made of it would be superior in strength and beauty to any canvas of our own country. The threads or filaments of this plant are formed by nature with the most exquisite delicacy, and they may be so minutely divided as to be small enough to make the finest cambrick; in color and gloss it resembles silk. After my true, though imperfect description of this plant, I need not enlarge on it, as a very singular acquisition, both to the arts of convenience and luxury.

This country may afford an asylum to those unfortunate American loyalists to whom Great Britain is bound by every tie of honour and gratitude to protect and support, where they may repair their broken fortunes, and again enjoy their former domestic felicity.

That the Government may run no risque nor be left to act in a business of this kind without sufficient information, it is proposed that one ship of the peace establishment (to incur the least possible expence) be directly sent to that country, for the discovery and allotment of a proper district, for the intended settlement; that one or two gentlemen of capacity and knowledge, as well in soil and situation, as in every other requisite, be sent in her, that there may be no imposition on the Government, nor upon the Americans, who, with their families, shall adventure there.

If the Government be disposed to extend this plan, two vessels may be sent with two companies of marines, selected from among such of that corps as best understand husbandry, or manufactures, and about twenty artificers, who are all the emigration required from the parent State; these last to be chiefly such as are taken on board ships of war for carpenters' and armourers' crews, with a few potters and gardeners.

These twenty men and the marines, under a proper person to be left at the new settlement with materials and provisions, to prepare for the reception of the intended settlers, that their wants may be as few as possible on their arrival.

As the ship, or ships, stop at the Cape of Good Hope, a sufficient stock to begin with of cows, sheep, goats, hogs, poultry, and seeds may be obtained there. A supply of the like articles, as well as cotton seeds, plantains, grapes, grain, &c., &c., may be had in any quantity at Savu or any of the Moluccas, which are very near New South Wales.

When the landing is effected the smaller vessel may be dispatched home with the intelligence; and while the party designed to be left are superintending the gardens and increase of live stock, the other ship may, if thought proper be despatched to New Caledonia, Otahite, and the neighbouring islands to procure a few families there, and as many women as may serve for the men left behind. There is every reason to believe they may be obtained without difficulty. If but one vessel goes, the party with their stock may be left without apprehension of danger from the natives.

Sir Joseph Banks is of opinion that we may draw any number of useful inhabitants from China, agreeably to an invariable custom of the Dutch in forming or recruiting their Eastern settlements.

As it is intended not to involve the Government in either a great or a useless expense (for the settlement is designed to increase the wealth of the parent country, as well as for the emolument of the adventurers), a sum not exceeding £3,000 will be more than adequate to the whole expense of Government. Most of the tools, saws, axes, &c., &c., for the use of the party left may be drawn from the ordnance and other public stores, where at present they are useless; and the vessels also, being part of the peace establishment, neither can, nor ought to be, fairly reckoned in the expenditure.

That the Ministry may be convinced that this is not a vain, idle scheme, taken up without due attention and consideration, they may be assured that the matter has been seriously considered by some of the most intelligent and candid Americans, who all agree that, under the patronage and protection of Government, it offers the most favourable prospects that have yet occurred to better the fortunes and to promote the happiness of their fellow-sufferers and countrymen.

Sir Joseph Banks highly approves of the settlement, and is very ready to give his opinion of it, either to his Majesty's Ministry or others, whenever they may please to require it.

Should this settlement be made, we may enter into a commerce that would render our trade to China, hitherto extremely against us, very favourable. The Aleutian and Foxes islands, situated between Asia and America, which abound with the choicest furs, lie nearly north of New South Wales. It is from these islands the Russians get the most and best of their furs, with which they carry on a very lucrative trade by land with the Chinese. Our ships that sailed under the command of Captain Cook and Clerke stopped at some of them, and the skins which they procured then sold in China at 400 hard dollars each, though for the few they brought home, of the same quality, they only received about ten pounds each. As our situation in New South Wales would enable us to carry on this trade with the utmost facility, we should be no longer under the necessity of sending such immense quantities of silver for the different articles we import from the Chinese Empire.

There is also a prospect of considerably extending our woollen trade. We know that large quantities of woollen cloth are smuggled to Japan by the Russians, which, as it is taken by land carriage from St. Petersburg to Kamschatka, and then to the islands by a very precarious navigation in boats, must be extremely dear. The Japanese, however, go in their junks to the islands and purchase great quantities of it.

The peninsula of Korea, a kingdom tributary to the Chinese, and unvisited by Europeans, has its supply at second-hand chiefly from the Japanese. No ship has ever attempted this commerce, excepting once or twice that the Spaniards ventured thither from their American dominions; but as the inhabitants of New Spain are but indifferent navigators for the high, cold latitudes, they could not oftener repeat the enterprise.

It may be seen by Captain Cook's voyage that New Zealand is covered with timber of size and every quality that indicates long duration; it grows close to the water's edge, and may be easily obtained. Would it not be worth while for such as may be dispatched to New South Wales to take in some of this timber on their return, for the use of the King's yards? As the two countries are within a fortnight's run of each other, and as we might be of the utmost service to the New Zealanders, I think it highly probable that this plan might become eminently useful to us as a naval power, especially as we might thus procure masts, a single tree of which would be large enough for a first-rate ship, and planks superior to any that Europe possesses.

By the preliminary articles of peace with Holland we are entitled to a free navigation in the Molucca Seas. Without a settlement in the neighbourhood, the concession is useless; for the Dutch have an agent almost on every island in those seas. If we have a settlement, it is unnecessary; for as spices are the only articles we could expect by it, it is probable we should stand in no need of their indulgence, for as part of New South Wales lies in the same latitude with the Moluccas, and is even very close to them, there is every reason to suppose that what nature has so bountifully bestowed on the small islands may also be found on the larger. But if, contrary to analogy, it should not be so, the defect is easily supplyed, for, as the seeds are procured without difficulty, any quantity may speedily be cultivated.

To those who are alarmed at the idea of weakening the mother country by opening a channel for emigration, I must answer that it is more profitable that a part of our countrymen should go to a new abode, where they may be useful to us, than to the American States. If we cannot keep our subjects at home, it is sound policy to point out a road by following of which they may add to the national strength.

The place which New South Wales holds on our globe might give it a very commanding influence in the policy of Europe. If a colony from Britain was established in that large tract of country, and if we were at war with Holland or Spain, we might very powerfully annoy either State from our new settlement. We might, with a safe and expeditious voyage, make naval incursions on Java and the other Dutch settlements; and we might with equal facility invade the coast of Spanish America, and intercept the Manilla ships, laden with the treasures of the west. This check which New South Wales would be in time of war on both those powers makes it a very important object when we view it in the chart of the world with a political eye.

Sir Joseph Banks' high approbation of the scheme which I have here proposed deserves the most respectful attention of every sensible, liberal, and spirited individual amongst his countrymen. The language of encoumium, applied to this gentleman, would surely be inequitably censured as the language of adulation. To spurn the alluring pleasures which fortune procures in a frivolous and luxurious age, and to encounter extreme difficulties and dangers in pursuit of discoveries, which are of great benefit to mankind, is a complicated and illustrious event, as useful as it is rare, and which calls for the warmest publick gratitude and esteem ...

JAMES M. MATRA

August 23rd, 1783.

'... to our trusty and well-beloved Captain Arthur Phillip'

GOVERNOR PHILLIP'S FIRST COMMISSION

ABOVE *Arthur Phillip, captain-general of the expedition to New South Wales.*

On 12 October 1786 Captain Arthur Phillip (1738–1814) was appointed captain-general of the proposed expedition to New South Wales and governor of the projected convict settlement at Botany Bay. The selection of this dutiful but generally little-known naval officer, retired on half-pay and living in the English countryside, was made by Lord Sydney, Secretary of State for the Home Department. To some the appointment came as a surprise. Lord Howe, First Lord of the Admiralty, wrote to Lord Sydney, 3 September 1786: 'I cannot say the little knowledge I have of Captain Philips would have led me to select him for a service of this complicated nature'. But to those who did know him, either in person or by reputation, there was confidence that in this quiet, efficient, methodical and intellectual man was a practical and capable administrator of the highest capacity. And so it proved in New South Wales, where Phillip was sustained by a positive vision of the colony's future and its prospects.

Phillip's first commission is brief—merely a statement of his appointment and its broad geographic span over a vast area of largely unknown territory. But it is one of a suite of foundation documents that constitute what might be called Australia's birth certificates.

George the Third, &c., to our trusty and well-beloved Captain Arthur Phillip, greeting:—

We, reposing especial trust and confidence in your loyalty, courage, and experience in military affairs, do, by these presents, constitute and appoint you to be Governor of our territory called New South Wales, extending from the northern cape or extremity of the coast called Cape York, in the latitude of 10° 37' south, to the southern extremity of the said territory of New South Wales or South Cape, in the latitude of 43° 39' south and of all the country inland to the westward as far as the one hundredth and thirty-fifth degree of longitude, reckoning from the meridian of Greenwich, including all the islands adjacent in the Pacific Ocean, within the latitude aforesaid of 10° 37' south and 43° 39' south, and of all towns, garrisons, castles, forts, and all other fortifications or other military works, which now are or may hereafter be erected upon this said territory. You are therefore carefully and diligently to discharge the duty of Governor in and over our said territory by doing and performing all and all manner of things thereunto belonging, and we do hereby strictly charge and command all our officers and soldiers who shall be employed within our said territory, and all others whom it may concern, to obey you as our Governor thereof; and you are to observe and follow such orders and directions from time to time as you shall receive from us, or any other your superior officer according to the rules and discipline of war, and likewise such orders and directions as we shall send you under our signet or sign manual, or by our High Treasurer or Commissioners of our Treasury for the time being, or one of our Principal Secretaries of State, in pursuance of the trust we hereby repose in you.

Given at our Court at St. James's, the twelfth day of October, 1786, in the twenty-sixth year of our reign.

By his Majesty's command,
SYDNEY.

'... those who behave well will be rewarded'

ARTHUR PHILLIP ON THE TREATMENT OF CONVICTS IN THE NEW COLONY

Following his commissioning in October 1786 as the foundation governor of the penal settlement in New South Wales, Arthur Phillip was closely and intimately involved in all the detailed planning necessary for what has been described as a 'stupendous' undertaking: the transportation of more than 1000 convicts to a remote and little-known location, without amenities of any kind. George Mackaness, Phillip's first Australian biographer, noted that during the five months and more that passed before the First Fleet sailed, 'scarcely a week passed without a letter or letters from Phillip to the Minister [Lord Sydney, secretary of state for the Home Department] or to one of the other under secretaries, touching upon various details that needed consideration; letters which show that to Phillip alone ... is due the credit for the whole of the preparations for the expedition'. Working only with a general plan and with little more than a general blessing from his political masters, it was Phillip who meticulously considered every detail necessary for a smooth transition to life in New South Wales.

Not the least of his concerns was the well-being of his 'human cargo' of convicts—the foundation European settlers of Australia. To this end he offered a detailed and constructive set of suggestions. If these had been accepted and implemented, they might have prevented many of the difficulties that were encountered on the ground, initially at Botany Bay and then at Port Jackson, to which Phillip quickly relocated the settlement.

Phillip's memorandum 'On the Conduct of the Expedition and the Treatment of Convicts' is undated, but was apparently set down soon after his appointment. It survives in the Public Record Office in London: the first small sheets of paper were handwritten by Phillip himself and the rest of the text is on foolscap sheets in an unknown clerical hand. The memorandum is a clear-sighted, thoughtful document, touching not only on the needs and welfare of the convicts in Phillip's charge but also anticipating the practical needs of the colony itself. It offers an insight into the character and capability of a man whose large authority and responsibilities laid the foundations of European settlement in Australia.

One of Phillip's suggestions was that an advance party be sent to arrive at the new settlement some two or three months ahead of the convict transports. While this idea was not adopted, presumably for reasons of cost, on the voyage itself Phillip sought to apply a local version of his original proposal. Two weeks out from Cape Town, Phillip transferred from the flagship *Sirius* to the *Supply*. Leaving the slower vessels to travel under the command of Captain John Hunter on board *Sirius*, Phillip divided the fleet. Sailing with three of the faster ships, his strategy was to reach Botany Bay in sufficient time to prepare storehouses and erect the first huts. However, the final leg of the journey was slower than expected, and Phillip's party reached its destination only two days before the main body of the fleet.

By arriving at the settlement two or three months before the transports many and very great advantages would be gained. Huts would be ready to receive the convicts who are sick, and they would find vegetables, of which it may naturally be supposed they will stand in great need, as the scurvy must make a great ravage amongst people naturally indolent and not cleanly.

Huts would be ready for the women; the stores would be properly lodg'd and defended from the convicts in such manner as to prevent their making any attempt on them. The cattle and stock would be likewise properly secured, and the ground marked out for the convicts; for lists of those intended to be sent being given to the commanding officers, mentioning their ages, crimes, trades, and characters, they might be so divided as to render few changes necessary, and the provisions would be ready for issuing without any waste. But if convicts' provisions, &c., must be landed a few days after the ship's arrival, and consequently mostly at the same time, great inconvenience will arise, and to keep the convicts more than a few days on board after they get into a port, considering the length of time which they must inevitably be confined, may be attended with consequences easier to conceive than to point out in a letter. Add to this, fever of a malignant kind may make it necessary to have a second hospital.

A ship's company is landed, huts rais'd, and the sick provided for in a couple of days; but here the greater number are convicts, in whom no confidence can be placed, and against whom both person and provision is to be guarded. Everything necessary for the settlement should be received at the Cape on board with the commanding officer, and nothing left for the transports but a certain proportion of live stock.

I may add, the short space of time left to choose a proper situation.*
The confineing the convicts on board the ships requires some consideration. Sickness must be the consequence in so long a voyage (six months may be allow'd for the voyage—that is, from the time of leaveing England to the arrival in Botany Bay) and disagreeable consequences may be feared if they have the liberty of the deck. The sooner the crimes and behaviour of these people are known the better, as they may be divided, and the greatest villains particularly guarded against in one transport.

The women in general I should suppose possess neither virtue nor honesty. But there may be some for thefts who still retain some degree of virtue, and these should be permitted to keep together, and strict orders to the master of the transport should be given that they are not abused and insulted by the ship's company, which is said to have been the case too often when they were sent to America.

At the ports we put into for water, &c., there may be some sick that may have fever of such a nature that it may be necessary for the sake of the rest to remove them out of the ship. In such a case, how am I to act?

The greatest care will be necessary to prevent any of the convicts from being sent that have any venereal complaints.

During the passage, when light airs or calms permit it, I shall visit the transports to see that they are kept clean and receive the allowance ordered by Government; and at these times shall endeavour to make them sensible of their situation, and that their happiness or misery is in their own hands,—that those who behave well will be rewarded by being allow'd to work occasionally on the small lotts of land set apart for them, and which they will be put in possession of at the expiration of the time for which they are transported.

On landing in Botany Bay it will be necessary to throw up a slight work as a defence against the natives—who, tho' only seen in small numbers by Captn. Cook, may be very numerous on other parts of the coast—and against the convicts; for this my own little knowledge as a field engineer will be sufficient, and will be the work of a few days only; but some small cannon for a redoubt will be necessary. Within the lines the stores and provisions will be secured; and I should hope that the situation I should be able to take may admit of having the small rivers between the garrison and the convicts so situated that I may be able to prevent their having any intercourse with the natives.

I shall think it a great point gained if I can proceed in this business without having any dispute with the natives, a few of which I shall endeavour to persuade to settle near us, and who I mean to furnish with everything that can tend to civilize them, and to give them a high opinion of the new guests, for which purpose it will be necessary to prevent the transports' crews from having any intercourse with the natives, if possible. The convicts must have none, for if they have, the arms of the natives will be very formidable in their hands, the women abused, and the natives disgusted.

The keeping of the women apart merits great consideration, and I don't know but it may be best if the most abandoned are permitted to receive the visits of the convicts in the limits allotted them at certain hours, and under certain restrictions; something of this kind was the case in Mill Bank formerly. The rest of the women I should keep apart, and by permitting the men to be in their company when not at work, they will, I should suppose, marry, in which case they should be encouraged, if they are industrious, by one day in the week more than the unmarried on their own lotts of ground.

The natives may, it is probable, permit their women to marry and live with the men after a certain time, in which case I should think it necessary to punish with severity the men who use the women ill, and I know of no punishment likely to answer the purpose of deterring others so well as exiling them to a distant spot, or to an island, where they would be obliged to work hard to gain their daily subsistance, and for which they would have the necessary tools, but no two to be together, if it could be avoided.

Rewarding and punishing the convicts must be left to the Governor; he will be answerable for his conduct, and death, I should think, will never be necessary—in fact, I doubt if the fear of death ever prevented a man of no principle from committing a bad action. There are two crimes that would merit death—murder and sodomy. For either of these crimes I would wish to confine the criminal till an opportunity offered of delivering him as a prisoner to the natives of New Zealand, and let them eat him. The dread of this will operate much stronger than the fear of death.

As the getting a large quantity of stock together will be my first great object, till that is obtained the garrison should, as in Gibraltar, not be allowed to kill any animal without first reporting his stock, and receiving permission. This order would only be necessary for a certain time, and I mention it here only to show the necessity of a military government; and as I mean in every matter of this kind to sett the example, I think that I can say this will never occasion any uneasiness, but if it should, it will be absolutely necessary, otherwise we shall not do in ten years what I hope to do in four.

Women may be brought from the Friendly and other islands, a proper place prepared to receive them, and where they will be supported for a time, and lots of land assigned to such as marry with the soldiers of the garrison.

As I would not wish convicts to lay the foundations of an empire, I think they should ever remain separated from the garrison, and other settlers that may come from Europe, and not be allowed to mix with them, even after the 7 or 14 years for which they are transported may be expired.

The laws of this country will, of course, be introduced in New South Wales, and there is one that I would wish to take place from the moment his Majesty's forces take possession of the country: That there can be no slavery in a free land, and consequently no slaves.

The cloathing for the convicts will last for a certain time, after which what means should I have of furnishing them with materials for their making their own cloaths?

It will be necessary to know how far I may permit the seamen and marines of the garrison to cultivate spots of land when the duty of the day is over, and how far I can give them hopes that the grounds they cultivate will be secured to them hereafter; likewise, how far I may permit any of the garrison to remain, when they are ordered Home in consequence of relief.

By what I am informed, hatchets and beads are the articles for barter—a few small grindstones for the chiefs; and as they use a light they hold it in their hands, small tin lamps on a very simple construction must be very acceptable.

Ships may arrive at Botany Bay in future. On account of the convicts, the orders of the port for no boats landing but in particular places, coming on shore and returning to the ships at stated hours, must be strictly inforced.

The saddles I mentioned will be absolutely necessary, for two horsemen will examine the country to a certain distance, when it might be dangerous to attempt it with half the garrison, for I am not of the general opinion that there are very few inhabitants in this country, at least so few as have been represented—but this article I take upon myself, as likewise the knifes, &c., that I mentioned.

Such fruit trees and cuttings that will bear removing should be added to the seeds carried from England, as likewise roots that will bear keeping that length of time out of the ground.

Two or three of the houses in question will be highly necessary, and there is no time to lose in giving the orders, if intended.

A certain quantity of the articles of husbandry, stores, corn, seeds, &c., of the articles for traffick, should be put on board the Berwick,† that in case of an accident we may not be in immediate want of those things, and the same on board the store-ship in which the Lt.-Gouvrnour goes.

* The manuscript is continued, on foolscap, in another hand—evidently a copy of Phillip's paper.
† Renamed *Sirius*.

'I never heard of any one Single Person having So great a Power in vest'd in him'

GOVERNOR PHILLIP'S SECOND COMMISSION

As his second commission reveals, in taking up his appointment in New South Wales Arthur Phillip was endowed with almost absolute powers. Lieutenant Ralph Clark commented that 'I never heard of any one Single Person having So great a Power in vest'd in him as the Govenour has by his commission'. Phillip, however, exercised his powers with discretion and restraint, notwithstanding the difficulties inherent in this most remote and initially under-resourced of British outposts.

The group of ships that came to be known as the First Fleet arrived at Botany Bay on 18 January 1788, but it was not until 7 February that a ceremony was held to read Phillip's commission and formally establish a government in the name of His Majesty King George the Third.

On reaching Botany Bay, Phillip had quickly recognised its unsuitability as a site for the permanent settlement. Several days were occupied in examining the site and in surveying and occupying an alternative. A crucial factor guiding the choice of the new site at Sydney Cove in Port Jackson was the presence of 'that grand essential fresh water'. On 26 January at Sydney Cove, Phillip presided over a flag-raising ceremony that was a belated declaration of arrival and of beginning. While that anniversary is today honoured (but mourned by many Aboriginal Australians) as the official Australian birthday, the significance of 7 February as 'the memorable day which established a regular form of Government on the coast of New South Wales' has been largely forgotten.

According to the contemporary accounts, the ceremony of 7 February 1788 was conducted with high solemnity and even a little pomp. It provided the occasion for the public reading of both the governor's commission and the commission constituting the courts of civil, military and criminal jurisdiction in the territory. On arrival, the governor was received by a party of soldiers under arms. With him were the principal office-holders of the new administration—the lieutenant governor, the judge-advocate, the surveyor-general and the chaplain. Formal compliments were exchanged between the marine officers and the officers of the military, who together then formed a circle around the company at their place on the recently cleared parade ground. All gentlemen present were invited to join the official party within the enclosure. The judge-advocate, David Collins, opened the red leather cases containing the commissions and broke the seals before reading the documents to the assembled gathering. The troops fired three volleys before Phillip thanked the soldiers and made a short address to the convicts. He then reviewed the different companies of the marines. At intervals in the ceremony, the band played airs on fifes and drums, finishing with 'God save the King'. At the conclusion, the convicts were dismissed to their quarters; a public holiday was declared; and the governor and his party adjourned to a marquee to partake of a celebratory luncheon. The mutton was flyblown, but many loyal and public toasts were proposed and drunk.

All which being duly performed you shall administer unto our Lieutenant-Governor if there be any upon the place and to our Judge-Advocate the oaths mentioned in the first-recited Act of Parliament altered as above as also cause them to make and subscribe the afore-mentioned declaration.

And Wee do hereby authorize and empower you to keep and use the public seal which will be herewith delivered to you or shall be hereafter sent to you for sealing all things whatsoever that shall pass the Great Seal of our said territory and its dependencies.

We do further give and grant unto you the said Arthur Phillip full power and authority from time to time and at any time hereafter by yourself or by any other to be authorized by you in that behalf to administer and give the oaths mentioned in the said first-recited Act of Parliament altered as above to all and every such person or persons as you shall think fit who shall at any time or times pass into our said territory or its dependencies or shall be resident or abiding therein.

And Wee do hereby authorize and empower you to constitute and appoint justices of the peace coronors constables and other necessary officers and ministers in our said territory and its dependencies for the better administration of justice and putting the law in execution and to administer or cause to be administered unto them such oath or oaths as are usually given for the execution and performance of offices and places.

And Wee do hereby give and grant unto you full power and authority where you shall see cause or shall judge any offender or offenders in criminal matters or for any fine or fines or forfeitures due unto us fit objects of our mercy to pardon all such offenders and to remit all such offences fines and forfeitures treason and wilful murder only excepted in which cases you shall likewise have power upon extraordinary occasions to grant reprieves to the offenders untill and to the intent our royal pleasure may be known therein.

And whereas it belongeth to us in right of our Royal Prerogative to have the custody of ideots and their estates and to take the profits thereof to our own use finding them necessaries and also to provide for the custody of lunaticks and their estates without taking the profits thereof to our own use.

And whereas while such ideots and lunaticks and their estates remain under our immediate care great trouble and charges may arise to such as shall have occasion to resort unto us for directions respecting such ideots and lunaticks and their estates Wee have thought fit to entrust you with the care and committment of the custody of the said ideots and lunaticks and their estates and Wee do by these presents give and grant unto you full power and authority without expecting any further special warrant from us from time to time to give order and warrant for the preparing of grants of the custodies of such ideots and lunaticks and their estates as are or shall be found by inquisitions thereof to be taken by the Judges of our Court of Civil Jurisdiction and thereupon to make and pass grants and committments under our Great Seal of our said territory of the custodies of all and every such ideots and lunaticks and their estates to such person or persons suitors in that behalf as according to the rules of law and the use of practice in those and the like cases you shall judge meet for that trust the said grants and committments to be made in such manner and form or as nearly as may be as hath been heretofore used and accustomed in making the same under the Great Seal of Great Britain and to contain such apt and convenient covenants provisions and agreements on the parts of the committees and grantees to be performed and such security to be by them given as shall be requisite and needful.

And Wee do hereby give and grant unto you the said Arthur Phillip by yourself or by your captains or commanders by you to be authorized full power and authority to levy arm muster and command and employ all persons whatsoever residing within our said territory and its dependencies under your government and as occasion shall serve to march from one place to another or to embark them for the resisting and withstanding of all enemies pirates and rebels both at sea and land and such enemies pirates and rebels if there shall be occasion to pursue and prosecute in or out of the limits of our said territory and its dependencies and (if it shall so please God) them to vanquish apprehend take and being so taken according to law to put to death or keep and preserve alive at your discretion.

And to execute martial law in time of invasion or other times when by law it may be executed and to do and execute all and every other thing and things which to our Captain-General and Governor-in-Chief doth or ought of right to belong.

And Wee do hereby give and grant unto you full power and authority to erect raise and build in our said territory and its dependencies such and so many forts and platforms castles cities boroughs towns and fortifications as you shall judge necessary and the same or any of them to fortify and furnish with ordnances and ammunition and all sorts of arms fit and necessary for the security and defence of the same or any of them to demolish or dismantle as may be most convenient.

And forasmuch as divers mutinies and disorders may happen by persons shipped and employed at sea during the time of war and to the end that such as shall be shipped and employed at sea during the time of war may be better governed and ordered Wee do hereby give and grant unto you the said Arthur Phillip full power and authority to constitute and appoint captains lieutenants masters of ships and other commanders and officers and to grant to such captains lieutenants masters of ships and other commanders and officers commissions to execute the law-martial during the time of war according to the directions of an Act passed in the twenty-second year of the reign of our late royal grandfather ...

And to use such proceedings authorities punishments corrections executions upon any offender or offenders who shall be mutinous seditious disorderly or any way unruly either at sea or during the time of their abode or residence in any of the ports harbours or bays of our said territory as the case shall be found to require according to martial law and the said directions during the time of war as aforesaid.

Provided that nothing herein contained shall be construed to the enabling you or any by your authority to hold plea or have any jurisdiction of any offence cause matter or thing committed or done upon the high sea or within any of the havens rivers or creeks of our said territory and its dependencies under your Government by any captain commander lieutenant master officer seaman soldier or other person whatsoever who shall be in actual service in pay in or on board any of our ships of war or other vessels acting by immediate commission or warrant from our Commissioners for executing the office of our High Admiral of Great Britain or from our High Admiral of Great Britain for the time being under the seal of our Admiralty.

But that such captain commander lieutenant master officer seaman soldier or other person so offending shall be left to be proceeded against and tried as the merits of their offences shall require either by commission under our Great Seal of Great Britain as the statute of the Twenty-eighth of Henry the Eighth directs by commission from our Commissioners for executing the office of our High Admiral of Great Britain or from our High Admiral of Great Britain for the time being according to the aforesaid Act …

Provided nevertheless that all disorders and misdemeanors committed on shore by any captain commander lieutenant master officer seaman soldier or any other person whatsoever belonging to any of our ships of war or other vessels acting by immediate commission or warrant from our Commissioners for executing the office of our High Admiral of Great Britain or from our High Admiral of Great Britain for the time being under the seal of our Admiralty may be tried and punished according to the laws of the place where any such disorders offences and misdemeanors shall be committed on shore notwithstanding such offender be in our actual service and borne in our pay on board any such our ships of war or other vessels acting by immediate commission or warrant from our Commissioners for executing the office of our High Admiral of Great Britain or from our High Admiral of Great Britain for the time being as aforesaid so as he shall not receive any protection from the avoidance of justice for such offences committed on shore from any pretence of his being employed in our service at sea.

Our will and pleasure is that all public monies which shall be raised be issued out by warrant from you and disposed of by you for the support of the Government or for such other purpose as shall be particularly directed and not otherwise.

And Wee do hereby likewise give and grant unto you full power and authority to agree for such lands tenements and hereditaments as shall be in our power to dispose of and them to grant to any person or persons upon such terms and under such moderate quit rents services and acknowledgments to be thereupon reserved unto us according to such instructions as shall be given to you under our sign manual which said grants are to pass and be sealed by our seal of our said territory and its dependencies and being entered upon record by such officer or officers as you shall appoint thereunto shall be good and effectual in law against us our heirs and successors.

And Wee do hereby give you the said Arthur Phillip full power to appoint fairs marts and markets as also such and so many ports harbours bays havens and other places for conveniency and security of shipping and for the better loading and unloading of goods and merchandizes as by you shall be thought fit and necessary.

And Wee do hereby require and command all officers and ministers civil and military and all other inhabitants of our said territory and its dependencies to be obedient aiding and assisting you the said Arthur Phillip in the execution of this our commission and of the powers and authorities herein contained and in case of your death or absence out of our said territory to be obedient aiding and assisting to such person as shall be appointed by us to be our Lieutenant-Governor or Commander-in-Chief of our said territory and its dependencies to whom Wee do therefore by these presents give and grant all and singular the powers and authorities herein granted to be by him executed and enjoyed during our pleasure or until your arrival within our territory and its dependencies.

And if upon your death or absence out of our said territory and its dependencies there be no person upon the place commissioned or appointed by us to be our Lieutenant-Governor or Commander-in-Chief of our said territory and its dependencies our will and pleasure is that the officer highest in rank who shall be at the time of your death or absence upon service within the same and who shall take the oaths and subscribe the declaration appointed to be taken and subscribed by you or by the Commander-in-Chief of our said territory and its dependencies shall take upon him the administration of the Government and execute our said commission and instructions and the several powers and authorities therein contained in the same manner and to all intents and purposes as other our Governor or Commander-in-Chief should or ought to do in case of your absence until your return or in all cases untill our further pleasure be known therein.

And Wee do hereby declare ordain and appoint that you the said Arthur Phillip shall and may hold execute and enjoy the office and place of our Captain-General and Governor-in-Chief in and over our said territory and its dependencies together with all and singular the powers and authorities hereby granted unto you for and during our will and pleasure.

In witness &c.

Witness ourself at Westminster the second day of April in the twenty-seventh year of our reign.

By writ of Privy Seal.

'open an intercourse with the natives, and to conciliate their affections'

PHILLIP'S INSTRUCTIONS

While Arthur Phillip's two commissions gave him the authority he needed to establish a British government in New South Wales, he also had to lay the physical foundations of the settlement itself. That large and onerous task was defined in a detailed set of instructions issued with his commission and dated 25 April 1787 that provided the directions for his administration of the colony. This document is perhaps the most crucial of those that shaped and defined the style and character of the settlement in its foundation period, and its influence continued to be felt for some years after Phillip's departure. In their transmission of British institutions to Australia, Phillip's commissions and his official instructions stand as Australia's founding documents.

In abandoning Botany Bay as the site of the settlement, Phillip departed from the literal direction of his instructions. In doing so, he achieved from the outset an infinitely better-suited site for the settlement—one protected within the confines of a magnificent harbour.

Especially significant were the directions to 'open an intercourse with the natives, and to conciliate their affections, enjoining all our subjects to live in amity and kindness with them'. Phillip took the greatest of care to honour this broad, but probably impossibly idealistic, direction. In a recent judgment, the historian David Andrew Roberts has noted that Phillip's enterprise was characterised by the failure to recognise and define the status of the Australian Aboriginal people. Almost from the beginning relations between the Aboriginal inhabitants and the European settlers disintegrated—the product not merely of displacement but also of a profound and mutual incomprehension between the two peoples. While knowledge and understanding gradually increased, the scars inflicted from the time of the first settler contacts remained.

George R.

(L.S.)

Instructions for Our Trusty and wellbeloved Arthur Phillip Esq'. Our Captain General and Governor in Chief, in and over Our Territory of New South Wales and its Dependencies, or to the Lieutenant Governor or Commander in Chief of the said Territory for the time being. Given at Our Court at S.t James's, the 25.th day of April 1787. In the Twenty Seventh Year of Our Reign.

With these Our Instructions you will receive Our Commission under Our Great Seal constituting and appointing you to be Our Captain General and Governor in Chief of Our Territory called New South Wales extending

ABOVE *Manuscript draft of the instructions to Phillip.*

G.R.

Instructions for Our Trusty and well beloved Arthur Phillip Esq., Our Captain-General and Governor-in-Chief, in and over our territory of New South Wales and its Dependencies, or to the Lieutenant-Governor or Commander-in-Chief of the said Territory for the time being. Given at Our Court at St. James the 25th day of April, 1787, in the twenty seventh year of our reign.

With these our instructions you will receive our commission under our Great seal constituting and appointing you to be our Captain General and Governor-in-Chief of our territory called New South Wales, extending from the northern cape or extremity of the coast, called Cape York, in the latitude of ten degrees thirty-seven minutes south, to the southern extremity of the said territory of New South Wales, or South Cape, in the latitude of forty-three degrees thirty-nine minutes south, and of all the country inland to the westward as far as the one hundred and thirty-fifth degree of east longitude, reckoning from the meridian of Greenwich including all the Islands adjacent in the Pacific Ocean within the latitudes aforesaid, of 10° 37' South, and 43° 39' South, and of all towns, garrisons, castles, forts, and all other fortifications, or other military works which may be hereafter erected upon the said territory, or any of the said Islands, with directions to obey such Orders and Instructions as shall from time to time be given to you, under our signet and sign manual, or by our order in our Privy Council.

You are, therefore, to fit yourself with all convenient speed, and to hold yourself in readiness to repair to your said command, and being arrived, to take upon you the execution of the trust we have reposed in you, and as soon as conveniently may be, with all due solemnity to cause our said Commission under our Great Seal of Great Britain constituting you our Governor and Commander-in-Chief as aforesaid to be read and published.

And whereas we have ordered that about 600 male, and 180 female convicts now under sentence or order of transportation whose names are contained in the list hereunto annexed, should be removed out of the gaols and other places of confinement in this our kingdom, and be put on board of the several transport ships which have been taken up for their reception, it is our royal will and pleasure that as soon as the said convicts, the several persons composing the civic establishments, and the stores, provisions &c., provided for their use, shall be embarked on board the Supply, tender, and the transport ships named in the margin [*Alexander, Charlotte, Scarborough, Friendship, Prince of Wales, Lady Penrhyn*], and be in readiness to depart, that you do take them under your protection and proceed in the Sirius with the said tender and transports to the port on the Coast of New South Wales, situated in the latitude of 33° 41', called by the name of Botany Bay, agreeably to the instructions with which you will be furnished by the Commissioners of our Admiralty, in pursuance of our royal commands already signified to them.

And whereas it may happen upon your passage to New South Wales that you may find it necessary and expedient to call with the ships and vessels under your convoy, at the island of Teneriffe, at the Rio de Janeiro, and also at the Cape of Good Hope, for supplies of water and other refreshments for the voyage, it is our further will and pleasure that you do, upon your arrival at the former of those places take on board any of the ships of the convoy which you may think proper such quantities of wine as may be requisite for the supply of the said settlement, according to the instructions with which the Commissary of Stores and Provisions will be furnished by the Commissioners of our Treasury, taking care that the quantities purchased do not exceed the proportions to be issued to the several persons composing the said settlements entitled thereto, agreeably to the said instructions, for the time to which they have confined the supply of that article; and for the amount of such purchases, you will direct the Commissary to draw bills of exchange upon them properly certified by you, or our Lieut.-Governor of the said intended settlement, with the other usual attestations that the same has been obtained at the most reasonable rates, transmitting at the same time an account thereof to them, in order that you may be released from any imprest which such purchases might occasion.

Notwithstanding there is already a considerable quantity of corn and other seed-grain put on board the ships of the convoy, probably more than may be immediately necessary for raising supplies for the settlement, We are disposed to guard as much as possible against accidents which may happen, or injuries which these articles might sustain during the Passage: It is, therefore, our further will and pleasure that you, upon your arrival at any of the places you may have occasion to touch at, endeavour to obtain such further quantities of seed-grain as You may think requisite for the tillage of the land, at the place of your destination: And also that you do take onboard any number of black cattle, sheep, goats, or hogs which you can procure, and the ships of the convoy can contain, in order to propagate the breed of these animals for the general benefit of the intended settlement, causing the Commissary of Stores and Provisions to draw bills for the same as is before directed for such supplies, as well as for any fresh provisions which it may be requisite to procure for the use of the marines or convicts, at those places, and transmitting information to the Commissioners of our Treasury such proceedings.

And whereas it is intended that several of the transport ships and victuallers which are to accompany you to New South Wales, should be employed in bringing home cargoes of tea, and other merchandize, from China, for the use of the East India Company, provided they can arrive at Canton in due time whereby a very considerable saving would arise to the public in the freight of these vessels: It is our royal will and pleasure that upon your arrival at Botany Bay, on the said Coast of New South Wales, you do cause every possible exertion to be made for disembarking the officers and men composing the civil and military establishments, together with the convicts, stores, provisions, &c., and having so done, you are to discharge all the said transports or victuallers, in order that such of them as may be engaged by the East India Company may proceed to China, and that the rest may return home. You will, however, take care, before the said transport ships are discharged, to obtain an assignment to you or the Governor-in-Chief for the time being, from the masters of them, of the servitude of the several convicts for the remainder of the times or terms specified in their several sentences or orders of transportation.

According to the best information which we have obtained, Botany Bay appears to be the most eligible situation upon the said coast for the first establishment, possessing a commodious harbour and other advantages which no part of the coast hitherto discovered affords. It is therefore our will and pleasure that you do immediately upon your landing, after taking measures for securing yourself and the people who accompany you as much as possible from any attacks or interruptions of the natives of that country, as well as for the preservation and safety of the public stores, proceed to the cultivation of the land, distributing the convicts for that purpose in such manner, and under such inspectors or overseers, and under such regulations as may appear to you to be necessary and best calculated for procuring supplies of grain and ground provisions. The assortment of tools and utensils which have been provided for the use of the convicts and other persons who are to compose the intended settlement are to be distributed according to your discretion, and according to the employment assigned to the several persons. In the distribution however, you will use every proper degree of economy, be careful that the Commissary do transmit an account of the issues from time to time to the Commissioners of our Treasury, to enable them to judge of the propriety or expediency of granting further supplies. The clothing of the convicts and the provisions issued to them, and the civil and military establishments, must be accounted for in the same manner.

And whereas the Commissioners of our Admiralty have appointed Capt. Hunter to repair on board the Sirius to assist you in the execution of your duty, and to take the command of the ship whenever you may see occasion to detach her from the settlement, and also to station the Supply, tender, under your orders, and to be assisting to you upon occasional services after your arrival. And whereas it is our royal intention that measures should be taken, in addition to those which are specified in the article of these our instructions, for obtaining supplies of live stock, and having, in consequence of such intention, caused a quantity of arms and other articles of merchandize to be provided, and sent out in the ships under your convoy, in order to barter with the natives either on the territory of New South Wales or the islands adjacent: It is our will and pleasure that as soon as either of these vessels can be spared with safety from the settlement you do detach one or both of them for that purpose, confining their intercourse as much as possible to such parts as are not in the possession or under the jurisdiction of other European powers.

The increase of the stock of animals must depend entirely upon the measures you may adopt on the outset for their preservation; and as the settlement with be amply supplied with vegetable productions, and most likely with fish, fresh provisions, excepting for the sick and convalescents, may in a great degree be dispensed with. For these reasons it will become you to be extremely cautious in permitting any cattle, sheep, hogs, &c., intended for propagating the breed of such animals to be slaughtered, until a competent stock may be acquired, to admit of your supplying the settlement from it with animal food without having further recourse to the places from whence such stock may have originally been obtained.

It is our will and pleasure that the productions of all descriptions acquired by the labour of the convicts shall be considered as a public stock, and which we so far leave to your disposal that such parts thereof as may be requisite for the subsistence of the said convicts and their families, or the subsistence of the civil and military establishments of the settlement, may be applied by you to that use. The remainder of such productions you will reserve as a provision for a further number of convicts, which you may expect will shortly follow you from hence, to be employed under your direction in the manner pointed out in these our instructions to you.

From the natural increase of corn and other vegetable food from a common industry, after the ground has been once cultivated, as well as of animals, it cannot be expedient that all the convicts which accompany you should be employed in attending only to the object of provisions. And, as it has been humbly represented unto us that advantages may be derived from the flax-plant which is found in the islands not far distant from the intended settlement, not only as a means of acquiring clothing for the convicts and other persons who may become settlers, but from its superior excellence for a variety of maritime purposes, and as it may ultimately become an article of export, it is therefore our will and pleasure that you do particularly attend to its cultivation, and that you do send home by every opportunity which may offer samples of that article, in order that a judgment may be formed whether it may not be necessary to instruct you further upon this subject.

And whereas we are desirous that some further information should be obtained of the several ports or harbours upon the coast, and the islands contiguous thereto, within the limits of your government, you are, whenever the Sirius or the Supply, tender, can conveniently be spared, to send one, or both of them, upon that service.

Norfolk Island ... being represented as a spot which may hereafter become useful, you are, as soon as circumstances will admit of it, to send a small establishment thither to secure the same to us, and prevent its being occupied by the subjects of any other European power; and you will cause any remarks or observations which you obtain in consequence of this instruction to be transmitted to our Principal Secretary of State for Plantation Affairs for our information.

And whereas it may happen, when the settlement shall be brought into some state of regulation, that the service of the Sirius may not be necessary at the said settlement, and as we are desirous to diminish as much as possible the expences which the intended establishment occasions, You will, whenever the service of the said ship can be dispensed with, order Capt. Hunter to return with to England. And as from such an arrangement the emoluments of your station will be diminished it is our royal intention, that the same shall be made good to you by bills to be drawn by you upon the Commissioners of our Treasury.

You are to endeavour by every possible means to open an intercourse with the natives, and to conciliate their affections, enjoining all our subjects to live in amity and kindness with them. And if any of our subjects shall wantonly destroy them, or give them any unnecessary interruption in the exercise of their several occupations, it is our will and pleasure that you do cause such offenders to be brought to punishment according to the degree of the offence. You will endeavour to procure an account of the numbers inhabiting the neighbourhood of the intended settlement, and report your opinion to one of our Secretaries of State in what manner our intercourse with these people may be turned to the advantage of this colony.

And it is further our royal will and pleasure that you do by all proper methods enforce a due observance of religion and good order among all the inhabitants of the new settlement and that you do take such steps for the due celebration of publick worship as circumstances will permit.

And whereas, from the great disproportion of female convicts to those of the males, who are put under your superintendance, it, appears advisable that a further number of the latter should be introduced into the new intended settlements, you are, whenever the Sirius or the tender shall touch at any of the islands in the seas, to instruct their commanders to take on board any of the women who may be disposed to accompany them to the said settlement. You will, however, take especial care, that the officers who may happen to be employed upon this service do not, upon any account, exercise any compulsive measures, or make use of fallacious pretences, for bringing away any of the said women from the places of their present residence.

And whereas we have by our Commission, bearing date [2nd April] 1787, given and granted upon you full power and authority to emancipate and discharge from their servitude, any of the convicts under your superindendance who shall, from their good conduct and a disposition to industry, be deserving of favor: It is our will and pleasure that in every such case you do issue your warrant to the Surveyor of Lands to make surveys of and mark out in lots such lands upon the said territory as may be necessary for their use; and when that shall be done, that you do pass grants thereof with all convenient speed to any of the said convicts so emancipated, in such proportions and under such conditions and acknowledgements, as shall hereafter be specified, viz.:—to every male shall be granted, 30 acres of land, and in case he shall be married, 20 acres more; and for every child who may be with them at the settlement at the time of making the said grant, a further quantity of 10 acres, free of all fees, taxes, quit rents, or other acknowledgments whatsoever, for the space of Ten years: Provided that the person to whom the said land shall have been granted shall reside within the same and proceed to the cultivation and improvement thereof; reserving only to us such timber as may be growing, or to grow hereafter, upon the said land which may be fit for naval purposes, and an annual quit rent of [blank in manuscript] after the expiration of the term or time before mentioned. You will cause copies of such grants as may be passed to be preserved, and make a regular return of the said grants to the Commissioners of our Treasury and the Lords of the Committee of our Privy Council for Trade and Plantations.

And Whereas it is likely to happen that the Convicts who may after their Emancipation, in consequence of this Instruction, be put in possession of Lands will not have the means of proceedings to their Cultivation without the Public Aid; It is our will and pleasure that you do cause every such person you may so emancipate to be supplied with such a quantity of provisions as may be sufficient for the subsistence of himself, and also of this family, for twelve months, together with an assortment of tools and utensils, and such a proportion of seed-grain, cattle, sheep, hogs, &c., as may be proper, and can be spared from the general stock of the settlement.

And whereas many of our subjects employed upon military service at the said settlement, and others who may resort thither upon their private occupations, may hereafter be desirous of proceeding to the cultivation and improvement of the land, and as we are disposed to afford them every reasonable encouragement in such an undertaking: It is our will and pleasure that you do with all convenient speed, transmit a report of the actual state and quality of the soil at and near the said intended settlement, the probable and most effectual means of improving and cultivating the same, and of the mode, and upon what terms and conditions, according to the best of your judgment, the said lands should be granted, that proper instructions and authorities may be given to you for that purpose.

And whereas it is our royal intention that every sort of intercourse between the intended settlement at Botany Bay, or other places which may be hereafter established on the coast of New South Wales, and its dependencies, and the settlements of our East India Company, as well as the coast of China, and the islands situated in that part of the world, to which any intercourse has been established by any European nation, should be prevented by every possible means: It is our royal will and pleasure that you do not upon any account allow craft of any sort to be built for the use of private individuals which might enable them to effect such intercourse, and that you do prevent any vessels which may at any time hereafter arrived the said settlement from any of the ports before mentioned from having communication with any of the inhabitants residing within your Government, without first receiving especial permission from you for that purpose.

G.R.

Whereas by an act made and passed in the twenty-fourth year of his present Majesty's reign intituled "an act for the effectual transportation of felons and other offenders and to authorise the removal of prisoners in certain cases and for other purposes therein mentioned" it is enacted that from and after the passing of that act when any person or persons at any sessions of oyer or terminer or gaol delivery or at any quarter or other general session of the peace to be holden for any county, riding, division, city, town, borough, liberty or place within that part of Great Britain called England or at any great session to be holden for the county palatine of Chester or within the principality of Wales shall be lawfully convicted of grand or petit larceny or any other offence for which such person or persons shall be liable by the laws of this realm to be transported it shall and may be lawful for the court before which any such person or persons shall be convicted as aforesaid or any subsequent court holden at any place for the same county, riding, division, city, town, borough, liberty or

ABOVE *The first page of the New South Wales Courts Act.*

The rule of law in a penal colony

NEW SOUTH WALES COURTS ACT

In *An Act to enable His Majesty to establish a Court of Criminal judicature on the Eastern Coast of New South Wales, and the Parts Adjacent*, provision was made for British law to travel to Australia with the First Fleet in 1788. The act established a criminal court (known generally as the Court of Criminal Jurisdiction) and ensured that the new colony had the basis for the enforcement of law; but it allowed for a more 'summary' legal proceeding than was usual, recognising the particular needs of a colony that had been established as a penal settlement. Historians have been unanimous in pointing to the severity and partisan nature of the first Australian court of law. Alex Castles described it as 'the best known and often the most dreaded tribunal in New South Wales', commenting also that 'for thirty-six years it arbitrated on life and death under the severe penal code of the day'. David Neal has noted that while Britain provided convicts and free settlers alike with the due process of law in serious criminal cases, similar to the system then prevailing in England, there were a number of serious differences, including the absence of a jury system.

The severity of the first court was compounded by its military appearance. Its principal functionary was described officially as a deputy judge-advocate (but was known in the colony as judge-advocate); he sat with 'six officers of His Majesty's forces by sea and land'. Together, the judge-advocate and these officers were the sole arbiters of fact and law in the cases that came before the court, and no provision was made for appeals against convictions. The court did not have to reach a decision unanimously, but by a majority of four of its members (though in cases involving a sentence of death, a majority of five was needed, or four together with approval from England). In the various processes of the court, the judge-advocate's opinion on matters of law counted no more than that of any other member of the bench.

The first hearings of the court were held on 11 February 1788, a bare fortnight after the official landing of the First Fleet; those hearings were presided over by David Collins in his official capacity as judge-advocate. In his *Account of the English Colony in New South Wales* (published in 1798; see page 52), Collins left a record of the court's first session when its members gathered 'in their military habits, with the insignia of duty the sash and the sword'.

As the first phase of the administration of justice in New South Wales, this system remained in force until 1824, when it was largely dismantled and replaced. Through this foundation period the British government sought to give an authoritarian character to the government of its penal settlement. Even as late as 1815, when J.T. Bigge was commissioned to inquire into the administration and governance of New South Wales, the prevailing British view was that the colony 'did not appear to His Majesty's Government sufficiently advanced to admit of withdrawing that appearance of military constraint which had been found necessary on its first formation, and which the composition of the population had rendered it indispensable ... to maintain'.

And whereas it may be found necessary that a colony and a civil Government should be established in the place to which such convicts shall be transported under and by virtue of the said Act of Parliament, the said two several Orders of Council, and other the said above-recited Orders, and that a Court of Criminal Jurisdiction should also be established within such place as aforesaid, with authority to proceed in a more summary way than is used within this realm, according to the known and established laws thereof.

Be it therefore enacted by the King's Most Excellent Majesty, by and with the advice and consent of the Lords Spiritual and Temporal and Commons in this present Parliament assembled, and by the authority of the same that his Majesty may by his Commission under the Great Seal authorise the person to be appointed Governor or the Lieutenant-Governor in the absence of the Governor, at such place as aforesaid to convene from time to time, as occasion may require, a Court of Judicature for the trial and punishment of all such outrages and misbehaviours as, if committed within this realm would be deemed and taken, according to the laws of this realm, to be treason or misprision thereof, felony or misdemeanour, which Court shall consist of the Judge-Advocate, to be appointed in and for such place, together with six officers of his Majesty's forces by sea or land:

Which court shall proceed to try such offenders by calling such offenders respectively before that Court, and causing the charge against him, her or them respectively to be read over, which charge shall always be reduced into writing, and shall be exhibited to the said Court by the Judge-Advocate, and by examining witnesses upon oath, to be administered by such Court, as well for as against such offenders respectively, and afterwards adjudging by the opinion of the major part of the persons composing such Court, that the party accused is or is not (as the case shall appear to them) guilty of the charge, and by pronouncing judgment therein (as upon a conviction by verdict) of death, if the offence be capital, or of such corporal punishment not extending to capital punishment as to the said Court shall seem meet and in cases not capital, by pronouncing judgment of such corporal punishment, not extending to life or limb, as to the said Court shall seem meet.

II. And be it further enacted that the Provost-Marshal, or other officer to be for that purpose appointed by such governor or lieutenant governor shall cause due execution of such judgement to be had and made under and according to the warrant of such Governor or Lieutenant-Governor, shall cause due execution of such judgment to be had and made under and according to the warrant of such Governor or Lieutenant-Governor in the absence of the Governor, under his hand and seal, and not otherwise.

Provided always that execution shall not be had or done on any capital convict or convicts unless five persons present in such Court shall concur in adjudging him, her, or them, so accused and tried as aforesaid, to be respectively guilty, and until the proceedings shall have been transmitted to his Majesty and by him approved.

And be it also enacted by the authority aforesaid that the said Court shall be a court of record and shall have all such powers as by the laws of England are incident and belonging to a court of record.

Bringing British law to Australia

CHARTER OF JUSTICE

As well as creating a criminal court in New South Wales, the British government provided the colony with a civil court to be known as the Court of Civil Jurisdiction. It was established by a charter of 2 April 1787, known historically as the first Charter of Justice (later charters were issued in 1814 and 1823 to reflect changes in the administration of the law in New South Wales). The court comprised the judge-advocate and two 'fit and proper persons' who were appointments of the governor. The court had the power to deal with disputes over property and had jurisdiction in matters concerning wills and estates.

Historian David Neal has noted that while it was the presence of free people in the infant colony of New South Wales that gave this court its rationale, the court was in fact open to convicts. Indeed, the first writ issued by the new court, when it sat on 1 July 1788, concerned a complaint by convict couple Henry and Susannah Kable that a parcel of their property loaded onto the transport ship *Alexander* in England had not been delivered to them in Sydney, even after numerous enquiries and complaints. Their writ named the ship's captain, Duncan Sinclair, as defendant. Directed by the judge-advocate, the court issued a warrant to the provost-marshall ordering that Captain Sinclair be brought to the court the next day to answer the complaint against him.

In what was the first civil case ever held in Australia, Henry Kable—who later prospered as a ship owner in Sydney—swore that his missing goods were worth fifteen pounds. In hearing this matter, the court found for Kable and entered a verdict against the ship's captain for that amount. As Neal emphasises, not only did this case vindicate the property rights of two convicts, but the handling of the matter by the court also offered a public demonstration that under the Charter of Justice even convicts had the ability to invoke the processes of the law.

Whereas by virtue of An Act of parliament passed in the Twenty Fourth Year of the Reign, Wee have judged fit, by and with the advice of Our Privy Council ... to declare and appoint the place to which certain Offenders should be transported for the time or Terms in their several Sentences mentioned, to be the Eastern Coast of New South Wales, or some one or other of the Islands adjacent.

And Whereas Wee find it Necessary that a Colony and Civil Government should be Established in the place, to which such Convicts shall be transported, and that sufficient Provision should be made for the Recovery of Debts and determining of private Causes between party and party in the place aforesaid. We taking the same into our Royal Consideration and being desirous that Justice may be Administered to all our Subjects, have ... thought fit to grant ordain direct and appoint ... a Court to be called the Court of Civil Jurisdiction; and that such Court shall consist of the Judge Advocate for the time being, together with two fit and proper persons, Inhabiting the said place, to be appointed from time to time by our Governor or ... by our Lieutenant-Governor for the time being, or of any two of them (whereof the Judge Advocate to be one); to which Court, Wee hereby give full power and Authority to hold plea of, and to hear and determine in a Summary way all pleas, concerning Lands, Houses, Tenements, and Hereditaments, and all manner of interests therein, and all pleas of Debt, Account or other Contracts, Trespasses, and all manner of other personal pleas whatsoever. And Wee do further Will, Ordain and Grant to the Said Court full power and Authority to Grant probates of Wills and Administration of the personal Estates of Intestates dying within the place or Settlement aforesaid. And our further Will and pleasure is and Wee do, by these presents, for Us, our Heirs and Successors, Direct, Ordain and Appoint that, upon Complaint to be made in writing to the said Court by any person or persons against any other person or persons residing or being within said place, of any Cause of Suit, The said Court shall or may Issue a Warrant in Writing under the Hand and Seal of the said Judge Advocate for the time being to be directed to the provost Marshall, or such other Officer as shall be appointed by Our Governor, to Execute the process thereof, which Warrant shall contain shortly the Substance of the Complaint, and shall either command such Officer to Summon the Defendant or Defendants to appear, or in case the Value of the Demand be Ten pounds or upwards (of which Oath shall first be made) Command him to bring his, her or their Body or Bodies, or take Bail for his or their Appearance before the Court ... to Answer to the said complaint, and to find Sufficient Security for his, her or their performance of such Judgment, Sentence or Decree, as shall be pronounced thereupon, or finally given upon Appeal; and upon Appearance, Arrest or Non Appearance, or Return by the Officer that the Defendant or Defendants cannot be found, Wee hereby ... Ordain, Direct and Authorize the said Court to proceed to the Examination of the Matter and cause of such Complaint, and upon due proof made thereof ... to give Judgment and Sentence according to Justice and Right, and to award and Issue out a Warrant or Warrants of Execution ... And if either party shall find him or themselves aggrieved by any Judgment or Decree to be given or pronounced by the said Court, Our Will and Pleasure is that he, she or they shall and may appeal to the Governor of the Eastern Coast of New

South Wales and the parts adjacent ... whom Wee do hereby Empower and Authorize to hear and determine the same, and to Issue process of Summons to answer to such an Appeal, and the like process of Execution as the Court is hereby directed and empowered to Issue. And if either party shall find him her or themselves aggrieved by the Judgment or Determination of the said Governor in any Case where the Debt or thing in Demand shall exceed the value of three hundred pounds and not otherwise, Our Will and pleasure also is that such party so aggrieved may Appeal to Us or Our Heirs and Successors in Council ... And whereas it is necessary that a Court of Criminal Jurisdiction should also be Established within the Colony or Settlement ... with authority to proceed in a more Summary way than is used within this Realm according to the known and Established Laws thereof ... It is Enacted that his Majesty may, by his Commission under the Great Seal, Authorize the person to be appointed Governor ... to Convene from time to time, as occasion may require, a Court of Judicature for the Trial and Punishment of all such Outrages and Misbehaviours, as, if Committed within this Realm would be deemed and taken according to the Laws of this Realm to be Treason or Misprision thereof, Felony or Misdemeanour, which Court shall consist of the Judge Advocate ... together with Six Officers of His Majesty's Forces by Sea or Land, which Court shall proceed to try such Offenders ... Now Know ye that Wee, ... Grant, Direct, Ordain and Appoint that there shall be within the Settlement and Colony aforesaid a Court which shall be called the Court of Criminal Jurisdiction ... and that the said Court of Criminal Jurisdiction shall have the power to enquire of bear determine and punish all Treasons or Misprision thereof, Murders, Felonies, Forgeries, Perjuries, Trespasses and other Crimes whatsoever, committed [in New South Wales] such punishment so to be Inflicted being according to the Laws of that part of Our Kingdom of Great Britain called England, as nearly as may be, considering and allowing for the Circumstances and Situation of the place and Settlement aforesaid and the Inhabitants thereof ... And if [the offender or offenders be] adjudged Guilty, that the Court shall proceed to pronounce Judgment of Death, if the Offence be Capital, in like manner as if the prisoner had been found Guilty by Verdict of a Jury in England, or by pronouncing Judgment of such Corporal Punishment, not extending to Capital Punishment, as to the said Court ... shall seem meet. ... And further Know Ye that Wee, for preserving the peace of our said Settlement and the Islands thereunto adjacent ... do grant, Ordain, direct and appoint that our present and all Our future Governors and Lieutenant Governors and our Judge Advocate for the time being shall be Justices of the peace within the said place or Settlement, and that all and every such Justice and Justices of the peace shall have the same power to keep the peace, arrest, take Bail, bind to good behaviour, Suppress and punish Riots, and to do all other Matters and Things with respect to the Inhabitants ... as Justices of the peace have within that part of the Kingdom of Great Britain called England within their respective Jurisdictions ... And lastly Our will and pleasure is, And Wee do hereby declare that this Our Charter shall be and remain in force only and untill Wee shall be pleased to revoke and determine the same ...

George the T[hird]

...King of Great Britain France and Ireland...
...by virtue of an Act of Parliament passed in...
...Privy Council by two several Orders bearing...
...to declare and appoint the place to which...
...mentioned to be the Eastern Coast of New South Wales or some one or other...
...Civil Government should be established in the place to which such Courts...
...and determining of private Causes between party and party in the place aforesaid...
...may be administered to all our Subjects have of our especial Grace certain know[ledge]...
...do for us our Heirs and Successors Will grant ordain direct and appoint that the...
...that such Court shall consist of the Judge Advocate for the time being together with...
...by our Governor or in case of his Death or Absence by our Lieutenant Gov[ernor]...
...which Court We do hereby give full power and Authority to hold plea of all...
...and Hereditaments and all manner of Interests therein and all pleas of Debt or...
And We do further Will ordain and grant to the said Court full power...
...intestates dying within the place or settlement aforesaid And our further Wi[ll]...
...ordain and appoint that upon Complaint to be made in writing to the said...
...within the said place of any Cause of Suit the said Court shall or may issue a [warrant]...
...to be directed to the Provost Marshall or such other Officer as shall be appointed...
...of the Complaint and either command such Officer that the Defendant or Defenda[nts]...
...shall first be made command them to bring his her or their Body or Bodies...
...place therein to be named to answer the said Complaint and to find sufficient...
...be pronounced thereupon or finally given upon an Appeal and upon Appearan[ce]...
...cannot be found We do thereby for us our Heirs and Successors ordain direct...
...Cause of such Complaint and upon...

ABOVE *The 1787 Charter of Justice for New South Wales.*

AN ACCOUNT

OF THE

ENGLISH COLONY

IN

NEW SOUTH WALES:

WITH

REMARKS ON THE DISPOSITIONS, CUSTOMS, MANNERS, &c. OF
THE NATIVE INHABITANTS OF THAT COUNTRY.

TO WHICH ARE ADDED,

SOME PARTICULARS OF NEW ZEALAND;

COMPILED, BY PERMISSION,

FROM THE MSS. OF LIEUTENANT-GOVERNOR KING.

By DAVID COLLINS, Esquire,
LATE JUDGE ADVOCATE AND SECRETARY OF THE COLONY.

ILLUSTRATED BY ENGRAVINGS.

"Many might be saved who now suffer an ignominious and an early death; and many
might be so much purified in the furnace of punishment and adversity, as to
become the ornaments of that society of which they had formerly been the bane. The
vices of mankind must frequently require the severity of justice; but a wise State will
direct that severity to the greatest moral and political good." ANON.

LONDON:
PRINTED FOR T. CADELL JUN. AND W. DAVIES, IN THE STRAND.
1798.

At anchor in Botany Bay

THE ARRIVAL OF THE FIRST FLEET

Several diarists and journal keepers were among those who travelled to Australia on board the ships of the First Fleet. It is in their accounts that we find much detail about the journey itself, the character and temperament of the leading personalities, the sequence of events that marked the first days after the landing at Botany Bay and the gradual bedding down of the new settlement. And here Australians can observe, through the eyes of those who were present, the steps taken to establish British authority in New South Wales and to lay the foundations of the convict settlement that would eventually be transformed into an independent nation. Whether written for publication or as private records kept for the writer's own pleasure and satisfaction, or as consolations against loneliness and despair, these various accounts are among the most precious of Australian documents.

Some of the First Fleet accounts were written as private journals. Others—those prepared by Governor Phillip's senior officers—were kept to honour publishing agreements negotiated before the fleet had sailed from England. Following the immense success of the published accounts of Cook's voyages, enterprising publishers in London were keen to profit from a public eager to read of new lands, new discoveries and the curiosities of exotic plants, animals and peoples. Phillip himself undertook to write an account of the voyage to Botany Bay, but he was not alone. Others were Captain John Hunter (1737–1821), commander of the fleet's flagship *Sirius*, and Surgeon-General John White (1757/8–1832). Another in the company of writers was the relatively junior Watkin Tench (1758?–1833), a captain-lieutenant of the marines, who created two especially engaging accounts. He scored something of a coup when his *A Narrative of the Expedition to Botany Bay* was published in London on 24 April 1789— the first to reach the public. He followed this in 1793 with *A Complete Account of the Settlement at Port Jackson*.

Yet another writer emerged in the judge-advocate, David Collins (1756–1810), who maintained a private journal during the voyage to New South Wales and at the settlement itself. At the outset, it was a record intended for himself and for the interest of his family and friends in England. But, no doubt alert to the publishing commitments of his colleagues and the potential prospects of good sales, after only a few months Collins, too, began to think of producing a book. Returning to England in June 1797, he was in great demand for information about the colony and as a source of news about those who were now effectively exiled in New South Wales. In 1798 Collins published from his personal records the first volume of *An Account of the English Colony in New South Wales*; as a prologue or introduction he narrated the course of the journey from England and the arrival in Botany Bay. A second volume of his *Account* appeared in 1802. Regarded still as the most complete and optimistic record of the first decade of English settlement in Australia, Collins' account is perhaps more dutiful and sober than it is entertaining or animated. Indeed, historian Inga Clendinnen has characterised Collins—perhaps a little unfairly—as a 'Master of Plod' for his weight of factual detail. But it should not be forgotten that Collins was moved by a larger purpose: to dissuade his countrymen from viewing the penal colony with 'odium and disgust', and in this he might be seen as one of the earliest Australian patriots.

In the extract selected here, Collins provides a quietly moving account of the arrival of the First Fleet to its 'anchor in Botany Bay'. He also records the steps Governor Phillip took shortly afterward to relocate the infant colony to Port Jackson inside the 'noble and capacious' harbour where a more certain supply of fresh water was found. It will be seen, too, that Collins is not insensitive to the anger expressed by the local Eora people, whose shouts and gestures left little doubt that no welcome was being extended to the new arrivals.

OPPOSITE *Title page of* An Account of the English Colony in New South Wales.

When the *Sirius* anchored in the bay, Captain Hunter was informed that the *Supply* had preceded him in his arrival only two days; and that the agent Lieutenant Shortland, with his detachment from the fleet, had arrived but the day before the *Sirius* and her convoy.

Thus, under the blessing of God, was happily completed, in eight months and one week, a voyage which, before it was undertaken, the mind hardly dared venture to contemplate, and on which it was impossible to reflect without some apprehensions as to its termination. This fortunate completion of it, however, afforded even to ourselves as much matter of surprise as of general satisfaction; for in the above space of time we had sailed five thousand and twenty-one leagues; had touched at the American and African Continents; and had at last rested within a few days of the antipodes of our native country, without meeting any accident in a fleet of eleven sail, nine of which were merchantmen that had never before sailed in that distant and imperfectly explored ocean: and when it is considered, that there was on board a large body of convicts, many of whom were embarked in a very sickly state, we might be deemed peculiarly fortunate, that of the whole number of all descriptions of persons coming to form the new settlement, only thirty-two had died since their leaving England, among whom were to be included one or two deaths by accidents; although previous to our departure it was generally conjectured, that before we should have been a month at sea one of the transports would have been converted into a hospital ship. But it fortunately happened otherwise; the high health which was apparent in every countenance was to be attributed not only to the refreshments we met with at Rio de Janeiro and the Cape of Good Hope, but to the excellent quality of the provisions with which we were supplied by Mr. Richards junior, the contractor; and the spirits visible in every eye were to be ascribed to the general joy and satisfaction which immediately took place on finding ourselves arrived at that port which had been so much and so long the subject of our most serious reflections, the constant theme of our conversations.

The governor, we found, had employed the time he had been here in examining the bay, for the purpose of determining where he should establish the settlement; but as yet he had not seen any spot to which some strong objection did not apply. Indeed, very few places offered themselves to his choice, and not one sufficiently extensive for a thousand people to sit down on. The southern shore about Point Sutherland seemed to possess the soil best adapted for cultivation, but it was deficient in that grand essential fresh water, and was besides too confined for our numbers. There was indeed a small run of water there; but it appeared to be only a drain from a marsh, and by no means promised that ample or certain supply which was requisite for such a settlement as ours. The governor, therefore, speedily determined on examining the adjacent harbours of Port Jackson and Broken Bay, in one of which he thought it possible that a better situation for his young colony might be found ...

The governor set off on Monday the 21st, accompanied by Captain Hunter, Captain Collins (the judge advocate), a lieutenant, and the master of the *Sirius*, with a small party of marines for their protection, the whole being embarked in three open boats. The day was mild and serene, and there being but a gentle swell without the mouth of the harbour, the excursion promised to be a pleasant one. Their little fleet attracted the attention of several parties of the natives, as they proceeded along the coast, who all greeted them in the same words, and in the same tone of vociferation, shouting every where "Warra, warra, warra,"—words, which, by the gestures that accompanied them, could not be interpreted into invitations to land, or expressions of welcome. It must however be observed, that at Botany Bay the natives had hitherto conducted themselves sociably and peaceably toward all the parties of our officers and people ... and by no means seemed to regard them as enemies or invaders of their country and tranquillity. [Collins later had cause to revise this opinion.]

The coast, as the boats drew near Port Jackson, wore so unfavourable an appearance, that Captain Phillip's utmost expectation reached no farther than to find what Captain Cook, as he passed by, thought might be found, shelter for a boat. In this conjecture, however, he was most agreeably disappointed, by finding not only shelter for a boat, but a harbour capable of affording security to a much larger fleet than would probably ever seek for shelter or security in it. In one of the coves of this noble and capacious harbour, equal if not superior to any yet known in the world, it was determined to fix the settlement ...

By Permission of His Excellency.

FOR THE BENEFIT OF J. BUTLER
AND W. BRYANT.

At the THEATRE, SYDNEY,

On Saturday, July 30, 1796. will be Performed

JANE SHORE.

Hastings	I. Sparrow.
Belmour	R. Evans
Catesby	H. Lavell.
Ratcliffe	L. Jones.
Gloster	W. Chapman
And Shore	H. Green.
Alicia	Mrs. Davis.
And Jane Shore	Mrs. Greville.

After the Play

The Wapping Landlady.

Sailors	Hughes and Evans.
And Mother Doublechalk	W. Fokes.

To which will be added

THE MIRACULOUS CURE.

Front Boxes 3s. 6d. Pit 2s. 6d. Gallery 1s.

Doors to be opened at Half past Five, begin at Six.

Tickets to be had of Mrs Greville, of W. Bryant and a Saturday at the House adjoining the Theatre.

ABOVE *The playbill, the reverse of which features a handwritten note listing two plays performed earlier in Sydney and Norfolk Island:* The Recruiting Officer *and* Richard III.

A place for the arts in Australia

A TRIO OF THEATRE PERFORMANCES IN SYDNEY

On 11 September 2007, Canadian Prime Minister Stephen Harper presented a rare document commemorating the early history of cultural endeavour in Australia to Prime Minister John Howard as a gift to the nation. This single-sheet broadside playbill is an advertisement for a theatrical performance at the Sydney Theatre on 30 July 1796. The work of Australia's first printer John (known as George) Hughes (active 1796–1800), the playbill is the earliest surviving example of a document printed in Australia. It was found in a scrapbook in the Library and Archives Canada, but as a result of Canadian generosity it now has a home in the National Library of Australia in Canberra.

The playbill advertises a trio of performances: *Jane Shore*, a popular drama of sin and redemption; *The Wapping Landlady*, a pantomime dance offered as a distraction to a rowdy crowd during interval; and a farce, *The Miraculous Cure*. The playbill lists company members, all convicts, with the printer Hughes appearing as a sailor in *The Wapping Landlady*. While these were not the first plays to be performed in Sydney, the playbill of 1796 is a rare survival representing a lively popular theatrical culture in Australia that began with a production of George Farquhar's comedy *The Recruiting Officer*, offered on 4 June 1789 to mark the birthday of King George III.

In *An Account of the English colony of New South Wales* (1798; see page 52), David Collins mentions that a small printing press had been brought to Australia by Arthur Phillip in 1788. But with no suitable paper or printers' ink, or even a skilled printer, the press remained unused until late in 1795. As David Collins tells it, one George Hughes was eventually 'found equal' to the task of using the press. A 'very decent young man ... of some abilities in the printing line', Hughes had arrived in Sydney on the *Pitt* in February 1792 to serve a seven-year sentence for stealing. Working in a small printery behind the first Government House, Hughes began printing government orders and other printed matter, including playbills. He worked in Sydney until at least 1800, but after this date there is no further mention of him. It is possible he left the colony when his sentence expired. The ephemeral printings by George Hughes predate the appearance of the first Australian printed book, *New South Wales Standing Orders* (1802) and the first Australian newspaper, the *Sydney Gazette and New South Wales Advertiser*, issued on 5 March 1803, both of them the work of George Howe (1769–1821), who was transported for shoplifting and appointed as the first government printer after his arrival in 1800. A rare and fortuitous survival, the modest Sydney playbill of 1796 points the way to the larger aspirations of European culture in Australia.

Naming Australia

MATTHEW FLINDERS WRITES TO SIR JOSEPH BANKS

In August 1804 the maritime explorer Matthew Flinders (1774–1814) completed his *General Chart of Terra Australis or Australia*. This map, the first complete record of the Australian coastline and the product of Flinders' intrepid surveys from 1801 to 1803, has been described by historian Paul Brunton as 'the summary of his life's work and his memorial'.

When it came to the choice of a name for the great island continent, Flinders made the bold decision to call it 'Australia or Terra Australis', though he was not the first to have used the term, which had had some currency from the seventeenth century. From about 1786, official usage in England preferred Cook's name of New South Wales for everything east of the 135° meridian of longitude and New Holland for everything west of it.

Flinders' reasons for giving primacy to the name 'Australia' were argued in detail in a private letter written in London in 1813 to Sir Joseph Banks. Flinders' Mauritian exile had ended and he had returned to England in 1810 to prepare for publication the account of his voyages and the accompanying volume of charts. He was dismayed that Banks was unwilling to support his choice of name, though others certainly did. When Flinders' account was published on 18 July 1814—the day before his death—it appeared as *A Voyage to Terra Australis*, but with a statement that it had been his preference to use the title *A Voyage to Australia*.

Prompted by the logic Flinders had applied to the description of his chart, it was Lachlan Macquarie, the fifth governor of New South Wales, who later formally advocated the adoption of the name Australia for the continent and began to popularise its use as a fitting designation for the country itself. In an official dispatch of 21 September 1817, Macquarie made clear his preference: 'I hope [Australia] will be the Name given to this Country in future, instead of the very erroneous and misapplied name hitherto given to it of "New Holland" which properly speaking only applies to a part of this immense Continent'. While Macquarie's use of the name contributed to its gradual adoption and to a sparking of the sentiments of a native patriotism, Flinders' view—informed by his achievements in the circumnavigation of the continent—has a special authority.

ABOVE *Matthew Flinders, 1806.*

17 August 1813
Joseph Banks
7 Upper Fitzroy Street, 17 August 1813

Sir

In consequence of the high value I set upon your approbation, your obliging note of the 13th. gave me very particular pleasure; but I will not disguise, that my chagrin was no less, to learn, from the postscript, that the term Terra Australis, as a name for New Holland and New South Wales collectively was not approved.

The opinion that the British discoveries ought not, in justice, to be comprehended under the name given by the Dutch to the parts discovered by them, originated, I believe with myself; but had it not met with the approbation of others whose opinions had great weight with me, and would be respected by the public, I should not have ventured upon making use, even of the original Terra Australis, in the publication of my charts and voyage. You, Sir Joseph, were the first person whom I thought it essential to consult, upon the propriety of calling the new continent Australia, and it appeared to be approved; but that it might be done upon due consideration, you were good enough, as I then understood, to request Major Rennell would call in Soho Square. I then proposed my reasons for not including the British discoveries as a part of New Holland, and they were so far approved that *Australia*, as a general name for the Continent, was judged a proper one by the gentleman present. A short time after, when I had the honour of shewing my charts to you and to Admiral Bligh, the name was again a subject of conversation, and appeared to meet the approbation of the admiral also.

But not to be precipitate, you took the trouble, to present the first sheets of my manuscript to the Earl of Liverpool, then secretary for the colonies, with a request that he would point out any thing therein, that he might wish corrected or erased; and in Mr. Peel's answer, the discussion upon the propriety of including Carpentaria as part of N.S. Wales, was pointed out as one which the Earl did not wish to be made; and it was erased; but no exception was taken to the term Australia; and I, therefore, thought it approved by him. I also mentioned the subject to the hydrographer of the Admiralty, with my reasons for using the name Australia. He did not enter into any discussion upon it, but said, that if I used it, it would be adopted in his office.

I then ventured to use the word without reserve; but on speaking to captain Burney, he thought that many persons might object to it from being new; but that *Terra Australis*, the original name, was not liable to the same objection, and would, most probably, be adopted by geographers. This I mentioned to you;—captain Burney's reasoning you thought to be good,— and, in consequence, I altered Australia in my manuscript to Terra Australis; and thus fortified, as I thought; my mind was made up to use it; although I found, and it was an unpleasant thing, that Mr. Brown and Mr. Arrowsmith, who had called it New Holland in their publications, did not approve of the alteration.

Such, Sir, were the steps I took to ascertain the most essential opinions, upon the renovation of the name Terra Australis. That captain Cook speaks of his New South Wales as a part of New Holland is certain; but I cannot help thinking that had Tasman's Instructions of 1644 been known to him, wherein Terra Australis or the Great South Land, is the name always used, and had he known that when *New Holland* was afterwards applied, the Dutch were so far from extending it beyond their own discoveries that even Carpentaria was not included;—had he been aware of these, I conceive his New South Wales would have been considered a part of Terra Australis and not of New Holland; and therefore, that what I proposed to do, was what he would have done, had he possessed the same documents.

I have no prejudice against comprehending the British discoveries under the term New Holland, except what I feel as an Englishman, and certainly no partiality to gratify in using Terra Australis; and could I have been aware that the latter would not meet your approbation, my own opinion would have been given up instantly. I am now in a disagreeable predicament; the name runs through my charts and narrative, and is interwoven in the general arrangement; and from the opinions asked, and approbation given, I am in some degree under an implied obligation to use it; yet to do so, appears to be contrary to that *opinion*, of which I make the greatest account. A hope remains to me, that it is rather from the imperfection of the reasoning in my printed sheet, than from the demerit of the name itself; and that on considering the subject in all its bearings, you may see cause to think that the name may remain without geographical impropriety, or a want of respect to the authority of captain Cook. Should such be the case, it would afford much gratification to, Sir

Your very faithful and obliged humble servant

P.S. Not having made any notes of who were present at the first discussion mentioned above, I wrote to Major Rennell upon the subject, and have the honour to inclose a copy, both my letter and of his answer.

From a settlement to a country

FIRST CROSSING OF THE BLUE MOUNTAINS

One of the landmark events in the history of European settlement and exploration in Australia was the successful crossing of the Blue Mountains by a party comprising army lieutenant William Lawson (1774–1850), settler Gregory Blaxland (1778–1853) and W.C. Wentworth (1790–1872), the future author, barrister, landowner and statesman. Blaxland's account of the expedition in *A Journal of a Tour of Discovery across the Blue Mountains in New South Wales* was published in 1823; it is today one of the most desirable books for collectors of the literature of Australian exploration. The journey commenced on 11 May 1813, with the exploring party accompanied by four servants, five dogs and five horses laden with provisions, ammunition and other necessities.

With the breaching of the once seemingly impenetrable barrier of mountains to the west of Sydney on 31 May 1813, a trail was blazed to the magnificent pastures of the Bathurst Plains. The following year, Governor Lachlan Macquarie made the same journey to the western edge of the Blue Mountains, there 'to feast our eyes with the grand and pleasing prospect of the fine low country below us'. Macquarie's journey, under the leadership of George W. Evans (1780–1852), one of the colony's assistant land surveyors, was undertaken to evaluate the prospects for the productive expansion of the colony. Within a year a road had been completed to the new territories, and by 1815 a settlement had been established at Bathurst. These were achievements that helped to define the years of Macquarie's administration as a remarkable period of exploration, growth and consolidation. These were the years that, in the words of Macquarie's biographer, M.H. Ellis, saw New South Wales cease to be a settlement and begin to be a country.

In an order issued from Government House in Sydney on 12 February 1814, Macquarie's official secretary announced and celebrated the new discoveries west of the Blue Mountains, while also promulgating the news of the rewards and grants of land that had been made to those involved in opening up the new country.

Government House,
Sydney. Feb. 12, 1814.

It having been long deemed an object of great importance, by His Excellency the Governor, to ascertain what resources this colony might possess in the interior, beyond its present known and circumscribed limits, with a view to meet the necessary demands of its rapidly increasing population; and the great importance of the discovery of new tracks of good soil, being much enhanced by the consideration of the long-continued droughts of the present season, so injurious in their effects to every class of the community in the colony: His Excellency was pleased, some time since, to equip a party of men, under the direction of Mr. George W. Evans, one of the Assistant Land Surveyors, (in whose zeal and abilities for such an undertaking he had well-founded reason to confide,) and to furnish him with written instructions for his guidance, in endeavoring to discover a passage over the Blue Mountains, and ascertaining the qualities and general properties of the soil he should meet with to the westward of them.

This object having been happily effected, and Mr. Evans returned with his entire party, all in good health: the Governor is pleased to direct that the following summary of his tour of discovery, extracted from his own journal, shall be published for general information:—

Mr. Evans, attended by five men, selected for their general knowledge of the country, and habituated to such difficulties as might be expected to occur, was supplied with horses, arms, and ammunition, and a plentiful store of provisions for a two months' tour. His instructions were, that he should commence the ascent of the Blue Mountains, from the extremity of the present known country at Emu Island, distant about thirty-six miles from Sydney, and thence proceed in as nearly a west direction as the nature of the country he had to explore would admit, and to continue his journey as far as his means would enable him.

On Saturday, the 20th of November last, the party proceeded from Emu Island; and on the fifth day, having then effected their passage over the Blue Mountains, arrived at the commencement of a valley on the western side of them, having passed over several tracks of tolerably good soil, but also over much rugged and very difficult mountain: proceeding through this valley, which Mr. Evans describes as beautiful and fertile, with a rapid stream running through it, he arrived at the termination of the tour lately made by Messrs. G. Blaxland, W.C. Wentworth, and Lieutenant Lawson. Continuing in the Western direction, prescribed in his instructions, for the course of twenty-one days from this station, Mr. Evans then found it necessary to return; and on the 8th of January he arrived back at Emu Island, after an excursion of seven complete weeks. During the course of this tour Mr. Evans passed over several plains of great extent, interspersed with hills and valleys, abounding in the richest soil, and with various streams of water and chains of ponds. The country he traversed measured ninety-eight miles and a half beyond termination of Messrs. Blaxland, Wentworth, and Lawson's tour, and not less than one hundred and fifty miles from Emu Island. The greater part of these plains are described as being nearly free of timber and brushwood, and in capacity equal (in Mr. Evans's opinion) to every demand which this colony may have for extension of tillage and pasture lands for a century to come. The stream already mentioned continues its course in a westerly direction, and for several miles, passing through the valleys, with many and great accessions of other streams becomes a capacious and beautiful river, abounding in fish of very large size and fine flavour, many of which weighed not less than fifteen pounds. The river is supposed to empty itself into the ocean, on the western side of New South Wales, at a distance of from two to three hundred miles from the termination of the tour. From the summits of some very high hills, Mr. Evans saw a vast extent of flat country, lying in a westerly direction, which appeared to be bounded at a distance of about forty miles by other hills. The general description of these hitherto unexplored regions, given by Mr. Evans, is, that they very far surpass, in beauty and fertility of soil, any he has seen in New South Wales or Van Diemen's Land.

In consideration of the importance of these discoveries, and calculating upon the effect they may have on the future prosperity of this colony, His Excellency the Governor is pleased to announce his intention of presenting Mr. Evans with a grant of one thousand acres of land in Van Diemen's Land, where he is to be stationed as Deputy Surveyor; and, further, to make him a pecuniary reward from the Colonial Funds, in acknowledgement of his diligent and active services on this occasion.

His Excellency also means to make a pecuniary reward to the two free men who accompanied Mr. Evans, and a grant of land to each of them. To the three convicts who also assisted in this excursion the Governor means to grant conditional pardons, and a small portion of land to each of them, these men having performed the services required of them entirely to the satisfaction of Mr. Evans.

The Governor is happy to embrace this opportunity of conveying his acknowledgments to Gregory Blaxland and William Charles Wentworth, Esqs., and Lieutenant William Lawson of the Royal Veteran Company, for their enterprising and arduous exertions on the tour of discovery which they voluntarily performed in the month of May last, when they effected a passage over the Blue Mountains, and proceeded to the extremity of the first valley, particularly alluded to in Mr. Evans's Tour, and being the first Europeans who had accomplished the passage over the Blue Mountains. The Governor, desirous to confer on these gentlemen substantial marks of his sense of their meritorious exertions on this occasion, means to present each of them with a grant of one thousand acres of land in this newly discovered country.

By command of His Excellency the Governor
J.T. Campbell
Secretary.

1817

Creating Australia's first bank

A CHARTER FOR BANKING IN AUSTRALIA

In Sydney on 29 January 1817 Lachlan Macquarie, as governor of New South Wales, signed the charter incorporating the Bank of New South Wales. It was the first Australian bank and as such the cornerstone of the country's financial system. The charter was delivered to the bank's directors on 22 March 1817. As the bank's historian, R.F. Holder, noted in 1970, the charter was granted to reassure the prospective proprietors that their liability was limited. Without such an assurance it was believed the project would not get off the ground.

Macquarie signed the charter at the urging of the New South Wales deputy judge-advocate, John Wylde (1781–1859), and supported by Barron Field (1786–1846), a judge of the Supreme Court, while recognising that in doing so he might be exceeding the powers of his commission as governor. In a dispatch to London he sought confirmation of his actions in case 'it should be considered that I have overstepped the just bounds of my authority'. As a matter of policy, however, Macquarie was in no doubt that the bank would bring a needed stability and certainty to the financial and commercial life of the colony.

In England in March 1818 the charter was referred to the Crown's law officers, who in August declared it null and void on the grounds that the governor had not been legally empowered either by his commission or instructions to grant it. But by that stage, the Bank of New South Wales was fully operational and was generally perceived to have added greatly to the commercial facilities of the colony.

Macquarie's successor, Sir Thomas Brisbane, was advised that while the bank could continue in operation subject to the ordinary risks of a commercial partnership, it might do so without a charter of incorporation. In the event, however, Brisbane signed a revised charter on 31 October 1823. But while it was flawed, not in substance but in execution, Macquarie's charter of 1817 remains the crucial pioneering document of Australia's banking industry and a treasured possession of Westpac, the successor body to the Bank of New South Wales.

GEORGE THE THIRD by the Grace of God of the United Kingdom of Great Britain and Ireland King Defender of the Faith

TO ALL WHOM THESE PRESENTS SHALL COME

GREETING

WHEREAS HIS MAJESTY'S subjects trading to and residing in the Colony of New South Wales and its Dependencies lie under great Difficulties for Want of a due Supply of Money and an improved certain and increased circulating Medium with the same.

AND WHEREAS it is expedient that those Difficulties should be removed and the same will be removed in a great Degree by the Establishment of a Colonial Bank upon a funded Joint Stock Capital and under certain Laws Liberties Provisions and Regulations in that Respect NOW KNOW YE THAT I LACHLAN MACQUARIE Esquire Captain General Governor and Commander in Chief in and over His said Majesty's Territory of New South Wales and its dependencies aforesaid by Virtue of and as far as the Powers and Authorities vested in me extend in Consideration of the Premises and of the Memorial and Petition of JOHN THOMAS CAMPBELL, D'ARCY WENTWORTH, ALEXANDER RILEY, THOMAS WYLDE, JOHN HARRIS, WILLIAM REDFERN and ROBERT JENKINS Esquires for and on Behalf of themselves and other Subscribers for raising a Fund for establishing a Bank in Sydney ... to be called or DENOMINATED "THE BANK OF NEW SOUTH WALES" praying me as such Governor as aforesaid to give grant ordain and permit to and on Behalf of themselves and other the Subscribers to and Proprietors in the said Bank Stock certain Rights Immunities and Privileges so as to indemnify and secure them and other the said Subscribers to the said Bank their Heirs Successors and Assigns against all Risk or Liability beyond the Amount of the Shares so respectively taken by each of and in the said Capital Stock of the said Bank HAVE THOUGHT FIT to give grant ordain and permit that the said John Thomas Campbell, D'Arcy Wentworth, Alexander Riley, Thomas Wylde, John Harris, William Redfern and Robert Jenkins Esquires and all other the Subscribers contributing to and Proprietors in and of the Fund hereby and herein now declared limited and set forth shall and may and the said John Thomas Campbell, D'Arcy Wentworth, Alexander Riley, Thomas Wylde, John Harris, William Redfern and Robert Jenkins and other the subscribers and proprietors ... are hereby authorized and permitted to raise constitute and establish at Sydney in the Territory a Bank to be denominated "THE BANK OF NEW SOUTH WALES" for the general and the customary Uses and Purpose of Deposit Loan and Discount charging and claiming in Respect thereof no higher rate than Ten per Cent per Annum on a Fund and Capital Stock of TWENTY THOUSAND POUNDS Sterling to be collected raised and funded in and by Two Hundred Shares or Subscriptions of One Hundred Pounds each in Respect of the said Capital Stock Certificates whereof under the Signatures of three or more of the Directors be appointed as herein after mentioned shall be duly made and granted and become transferable by Indorsement or otherwise provided

A charter for banking in Australia.

the same be registered in the Bank Books to be kept for that Purpose ...

AND PROVIDED ALSO that each of the said seven Directors so appointed on the Part of and by the Proprietors reside during the said Office in the Town of Sydney or within two miles of the same and be and are absolutely and unconditionally free ...

IN WITNESS where of I have set my Hand and caused the Great Seal of the Colony to be affixed to these Presents at Sydney this Twelfth day of February One Thousand Eight hundred and seventeen.

LACHLAN MACQUARIE

ABOVE *Bank of New South Wales on George Street, 1870s.*

An enquiry into the settlements in New South Wales

THE BIGGE REPORT

On 5 January 1819 the British government appointed John Thomas Bigge (1780–1843) to conduct a commission of inquiry into the colony of New South Wales. The assignment arose from a decision by Lord Bathurst, Secretary of State for the Colonies, to examine the effectiveness of transportation as a deterrent to felons. Bathurst was worried that 'transportation to New South Wales was becoming neither an object of Apprehension ... nor the means of Reformation', and that the colony itself had become too expensive. Bigge brought to his task the skills of a professional lawyer, the social assumptions (and prejudices) of an aristocrat and a disposition to judge all that he saw by English standards. Before his appointment in New South Wales, he had served four years as chief justice of the former Spanish colony of Trinidad, where he had exposed many flaws in the administration of the judicial system. It was this analytical capacity that commended Bigge to the British authorities to carry out the wide-ranging inquiry that Bathurst now believed to be essential in New South Wales.

Under the terms of his commission, Bigge was authorised to investigate 'all the laws regulations and usages of the settlements'. Notably, that included those affecting civil administration, management of convicts, development of the courts, the Church, trade, revenue and natural resources. This wide-ranging investigation—which was to bring Bigge into direct conflict with Governor Lachlan Macquarie—reflected what historian Raymond Evans has pointed to as 'a renewed interest in the Australian settlements, after thirty years of near neglect by Great Britain and languid local progress'.

The task was defined in broad terms in Bigge's commission of appointment, with considerably more detail added in three letters of instructions (entitled Enclosures 2–4). In the instructions, Bathurst suggested the criteria by which the inquiry should operate. At their core was his requirement that convict transportation to New South Wales and Van Diemen's Land should be made 'an Object of real Terror'. Bigge was also directed to root out evidence of 'ill considered Compassion' in Macquarie's administration of the penal system. Bigge's instructions vested him with enormous power and a status second in rank to the governor himself. But since the governor was under scrutiny, Bigge's authority during the course of his inquiry was absolute. It has been remarked that when Bigge sailed from England he did so 'in the dual guise of public commissioner of the Crown and private inquisitor for the government'.

Bigge's investigations throughout the Australian settlements were conducted over sixteen months. The result of his work was three detailed reports published by the House of Commons in the years 1822–1823. In the implementation of the reports' recommendations over the ensuing decade, Raymond Evans has noted the transformation of New South Wales from a minor and inadequate penal settlement into a thriving economic and social concern. New policies adopted in the wake of the reports allowed for the beginnings of mass convict transportation and the influx of substantial private capital. A new system emerged for the management of convict labour, including what Evans has enumerated as more privatisation through assignment, a more purposeful application of public labour and strategies for opening up new frontiers of white settlement.

But Evans has identified another and pervasive effect of the Bigge Reports—the setting of a new tone for penal administration in Australia. While the post-Bigge innovations led to an expansion of colonial industry and wealth, there was also a hardening of the reputation of the Australian colonies as places of dire punishment, deprivation and immorality. For those undergoing sentence, life worsened after 1822 as administrations applied a harsher penal regime. A free, prosperous and wealthy community would be built on the backs of a convict workforce, but it was a community that 'would long suffer the residual effects of embarrassment and uncertainty about its ignominious origins and character'. For many Australians, the 'stain' or the 'scar' of convict beginnings would survive as a mark of family and collective shame for generations. In the several documents that make up the commission issued to Bigge in 1819 (only the commission itself is published here) may be found the source of much that would prove beneficial to the future direction of the Australian colonies. Exposed there, too, are the dreadful strictures on crime and punishment that would inflict a grievous wound to the national psyche.

ABOVE *John Thomas Bigge.*

Enclosure No. 1.
COMMISSION OF JOHN THOMAS BIGGE

Commission of John Thomas Bigge.
   In the Name and on behalf of His Majesty.
   George. P.R.
   GEORGE the Third, by the Grace of God of the United Kingdom of Great Britain and Ireland, King, Defender of the Faith, To Our Trusty and Well-beloved John Thomas Bigge, Esqre., Greeting. Whereas We have judged it expedient to cause an Enquiry to be made into the present State of the Settlements in Our Territory of New South Wales and its Dependencies, and of the Laws, Regulations and Usages, Civil Military and Ecclesiastical prevailing therein, Now Know You that We, having especial Trust and Confidence in your approved Wisdom and Fidelity, have assigned, nominated and appointed and by these presents assign, nominate and appoint you, the said John Thomas Bigge, to be Our Commissioner to repair to Our said Settlements in Our said Territory in New South Wales, and by these Presents do give you full power and Authority to examine into all the Laws, Regulations and Usages of the Settlements in the said Territory and Dependencies, and into every other Matter or Thing in any way connected with the Administration of the Civil Government, the Superintendance and Reform of the Convicts, the State of the Judicial, Civil and Ecclesiastical Establishments, Revenues, Trade and internal Resources thereof, and to report to Us the Information, which You shall collect together, with your opinion thereupon, reducing your Proceedings, by Virtue of these Presents and your Observations touching and concerning the premises, into writing, to be certified under Your hand and Seal, and We do hereby require Our Governor of Our said Territory for the time being and all and every One, Officers and Minsters within the said Territory and its Dependencies to be aiding and assisting to you in the due execution of this Our Commission. In Witness, &ca. And for so doing this shall be Your Warrant.

   Given at Our Court at Carlton House this fifth day of
   January 1819, in the Fifty ninth Year of Our Reign.
   By the command of his Royal Highness The Prince Regent
   in the name and on Behalf of His Majesty.

BATHURST.

'A new Britannia in another world'

WILLIAM CHARLES WENTWORTH'S POEM *AUSTRALASIA*

With some notable Australian achievements already behind him, but with a rich public career still to be pursued at home in Sydney, the 32-year-old William Charles Wentworth (1790–1872)—explorer, author, barrister, landowner and statesman—entered Peterhouse at Cambridge in February 1823. In what he self-deprecatingly termed a crude effort of a 'poetic bantling', Wentworth submitted an entry to the Chancellor's Gold Medal competition for poetry in 1823. The theme that year was Australasia and, in a field of twenty-five entrants, Wentworth's 443-line meditation on place and national destiny was awarded second place. Though marred by the customary inflated rhetoric of the public poetry of its day, Wentworth's *Australasia* was immediately celebrated as an assertion of Australian identity. The poem occupies a special place as one of the first expressions in Australian literature of pride in country.

When the poem was published in 1823, Wentworth dedicated it to Lachlan Macquarie, whose long and productive governorship of New South Wales had recently ended in the dark shadow of the criticisms of the Bigge Reports (see page 67). Like the poem, the dedication is an emphatic statement of Wentworth's belief in Australia's promise. But it is also a powerful contemporary political judgment of Macquarie, which was written with an eye to the factions then jostling for power and influence in Sydney. In praising the old viceroy's contested achievements, the young Wentworth preferred to take the long view: and it is one that now carries the weight of historical opinion. While the dedication is usually mentioned and occasionally paraphrased in the historical and literary accounts of *Australasia*, it is rarely reproduced. Certainly it deserves to be more widely known, both as a formal introduction to the poem and as a clear statement of belief in a larger Australian future.

Historian Clive Faro has seen Wentworth's *Australasia* as part of a tradition of 'place-making', a literary looking upon the land and at a civilisation then in the process of creation. The poem and its dedication stand together as a single defining document of vision and of the imagination and as an expression of commitment to an Australian future, albeit one that saw the country indelibly shaped by its British inheritance.

ABOVE *W.C. Wentworth.*

My dear Sir,

Although I feel that I am scarcely warranted, without your permission, in thus bringing your name before the public; yet—as you are now travelling on the Continent, and as I could not, therefore, obtain that permission without some considerable delay—I have even ventured to inscribe to you this, the first fruits of Australasian poesy, without your sanction or privity. I have selected you for the patron of this crude effort, not because I could not have found another foster-father for this my poetic bantling, but because I cannot discover amidst the circle of my friends ... any one to whom its introduction to the public could be confided with equal propriety. In you, Sir, who for so many years have presided over the colonies which are included under the designation which is the subject of this poem; who have watched over and promoted their growth rather with the warm solicitude of a parent than the frigid superintendence of a governor; who have conducted them through the helplessness of infancy to the first dawn of youth and independence; and who, in resigning the task of their future guidance to other hands, have still left behind you the warmest wishes for their future welfare and prosperity,—I know that every thing Australasian, or connected with the honour and interests of Australasia, will ever find a steady friend and zealous advocate. I feel, therefore, that in this conjecture I could not apply to any one who would view this hasty production with equal partiality, and be likely to give it that warm countenance and support, which, I fear, will form its chief recommendation. But I will confess that a mere personal consideration of this nature is not the object of this dedication. An Australasian myself, I am anxious at a period when a few dastardly and privileged calumniators have dared ... to impugn the leading measures which characterized your administration of the government of my country, to testify my gratitude for the services which you have rendered to that country, and to assure you that, however those services may for the instant be underrated here, they will long live in the heartfelt recollection of those who were the objects of them, and who have had practical proof of their wisdom and humanity. Nor do I utter any doubtful prophecy when I predict that his Majesty's ministers will soon form a more correct estimate of the zeal, ability, and integrity, with which you have discharged the trust which your Sovereign reposed in you. Calumny is but the foul vapour of a day. As the envious mists that hide the sun quickly disappear, and the glorious luminary breaks forth with renewed force and splendour, thus it is with the benefactors of mankind. Their intentions and acts may be obscured for a season; but the light of their deeds remains behind, and warms and cheers through generations ...

I feel that the poem, to which I have thus annexed your name, would have been more complete, if it had contained some allusion, not to those astonishing monuments which you designed and executed in so short a period in the vast Austral wilderness,—the forests you levelled, the roads you formed, the bridges you built, the palaces you erected, and the towns you founded ... but to that high tone of feeling, that great moral reformation, of which, both by your precept, your example, and your institutions, you sowed the seeds among all classes of the colonists—seeds, the fruits of which will descend to their remotest posterity. Hereafter, when I shall revisit my country, when the beneficial results of your liberal principles and philanthropic labours shall be present to my senses, and when the sublimities of my native floods and forests shall lend their breathing inspiration to my verse, I shall be better qualified to do justice to such a theme; and am resolved ... to give this poem that extension of which the subject is susceptible, and of which I consider it to be deserving. This is a debt, Sir, which Australasia owes you, and which I, the humblest of her sons ... will do my utmost to discharge.

That you may at length find in the bosom of your family that repose which a long life of honourable exertion deserves, and which your declining years require, is the fervent prayer, not of myself alone but of all those of my compatriots who have Australasian hearts; and I am proud to say that there are few ... who do not fall under this denomination.

I remain,
My dear sir,
Your faithful and obedient Servant,

W.C. WENTWORTH.

AUSTRALASIA.

Land of my birth! though now, alas! no more
Musing I wander on thy sea-girt shore,
Or climb with eager haste thy barrier cliff,
To catch a glimmer of the distant skiff,
That ever and anon breaks into light,
And then again eludes the aching sight,
Till nearer seen she bends her foaming way
Majestic onward to yon placid bay,
Where Sydney's infant turrets proudly rise,
The new-born glory of the southern skies;—
Dear Australasia, can I e'er forget
Thee, Mother Earth? Ah no, my heart e'en yet
With filial fondness loves to call to view
Scenes which, though oft remember'd, still are new;
Scenes where my playful childhood's thoughtless years
Flew swift away, despite of childhood tears;
Where later too, in manhood's op'ning bloom;
The tangled brake, th'eternal forest's gloom,
The wonted brook, where with some truant mate
I loved to plunge, or ply the treach'rous bait;
The spacious harbour, with its hundred coves
And fairy islets—seats of savage loves,
Again beheld—restampt with deeper dye
The fading visions of my infancy:
And shall I now, by Cam's old classic stream,
Forbear to sing, and thou proposed the theme?
The native bard, though on a foreign strand,
Shall I be mute, and see a stranger's hand
Attune the lyre, and prescient of thy fame
Foretell the glories that shall grace thy name?
Forbid it, all ye Nine! 'twere shame to thee,
My Austral parent;—greater shame to me.

And, O Brittania! shouldst thou cease to ride
Despotic Empress of old Ocean's tide;—
Should thy tamed Lion—spent his former might,—
No longer roar the terror of the fight;—
Should e'er arrive that dark disastrous hour,
When bow'd by luxury, thou yield'st to pow'r;—
When thou, no longer freest of the free,
To some proud victor bend'st the vanquish'd knee;—
May all thy glories in another sphere
Relume, and shine more brightly still than here;
May this, thy last-born infant, then arise,
To glad thy heart and greet thy parent eyes;
And Australasia float, with flag unfurl'd,
A new Britannia in another world.

The birth of a free press

WENTWORTH AND WARDELL CREATE THE *AUSTRALIAN* NEWSPAPER

On 14 October 1824 the partnership of W.C. Wentworth and Robert Wardell (1793–1834) launched the *Australian* newspaper. Its independent stance, clearly stated in its first editorial, challenged the monopoly of the *Sydney Gazette*, the official voice of government in New South Wales since 1803. With its patriotic and assertive name, the *Australian* came into existence without the sanction of the governor, Sir Thomas Brisbane, who, notwithstanding the objections of the Colonial Office in London, thought it 'most expedient to try the experiment of full latitude of freedom of the Press'.

Brisbane's 'full latitude' was not without its severe discomforts either to the rulers of New South Wales or to the ambitions of the free settlers, the old 'exclusives' or 'pure merinos', who sought to maintain special privileges against those who had been transported and later pardoned. It was for these so-called emancipists and the native-born that Wentworth and Wardell spoke. Historian Peter Cochrane has characterised the *Australian*'s natural audience as 'an assortment of bond and free, indigent and wealthy, needy men and hangers-on, knockabouts and ne'er-do-wells'. A bitter dispute was waged against the paper by Brisbane's successor Sir Ralph Darling, who, vexed in his efforts to restrict a licentious press, eventually prosecuted the publishers for seditious libel.

For all its turbulent history, the *Australian* survived until 1848. It serialised novels by Charles Dickens and other English authors, while also giving voice to local writers, such as Henry Halloran, Charles Harpur, Richard Howitt and Charles Tompson. Its first editorial, reproduced here, contrived to be both brash and high-minded: with the tone of a manifesto, it is a document of colonial ambition charting the course of a new and more diverse Australia.

In presenting our Readers with the first number of THE AUSTRALIAN, we must be old-fashioned enough to give some account of our pretensions, and to state on what grounds we lay claim to their attention, or expect their favour. We do not enter upon our duties of Editors of this new Journal without feeling much of that diffidence which commonly attends the commencement of the anxious labours of periodical writers. Whatever obstacles however may arise, or whatever difficulties we may have to encounter, we flatter ourselves that The Australian appears at a period and under circumstances extremely propitious to such an undertaking. Were we simply to advert to the space of time during which this Colony has existed, we might be disposed to consider her in a state little likely to require the assistance of, or derive any benefit from the establishment of a free press. Infant societies, for the most part, have neither leisure nor inclination to bestow time or thought on objects that have no reference to their immediate wants or the necessities of the day. The elegancies of life are not courted until its conveniences are within their reach; literature is neglected while laborious occupation forms the principal ingredient in the concerns of a people; and the beneficial influence of regular, just and politic laws is not felt, because it is not needed in a community where a few simple regulations and ordinances are sufficient to guide individuals in their intercourse with each other, or a few rigid enactments are enforced for the protection of the peaceable from plunder or acts of violence. This, however, is a state of things beyond which the Colony of New South Wales has long since made considerable advancement: Her population and her possessions have encreased with a rapidity almost unexampled—individual enterprise has produced aggregate wealth—an immense extent of territory has yielded to the ameliorating hand of the husbandman—large plains are in a high state of cultivation—trackless deserts have given place to numerous and well inhabited towns—the active and varied industry of the settler has circulated life and movement through every vein and enriched and animated the country—those arts which embellish life and add to its comforts have become an object of considerable attention; they are cultivated and encouraged with a zeal proportioned to the resources of the country, and those artificial wants the offspring of prosperity and improvement prevail with all the force which marks their existence in polished and long established societies—thus affording every indication of a progressive advancement which nothing can retard, nothing can controul, but an illiberal policy on the part of government, impolitic public measures, or the ignorance and folly of public men. In a Colony whose energies are thus expanding, little doubt can be entertained of the utility and efficacy of an Independent Newspaper. The aggrandizement and the encreasing wealth of a people introduce a complexity in their affairs; conflicting opinions and conflicting interests arise, individual influence is apt to luxuriate and flourish where there exists no correction to check the exuberance or prevent its growth. A free Press is the most legitimate, and at the same time, the most powerful weapon that can be employed to annihilate such influence, frustrate the designs of tyranny, and restrain the arm of oppression. Without its active and liberal cooperation the biassed views of a party frequently preponderate, while the true interests of the public languish and are overlooked. In offering **THE AUSTRALIAN** to our Readers we pretend to no uncommon merit, we affect no singularity, we anticipate no triumphs. Aiming at something more than rendering it a mere miscellany of news or compilation of events, we are solicitous that it should become the medium of extensive and general communication among all members of the Colony, thereby concentrating public opinion and giving a tone and direction to public feeling. Whatever questions may arise involving the interests of the whole or any portion of the Colonists, whatever state measures may be promulgated they will each receive from us the attention and deliberation commensurate with their importance, at the same time that we afford every facility to an interchange of opinions among those who choose to become our Correspondents, as well as Readers. In the many topics that may come within the scope of our comments, we do not limit ourselves to any precise line of politics. Independent yet consistent—free yet not licentious ... without either a sycophantic approval of or a systematic opposition to acts of authority merely because they emanate from government. If, by any exercise of intellectual industry, we render **THE AUSTRALIAN** acceptable to our Readers or useful to the inhabitants of this Colony, we shall be pleased at this employment of our time and feel gratified at our success. Many beneficial improvements may be accomplished in the general condition of the country and in its political institutions. Much depends on the Colonists themselves—much is due from the British Government. The legislature of England knows and has acknowledged its worth and its rising importance, and surely such a useful lesson may be gleaned from the history of past times as may lead to an enlightened policy towards New South Wales. It is the happiness and welfare of colonies, their improvement and prosperity, that ought to be considered by the ministers of the parent state, not how they shall contribute to ministerial influence, ministerial patronage, or satisfy the crowd of needy dependents in the ministerial train.

In the sketch we have drawn, we have endeavoured to develop our sentiments and explain our views. Performance often falls short of promise, we have been careful therefore not to promise too much. We hope, however, that our Readers will always find something to entertain, something to instruct them in the pages of the **AUSTRALIAN**. Besides availing ourselves of the productions of occasional contributors, the aid of whose talents we court, we shall permanently attach to our establishment whatever literary worth is within our reach. We have adopted such precautionary steps as were necessary for securing a constant and early supply of intelligence from various parts of the world. We are also endeavouring to organize a system by which we shall be enabled to give an account of all domestic occurrences of immediate interest. Reporters will be employed to collect the news of the week from various sources. Indeed, as it is our wish to produce a publication which we can conscienciously invite the public to patronize, neither experience, nor labour, nor attention, shall, at any time, be wanting to make it as complete as it is possible for a Newspaper under existing circumstances to become. We must endeavour to amuse readers of all classes, and all tastes, and while we attend to objects of the first magnitude and importance, we shall be careful not to overlook those of minor consequence. Aware of the necessity that exists for the exercise of every diligence to avoid giving circulation to erroneous reports, we shall on no occasion insert any article of news that is not fully authenticated. And though we reserve to ourselves the utmost latitude in the expression of our opinions, we shall studiously abstain from individual attacks and personal invective, which can only be indulged in for the purpose of gratifying a malignant mind, or a rancorous spirit of revenge. It is the errors of a system—the vices of office that we condemn. It is measures not men that we assail; and our respect for the one will not restrain our animadversions on the other. A legal responsibility, we know, will attach to us for everything we may publish in the AUSTRALIAN—but we consider ourselves responsible in point of principles for such opinions only as appear in the leading articles, and our consistency cannot be impeached for admitting into our columns the letters of Correspondents, though they may militate with our own avowed sentiments. Indeed it would be in direct contravention of the spirit of a free Journal to exclude the writings of all whose views of a question happened not to coincide with our own.

A Newspaper carried on in undeviating conformity to these rules, must naturally meet with universal approbation, and eventually give rise to most important results in the Colony.

… From many of our friends we have the satisfaction of having received the kind assurances of assistance with whatever information it may from time to time be in their power to render us. To them and to those who have already flattered us with their patronage, not forgetting the many who have [generally?] and undisguisedly expressed their satisfaction on the commencement of the AUSTRALIAN; indeed, to all our patrons and well-wishers, we tender our best and most sincere acknowledgments, and beg to assure them, that whether we be designated Radicals, or Reformers, or Whigs, or Tories, or Republicans we do not the less seek to propitiate them.

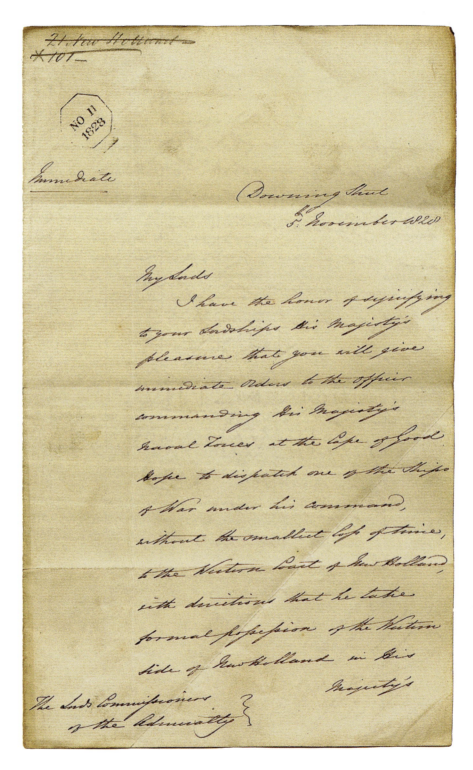

ABOVE *A facsimile of the instructions issued to the Admiralty, held in the National Archives (UK).*

Beginning of the Swan River Colony

INSTRUCTIONS TO TAKE POSSESSION OF WESTERN AUSTRALIA

Although the first formal claim of possession for Britain of what is now known as Western Australia was made by Commander George Vancouver in September 1791, the British government itself took no action to formalise that claim until the 1820s. It did so at that time motivated by a concern that the French might establish a colony on the coast of western Australia and by a growing demand at home for a new colony that would provide rich new opportunities for pastoral expansion. Captain James Stirling (1791–1865) of the Royal Navy had inspected the Swan River in 1827 and was glowing in his reports of its prospects for settlement; he would preside over the fortunes of the first settlement at Swan River from June 1829 to August 1832. As a result in part of Stirling's advocacy, several colonising schemes were being pushed by financiers and speculators, but the British government was unwilling to grant a charter to a private colonising company. The solution was to establish a colony of the Crown under direct government supervision. In 1826 the New South Wales governor, Ralph Darling, had established an informal pre-emptive settlement at King George Sound. Headed by Edmund Lockyer, it comprised eighteen soldiers, a medical officer, a storekeeper and a labour force of twenty-three convicts. However, such a toe-hold was not sustainable. It survived until 1831 when the troops and convicts were withdrawn to Sydney, but by then the Swan River Colony had been brought into existence.

Following the instructions issued to the Admiralty, the declaration formally establishing the new colony was effected by Captain Charles Fremantle of HMS *Challenger* on 2 May 1829. At a ceremony that day he unfurled the Union Jack at Arthur's Head at the mouth of the Swan River; in doing so, he took possession of the whole of that part of Australia that had not been included within the boundaries of New South Wales. This amounted to one-third of the Australian continent. On 2 June 1829 James Stirling arrived in Cockburn Sound on board the *Parmelia* to take up his responsibilities as lieutenant-governor. He was accompanied by his family and joined by sixty-nine intending settlers. It was a small beginning in a vast isolation. Historian Frank Crowley has noted the first steps of occupation—the erection of a small fort 'to assert British sovereignty over one million square miles of land, and the 4300 miles of coastline which had just been annexed, a country more than ten times as large as the British Isles'.

The sheer scale of the new territory unleashed a fever of interest in the prospects it offered for land and opportunity. The press in England reported an outbreak of 'Swan River Mania' while the Colonial Office was swamped with enquiries, the majority of them from 'highly respectable and independent persons', those Crowley has described as moneyed gentlefolk, practical farmers seeking larger properties, professional men, tradesmen and numbers of military and naval officers who had been on half pay since the end of the Napoleonic Wars. But the early optimism was short-lived. The new settlement failed to thrive. Within a few years most of the settlers had departed, and even twenty years later the European population was only 5000.

The modest document published here is the official instrument by which Charles Fremantle was empowered to take the western side of New Holland in the name of the king. It marks the formal beginnings of the present state of Western Australia.

Downing Street
5 November 1828

My Lords

I have the honour of signifying to your Lordships His Majesty's pleasure that you will give immediate orders to the officer commanding His Majesty's Naval Forces at the Cape of Good Hope to dispatch one of the Ships of War under his command, without the smallest loss of time, to the Western Coast of New Holland, with directions that he take formal possession of the Western side of New Holland in His Majesty's name. It is desirable that the place, on which he shall take the possession, be at, or as near as possible to Swan River, and that he maintain, on that spot, an uninterrupted Possession, on behalf of His Majesty, until the arrival of further instructions, which I will very shortly enable your Lordships to communicate.

I am, My Lords
Your Lordships
Most obedient
Humble Servant
G. Murray

Destruction of a people and their culture

A DECLARATION OF MARTIAL LAW IN VAN DIEMEN'S LAND

In Australia's long, contentious and traumatic history of relations between the Indigenous population and European settlers, Tasmania in the nineteenth century was one of the most intense and troubling centres of conflict. In Van Diemen's Land (as Tasmania was first known by the Europeans), the exercise of increasingly repressive measures by the colonial administration led in time to the decimation of a people and their culture.

In the 1820s, as violence increased between settlers and the Aborigines, the lieutenant governor, George Arthur (1784–1854), pursued what was in effect a policy of war in his efforts to impose order on chaos. While careful always to cast a nod to the official British policy of humane care to the Indigenous inhabitants, Arthur's policies were drastic. In the words of one observer, they amounted to a 'war of extermination'. Martial law was declared in 1830, followed almost immediately by the infamous 'Black Line' intended to drive the Aborigines from the settled districts into enforced captivity on the Tasman Peninsula.

A wealth of contemporary documents provides a richly detailed account of policies that evolved in the face of an apparently irreconcilable conflict between those exercising official authority and the Aborigines who, in defending their territory, had resort only to violence. It was an unequal equation. On 30 October 1828 the executive council concluded that 'the outrages of the Aboriginal natives amount to a complete declaration of hostilities against the settlers generally'. Its response was the imposition of martial law in prescribed areas of the colony. In his proclamation of 1 October 1830, published in the *Hobart Town Gazette* of 9 October, the lieutenant governor extended martial law beyond the settled districts to cover the whole of the island and apply to all Aborigines until what he called the 'cessation of hostilities'. There was no alternative, Arthur declared, to 'an active and extended system of Military operations against the Natives generally throughout the Island, and every portion thereof, whether actually settled or not'.

ABOVE *Pictograph from 1828 of Governor Arthur's declaration, painted on huon pine (36 x 22.8 cm).*

By His Excellency Colonel George Arthur, Lieutenant Governor of the Island of Van Diemen's Land and its Dependencies.

A PROCLAMATION.

WHEREAS, by my Proclamation bearing date the first day of November, One thousand eight hundred and twenty-eight, RECITING (amongst other things) that the Black or Aboriginal Natives of this Island, had for a considerable time, carried on a series of indiscriminate attacks upon the person and property of His Majesty's Subjects, and that repeated inroads were daily made by such Natives into the settled Districts, and that acts of hostility and barbarity were there committed by them, as well as at the more distant stock runs, and in some instances upon unoffending and defenceless women and children, and that it had become unavoidably necessary for the suppression of similar enormities, to proclaim Martial Law in the manner thereinafter directed, I the said Lieutenant Governor, did declare and proclaim, that from the date of that my Proclamation, and until the cessation of hostilities, Martial Law was and should continue to be in force against the said Black or Aboriginal Natives within the several Districts of this Island, excepting always the places and portions of this Island in the said Proclamation aforementioned:—And whereas, the said Black or Aboriginal Natives, or certain of their Tribes, have of late manifested, by continued repetitions of the most wanton and sanguinary acts of violence and outrage an unequivocal determination indiscriminately to destroy the White Inhabitants whenever opportunities are presented to them for doing so:—And whereas, by reason of the aforesaid exceptions so contained in the said Proclamation, no Natives have been hitherto pursued or molested in any of the places or portions of the Island so excepted, from whence they have accordingly of late been accustomed to make repeated incursions upon the settled districts with impunity, or, having committed outrages in the settled Districts, have escaped into those excepted places, where they remain in security; And whereas therefore, it hath now become necessary, and because it is scarcely possible to distinguish the particular Tribe or Tribes by whom such outrages have been in any particular instance committed, to adopt immediately, for the purpose of effecting their capture if possible, an active and extended system of Military operations against the Natives generally throughout the Island, and every portion thereof, whether actually settled or not.

Now, therefore, by virtue of the powers and authorities in me in this behalf vested, I the said Lieutenant Governor do, by these presents declare and proclaim, that from and after the date of this my Proclamation, and until the cessation of hostilities in this behalf shall be by me hereafter proclaimed and directed, Martial Law is and shall continue to be in force against all the Black or Aboriginal Natives, within every part of this Island, (whether excepted from the operation of the said Proclamation or not,) excepting always such Tribes, or Individuals of Tribes, as there may be reason to suppose are pacifically inclined, and have not been implicated in any of such outrages: And for the purpose aforesaid, all Soldiers and other His Majesty's Subjects Civil and Military, are hereby required and commanded to obey and assist their lawful Superiors in the execution of such measures as shall from time to time be in this behalf directed to be taken. But I do, nevertheless, hereby strictly order enjoin, and command, that the actual use of arms be in no case resorted to, by firing against any of the Natives or otherwise, if they can by other measures be captured; that bloodshed be invariably be checked as much as possible; and that any tribes or individuals captured, or involuntarily surrendering themselves up, be treated with the utmost care and humanity; And all Officers Civil and Military, and other persons whatsoever, are hereby required to take notice of this my Proclamation, and to render obedience and assistance accordingly.

Given under my hand and seal At arms, at the Government House, Hobart-Town, this first day of Oct. in the Year of our Lord, One Thousand Eight Hundred and Thirty.

GEORGE ARTHUR, (L.S)
By His Excellency's Command,
J. Burnett
GOD SAVE THE KING.

Settling wild and unoccupied lands

AN ACT FOR THE GOVERNMENT OF HIS MAJESTY'S SETTLEMENTS IN WESTERN AUSTRALIA

When it was established in June 1829, the Swan River Colony of Western Australia was the first British colony in Australia to be founded exclusively for private settlement. The official 'Conditions of Settlement', drafted in 1828 and issued in 1829, had three objectives: to minimise government expenditure; to attract private investors; and to ensure the productive utilisation of land grants, in order to avoid the problems of speculation and absenteeism that had been a problem in other colonies.

The act of the British Parliament establishing a government for the British settlement in Western Australia passed through the House of Commons even as the two ships carrying the first settlers, officials and a military complement were on their way to the new colony. Apart from its picturesque reference to the 'wild and unoccupied Lands on the Western Coast of New Holland' (and with no mention of the Indigenous inhabitants), the act specified that the colony stood alone and not as a part of the colonies of New South Wales or Van Diemen's Land. Whether intended or not, this provision gave an emphasis to the geographic isolation of Western Australia that has marked its character and outlook throughout its history. The new settlement did not prosper. Within a few years most of its foundation settlers had departed, and by 1850 the colony's total population had reached only 5254. Although convicts had been explicitly forbidden in the official 'Conditions of Settlement', that clause was set aside in 1850 so that an intake of felons might provide a stable labour force. The transportation of convicts to Western Australia ceased in 1868.

The founding act of government was extended over time by other legislative arrangements until it was formally repealed by the *Australian Constitutions Act 1850*, which provided for the governance of all the Australian colonies.

An Act to provide until the Thirty-first Day of *December* One thousand eight hundred and thirty-four, for the Government of His Majesty's Settlements in *Western Australia*, on the Western Coast of *New Holland*, 10 Geo. IV. c.22. (14th May 1829)

Whereas divers of His Majesty's Subjects have, by the Licence and Consent of His Majesty, effected a Settlement upon certain wild and unoccupied Lands on the Western Coast of *New Holland* and the Islands adjacent, which Settlements have received and are known by the Name of *Western Australia*: And whereas it is necessary to make some temporary Provision for the Civil Government of the said Settlement, until the said Undertaking shall be further matured, and the Number of Colonists in the said Settlements increased; Be it therefore enacted by the King's most Excellent Majesty, by and with the Advice and Consent of the Lords Spiritual and Temporal, and the Commons, in this present Parliament assembled, and by the authority of the same, That it shall and may be lawful for His Majesty, His Heirs and Successors, by any Order or Orders to be by Him or them made, with the Advice of His or their Privy Council, to make, ordain, and (subject to such Conditions and Restrictions as to Him or them shall seem meet) to authorize and empower any Three or more Persons resident and being within the said Settlements to make, ordain, and establish all such Laws, Institutions, and Ordinances, and to constitute such Courts and Officers, as may be necessary for the Peace, Order, and good Government of His Majesty's Subjects and others within the said Settlements; provided that all such Orders in Council, and all Laws and Ordinances so as to be made as aforesaid, shall be laid before both Houses of Parliament as soon as conveniently may be after the making and Enactment thereof respectively: Provided also, that no Part of the Colonies of *New South Wales* and *Van Diemen's Land*, as at present established, shall be comprised within the said New Colony or Settlements of *Western Australia*.

II. And be it further enacted, That this Act shall continue in force until the Thirty-first Day of *December* One thousand eight hundred and thirty-four, and thence forward until the End of the then next ensuing Session of Parliament, and no longer.

ABOVE *King George's Sound, part of the Swan River Colony, painted by Robert Havell in 1834.*

An Act for the government of His Majesty's settlements in Western Australia.

'The most extraordinary sale and purchase'

JOHN BATMAN'S MELBOURNE DEED

In May 1835, in a private initiative supported by a consortium soon to be called the Port Phillip Association, John Batman (1801–1839) sailed from Tasmania on the schooner *Rebecca*. He planned to sign a deed or treaty with the local Aboriginal people to secure rights to vast tracts of grazing land in the then little-explored Port Phillip district. He carried with him documents drafted by the lawyer Joseph Tice Gellibrand (1792?–1837). Batman's party included a group of seven Aborigines referred to affectionately as 'my Sydney natives', who would serve as intermediaries in negotiating the proposed purchase. Landfall was made at Indented Head on the Geelong side of Port Phillip Bay on 29 May 1835.

On 6 June, Batman negotiated two deeds (known later as the Melbourne and Geelong deeds) to secure rights to 600,000 acres (242,814 hectares), comprising the whole of the Bellarine Peninsula and the coastal strip between Geelong and the Yarra River. What Batman himself called the 'most extraordinary sale and purchase' was sealed with the exchange of signatures and markings on parchment, an immediate payment of blankets, knives, mirrors, tomahawks, beads, scissors and flour, and a commitment to an annual rental to be paid in the form of goods. After the deeds had been signed, Batman recorded that each of the chiefs handed him a portion of soil thus conferring on him 'full possession of the tracts of land I had purchased'. When he returned to Tasmania on 13 June John Batman was hailed in the press as 'the greatest landowner in the world'.

If Batman's deeds of settlement are derided now as an outrageous and unequal exploitation of the rights and interests of the Indigenous owners, in their day they were seen to confer the dangerous recognition that indeed the Aboriginal occupants had an established proprietary connection to the land on which they lived. While it is true that Batman and his partners were moved by commercial ambition, in their own way they had planned an exemplary invasion. In this they hoped for—but were denied—swift government sanction. In withholding that sanction, the authorities determined finally to define the rights of the Crown over the rights of the Aboriginal occupants. The Batman deeds may be seen not simply as curiosities but also as the catalysts that would lead to a formal enunciation by the Crown of the concept of *terra nullius* (see page 95).

Know all Persons that We, Three Brothers, Jagajaga, Jagajaga, Jagajaga, being the Principal Chiefs, and also Cooloolock, Bungarie, Yanyan, Moowhip, and Mommarmalar also, being the Chiefs of a certain Native Tribe, called Dutigallar, situate at and near Port Phillip, called by us, the above mentioned Chiefs, Irumao, being possessed of the Tract of Land hereinafter mentioned, for and in consideration of Twenty pairs of Blankets, Thirty Tomahawks, One Hundred Knives, Fifty pair Scissors, Thirty Looking Glasses, Two Hundred Handkerchiefs, and One Hundred Pounds Flour, and Six Shirts, delivered to us by John Batman, residing in Van Diemen's Land, Esquire, but at present sojourning with us and our Tribe, Do for ourselves, Our Heirs and Successors, Give, Grant, Enfeoff, and Confirm unto the said John Batman, His Heirs and Assigns, All that Tract of Country situate and being at Port Phillip ... containing about Five Hundred Thousand more or less Acres, as the same hath been, before the execution of these presents, delineated and marked out by us, according to the custom of our Tribe, by certain marks made upon the Trees growing along the boundaries of the said tract of land, To Hold the said tract of Land with all advantages belonging thereto, unto, and To the Use of the said John Batman, His Heirs and Assigns for ever, to the intent that the said John Batman, his Heirs and Assigns, may occupy and possess the said tract of Land, and place thereon Sheep and Cattle. Yielding and delivering to us, and our Heirs and Successors the yearly Rent or Tribute of One Hundred pairs of Blankets, One Hundred Knives, One Hundred Tomahawks, Fifty Suits of Clothing, Fifty Looking Glasses, Fifty pairs Scissors, and Five Tons Flour. In Witness whereof We Jagajaga, Jagajaga, Jagajaga, the before mentioned principal Chiefs and Cooloolock, Bungarie, Yanyan, Moowhip, Mommarmalar, being the Chiefs of the said Tribe, have hereunto affixed our Seals to those presents, and have signed the same. Dated according to the Christian Era, this Sixth day of June, One Thousand Eight Hundred and Thirty five.

John Batman's Melbourne Deed

Know all Persons that We Three Bro[thers]
Bungarie, Yangan, Moou[...]
being the Chiefs of a certain Native [Tribe]
by us the above mentioned Chiefs Tribe [...] being possessed of the tract [of land]
Tomahawks, One Hundred Knives [...] Scissors, Thirty Looking [Glasses]
[...] delivered to us by John Batman residing in Van D[iemen's Land]
Heirs and Successors **Give** Grant Enfeoff and confirm unto the said John [Batman]
from the branch of the River at the top of the Port about 7 Miles from the mo[uth]
Downs or Plains and from thence [...] South [...] across Mount [...]
and containing about Five Hundred Thousand more Acres as the same hath been b[ounded]
by certain marks made upon the Trees growing along the boundaries of the said [land]
To the Use of the said John Batman his heirs and Assigns for ever To [hold the]
said tract of Land and place thereon Sheep and Cattle **Yielding** and [...]
Blankets, One Hundred Knives, One Hundred Tomahawks, Fifty suits of [...]
whereof We Jagajaga, Jagajaga, Jagajaga, the above mentioned Principal [Chiefs of]
the said Tribe have hereunto affixed our seals to these presents and have sign[ed]
One Thousand eight hundred and thirty five

Signed Sealed and Delivered in the presence of Us the same having
been fully and properly interpreted and explained to the said Chiefs

James Gumm

Alexander Thompson

Wm Todd

Signed on the Banks of Batmans Creek
6th June 1835

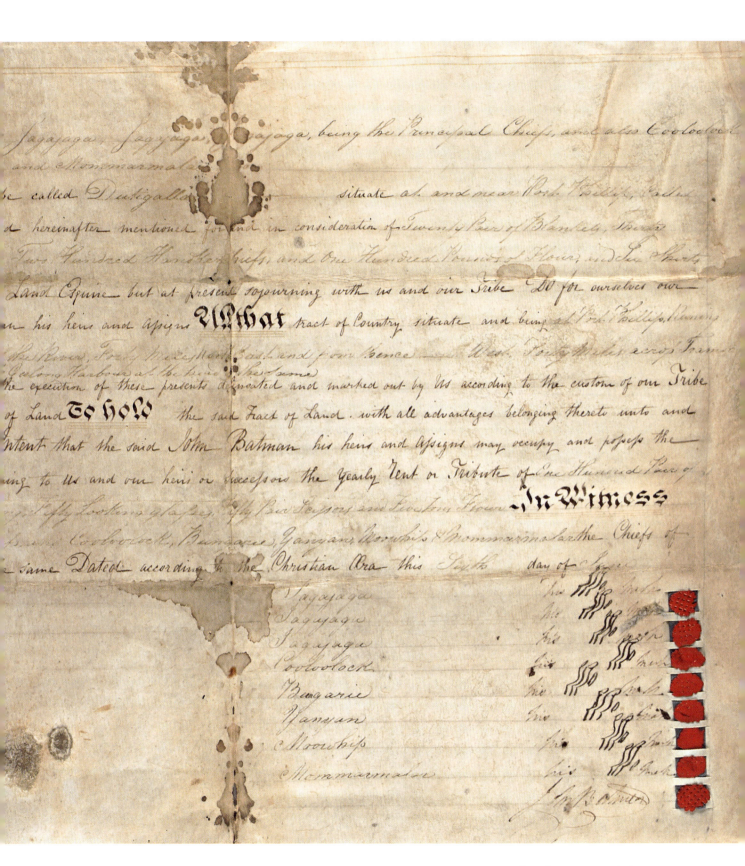

ABOVE *The Melbourne Batman deed.*

'the place for a Village'

JOHN BATMAN AND THE FOUNDING OF MELBOURNE

Who founded Melbourne? While John Batman famously recorded in his diary entry of 8 June 1835 'this will be the place for a village', historians of the early settlement of Victoria have long debated the rival claims of Batman and John Pascoe Fawkner (1792–1869) who lived longer, exercised greater influence and was tireless in claiming the founder's honours for himself. Historian A.G.L. Shaw has remarked that heated discussions on the question have overemphasised its importance. At the same time, he has pointed to the confusion between the ideas of establishing a pastoral settlement in the Port Phillip District and of establishing a village or township on the site of the present-day City of Melbourne. While a number of men had shown interest in settling near Port Phillip before 1835, John Batman was probably the most persistent. He had long thought about the venture, proposed a visit in 1825, sought a land grant there in 1827, suggested an expedition with official backing in 1833, and finally planned and executed his own private expedition in 1835 backed by a syndicate of supporters.

Having chartered the schooner *Rebecca*, Batman and his party sailed though Port Phillip Heads on the morning of 28 May 1835. On landing, they set out to make an extended reconnaissance of the area, which Batman described as a 'country possessing so many interesting features, and facilities so entirely congenial to the ripening of my intentions'. On 3 June Batman proceeded for several miles into the coastal hinterland, exploring its watercourses. On 6 June he presided at a ceremony where his treaty of purchase of the syndicate's land was signed with the Aboriginal occupants (see page 88).

With an extraordinary confidence in his new rights of 'ownership', Batman then proceeded with a further exploration of some part of his vast domain. His much-quoted line about a 'place for a Village' was written on 8 June, but whether this specified the actual site of what became Melbourne is doubtful. The surveyor and explorer John Helder Wedge (1793–1872), one of Batman's close associates and supporters, admitted later that on that first visit Batman did not see 'the present site of Melbourne', though he was the 'first who went and formed an establishment in Victoria'. Still, Batman's journal entry has been fondly regarded through the generations as a declaration that nicely combines the elements of prescience, romance, ambition and proximity. Melbournians especially have willingly embraced the legend and Batman has a place of honour as one of the founders of the city.

Tuesday 9th June 1835

We are now under way with a light wind for Indenture Head where I hope to Land all the things with the Men — about 6 PM. made Indenture Head and commenced Landing the Goods immediately as the Port was Very rough. and the wind increasing, we Landed all in four Boats full. every thing. pointed out the Spot where Gumm, is to commence a Garden, but &c House &c &c the whole of my Natives, at last wanted to Stop, however Bullett, Pegeon, and Joe the Marine, Stop with the other three Natives allready mentioned, making in all Eight persons they have got now three months Provisions. or more. with a

ABOVE *Batman's diary entry for 9 June 1835.*

Monday 8th June 1835
The wind foul this morning for Indenture Head—we tried but could not get out of the river—The Boat went up the large River I have spoken of which comes from the east, and I am glad to state about six miles up found the River all good water, and very deep—this will be the place for a Village—the Natives on shore

Tuesday 9th June 1835
We are now under way with a light wind for Indenture-Head whence I hope to Land all the things with the men—about P.M. made Indenture Head and commenced Landing the Goods immediately as the Port was very rough, and the wind increasing, we landed all in four Boats full—everything. I pointed out the Spot where Gumm, is to commence a garden, Hut or House &c. &c the whole of my Natives, at last wanted to stop, however I let Pigeon, and Joe the Marine, stop with the other three natives already mentioned making in all Eight persons they have got now three months Supply, or more, with a large quantity of Potatoes to put in the Ground, and all Kind of other Garden Seeds, as well as pips and stones fruit—I left apples & Oranges with them also the 6 Dog's, and gave *Gumm* written authority to put off any person or persons that may trespass on the Land I have purchased from the Natives—They got every thing Landed in an hour and we shook hands with them and off we came to the Heads which we got clear of by eight oclock, with a fair wind

Wednesday 10th June 1835
made a good run last Night got about 80 miles—the wind still fair—about 12 oclock last night saw V-D-Land

Thursday 11th June 1835
Got into George Town Heads at six oclock this morning with a fair wind up the River—we expect to be at Launceston with this Tide—

Defining *terra nullius*

GOVERNOR RICHARD BOURKE'S PROCLAMATION

The attempt by John Batman to buy land from the Port Phillip Aborigines by means of a treaty or a deed was denied by the Crown in a proclamation issued by the New South Wales governor, Sir Richard Bourke (1777–1855), on 10 October 1835. Bourke's proclamation effectively quashed Batman's treaty. The publication of the proclamation in Sydney meant that from that time, people found in possession of land without the authority of the government would be considered intruders or trespassers.

In thus defining the supremacy of the Crown in relation to so-called unoccupied lands, Bourke's proclamation formally implemented the doctrine of *terra nullius* upon which British settlement was based, reinforcing the notion that the land had belonged to no one before the British Crown took possession of it. It followed, therefore, that Aboriginal people had no rights to sell or assign the land on which they lived and that no individual or interests could acquire previously 'unoccupied' land other than through its distribution by the Crown.

Although there was an increasing understanding (both officially and more generally) that the Aboriginal occupants had rights in the land, the application and interpretation of the law followed, and almost always applied, the principles that had been enunciated in the 1835 proclamation. Indeed, these principles would remain unchanged until the decision of the High Court of Australia in the Mabo case in 1992 (see page 327).

Another consequence of Batman's attempt to negotiate a private treaty with the Port Phillip Aboriginal people and the new proclamation was the discretion given to Bourke to determine the form of an administration to be established to represent Crown interests in what would later become Victoria. In September 1836 Bourke sent Captain William Lonsdale to Port Phillip to assume the duties of police magistrate, military commander, head of civil administration, and protector of Aborigines. Thus were set in place the arrangements necessary for the orderly development of what later came to be called the Port Phillip District.

Proclamation

By His Excellency Major General Sir Richard Bourke, K.C.B. Commanding His Majesty's Forces, Captain General and Governor in Chief of the Territory of New South Wales and its dependencies, and Vice-Admiral of the same &c. &c. &c.

Whereas, it has been represented to me, that divers of His Majesty's Subjects have taken possession of vacant Lands of the Crown, within the limits of this Colony, under the pretence of a treaty, bargain, or contract, for the purchase thereof, with the Aboriginal Natives; Now therefore, I, the Governor, in virtue and in exercise of the power and authority in me vested, do hereby proclaim and notify to all His Majesty's Subjects, and others whom it may concern, that every such treaty, bargain, and contract with the Aboriginal Natives, as aforesaid, for the possession, title, or claim to any Lands lying and being within the limits of the Government of the Colony of New South Wales, as the same are laid down and defined by His Majesty's Commission; that is to say, extending from the Northern Cape, or extremity of the Coast called Cape York, in the latitude of ten degrees thirty seven minutes South, to the Southern extremity of the said Territory of New South Wales, or Wilson's Promontory, in the latitude of thirty nine degrees twelve minutes South, and embracing all the Country inland to the Westward, as far as the one hundred and twenty ninth degree of east longitude, reckoning from the meridian of Greenwich, including all the Islands adjacent, in the Pacific Ocean within the latitude aforesaid, and including also Norfolk Island, is void and of no effect against the rights of the Crown; and that all Persons who shall be found in possession of any such Lands as aforesaid, without the license or authority of His Majesty's Government, for such purpose, first had and obtained, will be considered as trespassers, and liable to be dealt with in like manner as other intruders upon the vacant Lands of the Crown within the said Colony.

Given under my Hand and Seal, at Government House, Sydney, this twenty sixth Day of August, One thousand eight hundred and thirty five.

(Signed) *Richard Bourke*
By His Excellency's Command

(Signed) *Alexander McLeay*
God Save the King!

OPPOSITE *Governor Richard Bourke's proclamation.*

(Copy)

Proclamation

By His Excellency Major General Sir Richard Bourke, K.C.B. Commanding His Majesty's Forces, Captain General and Governor in Chief of the Territory of New South Wales and its Dependencies, and Vice Admiral of the same &c. &c. &c.

Whereas, it has been represented to me, that divers of His Majesty's Subjects have taken possession of vacant Lands of the Crown, within the limits of this Colony, under the pretence of a treaty, bargain, or contract, for the purchase thereof, with the Aboriginal Natives; Now therefore, I the Governor, in virtue and in exercise of the power and authority in me vested, do hereby proclaim and notify to all His Majesty's Subjects, and others whom it may concern, that every such treaty, bargain, and contract with the Aboriginal Natives, as aforesaid, for the possession, title, or claim to any Lands lying and being within the limits of the Government of the Colony of New South Wales, as the same are laid down and defined by His

For the advancement of the Christian religion

THE *CHURCH ACT*

Although Australians are not noted as an especially spiritual people, and the country has evolved as a secular democracy, churches and church life have played a significant part in the life and traditions of the country. Many handsome nineteenth-century ecclesiastical buildings are prominent and familiar landmarks in the cities, towns and suburbs of Australia, even if congregations have shrunk as the numbers of the faithful have declined. But it was not always so. Churches once had their place as bastions of faith, as places of comfort and succour and—unwisely—as the guardians of sectarian divisions.

Sir Richard Bourke succeeded Ralph Darling as governor of New South Wales in 1831. With difficulty and in the face of opposition from conservative forces in the colony, Bourke nevertheless achieved some notable reforms. One of these was his *Church Act* of 1836. A liberal Anglican, Bourke especially abhorred sectarian intolerance, the dire effects of which he had seen in his native Ireland. He was convinced that there should be no attempt to establish a dominant colonial church. While he recognised that Anglicans were in the majority in New South Wales, he had noted that about a fifth of the population was Roman Catholic, and that Presbyterians and Dissenters formed an influential majority. He therefore proposed to give support from public funds to three major denominations in proportion to the numbers of their followers. By supporting the development of a diversity of religious communities in the colony, Bourke's *Church Act* diminished the power of the Anglican church. Originally intended to cover the Anglican, Catholic and Presbyterian denominations, Bourke later extended the act's provisions to other denominations, including the Jewish, Wesleyan and Baptist communities.

With public subsidies available for clerical salaries, for the housing of clergy and for the construction of new churches, the act led to increased numbers of clergy and to a spate of church-building throughout the colony. It also provided for the large convict constituency and for the poor to be recognised as part of their churches' communities.

A.D. 1836. 7° GUL. IV No. 3 719
No. III.

An Act to promote the building of Churches and Chapels, and to provide for the Maintenance of Ministers of Religion in New South Wales.
(29th July, 1836.)

Whereas, for the advancement of the Christian Religion and the promotion of good morals in the Colony of New South Wales, it is expedient to encourage the observance of Public Worship, and for this purpose to authorise the issue from the Revenue of the said Colony of sums to be applied in aid of the building of Churches and Chapels, and of the maintenance of Ministers of Religion: Be it therefore enacted, by His Excellency the Governor of New South Wales, with the advice of the Legislative Council thereof, That whenever a sum of not less than three hundred pounds shall have been raised by private contribution, and applied towards the building of a Church or Chapel and a dwelling where the same may be deemed necessary for the officiating Minister thereof, in any part of the said Colony, it shall be lawful for the Governor ... to issue from the Colonial Treasury in aid of the undertaking, any Sum of Money not exceeding the amount of the said private contribution: Provided always, that the whole amount so to be issued ... shall not exceed one thousand pounds, and that no sum shall be so issued in aid of any private contribution, unless such contribution shall be paid up and expended within three years from the date of the first issue from the Colonial Treasury, on behalf of the said undertaking: Provided further, that nothing herein contained shall prevent, or be construed to prevent the appropriation for the purposes aforesaid, of any sum exceeding one thousand pounds, by the Governor, with the advice and consent of the Legislative Council.

II. And be it enacted, That it shall be lawful for the said Governor with the advice of the Executive Council ... to authorise from time to time the issue from the Colonial Treasury of stipends towards the support of Ministers of Religion, duly appointed to officiate in any Churches or Chapels to be erected in manner aforesaid, or in any Churches or Chapels already erected, and of which Trustees shall be appointed for the maintenance thereof ... such stipends being issued at the several rates hereinafter mentioned; that is to say, in case it shall be shown to the satisfaction of the said Governor and Executive Council, that there is resident within a reasonable distance of the proposed Church or Chapel, a population of One Hundred adult Persons, and such Persons shall subscribe a Declaration, setting forth their desire to attend such Church or Chapel, it shall be lawful to issue to the Minister thereof ... One Hundred Pounds a-year; and in case there should appear ... Two Hundred adults ... then One Hundred and Fifty Pounds a-year; and in case there shall appear ... Five Hundred adults ... then Two Hundred pounds a-year; which shall be the highest stipend to be issued from the Colonial Treasury ... Provided always, that in estimating the number of adult attendants for the purpose aforesaid, there may be included the Convict Servants of any Master residing within a reasonable distance, who shall furnish a certificate setting forth the names of such Servants, and that they are of the Religious denomination for the use of which the said Church or Chapel is intended …

IX. And be it further enacted, That as soon as conveniently may be after the completion of any Church or Chapel under the provisions of this Act, pews, sittings, or benches in every such Church or Chapel, to be marked with the words "free seats," amounting to not less than one-sixth part of the whole of the sittings in every such Church or Chapel, shall also be appropriated and set apart for the use of poor persons resorting thereto, upon which pews, sittings or benches, so to be appropriated, no rent whatever shall at any time be charged or imposed …

Richard Bourke, Governor.

Passed the Council,
29th July, 1836.

E. DEAS THOMSON,

CLERK OF THE COUNCIL.

'a land free from all political patronage and the evils of a privileged church'

PROCLAIMING THE PROVINCE OF SOUTH AUSTRALIA

The province of South Australia was established in February 1836. Founded on the idea of 'systematic colonisation' advanced by the theorist Edward Gibbon Wakefield (1796–1862), South Australia was to be a new kind of British colony. Wakefield's theory proposed a 'contrived' balance between invested capital and labour, combined with concentrated agricultural settlement and a freedom from government interference. Such a balance, it was argued, would ensure maximum returns for British investors and better opportunities for emigrant labourers. Using these ideas, the promoters of settlement in the new colony negotiated a compromise in which control would reside with the British government, but colonisation commissioners would manage the survey and sale of land, the proceeds of which would be applied to the selection and transportation of labourers. Convicts would not be brought into the province, and there would be no established church. Non-conformism was free to flourish.

Historian Douglas Pike famously characterised the new South Australian colony as a 'paradise of dissent'. He has suggested that although the promoters had their worldly purposes, and although their ranks constantly changed as the South Australian project passed through its various stages of development, there was to be found, behind all of their plans, 'the idealistic hope that the new colony would be a land free from all political patronage and the evils of a privileged church'.

These ideas, though they are not explicitly stated, gave colour and character to the proclamation of South Australia by its first governor, Captain John Hindmarsh (1785–1860). On the afternoon of 28 December 1836, Hindmarsh was rowed ashore from his ship, the *Buffalo*, to meet a small gathering assembled on the sand hills of the beach at Glenelg. The wording of the proclamation was brief, but its message clear: there was an appeal to a sense of civic responsibility and obligation, not least in matters concerning the Aboriginal inhabitants although, as elsewhere in Australia, official aspirations often failed in practice. After the reading of the proclamation, a twenty-one gun salute was fired before the official party adjourned for lunch. The proclamation continues to be honoured in South Australia. In an act of civic renewal and commitment, it is publicly read at a ceremony that marks the annual anniversary of the first Proclamation Day of 1836.

Proclamation

By His Excellency John Hindmarsh, Knight of the Royal Hanoverian Order Governor and Commander in Chief of South Australia.

In announcing to the Colonists of His Majesty's Province of South Australia, the establishment of the Government, I hereby call upon them to conduct themselves on all occasions with order and quietness, duly to respect the laws, and by a course of industry and sobriety, by the practice of sound morality and a strict observance of the ordinances of Religion, to prove themselves worthy to be the Founders of a great and free Colony.

It is also, at this time, especially my duty to apprise the Colonists of my resolution to take every lawful means for extending the same Protection to the Native population as to the rest of His Majesty's Subjects and of my firm determination to punish with exemplary severity all acts of violence or injustice which may in any manner be practised or attempted against the Natives who are to be considered as much under the safeguard of the law as the Colonists themselves, and equally entitled to the Privileges of British Subjects. I trust, therefore, with confidence to the exercise of moderation and forbearance by all Classes, in their intercourse with the Native inhabitants, and that they will omit no opportunity of assisting me to fulfil His Majesty's most gracious and benevolent intentions towards them by promoting their advancement in Civilisation, and ultimately, under the blessing of Divine Providence their conversion to the Christian Faith. Given under my Hand at Glenelg this twenty-eighth day of December 1836.— J. Hindmarsh

By His Excellency's Command
Robert Gouger
Colonial Secretary

God Save the King.

ABOVE The Proclamation of South Australia 1836, *oil on canvas by Charles Hill.*

Australia Felix

THOMAS MITCHELL DESCRIBES THE COUNTRY OF VICTORIA

In 1839 Major Thomas Livingstone Mitchell (1792–1855), surveyor-general of New South Wales, published his account of his land explorations in eastern Australia under the title *Three Expeditions into the Interior of Eastern Australia; with descriptions of the recently explored region of Australia Felix, and of the present Colony of New South Wales*. Probably the best literary stylist among the Australian explorers, Mitchell had an eloquent turn of phrase as well as a large vision, qualities which enriched the painstaking competence he brought to the surveyor's task.

It was on the third of his journeys, commencing in March 1836, that Mitchell, having decided to abandon the survey of the deserts around the Darling River, set out to explore the more promising country along the Murray. At the junction of the Murray and Loddon rivers, he turned south-west into what is now Victoria. He was so enchanted by what he saw that he concluded his lyrical description of the landscape by assigning to it the name Australia Felix. This term, at once romantic and optimistic, would soon serve as a potent lure to the rapid occupation and settlement of Victoria.

Conjuring as it did the prospects of a bright Australian future, Mitchell's term Australia Felix was readily appropriated in other ways. It was frequently used in titles of literary, historical, geographical and biographical works in the nineteenth century, such as Richard Howitt's *Impressions of Australia Felix* of 1845 and the *Australia Felix Monthly Magazine* (1849). But probably its most famous appearance in literature came in the twentieth century, when Henry Handel Richardson used it as the title for the first volume of her great Australian trilogy *The Fortunes of Richard Mahoney*, published in 1917. Mitchell's eloquent and enduring phrase was perfectly attuned to Richardson's varied, densely packed portrait of Victorian colonial life.

ABOVE *Thomas Mitchell, depicted by an unknown painter.*

... Perhaps the greater portion of really good land, within the whole extent, will be found southward of the Murray, for there the country consists chiefly of trap, granite, or limestone. The amount of surface comprised in European kingdoms, affords no criterion of what may be necessary, for the growth of a new people in Australia. Extreme differences of soil, climate, and seasons, may indeed be usefully reconciled, and rendered available to one community there; but this must depend on ingenious adaptations, aided by all the facilities man's art can supply, in the free occupation of a very extensive region. Agricultural resources must ever be scanty and uncertain, in a country where there is so little moisture to nourish vegetation. We have seen, from the state of the Darling, where I last saw it, that all the surface water flowing from the vast territory west of the dividing range, and extending north and south between the Murray and the tropic, is insufficient to support the current of one small river. The country southward of the Murray is not so deficient in this respect, for there the mountains are higher, the rocks more varied, and the soil consequently, better; while the vast extent of open, grassy downs, seems just what was most necessary, for the prosperity of the present colonists, and the encouragement of a greater emigration from Europe.

Every variety of feature may be seen in these southern parts, from the lofty alpine region on the east, to the low grassy plains, in which it terminates on the west. The Murray, perhaps the largest river in all Australia, arises amongst those mountains, and receives in its course, various other rivers of considerable magnitude. These flow over extensive plains, in directions nearly parallel to the main stream, and thus irrigate and fertilize a large extent of rich country. Falling from mountains of great height, the current of these rivers is perpetual, whereas in other parts of Australia, the rivers are too often dried up, and seldom, indeed, deserve any other name than chains of ponds.

Hills, of moderate elevation, occupy the central country, between the Murray and the sea, being thinly or partially wooded, and covered with the richest pasturage. The lower country, both on the northern and southern skirts of these hills, is chiefly open; slightly undulating towards the coast on the south, and is, in general, well watered.

The grassy plains which extend northward from these thinly wooded hills, to the banks of the Murray, are chequered by channels of many streams falling from them, and by the more permanent and extensive waters of deep lagoons. These are numerous on the face of the plains near the river, as if intended by a bounteous Providence, to correct the deficiencies of too dry a climate. An industrious and increasing people, may always secure an abundant supply, by adopting artificial means to preserve it, and in acting thus, they would only extend the natural plan, according to their wants. The fine climate is worthy of a little extra toil, especially in those parts at a distance from the surplus waters of the large rivers, and in places, considered favourable in other respects, either for the rearing of cattle, or for cultivation.

In the western portion, small rivers radiate from the Grampians, an elevated and isolated mass, presenting no impediment, to a free communication, through the fine country, around its base. Hence that enormous labour necessary to obtain access to some parts, and for crossing continuous ranges, to reach others, by passes like those so essential to the prosperity of the present colony, might be, in a great degree, dispensed with, in that southern region.

Towards the sea-coast on the south, and adjacent to the open downs, between the Grampians and Port Phillip, there is a low tract consisting of very rich black soil, apparently the best imaginable, for the cultivation of grain, in such a climate.

On parts of the low ridges of hills near Cape Nelson and Portland Bay, are forests of very large trees of stringy-bark, iron-bark, and other useful species of eucalyptus, much of which are probably destined yet to float, in vessels on the adjacent sea.

The character of the country behind Cape Northumberland, affords fair promise of a harbour, in the shore to the westward. Such a port would probably possess advantages over any other on the southern coast; for a railroad thence, along the skirts of the level interior country, would require but little artificial levelling, and might extend to the tropical regions, or even beyond them, thus affording the means of expeditious communication between all the fine districts on the interior side of the coast ranges, and a sea-port, to the westward of Bass's Straits.

The Murray, fed by the lofty mountains on the east, carries to the sea a body of fresh water, sufficient to irrigate the whole country, which is, in general, so level, even to a great distance from its banks, that the abundant waters of the river, might probably be turned into canals, for the purpose, either of supplying deficiencies of natural irrigation at particular places, or of affording the means of transport, across the wide plains.

The high mountains in the east, have not yet been explored, but their very aspect is refreshing, in a country, where the summer heat is often very oppressive. The land is, in short, open and available in its present state, for all the purposes of civilized man. We traversed it in two directions with heavy carts, meeting no other obstruction than the softness of the rich soil; and, in returning, over flowery plains and green hills, fanned by the breezes of early spring, I named this region Australia Felix, the better to distinguish it from the parched deserts of the interior country, where we had wandered so unprofitably, and so long.

Thomas Mitchell describes the country of Victoria.

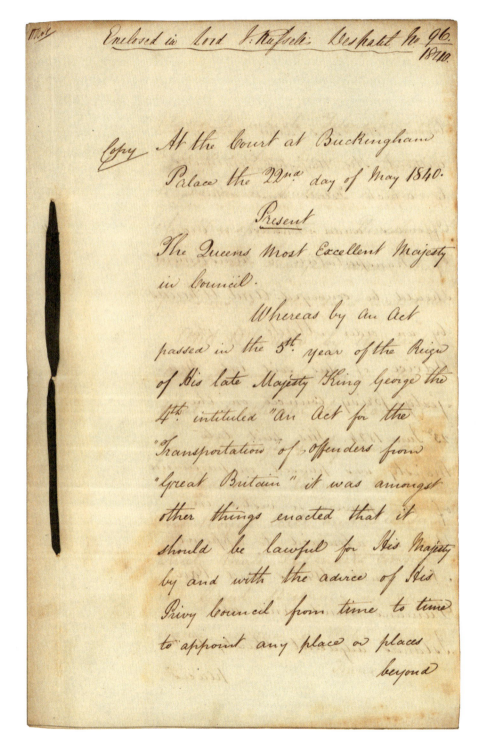

ABOVE *The first of the sixteen pages that make up the order-in-council ending transportation to New South Wales.*

Becoming a free colony

ENDING THE TRANSPORTATION OF CONVICTS TO NEW SOUTH WALES

New South Wales was established as a convict colony in December 1786, and the First Fleet arrived in Australia in January 1788, carrying its human cargo of 1480 men, women and children. When the Second Fleet arrived in 1790, its complement of 1000 prisoners had been devastated by nearly 300 deaths at sea, and many of the survivors were suffering from scurvy, dysentery and fever. Transportation would continue in New South Wales for a full fifty years, the source of a heavily subsidised cheap labour force.

Over time, transportation became the subject of much debate and controversy, particularly in the 1830s when demands for its cessation reached a crescendo. In 1837 a British parliamentary committee headed by Sir William Molesworth (1810–1855) recommended ceasing transportation to New South Wales, though convicts would continue to be sent to Van Diemen's Land until 1853. Convicts would also be sent to Western Australia, where transportation survived until 1868. The *Eden*, carrying 270 male convicts, was the last convict transport to reach New South Wales, arriving on 1 August 1840.

The British government acted on the Molesworth recommendations with the publication of an order-in-council. On 22 May 1840, New South Wales was removed from the list of places to which convicts could be sent. In 1848 there was an attempt to reintroduce a limited form of transportation to New South Wales, but it was so strenuously opposed in the colony that the plan was abandoned. The order-in-council remained in force, but it was left to Earl Grey, secretary of state for the colonies, to inform the governor of New South Wales, Sir Charles Fitzroy, on 18 November 1849, that no more convicts would be sent to the colony.

For New South Wales at least, the 1840 order-in-council stands as a symbolic landmark. In practical terms its promulgation brought to an end the apparatus of penal transportation, though it would take a long time for the machinery of the convict system to be dismantled. That system had imposed a heavy imprint on New South Wales: of a total population in 1839 of 114,386, one-third, or 38,035 people, were convicts—and this number does not include those whose sentences had expired or those with convict ancestry.

The order-in-council served to draw another line. It marked what might be seen as the closing of the first great formative period of the colony itself. Both personally and collectively, the legacy of the convict experience would continue to be felt for many years, but from 1840 New South Wales enjoyed the status of a free colony in which democratic institutions could evolve and flourish.

ORDER-IN-COUNCIL
At the Court at Buckingham Palace the 22nd day of May 1840.

Present
The Queens Most Excellent Majesty

Whereas by an Act passed in the 5th year of the Reign of His late Majesty King George the 4th intituled "An Act for the Transportation of Offenders from Great Britain" it was amongst other things enacted that it should be lawful for His Majesty by and with the advice of His Privy Council from time to time to appoint any place or places beyond the seas either within or without His Majesty's Dominions to which Felons and other Offenders under Sentence or Order of Transportation or Punishment should be conveyed. And Whereas by an order made by the advice of his said late Majesty's privy Council on the 23rd June 1824. His said late Majesty was pleased in pursuance of the powers so vested in Him as aforesaid to appoint New South Wales and Van Dieman's Land and all Islands adjacent thereto, to be places to which Felons and other offenders then being, or thereafter to be under Sentence, or order of Transportation or Punishment should be conveyed under the provisions of the said recited Act.

And Whereas by the said Act it was farther enacted that it should be lawful for His Majesty by any order or Orders in Council to declare His Royal Will and Pleasure that Male Offenders convicted in Great Britain and being under Sentence or Order of Transportation should be kept to labor in any part of His Majesty's Dominions out of England to be named in such Order or Orders in Council ...

And Whereas it hath seemed fit to Her Majesty on the advice of Her Privy Council to revoke the said recited Orders in Council, and to substitute in lieu thereof such other provisions as are hereinafter mentioned. Now therefore, in pursuance and exercise of the Powers vested in Her Majesty in Council by the said recited Acts of Parliament, Her Majesty by and with the advice of Her Privy Council doth Order ... upon and from the 1st day of August in this present year 1840 the said recited Orders in Council of the 23rd day of June 1824, and of the 11 day of November 1825 shall be and the same are hereby revoked so far as respects any act, matter, or thing to be done from and after the said first day of August, 1840, in the premises. And it is hereby further ordered by the advice aforesaid that, from and after the said 1st day of August 1840 the Island Van Diemans Land and Norfolk Island and the Islands adjacent to and comprised within the Government of Van Diemans Land shall be the places to which Felons and other Offendders in the United Kingdom ... shall be conveyed under the provisions of the said recited Act of the 5th year of the Reign of His late Majesty King George the 4th ... And the Most Noble the Marquis of Normanby and the Right Honourable Lord John Russell two of Her Majesty's principal Secretaries of State, are to give the necessary Instructions herein accordingly as to them may respectively appertain.

Signed Wm L. Bathurst

'We humbly pray Your Majesty the Queen will hear our prayer'

A PETITION OF THE FREE ABORIGINES OF VAN DIEMEN'S LAND

The writing of a petition addressed to Queen Victoria in February 1846 by a group of inhabitants from the Aboriginal settlement at Wybalenna on Tasmania's Flinders Island stands without precedent in Australian colonial history. Until a recent reappraisal by historians, the significance of the petition was largely overlooked or downplayed. Today, however, it is honoured as the earliest formal Aboriginal protest, a set of immediate complaints against abuse of power, an assertion of freedom and an emphatic statement of protest about the alienation from 'country'. In a careful examination of the issues, historian Henry Reynolds has described the petition as 'one of the most important, as well as one of the most neglected, documents relating to the history of relations between Indigenous and immigrant Australians'.

The petition was written as a complaint against the authoritarian regime of the settlement's superintendent, Dr Henry Jeanneret (1802–1886), whose behaviour and arbitrary use of his power had made the lives of community members a misery. Jeanneret had been dismissed as superintendent in 1844, but he had conducted a campaign in Hobart seeking a statement of reasons for the loss of his position and vindication of his character. Achieving no redress, he had taken his case to the secretary of state for the colonies in London, with a demand for reinstatement and compensation. Those claims were upheld in a dispatch dated 11 August 1845. With this victory, Jeanneret prepared to return to Wybalenna.

On hearing news of Jeanneret's intentions, a number of the Aboriginal residents, led by Walter George Arthur (c. 1820–1861), began to agitate against him. Their most significant action was to prepare a petition to Queen Victoria, in which they made a robust denunciation of Jeanneret and demanded that he should not be permitted to resume his post.

Dated 17 February 1846, the petition was signed by 'Walter G. Arthur, Chief of the Ben Lomond tribe' and seven others: John Allen, Davey Bruney, Neptune, King Alexander, Augustus, King Tippoo and Washington. As the leading signatory and one who later claimed major responsibility for the petition, Arthur is an especially interesting figure. As Henry Reynolds has noted, he was the son of Rolepa, a leading man of the Ben Lomond tribe, who had been known to the Europeans as King George. But he had been separated from his tribe in unknown circumstances and may have learnt little of the language, culture and traditions of his own people. Reynolds records that, at the Boys' Orphan School in Hobart from 1832 to 1835, Arthur learnt to read and write 'with a proficiency equal to that of the majority of [Tasmanian] colonists below the level of the professional and official elite'. Certainly Arthur was proud of his achievement and he was energetic in using it both on his own behalf and in the wider interests of his community. He seems also to have had a keen sense of justice and a determination to right wrongs as he saw them.

The petition itself was immediately controversial and has remained so in later historical accounts. While sympathetic to the document as an expression of Aboriginal protest, historian N.J.B. Plomley has cautioned that its relative sophistication both in method and expression indicates some active guidance or direction by those local officials at Wybalenna who had their own reasons for opposing the return of Dr Jeanneret. In this interpretation, the importance of the petition is diminished and its Aboriginal authors presented as lacking agency or independence. It is clear, however, that the petition uses the speech forms of Aboriginal English, and that it was treated seriously by the Tasmanian authorities, who sent it to England, where it was presented to Queen Victoria in March 1847.

An inquiry into the circumstances of the writing of the petition was conducted by Matthew Friend (1792–1871), the harbour master at George Town who had an interest in Aboriginal matters. This inquiry was carried out over three weeks in October 1846. Friend established that while the petitioners sought the assistance of several Europeans, the petition was largely their own work. Arthur's evidence to the inquiry was proprietorial and emphatic: 'The Petition to the Queen is really the wish of my Countrymen no one prompted me to write it, I did it of my own accord.'

Nor does the petition stand in isolation and without effect. It was followed almost immediately by a letter written by Arthur and others to the colonial secretary in which they enquired if their 'father the governor' had received the petition, and asking him 'to send some good men down to Flinders' to talk to them. Subsequently Walter Arthur together with his wife Mary Anne wrote several letters of their own to the governor seeking his support for their rights and those of their own people. Ultimately the petition played a part, if only indirectly, in the final termination of Jeanneret's appointment and the decision in 1847 to close the Flinders Island settlement. But as the symbol of a larger aspiration, the petition has an enduring importance as a document of protest. It was grounded in Walter Arthur's fundamental belief that it was the right of the Aboriginal people to be treated as equals in a free society.

ABOVE *The Flinders Island settlement of Wybalenna, 1847.*

The humble petition of the free Aborigines Inhabitants of Van Dieman's Land now living upon Flinders Island ... That we are your free children that we were not taken prisoners but freely gave up our country to Colonel Arthur then the Governor after defending ourselves.

Your petitioners humbly state to your Majesty that Mr Robinson made for us and with Colonel Arthur an agreement which we have not lost from our minds since and we have made our part of it good.

Your petitioners humbly tell Your Majesty that when we left our own place we were plenty of people, we are now but a little one.

Your petitioners state they are a long time at Flinders Island and had plenty of superintendents and were always a quiet and free people and not put in gaol.

Your Majesty's petitioners pray that you will not allow Dr Jeanneret to come again among us as our superintendent as we hear he is to be sent another time for when Dr Jeanneret was with us many moons he used to carry pistols in his pockets and threatened very often to shoot us and make us run away in fright. Dr Jeanneret kept plenty of pigs in our village which used to run into our houses and eat up our bread from the fires and take away our flour bags in their mouths also to break into our gardens and destroy our potatoes and cabbage.

Our houses were let fall down and they were never cleaned but were covered with vermin and not white-washed. We were often without clothes except a very little one and Dr Jeanneret did not care to mind us when we were sick until we were very bad. Eleven of us died when he was here. He put many of us into jail for talking to him because we would not be his slaves. He kept from us our rations when he pleased and sometimes gave us bad rations of tea and tobacco. He shot some of our dogs before our eyes and sent all the other dogs of ours to an island and when we told him that they would starve he told us they might eat each other. He put arms into our hands and made us to assist his prisoners to go to fight the soldiers we did not want to fight the soldiers but he made us go to fight. We never were taught to read or write or to sing to God by the doctor. He taught us a little upon the Sundays and his prisoner servant also taught us and his prisoner servant also took us plenty of times to jail by his orders.

The Lord Bishop seen us in this bad way and we told His Lordship plenty how Dr Jeanneret used us.

We humbly pray your Majesty the Queen will hear our prayer and not let Dr Jeanneret any more come to Flinders Island.

Anno Decimo Quarto
Victoriæ Reginæ
No. 31

By His Excellency Sir Charles Augustus Fitzroy Knight Companion of the Royal Hanoverian Guelphic order, Captain General and Governor in Chief of the Territory of New South Wales and its Dependencies, and Vice Admiral of the same, with the advice and consent of the Legislative Council.

An Act to incorporate and endow the University of Sydney.

Whereas it is deemed expedient for the better advancement of religion and morality and the promotion of useful knowledge, to hold forth to all classes and denominations of Her Majesty's subjects resident in the Colony of New South Wales, without any distinction whatsoever, an encouragement for pursuing a regular and liberal course of education: Be it therefore enacted by His Excellency the Governor of New South Wales, with the advice and consent of the Legislative Council thereof, That, for the purpose of ascertaining, by means of examination, the persons who shall acquire proficiency in Literature, Science, and Art, and of rewarding them by academical degrees as evidence of their respective attainments, and by marks of honor proportioned thereto, a Senate consisting of the number of persons hereinafter mentioned, shall within three months after the passing of this Act be nominated and appointed by the said Governor, with the advice of the Executive Council of the said Colony, by Proclamation to be duly published in the New South Wales Government Gazette, which Senate shall be and is hereby constituted from the date of such nomination and appointment a Body Politic and Corporate, by the name of "The University of Sydney," by which name such Body Politic shall have perpetual succession, and shall have a common Seal, and shall by the same name sue and be sued, implead and be impleaded, and answer and be answered unto in all courts of the said Colony, and shall be able and capable in law to take, purchase, and hold to them and their successors, all goods, chattels, and personal property whatsoever, and shall also be able and capable in law to take, purchase, and hold to them and their successors, not only such lands, buildings, hereditaments and possessions as may from time to time be exclusively used and required for the immediate requirements of the said University, but also any other lands, buildings, hereditaments, and possessions whatsoever. Provided that the said Colony or Successors, and that they and their successors shall be able and capable in law to grant, demise, alien, or otherwise dispose of all or any of the property, real or personal, belonging to the said University, and also to do all other matters and things incidental to or appertaining to a Body Politic.

II. Provided always and be it enacted, That it shall not be lawful for the said University to alienate, mortgage, charge, or demise any lands, tenements, or hereditaments to which it may become entitled, by grant, purchase, or otherwise, unless with the approval of the Governor and Executive Council of the said Colony for the time being, except by way of lease for any term not exceeding thirty-one years from the time when such lease is to commence, and by which there shall be reserved and made payable, during the whole of the term thereby granted, the best yearly rent that can be reasonably gotten for the same without any fine or forfeit.

III. And be it enacted, That by way of permanent endowment for the said University, the said Governor shall be, and is hereby empowered, by Warrant under his hand, to direct to be issued and paid out of the General or Ordinary Revenues of the said Colony, by four equal quarterly payments, on the first day of January, the first day of April, the first day of July, and the first day of October in every year, as a fund for building and for defraying the several stipends which shall be appointed to be paid to the several Professors or Teachers of Literature, Science, and Art, and to such necessary officers and servants as shall from time to time be appointed by the said University, and for defraying the expense of such prizes, Scholarships, and exhibitions as shall be awarded for the encouragement of Students in the said University, and for providing, gradually, a Library for the same, and for discharging all incidental and necessary charges connected with the current expenditure thereof, or otherwise, the sum of five thousand pounds in each and every year, the first instalment thereof to become due and payable on the first day of January, one thousand eight hundred and fifty one.

IV. And be it enacted, That the said Body Politic and Corporate shall consist of sixteen Fellows, twelve of whom at the least shall be laymen, and all of whom shall be members of and constitute a Senate, who shall have power to elect, out of their own body, by a majority of votes, a Provost of the said University for such period as the said Senate shall from time to time appoint, and whenever a vacancy shall occur in the office of Provost of the said University, either by death, resignation, or otherwise, to elect, out of their own body, by a majority of votes, a fit and proper person to be the Provost, instead of the Provost occasioning such vacancy.

V. And be it enacted, That until there shall be one hundred Graduates of the said University who have taken the degree of Master of Arts, Doctor of Laws, or Doctor of Medicine, all vacancies which shall occur by death, resignation, or otherwise among the Fellows of the said Senate, shall be filled up as they may occur, by the election of such other fit and proper persons as the remaining members of the said Senate shall, at meetings to be duly convened for that purpose, from time to time elect to fill up such vacancies: Provided always, that no such vacancy, unless created by death or resignation, shall occur for any cause whatever, unless such cause shall have been previously specified by some bye-law of the said Body Politic and Corporate, duly passed as hereinafter mentioned.

1850

An institution open to merit, not privilege

AN ACT TO INCORPORATE AND ENDOW THE UNIVERSITY OF SYDNEY

Established in 1850, the University of Sydney is the oldest tertiary foundation in Australia. It was followed by the University of Melbourne in 1853. Subsequently universities were established in Adelaide (1874), Tasmania (1890), Queensland (1909), and Western Australia (1910). It was not until the second half of the twentieth century that the Australian university sector expanded significantly.

In New South Wales and Victoria, especially, the universities created in the 1850s stood as important symbols of the cultural heritage of the colonial citizenry and as markers both of aspiration and ambition. The same coalition of public and private interest was joined later in the universities founded in the colonies of South Australia and Tasmania, and in the young states of Queensland and Western Australia. As Carolyn Rasmussen has suggested, the assumption underlying the establishment of the first generation of Australian universities was that a 'liberal education' would nurture the moral and social improvement that would smooth the transition to social and political maturity.

In forming their institutions, the founders of the new Australian universities drew on English, Scottish and Irish models. Of these, it was the ancient institutions of Oxford and Cambridge that stood as the most cherished exemplars—in symbolic forms of dress and ceremonies, in teaching, in the style of collegiate communities and in the physical forms of buildings. The Australian universities were urban in character and largely non-residential (though residential colleges were always an important part of the fabric of university life).

As the act for the new University of Sydney makes clear, the institution was to be open to merit, not privilege; and it was explicitly secular and predominantly state funded. Establishing a pattern that was followed elsewhere in Australia, Sydney's founding concern was more with the communication of knowledge and professional training than to induct its graduates into a privileged culture or to take responsibility for the development of character. For many years, however, the new universities catered to such small numbers that they inevitably created elites of their own. A true democracy in the availability of Australian tertiary education did not emerge until well into the twentieth century.

OPPOSITE *First page of the* University of Sydney Act 1850.

Anno Decimo Quarto
Victoria Regina No 31

By His Excellency Sir Charles Augustus Fitzroy Knight Companion of the Royal Hanoverian Guelphic Order Captain General and Governor in Chief of the Territory of New South Wales and its Dependencies, and Vice Admiral of the same, with the advice and consent of the Legislative Council

An Act to incorporate and endow the University of Sydney

Whereas it is deemed expedient for the better advancement of religion and morality and the promotion of useful knowledge, to hold forth to all classes and denominations of Her Majesty's subjects resident in the Colony of New South Wales, without any distinction whatsoever, an encouragement for pursuing a regular and liberal course of education: Be it therefore enacted by His Excellency the Governor of New South Wales with the advice and consent of the Legislative Council thereof, That for the purpose of ascertaining by means of examination, the persons who shall acquire proficiency in literature, science and art, and rewarding them by academical degrees as evidence of their respective attainments and by marks of honor proportioned thereto, a Senate consisting of the number of persons hereinafter mentioned, shall within three months after the passing of this Act be nominated and appointed by the said Governor, with the advice of the Executive Council of the said Colony, by Proclamation to be duly published in the New South Wales Government Gazette, which Senate shall be and is hereby constituted from the date of such nomination and appointment, a Body Politic and Corporate, by the name of "The University of Sydney", by which name such Body Politic, shall have perpetual succession and shall have a Common Seal, and shall by the same name sue and be sued, implead and be impleaded, and answer and be answered unto in all Courts of the said Colony, and shall be able and capable in law to take, purchase, and hold to them and their Successors, all goods, chattels, and personal property whatsoever, and shall also be able and capable in law to take, purchase, and hold to them and their Capable successors, only such lands, buildings, hereditaments, and possessions as may from time to time be exclusively used and occupied for the immediate requirements of the said University, but also to any other lands, buildings, hereditaments and possessions whatever situate in the said Colony or elsewhere, and that they and their successors shall be able and capable in law to grant, demise, alien or otherwise dispose of all or any of the property, real or personal, belonging to the said University, and also to do all other matters and things incidental to or appertaining to a Body Politic ...

III. And be it enacted, That by way of permanent endowment for the said University, the said Governor shall be and is hereby empowered, by Warrant under his hand, to direct to be issued and paid out of the General or Ordinary Revenues of the said Colony, by four equal quarterly payments, on the first day of January, the first day of April, the first day of July, and the first day of October, in every year, as a fund for building and for defraying the several stipends which shall be appointed to be paid to the several Professors or Teachers of literature, science, and art, and to such necessary officers and servants as shall be from time to time appointed by the said University, and for defraying the expense of such prizes, scholarships, and exhibitions as shall be awarded for the encouragement of Students in the said University, and for providing, gradually, a library for the same, and for discharging all incidental and necessary charges connected with the current expenditure thereof, or otherwise, the Sum of five thousand pounds in each and every year, the first instalment thereof to become due and payable on the first day of January, one thousand eight hundred and fifty-one.

IV. And be it enacted, That the said Body Politic and Corporate shall consist of sixteen Fellows, twelve of whom at the least shall be laymen and all of whom shall be members of and constitute a Senate, who shall have power to elect, out of their own body, by a majority of Votes, a Provost of the said University for such period as the said Senate shall from time to time appoint ...

VIII. And for the better government of the Students in the said University: Be it enacted, That no Student shall be allowed to attend the lectures or classes of the same, unless he shall dwell with his parent or guardian, or with some near relative or friend selected by his parent or guardian, and approved by the Provost or Vice Provost, or in some collegiate or other educational establishment, or with a tutor or master of a boarding House, licensed by the Provost or Vice Provost ...

XX. And be it enacted That no religious test shall be administered to any person in order to entitle him to be admitted as a Student of the said University or to hold any office therein, or to partake of any advantage or privilege thereof: Provided always that this enactment shall not be deemed to prevent the making of Regulations for securing the due attendance of the Students for Divine Worship at such Church or Chapel as shall be approved by their parents or guardians respectively.

An Act to incorporate and endow the University of Sydney

'the state of things in Australia'

WILLIAM HOWITT'S ADVICE TO EMIGRANTS AND GOLD SEEKERS

As the Australian colonies began to throw off the stigma of the convict past and as new prospects opened up for a better life and even—in the hectic decade of the 1850s—winning quick fortunes on the goldfields, there was a dramatic proliferation of interest in the country from abroad, especially from England. In the ten years 1851–1861, some 622,000 migrants came to Australia, 372,000 of them unassisted and 250,000 assisted.

Migration became an industry in its own right, stimulating a boom in the publication of news and intelligence about life in Australia: in the towns and cities; in the bush; and, of course, on the diggings. A proliferation of guide books offered advice to emigrants about the sea voyage to Australia, food and dress, the cost of living, the manners and ways of colonial Australians (already with a distinctive character of their own) and the differences to be found between town and 'up country' or 'the bush'. Information came in many forms, but especially valued was personal testimony, the constructive and thoughtful observations of the first-hand account.

The English author William Howitt (1792–1879) spent the years 1852–1854 in Australia. His hope was to improve the family fortunes. Accompanied by his sons Alfred William (the future explorer, natural scientist and pioneer authority on Aboriginal culture) and Charlton, their purpose was to sample life in the colony and win their fortunes in gold. But their success as diggers was modest and spasmodic. William gained from his experience in other ways. In a series of books on aspects of Australian life, he drew on the diaries and letters he had written during his travels. While highlighting many of the more obviously dramatic aspects of the colonial experience— towns and cities deserted because of gold fever, soaring inflation, the strangeness of colonial flora, fauna and climate, and life on the diggings—William had another purpose. At a time when new constitutions were being drawn up for New South Wales and Victoria, he saw it as a duty to give a candid and honest exposition of the social and political state of the colonies. His most important book *Land, Labour and Gold: Or Two Years in Victoria* (1855) is one of the most accurate and comprehensive of the travel books that became so popular during the nineteenth century, and it opened a window onto Australian life and prospects.

Here, in a published letter, William Howitt gives a lively, amusing (sometimes bemused) and informative narrative of a visit to the Ovens Valley gold diggings in Victoria. The letter appeared in *The Emigrant's Guide to the Australian Goldfields*, published in 1853, its standing as both testimony and a source of accurate information enhanced by what the publisher described as the 'known character and ability of the writer'. With this assurance, the letter was publicly circulated as 'a fair [but not always flattering] view of the state of things in Australia'.

December 15, 1852.
We are now among the Ovens Ranges, and are approaching the diggings ...

Singular groups pass us continually on the road. Here are five or six diggers on splendid horses, with their "swag" before them, consisting of a rug rolled around their damper, &c. Here again career along diggers of a more work-a-day description, on lanky horses with switch tails and a more weather-beaten swag; the men themselves in nothing but dirty cabbage-leaf hats, shirt and trousers, and belt round the waist, with a tin pannikin hanging behind. There, again, goes a train of bullock teams. They are all the property of one man, who travels from one digging to another with stores — sugar, flour, cheese, &c. See, they come to a creek. All halt, take out their bullocks, and let them graze. Out of one covered wagon comes a flock of children, from two to seven or eight years old, followed by their mother with her sun bonnet shading her neck with a broad flap. A fire is made and the kettle set on, and the frying-pan brought out. But there again. See what a train. It is like the retainers of some feudal baron. First rides a man in a cloth cap with a gold band and scarlet mantle that floats behind him. He has led a horse carrying swag in a leathern wrapper. Next comes another man in ordinary dress leading two horses; and finally, one with the cabbage-tree beehive helmet of the mounted police leading another horse. They belong to the officers of the mounted police ...

Ovens diggings

At length we have reached this point, after our arduous and eventful journey of nearly two months, over only 250 miles of ground. But such ground! Some people insist upon it that it is only 150, others 200 miles, but we know very well that in England it would measure 280.

Reaching the brow of the hill we see a broad valley lying below, and white tents scattered along it for a mile or more. The tents right and left glance out of the woods on all sides. In the open valley they stand thick, and there is a long stretch up the centre of the valley, where all the ground has been turned up, and looks like a desert of pale clay. After our long pilgrimage it seems as we ought never to arrive at our journey's end, but to go on and on ... We descend the hill. There stands a large, wide, open tent, with a pole and a handkerchief twisted round it. That is a store or shop. We go on. Huts, dusty ground all trodden, trees felled and withering in the sun; here and there a round hole like a well, a few feet deep, where they have been trying for gold. Down we go. More tents, more dust, more stores, heaps of trees felled and lying about, lean horses grazing on a sward that a goose could not lay hold of, hole after hole, where gold has been dug for, and now abandoned, linen hanging out to dry, horrid stenches from butchers' shops and holes into which they have flung their garbage. Along the valley to the left there grows a smooth sward. What there is, however, to indicate gold here more than in a thousand other places that we have walked over with unconscious feet, we cannot see. Up the valley hundreds of tents are clapped down in the most dirty and miserable places, and all the ground is perforated with holes, round or square—some deeper, some shallower, some dry, some full of water; but in very few of them does work seem to be going on. They have flitted to other holes. All between the holes the hard, clay-coloured sand lies in ridges, and you must thread your way carefully among them if you don't mean to fall in. Still horrid stenches of butchers' shops and garbage pits; stores after stores; tents and booths, and bark huts, like a fair. There is the creek, or little stream, no longer translucent, as it came from the mountains, but thick as a clay puddle, and rows of puddling tubs standing by it, and men busy washing their earth in tins and cradles.

Such is the first view of the diggings. But we turn up to the left into a green quiet glade of the forest, and there pitch a tent at a distance from the throng, and where there is feed for the horses. A hasty tea, and away we go to the commissioner's tent for our letters. It is on the other side of the creek; two of these stately tents, in fact, lined with blue cloth, and with other tents in the rear, the whole enclosed with palings ... If you could see our pots, pans, pannikins, our tin dishes, some for making loaves and puddings in, others for washing in, our knives, forks, spoons, lying on our bags of sugar, rice, flour, &c., standing about, our tea chest, our lantern, our tin teapot of capacious size, our teakettle in constant requisition, our American axes for chopping firewood, our lantern at night suspended from a string in the tent—the interior of our tent, with the beds spread out broad over part of the floor, and covered with grey rugs; the tent hung with pieces of dried salt beef, straw hats with veils round them, caps and so on; our guns standing in a corner, with books and writing cases and portfolios—you would say it was a scene at once curious and comfortable-looking.

I have taken a round among the diggings, and seen the people washing their gold. They seem to have a good deal. One man had, after pouring off the sand and water from his tin dish, a pound weight; another had five or six ounces, and so on ... As we were watching the people washing their gold at the creek we noticed that a great crowd gathered round a little green rocker as they called it — a little greenpainted cradle. They said that the party belonging to that rocker had washed out 7lb. of gold from nine dishes of stuff. All eyes, therefore, were on the watch to trace the party to the hole they came from, and then a desperate rush was made to that spot. In a few hours hundreds of claims had been marked out as near as possible to the golden hole. It was curious to see what swarms were at once on the place, engaged with their picks and spades. In a few hours a great space of many acres was marked out, and more people were flocking in, so that they bade fair speedily to come up our quiet glade to our very tent. Had much gold been found, the whole would soon have been turned over ...

The season has been frightfully unhealthy, and the journey to the gold fields has been fatal to many. Thousands have been struck down by sickness; hundreds have already returned, cursing the parties who sent them such onesided statements of the gold fields and the climate; hundreds are still lying ill from the insidious influence of this "fine salubrious climate." In a letter just received from Melbourne I hear that scarcely a soul there but has been ill, and all up the country it is the same. Gentlemen who have been in India, China, and over the whole continents of Europe and America, say that this is the worst climate they know. Without any apparent cause, people are everywhere attacked with dysentery, rheumatism, cramp, and influenza. All this ought to be fully and fairly stated. Onesided statements are a dishonest procedure—"a delusion, a mockery, and a snare." The little black fly of Australia is a perfect devil. The grass seeds in summer, which pierce your legs like needles ... the dust winds, and the violent variations of the atmosphere—often of no less than 100 degrees in a day—these are nuisances which ought to be well known. A deal is said about sending out young women to marry the men in the bush. God help such women as marry the greater portion of such fellows as the common class here. Their very language is perfectly measled with obscenity and the vilest oaths and the basest phraseology, and they drink all they can get. In short, this is a country to come to, as people go to India, to make money; as to spending it here, that, under present circumstances, would require different tastes to those of most cultivated men and women. The greatest thing that can be said of this country is, that the better classes are so exceedingly kind and hospitable, and, considering their isolated lives, not deficient in general information. I am sure we shall always have occasion to remember the kindness of the inhabitants of the bush. Every house, if we had desired it, would have opened itself to us as a home, and but for bush kindness I should, perhaps, not have been writing this.

Had I been aware before setting out to this place how formidable the journey was, and how unhealthy the season would prove, I would have deferred my visit; but, however, here we are now safe and sound, and as it is necessary for me to see all the diggings and as much of the country as I can, it will be right in the end ...

December 23.
At present the weather is very thundery and rainy. We were, by all accounts, to have been broiled alive here at Christmas, but there is no prospect of it at present. As I write, the thunder and hail are terrific. It is quite cool—often cold. We are all quite well. We shall make some sort of jollification on Christmas-day. We can buy dried apples. I shall have an apple pudding and roast beef, and drink all your healths in—a nobbler of brandy and water.

'Thou shalt not grow discouraged and think of going home'

THE DIGGERS' TEN COMMANDMENTS

Gold was discovered in Victoria in 1851, almost immediately stimulating a mass movement of humanity to the goldfields, which quickly became known as 'the diggings' and where gold-seekers were known as 'diggers'. That name was later applied with honour and affection to the Australian soldiers of two world wars, and the term survives in common usage. The mania for gold, the hopes for quick fortunes and eventually the extraordinarily rich yields of the precious metal fundamentally altered the nature of Australian society, throwing off the traditional dominance of the pastoralist. Life on the diggings developed a lively quality and character of its own as sober and law-abiding enterprise competed—often unequally—with human greed and criminal rapacity.

Something of the tone and character of goldfields life survives in a satirical code of rules, or Ten Commandments, drawn up 'by a digger' at Ballarat in Victoria for the guidance of those who had flocked to the goldfields from around the globe. Written in a quasi-biblical style, the commandments were posted about the diggings for guidance in matters of ethics and behaviour and perhaps also for amusement. Certainly the commandments have a light and humorous touch, but their purpose was to set down some of the more serious and generally unwritten rules of conduct governing the relations the diggers had with each other in the volatile circumstances of goldfields life. In their appeal to practical decency, the commandments stand as an expression of the concept of the 'fair go' that sits at the heart of Australia's egalitarian democracy. The printing and sale of the rules (price sixpence) by the *Ballarat Star* newspaper (established 1855) suggests that they had a wide circulation over several years, assuming their origins early in the gold rush era. The survival of the occasional early handwritten copy suggests that the commandments were sometimes transcribed and passed around by hand.

A version of the commandments was published by the journalist W.B. Withers (1823–1913) as an appendix to his pioneering book of 1870, *The History of Ballarat*. Withers himself had gone to try his luck on the diggings in 1852, but like so many others had found little success in the lottery of prospecting. Other occupations beckoned including, eventually, journalism, in which he built a satisfying career. As his Ballarat history suggests, he had a keen eye for the rich variety of life he had known at first hand on the diggings. And it was in this spirit that he offered the commandments to his readers. In their quaint text, a survival from Ballarat's early days, he saw that the commandments might let 'a little light in upon the modes of thought, the customs, the amusements, and the phrases in vogue then, and which are only partially known to the later comers'.

A man spake these words and said:— I am a digger, who wandered from my native home, and came to sojourn in a strange land and "see the elephant!" And behold, I saw him, and bear witness, and that from the key of his trunk to the end of his tail his whole body had passed before me; and I followed until his huge feet stood still before a Clapboard Store; then with his trunk extended, he pointed to a candle card tacked upon a shingle, as though he would say Read, and I read—

THE TEN COMMANDMENTS.

I.—Thou shalt have no other claim but one.

II.—Thou shalt not make to thyself any false claim nor any likeness to a mean man by "jumping" one, whatever thou findest on the top above, or on the rock beneath, or in a crevice underneath the rock, for I am a jealous Dog and will visit the Commissioner round with my presence to invite him on my side; and when he decides against thee thou shalt have to take thy pick, thy pan, thy shovel, and thy "swag", and all thou hast, and go "prospecting" both north and south, to seek good diggings—and thou shalt find none. Then, when thou hast returned in sorrow, thou shalt find that thine own claim is worked out and no pile made thee, to hide in the ground, or in an old boot beneath thy bunk or in buckskin or bottle beneath thy tent but best paid all that was in thy purse away, worn out thy boots and thy garments so that there is nothing good about thee but the pockets, and thy patience be like unto thy garments: and at last thou shalt hire thy body out to make thy board and save thy bacon.

III.—Thou shalt not go "shepherding" before thy claim is worked out. Thou shalt not take thy money, nor thy gold-dust, nor thy good name to the gaming table in vain, for Monte, Twenty-one, Roulette ... and Poker will prove to thee that the more thou puttest down the less thou shalt take up; and when thou thinkest of thy wife and children thou shalt not hold thyself ... but insane.

IV.—Thou shalt not remember what thy friends do at home on the Sabbath day lest the remembrance may not compare favorably with what thou doest; six days thou mayest dig or pick all that the body can stand under but the other day ... all thy stockings, ... all thy boots, drink all thy nobblers, mend all thy clothing, chop all thy firewood, make and bake thy bread, and boil thy pork and beans, that thou wait not when thou returnest from thy long tour weary. For in six days labor only thou canst not work out thy body in two years, but if thou workest hard on Sunday also thou canst do it in six months—and thy son and thy daughter, thy male friend, and thy female friend, thy morals and thy conscience be none the better for it, but reproach thee, shouldest thou ever return with thy worn-out body to thy mother's fireside and thou strive to justify thyself because the leaders, jews, and fossikers defy God and civilisation by keeping not the Sabbath day, and wish not for a day's rest, such as true digger's memory, youth, and home, make hallowed.

V.—Think more of, and how thou canst make it fastest, rather than how thou wilt enjoy it after thou hast ridden rough-shod over thy good old parents' precepts and examples, that thou mayest have something to reproach and sting thee when thou art left alone in the land where thy father's blessings and thy mother's love have sent thee.

VI.—Thou shalt not harm thyself by working in the rain, even though thou shalt make enough (out o' "core") to buy physic and attendance with. Neither shalt thou kill thy neighbor's body by shooting him, except he give thee offence, then, upon the principle of honor, without principle, thou mayest, though by "keeping cool" thou hadst saved his life and thy conscience.

VII.—Thou shalt not grow discouraged and think of going home before thou hast made thy "pile," because thou hast not "struck a lead," nor found a "nugget," nor sunk a hole on a "pocket," or the "gutter;" but in going home thou shalt be deemed a "shicer" and go to work ashamed, and serve thee right, for by staying here thou mightest strike a "lead," and thyself respect, and then go home with enough to make thyself and others happy.

VIII.—Thou shalt not fossick out specimens from thy mates' pan and put them in thy mouth, or in thy purse; neither shalt thou take from thy sleeping partner, or tent-mate, his gold to add to thine lest he find thee out, and straight-way call his fellow diggers together with the "traps" and put thee in limbo vile, or brand thee like a horse-thief with R upon thy cheek, to be known and feared of all men, Ballarat in particular; and if thou steal a shovel, pick, or pan from thy toiling fellow digger, hanging will be too good for thee, and the sooner thou makest thyself scarce the better, and forever hang down thy head.

IX.—Thou shalt not "blatherskite" about "new rushes" to thy neighbor that thou mayest benefit a storekeeper who hath a store with provisions, tools, swags, &c., he cannot sell, lest, in deceiving thy neighbor, that he may, returning through the bush with nought save his revolver, present thee with the contents thereof, and, like a dog, thou shalt fall down and perish, and die the death of a bushranger.

X.—Thou shalt "shepherd" but one hole at a time, nor covet thy neighbor's gold, nor his claim, nor move his stake, nor wilfully take washing-stuff not thy property, nor wash the tailings from his sluice's mouth, nor in any way molest him in his claim. And if thy neighbour have his family here, and thou love and covet his daughter's hand in marriage, thou shalt lose no time in seeking her affection, and when thou hast obtained it thou shalt "pop" the question like a man, lest another, more manly than thou art, should step in before thee, and thou covet her in vain; and, in the anguish of disappointment, thou shalt quote the language of the great, and say—"let her rip," and thy future life be that of a poor, lonely, despised, and comfortless bachelor!

THE END

Another Little One.—Thou shalt not dig up a public road unless thou canst afford to fix it up again as good as before, less thou injurest the drayman to benefit thyself, and he curse thee every time he passeth. Amen!

Last, But Not Least.—Thou shalt be particular not to leave thy swag at thy boarding-house without making satisfactory arrangements with the man whose grub thou hast eaten, for it is better to have a good name than much riches. Amen! Amen!!

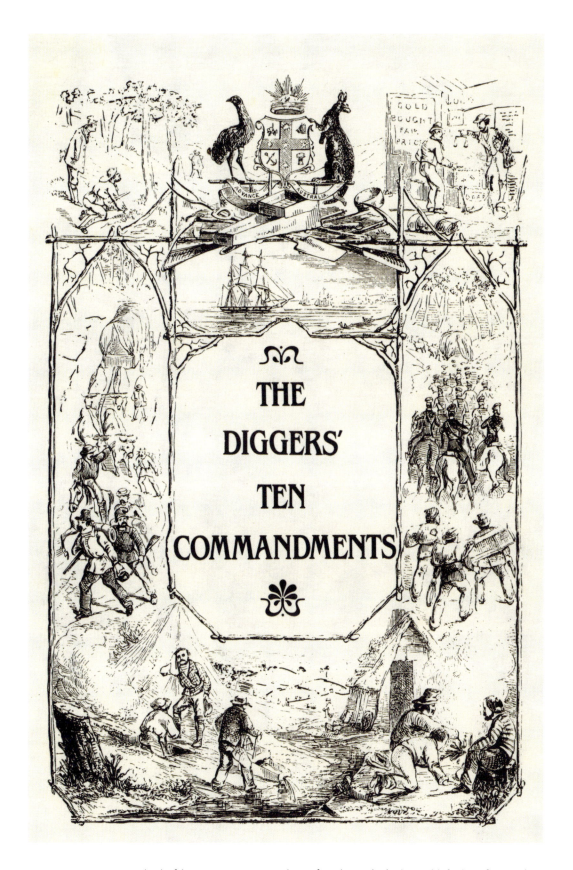

ABOVE *Sketch of the Diggers' Ten Commandments from the 1853 book* The Gold-finder of Australia.

To His Excellency Charles Joseph La Trobe Esquire Lieutenant Governor of the Colony of Victoria &c

The Humble Petition of the Undersigned Gold Diggers and other residents on the Gold Fields of the Colony

Sheweth

That Your Petitioners are the Loyal and Devoted Subjects of Her Most Gracious Majesty Queen Victoria the Sovereign Ruler of this Colony and of _____ the British Crown

That in the present impoverished condition of the Gold Fields the impost of Thirty Shillings a Month is more than Your Petitioners can pay as the fruit of labor at the Mines scarcely affords to a large proportion of the Gold Miners the common necessaries of life

That in consequence of the few Officials appointed to issue Licenses the Diggers Storekeepers and other residents lose ____ at each Monthly issue in procuring their Licenses

That the laborious occupation of Gold digging and the privations attendant on a residence on the Gold-fields entail much sickness and its consequent expenses on Your Petitioners

That in consequence of the Squatter Land Monopoly a large proportion of successful Diggers who desire to invest their earnings in a portion of land are debarred from so doing

That newly arrived Diggers must lose much time and money before they become acquainted with the process of Gold Mining

That in consequence of Armed Men (many of whom are notoriously bad in character) being employed to enforce the impost of Thirty Shillings a Month there is much ill feeling engendered amongst the Diggers against the Government

That in consequence of the non-possession by some of the Miners of a Gold Diggers License some of the Commissioners appointed to administer the Law on the Gold Fields have on various occasions Chained non-possessors to Trees and Condemned them to hard labor on the Public Roads of the Colony – A proceeding Your Petitioners maintain to be contrary to the spirit of the British Law which does not recognize the principle of the Subject being a Criminal because he is indebted to the State

That the impost of Thirty Shillings a Month is unjust because the successful and unsuccessful Digger are assessed in the same ratio

For these reasons and others which could be enumerated Your Petitioners pray Your Excellency to Grant the following Petition

First. To direct that the License Fee be reduced to Ten Shillings a Month

Secondly. To direct that Monthly or Quarterly Licenses be issued at the option of the Applicants

Thirdly. To direct that new arrivals or invalids be allowed on registering their names at the Commissioners Office fifteen clear days residence on the Gold Fields before the License is enforced

Fourthly. To afford greater facility to Diggers and others resident on the Gold Fields who wish to ____ in Agricultural Pursuits for investing their earnings in small allotments of land

The beginnings of the Eureka rebellion

THE BENDIGO GOLDFIELDS PETITION

The story of the great Victorian gold rushes of the 1850s and their dramatic impact on the colony is well known. By mid-1853 about 60,000 diggers, many with their families, were on the Victorian goldfields. Of this number, some 23,000 were at Bendigo. In June 1853 an Anti-Gold-Licence Association was formed at Bendigo to give voice to the many grievances of the diggers about their conditions and what was seen to be the unfair and inequitable impost of the licence fee of thirty shillings a month, which was harshly administered, imposed irrespective of success or failure on the diggings and conferred no rights to vote or of representation. The association was led by, among others, George Edward Thomson (1826–1889), who had been active in political and social protest movements in England before his migration to Australia in 1852 and his modest success on the diggings first at Forest Creek (modern Castlemaine) and then at Sandhurst (modern Bendigo).

At a meeting of the Anti-Gold-Licence Association held on 6 June 1853, Thomson and his associates presented a petition with demands for the reduction of the licence fee, reform of the police and the enfranchisement of the diggers. The petition was signed by diggers at Sandhurst, Ballarat, Forest Creek, McIvor (modern Heathcote), Mount Alexander (modern Stawell) and other diggings. Although a claim was made that 30,000 signatures were collected, the petition carried only 5000–6000 signatures (excluding those from the McIvor diggings, which were lost in a robbery from the gold escort).

Thomson then took the petition to Melbourne, where it was presented to the lieutenant governor, C.J. La Trobe (1801–1875), on 1 August 1853. Most of its demands, including the central plea for the reduction of the fee, were rejected. The diggers continued to protest peacefully, but in acts of civil disobedience, and the fee was increasingly evaded. Eventually, the accumulated grievances of the diggers erupted into angry demonstrations in Ballarat where the Ballarat Reform League issued demands for manhood suffrage, the abolition of the licence fee and the opening up of the land to small farming settlement. At a large public meeting on 11 November 1854 a resolution was passed declaring that 'it is the inalienable right of every citizen to have a voice in the making of laws he is called upon to obey—that taxation without representation is tyranny'.

Still the colonial administration refused to negotiate with the protesters, with the larger demands for the abolition of the licence fee having become mixed with protests over the maladministration of justice. A further protest meeting on 29 November saw the unfurling of the rebel Southern Cross flag, the burning of licences and the construction of a stockade. In the early hours of 3 December 1854 government troops attacked the stockade; some thirty diggers were killed, and five soldiers died and twelve were seriously wounded. The Eureka rebellion is probably Australia's most famous civil insurrection; it stands as a continuing symbol of democratic expression that is honoured still in the rebel Southern Cross or Eureka flag that has been adopted by other causes, not least as an expression of republican aspirations.

The Bendigo petition is 13 metres long and bound in green silk. Lost for many years, it was acquired in the 1980s by Dr John Chapman, a Melbourne collector of Australiana, who gave it to the State Library of Victoria on the occasion of the Australian Bicentenary in 1988.

OPPOSITE *Introduction to the Bendigo Goldfields Petition.*

The Humble Petition of the Undersigned Gold Diggers and other residents on the Gold Fields of the Colony

Sheweth

That your petitioners are the Loyal and Devoted Subjects of Her Most Gracious Majesty Queen Victoria the Sovereign Ruler of this Colony one of the dependencies of the British Crown

That in the present impoverished conditions of the Gold Fields the impost of Thirty Shillings a Month is more than Your Petitioners can pay as the fruit of labor at the Mines scarcely affords to a large proportion of the Gold Miners the common necessaries of life

That in consequence of the few Officials appointed to issue Licenses the Diggers Storekeepers and other residents lose much time at each Monthly issue in procuring their Licenses

That the laborious occupation of Gold digging and the privation attendant on a residence on the Gold fields entail much sickness and its consequent expenses on Your Petitioners

That in consequence of the Squatter Land Monopoly a large proportion of Successful Diggers who desire to invest their earnings in a portion of land are debarred from so doing

That newly arrived Diggers must lose much time and money before they become acquainted with the process of Gold Mining

That in consequence of Armed Men (many of whom are notoriously bad in character) being employed to enforce the impost of Thirty Shillings a Month there is much ill feeling engendered amongst the Diggers against the Government

That in consequence of the non-possession by some of the Miners of a Gold Diggers License some of the Commissioners appointed to administer the Law of the Gold Fields have on various occasions Chained non-possessors to Trees and Condemned them to hard labor on the Public Roads of the Colony—A proceeding Your Petitioners maintain to be contrary to the spirit of the British Law which does not recognise the principle of the Subject being a Criminal because he is indebted to the State

That the impost of Thirty Shillings a Month is unjust because the successful and unsuccessful Digger are assessed in the same ratio

For these reasons and others which could be enumerated Your Petitioners pray your Excellency to Grant the following Petition

First.—To direct that the Licence Fee be reduced to Ten Shillings a Month

Secondly.—To direct that Monthly or Quarterly Licenses be issued at the option of the applicants

Thirdly.—To direct that new arrivals or invalids be allowed on registering their names at the Commissioners Office fifteen clear days residence on the Gold Fields before the License be enforced

Fourthly.—To afford greater facility to Diggers and others resident on the Gold Fields who wish to engage in Agricultural Pursuits for investing their earnings in small allotments of land

Fifthly.—To direct that the Penalty of Five Pounds for non-possession of License be reduced to One Pound

Sixthly.—To direct that (as the Diggers and other residents on the Gold Fields of the Colony have uniformly developed a love of law and order) the sending of an Armed Force to enforce the License Tax be discontinued

Your Petitioners would respectfully submit to Your Excellency's consideration in favour of the reduction of the License Fee that many Diggers and other residents on the Gold-fields who are debarred from taking a license under the present System would if the Tax were reduced to Ten Shillings a Month cheerfully comply with the Law so that the License Fund instead of being diminished would be increased

Your Petitioners would also remind your Excellency that a Petition is the only mode by which they can submit their views to your Excellency's consideration as although they contribute more to the Exchequer than half the Revenue of the Colony they are the largest class of Her Majesty's Subjects in the Colony unrepresented

And your Petitioners as in duty bound will ever pray etc.

ABOVE *Some of the signatories to the petition.*

Towards a national game of football

RULES OF THE MELBOURNE FOOTBALL CLUB

The national game of Australian Rules Football is a uniquely Australian invention. While its first rules were drawn from various regional codes and conventions already established in the United Kingdom, in Australia the game evolved its own distinctive style. Allen Aylett, one of the sport's great players and administrators, has observed that the game 'is ours and ours alone, but has also become one of the most recognisable codes in the world. It is a sensational game, and watching young Australian Rules footballers displaying their skills, athleticism and courage on the field is an enjoyable activity for all spectators'.

The journalist Edmund Finn writing as 'Garryowen' documented the earliest recorded football game in Melbourne in 1844 but the code from which Australian football developed was first drafted at a meeting held on 17 May 1859 at the Parade Hotel in East Melbourne, a short walk from today's Melbourne Cricket Ground, one of the sport's great arenas. Four men drafted the rules: the sportsman Thomas Wentworth Spencer Wills (1835–1880) who chaired the meeting and who is credited by some as the father of the game; James Bogue Thompson (1829–1877), the Melbourne Football Club's inaugural secretary, who penned the document; sportsman and journalist William Hammersley (1826–1886); and Thomas Henry Smith (b. 1830), a master at Scotch College. From their simple ten rule platform, the code evolved into the game now known as Australian Rules Football.

For much of the twentieth century, followers of the Australian game knew nothing of the existence of the 1859 rules. For many years it was held that a set of rules drafted at a meeting presided over by H.C.A. Harrison (1836–1929) represented the earliest known laws of the game. But in 1980 all that changed in what has been described as 'a moment of serendipity and triumph for the history of Australian sport'. In that year, Bill Gray, then curator of the M.C.C. Museum at the Melbourne Cricket Ground, made a remarkable discovery. In a chance find he turned up the precious document of 1859 described recently by historians Rob Hess, Matthew Nicholson, Bob Stewart and Gregory De Moore as 'arguably the most important cultural landmark in Australian sporting history'. In the view of these writers, the so-called 'Melbourne Rules' may be seen as the 'clearest formal attempt to define the beginnings of a new sport in a new country'. The simplicity of the rules as first drafted created a game that was remarkably adaptable and readily accessible to new players. This accounted for its immediate popularity in Victoria at least though the game soon built a following in the southern states and Western Australia.

For all that the original rules of the game were so intimately connected with Melbourne, the supporters and defenders of the sport have always been ambitious to see the code expanded. Over 150 years the game has grown from a rough-and-tumble sport played in the parklands of Melbourne to a billion-dollar national industry. Throughout, administrators, players and spectators have not hesitated to promote the sport as a national code notwithstanding the presence of rival codes with ambitions and loyal constituencies of their own. These national ambitions have been reflected in the sport's various name changes. These have evolved from the 'Melbourne Rules' of 1859 to 'Victorian Rules' and finally to 'Australian Rules' as the game has earned its place as a truly national sport.

RULES OF THE MELBOURNE FOOTBALL CLUB, MAY 1859

I
The distance between the Goals and the Goal Posts shall be decided upon by the Captains of the sides playing.

II
The Captains on each side shall toss for the choice of Goal; the side losing the toss has the Kick off from the centre point between the Goals.

III
A Goal must be Kicked fairly between the posts, without touching either of them, or a portion of the person of any player on either side.

IV
The game shall be played within a space of not more than 200 yards wide, the same to be measured equally on each side of a line drawn through the centres of the two Goals; and two posts to be called 'Kick Off' posts shall be erected at a distance of 20 yards on each side of the Goal posts at both ends, and in a straight line with them.

V
In case the Ball is kicked behind Goal, any one of the side behind whose Goal it is kicked may bring it 20 yards in front of any portion of the space between the 'Kick off' posts, and shall kick it as nearly as possible in a line with the opposite Goal.

VI
Any player catching the Ball directly from the foot may call 'mark'. He then has a free kick; no player from the opposite side being allowed to come inside the spot marked.

VII
Tripping and pushing are both allowed (but no hacking) when any player is in rapid motion or in possession of the Ball, except in the case provided for in Rule VI.

VIII
The Ball may be taken in hand only when caught from the foot, or on the hop. In no case shall it be lifted from the ground.

IX
When a Ball goes out of bounds (the same being indicated by a row of posts) it shall be brought back to the point where it crossed the boundary-line, and thrown in at right angles with that line.

X
The Ball, while in play, may under no circumstances be thrown.

Rules for Play

I

The distance between the Goals and the Goal Posts shall be decided upon by the Captains of the sides playing.

II

The Captains on each side shall toss for choice of Goal; the side losing the toss has the kick off from the centre of point between the Goals

III

A Goal must be kicked fairly between the posts, without touching either of them, or a portion of the person of any player on either side.

IV

The game shall be played within

a space of not more than 200 yards wide, the same to be measured equally on each side of a line drawn through the centres of the two Goals; and two posts to be called the "Kick off" posts shall be erected at a distance of 20 yards on each side of the Goal posts at both ends, or in a straight line with them.

In case the Ball is kicked behind Goal, any one of the side behind whose Goal it is kicked may bring it 20 yards in front of any portion of the space between the "Kick off" posts, and shall kick it as nearly as possible in a line with the opposite Goal.

ABOVE *The 1859 Rules for Play of the Melbourne Football Club, penned by James Bogue Thompson.*

'I am now camped in the centre of Australia'

JOHN MCDOUALL STUART PLANTS THE BRITISH FLAG

Until the 1970s, the feats of both the maritime and land explorers of the continent were the staples of popular and school history. Generations of Australian school children traced the coastal triumphs of Tasman, Cook, Flinders and others, or learned by rote the names of men such as John Oxley, Thomas Mitchell, Charles Sturt, Edward Eyre, John McDouall Stuart, Ludwig Leichhardt, the Forrest brothers, and the famous pairings of Hume and Hovell and the tragic Burke and Wills. There were lessons to be learned as European Australians came to understand how the country was claimed for Britain's empire and how European civilisation came to take root in what was understood to be a vast emptiness. In this narrative of history, the explorers were to be celebrated as heroes, even if sometimes expeditions disappeared without trace or lives were lost in deserts of plenty, with the help of local Aboriginal people close at hand.

Not the least of the achievers was the Scottish-born surveyor John McDouall Stuart (1815–1866), whose four expeditions mounted out of Adelaide, between 1858 and 1862, gave South Australians a mighty sense of pride and enlarged their awareness of the further reaches of their colony. In April 1860 Stuart reached the geographical centre of the continent, marking the occasion in a small, proud ceremony recorded in his journal. The track of Stuart's successful south to north crossing of the continent later defined the course of another South Australian triumph, the construction of the Overland Telegraph line, completed in 1872 (see page 138).

The major record of Stuart's journeys is the volume edited for him by William Hardman, *The Journals of John McDouall Stuart during the years 1858, 1859, 1860, 1861 & 1862 when he fixed the Centre of the Continent and successfully crossed it from sea to sea*, and published in 1864. The extract here records Stuart's planting of the British flag in the centre of Australia on 23 April 1860 and his brief waterless sojourn in that spacious and beautiful landscape.

ABOVE *John McDouall Stuart plants the Union Jack on Central Mount Stuart.*

Sunday, 22nd April, Small Gum Creek, under Mount Stuart, Centre of Australia.—To-day I find from my observations of the sun, 111°00'30", that I am now camped in the centre of Australia. I have marked a tree and planted the British flag there. There is a high mount about two miles and a half to the north-north-east. I wish it had been in the centre; but on it to-morrow I will raise a cone of stones, and plant the flag there, and name it "Central Mount Stuart". We have been in search of permanent water to-day, but I cannot find any. I hope from the top of Central Mount Stuart to find something good to the north-west. Wind south. Examined a large creek; can find no surface water, but got some by scratching in the sand. It is a large creek divided into many channels, but they are all filled with sand; splendid grass all round this camp.

Monday, 23rd April, Centre.—Took Kekwick and the flag, and went to the top of the mount, but found it to be much higher and more difficult of ascent than I anticipated. After a deal of labour, slips, and knocks, we at last arrived on the top. It is quite as high as Mount Serle, if not higher. The view to the north is over a large plain of gums, mulga, and spinifex, with watercourses running through it. The large gum creek that we crossed winds round this hill in a north-east direction; at about ten miles it is joined by another. After joining they take a course more north, and I lost sight of them in the far-distant plain. To the north-north-east is the termination of hills; to the north-east, east and south-east are broken ranges, and to the north-north-west the ranges on the west side of the plain terminate. To the north-west are broken ranges; and to the west is a very high peak, between which and this place to the south-west are a number of isolated hills. Built a large cone of stones, in the centre of which I placed a pole with the British flag nailed to it. Near the top of the cone I placed a small bottle, in which there is a slip of paper, with our signatures to it, stating by whom it was raised. We then gave three hearty cheers for the flag, the emblem of civil and religious liberty, and may it be a sign to the natives that the dawn of liberty, civilization, and Christianity is about to break upon them. We can see no water from the top. Descended, but did not reach the camp till after dark. This water still continues, which makes me think there must certainly be more higher up. I have named the range "John Range," after my friend and well-wisher, John Chambers, Esq., brother to James Chambers, Esq., one of the promoters of this expedition.

Tuesday, 24th April, Central Mount Stuart.—Sent Kekwick in search of water, and to examine a hill that has the appearance of having a cone of stones upon it; meanwhile I made up my plan, and Ben mended the saddle-bags, which were in a sad mess from coming through the scrub. Kekwick returned in the afternoon, having found water higher up the creek. He has also found a new rose of a beautiful description, having thorns on its branches, and a seed-vessel resembling a gherkin. It has a sweet, strong perfume; the leaves are white, but as the flower is withered, I am unable to describe it. The native orange-tree abounds here. Mount Stuart is composed of hard red sandstone, covered with spinifex, and a little scrub on the top. The white ant abounds in the scrubs, and we even found some of their habitations near the top of Mount Stuart.

ABOVE *Print of an 1860 engraving of the expedition setting out from Royal Park, Melbourne. Members of the team are on camels and horses.*

Crossing the Australian continent

ROBERT O'HARA BURKE'S SPEECH AND THE LAST LETTER OF WILLIAM JOHN WILLS

Extravagantly equipped but disastrously executed, the Burke and Wills Expedition (1860–1861) set out to make the first south–north crossing of the Australian continent. Organised as the Victorian Exploring Expedition by the Royal Society of Victoria and supported by the Victorian government, the venture was led by Robert O'Hara Burke (1821–1861), an Irish-born superintendent of police, and his second-in-command William John Wills (1834–1861). Hot-headed, impetuous and woefully inexperienced in bushcraft, Burke's leadership was a disaster. He quarrelled with expedition members and eventually made the fatal decision to divide his party so that he—together with Wills, John King (1841–1872) and Charles Gray (d. 1861)—could push on to the Gulf of Carpentaria and so achieve the objective of crossing the continent. In a chapter of accidents, Burke and his companions failed to meet again with the back-up party they had left behind at Cooper's Creek. Burke, Wills and Gray all perished; only John King survived to bear witness to the ignominious end of what had promised to be a glorious adventure.

Burke's farewell speech given in Melbourne on the day the expedition departed is a brief prologue to a venture that began with high hopes but ended nine months later in tragedy. The speech was the forced climax of the shambles of the expedition's delayed departure from Royal Park, just outside Melbourne, late in the afternoon of 20 August 1860. A royal commission later condemned Burke's leadership, though the expedition itself would find a place in the Australian imagination as a glorious failure and as a metaphor for disaster. The expedition contributed virtually nothing to geographical knowledge, but its epic failure has stimulated the imagination of several artists and writers, including the painter Sidney Nolan (1917–1992).

Historian Tim Bonyhady has remarked that the departure 'was more to still the crowd's impatience than because the expedition was ready'. Still, it lumbered away with Burke mounted on his favourite horse, Billy, at the head of a caravan that should have comprised twenty-seven camels, twenty-three horses and 21 tonnes of equipment, including around 270 litres of rum. Only some of the packhorses departed at the time, and none of the wagons, though these followed later. Even as the expedition lurched its way towards Sydney Road to the tune of 'Cheer, Boys, Cheer', played by a band of musicians, three members of the expedition were still packing the scientific equipment.

Burke's speech was delivered in response to a call from the Mayor of Melbourne who had mounted a wagon to wish the explorers 'God speed'. After three cheers, Burke delivered his response in a 'clear, earnest voice that was heard all over the crowd'. The moment itself is commemorated in a single surviving photograph of the expedition's departure—and in Burke's own words that in hindsight carry the taste of ashes. The bodies of Burke and Wills were recovered and returned to Melbourne for burial in January 1863. A commemorative monument by the sculptor Charles Summers was erected in their honour; it stands today at the intersection of Swanston and Collins streets in central Melbourne.

A companion to Burke's short and optimistic speech is the last letter written by Wills before his lonely death at Cooper's Creek in South Australia. Addressed to his father, Dr William Wills, this stoic epistle, dated 27 June 1861, is a poignant testimony to the disaster that befell the exploration party. That was brought back to Melbourne after the recovery of the explorers' remains and published in *A Narrative of a Successful Exploration through the Interior of Australia* (1862), the book Dr Wills wrote to vindicate his son and assert the enterprise's success. The letter is held by the State Library of Victoria in Melbourne, which also holds the records of the Royal Society of Victoria as principal organisers of the expedition.

ABOVE *The only surviving photograph of the expedition members at Royal Park, with Burke standing in the centre making his farewell speech.*

Mr Mayor, On behalf of myself and the expedition I beg to return to you my most sincere thanks. No expedition has ever started under such favourable circumstances as this. The people, the Government, the Committee [of the Royal Society of Victoria]—all have done heartily what they could do. It is now our turn, and we shall never do well until we entirely justify what you have done in showing what we can do. (Cheers).

27 June 1861
My dear Father

These are probably the last lines you will ever get from me. We are on the point of starvation not so much from absolute want of food but from the want of nutriment in what we can get.

Our position although more provoking is probably not so disagreeable as that of poor Harry & his companions [a reference to Lieutenant Harry Le Vescomte, a cousin of Wills who had perished in the Arctic]; We have had every good luck and made a most successful trip to Carpentaria and back to where we had every right to consider ourselves safe. Having left a Depot here consisting of four men twelve horses and six camels, they had sufficient provisions to have lasted them for twelve months with proper economy. We had also every right to expect that we should have been immediately followed up from [Miniminka?] by another party with additional provisions and every thing necessary for forming a permanent Depot at Coopers Creek. The party we left here had special instructions not to leave until our return, unless from absolute necessity. We left the Creek with, nominally, three months supply, but they were reckoned at little over the rate of half rations & we calculated on having to eat some of the Camels. By the greatest good luck at every turn we crossed to the Gulf through a good deal of fine country almost in a straight line from here. On the other side the camels suffered considerably from wet & we had to kill & jerk one soon after starting back. We had now been out a little more than two months and found it necessary to reduce the rations considerably, and this began to tell on all hands, but I felt it by far less than either of the others. The great scarcity & shyness of game & our forced marches prevented our supplying the deficiency from external sources to any great extent but we never could have held out but for the Crows & Hawks & the Portulac. The latter is an excellent vegetable and I believe secured our return to this place. We got back here in four months & four days and found that the party had left the creek the same day & we were not in a fit state to follow them.

I find I must close this that it may be planted but I will write some more although it has not so good a chance of reaching you …

You have great claim on the Committee for their neglect. I leave you the sole charge of what is coming to me the whole of my money. I desire to leave it to my sisters. Other matters I will leave for the present.

Adieu my dearest father
W.J. Wills

I think to live about four or five days. My religious views are not the least changed and I have not the least fear of their being so. My spirits are excellent.

Ending the silence

JOINING THE OVERLAND TELEGRAPH LINE BETWEEN ADELAIDE AND PORT DARWIN

ABOVE *Landing the cable at Port Darwin on 7 November 1871.*

On 22 August 1872, after one year and eleven months of taxing construction, the Overland Telegraph Line between Adelaide and Port Darwin was successfully joined. For its architect, electrical engineer Charles Todd (1826–1910), joining the cable was a personal triumph. For the tiny colony of South Australia, which had built and paid for the construction of a cable extending over more than 3000 kilometres, the enterprise was a magnificent feat of vision and commitment to the building not simply of a local amenity but a prime piece of national infrastructure.

At the moment of its joining, the Overland Telegraph Line transformed life in the Australian colonies. Historian Peter Taylor has observed that the cable ended Australia's isolation: a messsage could now be telegraphed from Sydney to London in just seven hours, where a letter might take three months to travel the same distance. The achievement was little short of miraculous.

With the connection a success, celebrations erupted. At the final construction site of Frews Ponds, where the cable was joined, the men fired a salute of twenty-one shots from their revolvers and a bottle of 'brandy' (but probably cold tea) was broken over one of the poles. At Todd's camp at the foot of Central Mount Stuart, three hearty cheers rang out. In distant Adelaide, the red ensign fluttered from the Post Office tower and flags were flown across the city; the Town Hall bells pealed; and bunting decorated ships in the port. Adelaide was in holiday mood.

Messages flowed down the line. From Port Darwin, the acting government resident cabled a greeting to the South Australian governor, Sir James Fergusson, in Adelaide.

In the absence of the Government Resident, I have the honour to congratulate Your Excellency on the completion and opening of the Overland Telegraph Line. I trust this great undertaking will increase the trade, and develop the varied resources of the Colony, and prove the pioneer of still greater works, uniting more firmly the various Australian Colonies to each other and them to the mother country. God save the Queen!

To Todd himself, the chief secretary reported:

We opened the line at 1.00 p.m. this day as it was completed ... I took that opportunity of sending a message in the name of the Government of this Colony thanking the officers and men of the Construction Party for the praiseworthy efforts and untiring diligence that they have displayed in bringing to a successful conclusion this great work, under your able superintendence. Accept my congratulations that your troubles are now over.

From his camp at the centre of the continent, Todd replied:

Many thanks for your kind congratulations on the completion of the Adelaide and Port Darwin telegraph, which, as an important link in the electric chain of communication connecting the Australian Colonies with the mother country and the whole of the civilised and commercial world, will, I trust, redound to the credit of South Australia.

In 1954, more than eighty years later, the then Postmaster General's Department, set in place a permanent memorial to the achievement of those who had built the telegraph line. A marble column was erected on the Stuart Highway between Elliott and Dunmara. The inscription reads:

The Overland Telegraph Line
This column was erected to the memory of Sir Charles Todd, KCMG, MA, FRS, FRAS, FRMS, FSTE, Postmaster General of the Province of South Australia. His gallant construction teams, operators, and linemen under R.C. Patterson, A.T. Woods, W.H. Abbott, B.H. Babbage, R.C. Burton, W. Harvey, R.R. Knuckey, G.G. MacLachlan, G.R. McMinn, W. McMinn, W.W. Mills, A.J. Mitchell, W. Rutt and explorer John Ross. The northern and southern parts of this epic Overland Telegraph Line were finally joined about one mile west of this spot, by R.C. Patterson, engineer, at 3.15 p.m. on Thursday, August 22nd 1872, thus making possible for the first time instantaneous telegraph communication between Australia and Great Britain.

FINIS CORONAT OPUS

ABOVE *Lyrics and score for 'Advance Australia Fair'.*

Bold, stirring and decidedly patriotic

A NEW ANTHEM: 'ADVANCE AUSTRALIA FAIR'

'Advance Australia Fair' was composed by Sydney school teacher and songwriter Peter Dodds McCormick (1834?–1916) under the pen-name 'Amicus'. It was first sung in public by Andrew Fairfax at the St Andrew's Day concert of the Highland Society in Sydney on 30 November 1878. The *Sydney Morning Herald* described Dodds' music as 'bold and stirring' and the words as 'decidedly patriotic'. It was predicted that the song was likely to become a popular favourite and indeed it did.

The song also quickly assumed some standing as a quasi-Australian anthem. At the inauguration of the Commonwealth of Australia in 1901 'Advance Australia Fair' was sung by a choir of 10,000 voices, and in 1913 it was played by massed bands at the celebrations to mark the naming of Canberra as the federal capital. For many years, the Australian Broadcasting Commission used the song to announce its news bulletins. But it was not until 1984 that 'Advance Australia Fair' was adopted officially as the Australian national anthem, finally displacing the British royal anthem, 'God Save the Queen', and dispatching another popular contender, the perennially popular but contentious 'Waltzing Matilda' (see page 173).

In the form in which it is known in Australia today, the anthem differs from the original composition by Peter Dodds McCormick. But even with modifications for official use, the modern lyrics seem to many not merely old fashioned but also archaic, and the melody is banal. The words still seem to elude many members of the public and especially those in sporting teams, who must stand to attention when the anthem is played at cricket matches or at football grand finals. Even so, 'Advance Australia Fair', even if it is not greatly loved, seems to have gained a place in the affections of the nation. McCormick's original words, published for the first time in 1879, are rich in the prevailing British sentiment of their time.

Australia's sons, let us rejoice,
For we are young and free;
We've golden soil and wealth for toil,
Our home is girt by sea;
Our land abounds in nature's gifts
Of beauty rich and rare;
In history's page, let every stage
Advance Australia Fair.
In joyful strains then let us sing
Advance Australia Fair.

When gallant Cook from Albion sailed,
To trace wide oceans o'er;
True British courage bore him on,
Till he landed on our shore;
Then here he raised Old England's flag,
The standard of the brave;
With all her faults we love her still
Britannia rules the wave.
In joyful strains then let us sing
Advance Australia Fair.

While other nations of the globe
Behold us from afar,
We'll rise to high renown and shine
Like our glorious southern star;
From England, Scotia, Erin's isle,
Who come our lot to share,
Let all combine with heart and hand
To Advance Australia Fair.
In joyful strains then let us sing
Advance Australia Fair.

Should foreign foe e'er sight our coast,
Or dare a foot to land,
We'll rouse to arms like sires of yore,
To guard our native strand;
Britannia then shall surely know,
Though oceans roll between,
Her sons in fair Australia's land
Still keep their name serene.
In joyful strains then let us sing
'Advance Australia Fair!'

Fearless, free and bold

NED KELLY'S JERILDERIE LETTER

Edward 'Ned' Kelly (1855–1880) was born in Beveridge, Victoria, the eldest son of John and Ellen Kelly. Following the death of John Kelly, the family moved to a hut near Greta in north-eastern Victoria. There the young Ned fell in with the larrikin boys of the township and at the age of 14 was arrested on a charge of assault. He had a brief spell in prison in 1870 and again in 1871–1874. In January 1876 a warrant was issued against him for horse stealing. That charge was eventually dismissed, but as Kelly historian Ian Jones has noted, the case set off a chain of events that brought his 'honest years' to an end. As the decade advanced, Kelly's grievances accumulated, not the least of them being a sense of victimisation and injustice at the hands of the police.

In April 1878 a policeman attempting to arrest Kelly's brother Dan was wounded at the Kelly home. In the aftermath, Ellen Kelly was arrested and imprisoned, together with two Kelly associates. With warrants issued for their arrest, Ned and Dan Kelly retreated with fellow gang members Joe Byrne (1856–1880) and Steve Hart (1859–1880) to the sanctuary of the Wombat Ranges near Mansfield. At nearby Stringybark Creek on 26 October, the Kelly gang ambushed and killed three policemen. In December they took to bushranging—robbing a homestead and then a bank at Euroa. In February 1879 the gang bailed up the New South Wales town of Jerilderie, compounding this outrage with the robbery of another bank. In June the following year, police informer Aaron Sherrit was murdered. This led two days later to a shoot-out with the police at Glenrowan. Ned Kelly escaped briefly but was captured shortly afterwards. He stood trial in Melbourne and was sentenced to death. He was hanged at the Melbourne gaol on the morning of 11 November 1880.

During the bank robbery at Jerilderie, Ned Kelly had pressed into the hand of the accountant, Edwin Living, a fifty-six-page letter that has become known as the Jerilderie Letter. Often described as a manifesto, it is a powerful and sometimes disturbing document. It pours scorn on the police, but it also gives voice to Kelly's accumulated grievances—what he saw as a vendetta against him by the police, as well as matters of social, economic and religious concern. Dictated by Ned Kelly and written down for him by Joe Byrne, the letter gives a powerful sense of Kelly's own voice and persona. In 7400 angry and sometimes incoherent words, Kelly defends his actions. He records the injustices and indignities he and his family suffered at the hands of the police, asserts his innocence and, in a broad but ill-defined political agenda, seeks justice for poor and vulnerable families such as his own. It was Kelly's wish to see the letter published, but this was denied while he lived; instead it was used against him at his trial.

In life, Ned Kelly was hunted down and punished as a notorious criminal, though even then he had his sympathisers. In death he became a legend, admired by many as a folk hero, failed revolutionary and Australian nationalist. For historian Bill Gammage this Ned Kelly is a young statesman but M.H. Ellis describes him as 'one of the most cold-blooded egotistical and utterly self-centred criminals who ever decorated the end of a rope in an Australian jail'. The legend of Ned Kelly survives in books, poetry, songs and images, including the narrative paintings (1946–1947) by artist Sidney Nolan. The stream of reportage, commemoration, analysis, criticism and celebration that began even while Kelly lived has never ceased to flow. Over the years, the Jerilderie Letter has been published in several forms, including a 2001 edition movingly introduced and analysed by the Melbourne historian Alex McDermott. Peter Carey drew extensively on it to write his Booker Prize–winning novel *True History of the Kelly Gang*. The Jerilderie Letter has a special place in the rich memorialising of Ned Kelly. At once artefact and document, a testimony and life story, it has a life now as icon and national treasure. It is the means, surely, by which we might know Ned Kelly himself and hear what is authentically his own voice.

... Is there not big fat-necked Unicorns enough paid to torment and drive me to do things which I don't wish to do, Without the public assisting them I have never interfered with any person unless they deserved it. And yet there are civilians who take firearms against me, for what reason I do not know unless they want me to turn on them and exterminate them with out medicine. I shall be compelled to make an example of some of them if they cannot find no other employment. If I had robbed and plundered and ravished and murdered everything I met young and old rich and poor the public could not do any more than take firearms and assisting the police as they have done, but by the light that shines pegged on an ant-bed with their bellies opened their fat taken out rendered and poured down their throat boiling hot will be cool to what pleasure I will give some of them. And any person aiding or harbouring or assisting the Police in any way whatever or employing any person whom they know to be a detective or cad or those who would be so deprived as to take blood-money will be Outlawed, And declared unfit to be allowed human buriel their property either consumed or confiscated And them theirs and all belonging to them exterminated off the face of the earth, the enemy I cannot catch myself I shall give a payable reward for, I would like to know who put that article that reminds me of a poodle dog half clipped in the lion fashion called Brooke. E. Smith Superintendent of Police he knows as much about commanding Police as Captain Standish does about mustering mosquitoes and boiling them down for their fat on the back blocks of the Lachlan for he has a head like a turnip a stiff neck as big as his shoulders narrow hipped and pointed towards the feet like a vine stake. And if there is anyone to be called a murderer regarding Kennedy, Scanlon and Lonigan it is that mis-placed poodle he gets as much pay as a dozen good troopers, if there is any good in them, And what does he do for it he cannot look behind him without turning his whole frame it takes three or four police to keep sentry while he sleeps in Wangaratta, for fear of body snatchers do they think he is a superior animal to the men that has to guard him if so why not send the men that gets big pay and reconed superior to the common police after me and you shall soon save the county of high salaries to men that is fit for nothing else but getting better men than himself shot and sending orphan children to the industrial school to make prostitutes and cads of them for the Detectives and other evil disposed persons. Send the high paid and men that received big salaries for year in a gang by themselves after me, As it makes no difference to them but it will give them a chance of showing whether they are worth more pay than a common trooper or not And I think the Public will soon find they are only in the road of good men And obtaining money under false pretences. I do not call McIntyre a coward for I reckon he is as game a man as wears the Jacket as he had the presence of mind to know his position, directly as he was spoken to, and only foolishness to disobey, it was cowardice that made Lonigan and the others fight it is only foolhardiness to disobey an outlaw as any Policeman or other man who do not throw up their arms directly as I call on them knows the consequence which is speedy dispatch to Kingdom Come, I wish those men who joined the stock protection society to withdraw their money and give it and as much more to the widows and orphans and poor of Greta district where I spent and will again spend many a happy day fearless free and bold as it only aids the police to procure false witnesses and go whacks with men to steal horses and lag innocent men. It would suit them far better to subscribe a sum and give it to the poor of the district And there is no fear of anyone stealing their property for no man could steal their horses without the knowledge of the poor if any man was mean enough to steal their property the poor would rise out to a man and find them if they were on the face of the earth it will always pay a rich man to be liberal with the poor And make as little enemies as he can As he shall find if the poor is on his side he shall loose nothing by it. If they depend in the police they shall be drove to destruction. As they can not And will not protect them if duffing and bushranging were abolished the police would have to cadge for their living I speak from experience as I have sold horses and cattle innumerable and yet eight head of the culls is all ever was found. I never was interfered with whilst I kept up this successful trade. I give fair warning to all those who has reason to fear me to sell out and give £10 out of every hundred towards the widow and orphan fund and do not attempt to reside in Victoria but as short a time as possible after reading this notice, neglect this and abide by the consequences, Which shall be worse than the rust in the wheat in Victoria or the druth of a dry season to the grasshoppers in New South Wales. I do not wish to give the order full force without giving timely warning but I am a widows son outlawed and my orders must be obeyed.

ABOVE *Ned Kelly standing shackled, from an undated photograph.*

37

going to shoot him and his mates. I told him no. I would shoot no man if he gave up his arms and leave the force he said the police all knew Fitzpatrick had wronged us. And he intended to leave the force. As he had bad health. And his life was insured, he told me he intended going home. And that Kennedy and Scanlan were out looking for our camp And also about the other Police he told me the N. S. W Police had shot a man for shooting Sergeant Walling I told him if they did, they had shot the wrong man And I expect your gang came to do the same with me he said no they did not come to shoot me they came to apprehend me I asked him what they carried spenceir rifles and breech loading fowling pieces and so much ammunition for as the Police was

Only supposed to carry one revolver and 6 cartridges in the revolver but they had eighteen rounds of revolver cartridges each three dozen for the fowling piece and twenty one spenceir-rifle cartridges and God knows how many they had away with the rifle this looked as if they meant not only to shoot me only to riddle me but I dont know either Kennedy Scanlan or him and had nothing against them, he said he would get them to give up their arms if I would not shoot them as I could not blame them, they had to do their duty I said I did not blame them for doing honest duty but I could not suffer them blowing me to pieces in my own native land, and they knew Fitzpatrick wronged

ABOVE Pages 37 and 38 of the 56-page Jerilderie Letter.

'The body will be cremated and the ashes taken to Australia'

THE LEGEND OF THE ASHES

In August 1882, on the hallowed ground of the Oval, colonial Australia won its first Test cricket victory on English soil. Out of this memorable Australian triumph emerged the concept of the Ashes, the Test cricket series played biennially between England and Australia.

With the dismissal of Ted Peate, England's last batsman, the Australian victory by a mere seven runs led to two mock obituaries in the English press. The first appeared in the magazine *Cricket* on 31 August 1882 and mourned the loss of 'England's Supremacy in the Cricket-Field'. The second—and more famous—written by Reginald Brooks, appeared in the *Sporting Times* in London on 2 September 1882. It lamented the death of English cricket and noted that 'the body will be cremated and the ashes taken to Australia'. In the week that the Australian team of 1882 returned to Australia, the Sydney *Bulletin* of 9 December 1882 referred to the 'revered ashes of English cricket which had been laid on the shelf of the Australian Eleven'. With the prospect of the next contest in Australia (1882–83), the English media began to write of 'the quest to regain The Ashes'. That contest evolved over the years into one of the most celebrated rivalries in international cricket. On both sides, the battle for the Ashes has generated an intense passion and interest that for some approaches fanaticism.

But on 28 September 1882, at a banquet held at the Criterion Hotel in London to farewell the victorious Australians, a whole-hearted toast was moved to 'The Australian Cricket Team'. Responding on behalf of his players and his country, the Australian captain, William 'Billy' Lloyd Murdoch (1854–1911), delivered a speech notable for its grace and generosity, its quiet pride in victory and its high sense of honour. Having bearded the English lion in its den, Murdoch was quick to acknowledge the debt owed by the Australians to their English mentors and exemplars. At the same time he asserted the determination of his countrymen to play the game with honour and to play the game to win.

ABOVE *The Australian Eleven in 1880.*

I feel my position tonight very keenly for it is one I cannot but be proud of, and I am sure it is one that will be envied by the sportsmen throughout Australia. I desire on behalf of myself and my colleagues to return you our warmest thanks for the very great honour you have done us in so kindly receiving the toast which Sir Henry Barkly proposed. It is very gratifying to us to find that our exertions in the cricket field are considered worthy of such generous recognition and such openhanded hospitality. When we quitted Australia we did so as a band of cricketers, determined to do our best to uphold the reputation of the land of our birth, to leave no stone unturned to gain the laurels so dear to every true sportsman. In this spirit we started on our daring enterprise to beard the English lion in his den. The result you know. Since landing here in May we have been constantly engaged in playing matches. On all occasions we simply did our best to play up to the true letter and spirit of the game, and we always tried our very hardest to win. I can assure you that on the few occasions we lost there were not fourteen more grieved men in the world. We knew very well that the eyes of all Australia were upon us, and that the honour of Australia had been entrusted to our hands. The laurels we have won we shall on our return place at the feet of our fellow countrymen, and hope that the verdict be that we have been tried and not found wanting. If I may be permitted to say so, I feel at present something like your very able General Wolseley must feel when he contemplated the result of the Egyptian campaign. He was sent out to do a certain thing—to crush Arabi—and he has done it. I was sent home as a captain of an Australian cricket team to beat England and I am proud of having done it. Personally I have attained the height of my ambition, having captained a team which has beaten a representative Eleven of England. Having done this, I do not wish any more to play cricket. I do not care any more to run the risk of commanding a team which may possibly sustain defeat, but if I am called upon to occupy such a position I shall only be too proud to do so, and shall do my very best to win.

There are several gentlemen present tonight who have played cricket in Australia perhaps forty years ago. They, I trust will feel gratified at witnessing the cordial reception given tonight to those who have followed their example. English teams which have visited these colonies have taught us what we know of cricket. When the first went out there we knew little or nothing of the game, but we have since improved, as we have endeavoured to show on our present tour. If we have attained any position as cricketers, you in England have yourselves to thank for it, for you have been our instructors. We have been very ready and willing to learn, for the cricketing spirit is as strong in Australia as in England. It is the national game of the colonies, and we shall always be ready to take up the willow and do battle with any who desire to meet us in the field ... Before resuming my seat I desire to propose the toast, 'The English Cricketers, and success to Cricket', coupled with the names of Mr A.N. Hornby and Mr C.I. Thornton [the English cricketers Albert Neilson Hornby (1847–1925) and Charles Inglis Thornton (1850–1929). Hornby captained England in the 1882 Test; Thornton offered generous encouragement to the early Australian teams]. Both these gentlemen have always exhibited the true spirit of the game, and I thank them for the cordiality of their relations with us.

'Here then is DAWN, the Australian Woman's Journal and mouthpiece'

A NEWSPAPER FOR WOMEN

When *The Dawn: A Journal for Women* appeared on 15 May 1888, it was the first Australian newspaper to cater to the interests of women who wanted to free themselves from the narrow confines of domesticity. Other women's magazines had appeared before, but their aim had been to entertain rather than deal with serious issues. *The Dawn* was the brainchild of pioneer feminist and journalist Louisa Lawson (1848–1920). She had previously owned and published *The Republican* (1887–88), 'a truculent little paper', which included early contributions written by her son Henry Lawson (1867–1922), who would eventually become one of Australia's best-loved writers.

Louisa Lawson's newspaper for women would run as a monthly from 1888 to 1905. Over those seventeen years, its entire contents would be written or edited by Lawson herself, except for a ten-month period in 1900 when she was incapacitated. Initially, the paper was edited under the pseudonym Dora Falconer, a convention Lawson maintained until January 1891, but it was always clear that Louisa Lawson was the owner and publisher of the newspaper. As Lawson's first editorial announcement—the document published here—declares, *The Dawn* had an emphatic and unapologetic reformist and feminist agenda. The paper regularly published articles on social issues, such as divorce reform and women's suffrage, together with news, fiction and poetry. Another innovation, radical in its time, was Lawson's policy, where possible, of employing women to produce the paper. In the early years, this led to a boycott being imposed by male printers in Sydney, who opposed the admission of female employees to membership of the Typographical Association. Louisa Lawson fought this battle head on, and subsequent issues of the paper detailed the progress of its female compositors towards their eventual admission to the union.

Summing up the contribution made by *The Dawn*, historian Olive Lawson (herself the great granddaughter of Louisa Lawson), has noted that the newspaper's political influence and social impact were considerable: '[it] played a significant role in promoting those legislative changes which most affected the lives of Australian women at the turn of the [nineteenth] century—the laws on female suffrage, on marriage and divorce, on property ownership, on women's conditions of work and unionism, on women's education and equal opportunity in the workforce'.

ABOVE *Louisa Lawson around 1880.*

About Ourselves.

"Woman is not uncompleted man, but diverse.", says Tennyson, and being diverse why should she not have her journal in which her divergent hopes, aims, and opinions may have representation. Every eccentricity of belief, and every variety of bias in mankind allies itself with a printing-machine, and gets its singularities bruited about in type, but where is the printing-ink champion of mankind's better half? There has hitherto been no trumpet through which the concentrated voices of womankind could publish their grievances and their opinions. Men legislate on divorce, on hours of labor, and many another question intimately affecting women, but neither ask nor know the wishes of those whose lives and happiness are most concerned. Many a tale might be told by women, and many a useful hint given, even to the omniscient male, which would materially strengthen and guide the hands of law-makers and benefactors aspiring to be just and generous to weak and unrepresented womankind.

Here then is DAWN, the Australian Woman's Journal and mouthpiece—

A newspaper for women

'a turning point in the art of Australia'

THE 9 × 5 IMPRESSION EXHIBITION IN MELBOURNE

On Saturday 17 September 1889, the 9 × 5 Impression Exhibition was opened to the public at Buxton's Art Gallery in Swanston Street, Melbourne, opposite the town hall. One of the participants, Arthur Streeton (1867–1943), later described the show as 'a turning point in the art of Australia'. It laid the foundations of the golden era of Australian plein-air painting, itself part of a larger expression of national self-awareness that flourished in the 1890s. The exhibition of 182 works, presented on the lids of cigar boxes in the place of canvas, offered fleeting impressions of landscape painted in the open air. Here was both a challenge to the established conventions of studio painting and the beginning of a new and vital era in Australian art in which the names of Streeton, Tom Roberts (1856–1931) and Charles Conder (1868–1909) are now among the most famous.

The task of designing the exhibition catalogue—now extremely rare and one of the most precious documents in the history of Australian art—was assigned to the young Charles Conder, then only 20 years of age. If his design lacked what one later commentator called a 'propagandist clarity', Conder's chosen symbols nevertheless nicely suggested the prevailing theme of the show. As art historian Terence Lane has pointed out, the figures of Art and Convention are surrounded by symbols of the fleeting nature of life—blossoms, the sun, a dragonfly, an extinguished torch. On the title page was a quotation from the French painter and teacher Jean-Léon Gérôme: 'When you draw, form is the important thing; but in painting the *first* thing to look for is the *general impression* of colour.' This was followed by the artists' own statement of intent.

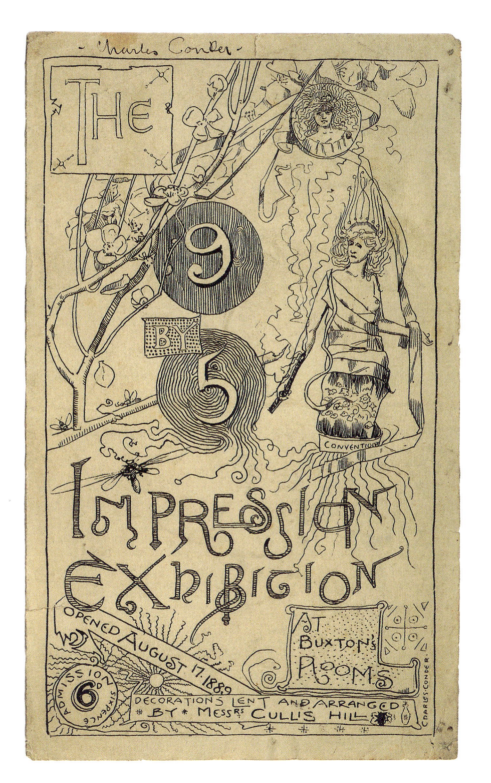

ABOVE *Charles Conder's design for the exhibition catalogue.*

TO THE PUBLIC.

An Effect is only momentary: so an impressionist tries to find his place. Two half-hours are never alike, and he who tries to paint the sunset on two successive evenings, must be more or less painting from memory. So, in these works, it has been the object of the artists to render faithfully, and thus obtain first records of effects widely differing, and often of very fleeting character.— * * *

On the morning of 17 August 1889, art critic James Smith of the *Argus* newspaper damned the show.

Such an exhibition of impressionist memoranda as will be opened today at Buxton's Art Gallery by Messrs. Roberts, Conder, Streeton, and others fails to justify itself. It has no adequate raison d'etre. It is as if a dramatist should give a performance on the stage of such scraps of dialogue, hints of character, ideas for incident, and suggestions of situations as had occurred to him while pondering over the construction of a play, or as if a musician should invite people to listen to crude and disconnected scraps of composition, containing the vaguely indicated theme for a cantata, a symphony, or an opera; or as if a sculptor should ask us to inspect masses of marble from which he had just blocked out the amorphous outlines of various pieces of statuary. None of these is to be regarded as a work of art. Neither is a painter's 'impression.' It is simply a record in colour of some fugitive effect which he sees, or professes to see, in nature. But, like primeval chaos, 'it is without form and void'. To the executant it seems spontaneous and forcible. To the spectator it appears grotesque and meaningless … The modern impressionist asks you to see pictures in splashes of colour, in slap-dash brushwork, and in sleight-of-hand methods of execution leading to the proposition of pictorial conundrums, which would baffle solution if there were no label or catalogue. In an exhibition of paintings you naturally look for pictures, instead of which the impressionist presents you with a varied assortment of palettes. Of the 180 exhibits catalogued on the present occasion, something like four-fifths are a pain to the eye. Some of them look like faded pictures seen through several mediums of thick gauze; others suggest that a paint-pot has been accidentally upset over a panel nine inches by five; others resemble the first essays of a small boy, who has been apprenticed to a house-painter; whilst not a few are as distressing as the incoherent images which float through the mind of a dyspeptic dreamer.

Defending themselves, the artists wrote an impassioned letter in response. It was published in the *Argus*, 3 September 1889. Rounding out the statement in the exhibition catalogue, it spelled out their Impressionist manifesto.

That we will not be led by any forms of composition or light and shade; that any effect of nature which moves us strongly by its beauty, whether strong or vague in its drawing, defined or indefinite in its light, rare or ordinary in colour, is worthy of our best efforts and of the love of those who love our art. Through and over all this we say we will do our best to put only the truth down, and only as much as we feel sure of seeing ... So in judging landscape work in Victoria, the mind is more or less influenced by familiar works. In looking at the works of modern European and American painters, who have in great measure discarded the studio for their painting ground, and whose aim has been to sacrifice no truth for effect, the spectator may feel a certain want as of finish or arrangement, and here let us leave our mind open, and forget for the moment our own idea of what ought to be in a picture, realise the intention of the artist, then judge if the impression given is true under the conditions represented, leaving the rest to time, for if the work is good it will grow upon us and hold us.

'we must unite as one great Australian people'

SIR HENRY PARKES ADDRESSES THE FEDERATION CONFERENCE

On the evening of 6 February 1890, four hundred guests attended the Grand Federal Banquet held in Queen's Hall, Parliament House, Melbourne. The occasion was the social climax of the Federation Conference, one of the landmarks on the road to the federation of the Australian colonies. Sir Henry Parkes (1815–1896)—by then five times premier of New South Wales—was present at the conference, where he was acknowledged as one of the leading proponents of federal unification. Rising to give the reply to the toast 'A United Australasia', Parkes was greeted with a roar of acclamation. His speech, with its famous line 'The crimson thread of kinship runs through us all', is honoured as one of the most persuasive and eloquent documents of the federation movement. The speech was presented at a time when it still seemed possible that New Zealand might join into a federal union with Australia, and, as the 'crimson thread' reference suggests, the connection to Britain and to the wider British empire was taken to be an essential part of the federal compact.

ABOVE *Sir Henry Parkes, photographed by Walter Barnett around 1893.*

In this human world of ours, so full of wise designs, mixed with so much failure and error, nothing is more noticeable than the delusions which lead men on to great crises. On the eve of that terrible convulsion which shattered France to atoms and startled the world, the ruling people and fashionable life went on as ever. There was marrying and giving in marriage, there was merry-makings and festivals, until the hidden elements burst out from under them and around them, and all the world wondered. No one supposed that they were standing on the brink of a terrible precipice. Without going to such examples as that, many and many is the occasion where men go on with their eyes closed, when only the far-seeing students of philosophy and history can see. And it may be at this moment that the people of these Australian colonies are going on with their bartering, rejoicing and merry-making—of which we know they are so fond—without being aware that they are standing on the imminence of an event that can only occur once in the whole world's history—the creation of a nation. [*Cheers.*] And in this country of Australia, with such ample space, with such inviting varieties of soil and climate, with such vast stores in the hidden wealth under the soil, with such unrivalled richness on all hands, and with a people occupying that soil unequalled in all the whole range of the human race in nation-creating properties, what is there that should be impossible to those people? By the closest calculation that I have been able to make, we, including New Zealand, want 200,000 souls to make four millions of a population. If four millions of a population cannot be the basis for national life, then there never will be a national life [*Cheers.*] Four millions of population, all of British origin, many and many thousands united to the soil by ties of birth, by ties of parentage, by ties of friendship and love, as well as by ties of marriage and ties of children, if they are not capable of making a nation—a united Australasia, why we are not fit hardly to occupy this bounteous country. [*Applause.*]

But if anyone supposes those are mere flights of imagination, let us come down to the barest possible calculation of facts. A hundred years ago the continent was occupied by a despairing group of outcast persons of British origin, and that British origin speaks volumes in every step of our calculation. Forty years ago the colony of Victoria had no existence. I had been an inhabitant of Australia ten years before Victoria was born; I was an inhabitant of Australia, and had a seat in a Legislature before the colony of Queensland was born. There is, however, no man in Victoria or Queensland who more rejoiced in their prosperous career, and in the grand results that followed, than I did [*Cheers.*] These two colonies, the great and the splendid ... are truly daughters of New South Wales [*Cheers.*] ... The mother colony knows too well ... that the prosperity of her two daughters means her own. [*Cheers.*] We know that it is a wise dispensation that these large colonies sprang into existence, and we admired them when they were fighting their own battles and working out their own prosperity independently of New South Wales, but the time has now arrived when we are no longer isolated. [*Cheers.*] The crimson thread of kinship runs through us all. Even the native-born Australians are Britons, as much as the men born within the cities of London and Glasgow. We know the value of their British origin. We know that we represent a race ... for the purposes of settling new colonies,

Sir Henry Parkes addresses the Federation Conference

which never had its equal on the face of the earth. [*Loud cheers*.] We know, too, that conquering wild territory, and planting civilized communities therein is a far nobler, a far more immortalizing achievement than conquest by feats of arms. We as separate communities have had to fight our way. We have had that which at times, I dare say, has degenerated into antagonism, naturally enough; but on the whole I do not believe that the thoughtful men of Victoria have ever lost sight of the good qualities of the men of New South Wales. [*Cheers*.] I do not believe that the people of the mother colony—and we have many men and women in the second and third generation born on the soil—have ever lost their admiration of the legitimate enterprise and fine emulation of the people of Victoria. What may be said of Victoria may be said of Queensland, South Australia, Tasmania ... Is there a man living in any part of Australasia who will say that it would be to the advantage of the whole that we should remain disunited—[*'No, no,' and cheers*.]—with our animosities, border Customs and all the frictions which our border Customs tend to produce, until the end of time. [*Cheers*.] I do not believe there is a sane man in the whole population of Australasia who will say such a daringly absurd thing. [*Cheers*.] If this is admitted, the question is reduced to very narrow limits, and it follows that at some time or other, we must unite as one great Australian people [*Cheers*.]

Let those who are opposed to the union now point out the advantage that would arise from one, five or ten years' delay. It is impossible for the human intellect to conceive that any advantage could arise. Do we not all see that the difficulties would be greater as years go on. If that reasoning is correct, we have now arrived at a time when we are fully justified by all the laws that regulate the growth of free communities in uniting under one government and one flag [*Cheers*.] The flag of United Australasia means to me no separation from the Empire. [*Prolonged cheering*.] It means no attempt to create a foreign political organization. Admitting, as I do, that the interests of the Australian people ought to be the first object of concern, still I say that our interests cannot be promoted by any rash, thoughtless and crude separation from the grand old country of which we are all so proud. [*Cheers*.] All free communities must have a political head, and I should like to ask any thoughtful student of history what supreme head we could have more attractive, more ennobling, more consonant with the true principles of liberty than our august Sovereign ... There is no reign of emperor, king or potentate, which has included such tremendous changes for the improvement of the world, for the spread of Christian civilization, and for increasing the happiness of the mass of the human family as that of Queen Victoria. [*Cheers*.] Let it not go forth a moment ... that in seeking complete authority over our own affairs in this fair land of Australia we are seeking any separation from the great Empire. [*Cheers*.]

Now what stands in the way of a federated Australasia? A common tariff. National life is a broad river of living water. Your fiscal notions ... on one side or the other, are as planting a few stones or piling up a sandbank to divert the stream for a little, in order to serve some local interest. This question of a common tariff is a mere trifle compared with the great overshadowing question of a living and eternal national existence. Free trade or protection, all must admit, is to a large extent but a device for carrying out a human notion; but there is no human notion at all about the eternal life of a free nation. I say then that what I understand about the sentiment of a united Australasia is a sinking of all subordinate questions. I speak for my colony, which is as great as the rest of you. [*Cheers.*] We are prepared ... to go into this national union without making any bargain whatsoever—[*cheers*]—without stipulating for any advantage whatever for ourselves, but trusting to the good faith and justice of a Federal Parliament. [*Cheers.*] We are praying that God will give us power to rise above these secondary considerations, and that we may be able to come to an agreement to create this united Australia which you are as much in favour of as I am. These smaller questions ought not to be considered at the present time, and they ought not to deter us from reaching the great consummation which we have in view. [*Hear, hear.*] ...

But supposing there should be a United Australia, what would be the benefit to us? Well, with one leap we should appear before the world as a nation. [*Hear, hear.*] As separate colonies we are of little consequence, but the potentate does not exist—the ruling authority in human affairs does not exist—who would lightly consider the decision of a United Australasia. [*Cheers.*] We should grow at once ... from a group of disunited communities into one solid, powerful, rich and widely respected power. [*Cheers.*] Believing, then, as I do, that every man in these colonies would be better off by this union, and that no injury could result to any honest interest in consequence, I am altogether in favour of no time being lost in carrying out the sublime object. [*Cheers.*] ... We are here a great people united by natural ties, and with all the capacities that civilized communities can possess. We are as capable of managing our own affairs as our countrymen in any other parts of the Empire. We are in a fruitful land, separated by the will of Providence from the rest of the world. [*Hear, hear.*] What has been difficult in other parts of the world ought not to be difficult with us, and the only obstacles that stand in the way of a united Australasia are those which arise from our unfortunate separation. Every conceivable difficulty is based upon the separation which we all deplore. Well, these are difficulties which it is to the benefit of all to get rid of. Remember, gentlemen, that no work worthy of achievement was ever attained without surmounting difficulties ... It cannot be shown that at some other period we shall be in a better position to bring about a United Australasia. [*Cheers.*] Gentlemen, I have tried to express my individual sentiments on this question. I shall endeavour, in friendly agreement with my colleagues, to do my best towards the same end. I wish to make it known to the world that, so long as I have power, I shall not cease to strive to bring about this glorious consummation. [*Cheers.*] I thank you gentlemen, for the manner in which you have received this toast ... I do hope that this meeting tonight ... reflects the sentiments of the great colony of Victoria, and that the time is coming when we shall all appear before the world as a United Australia. [*Loud and prolonged cheers.*]

'a stripling on a small and weedy beast'

ANDREW BARTON 'BANJO' PATERSON'S 'THE MAN FROM SNOWY RIVER'

ABOVE *Andrew Barton 'Banjo' Paterson, photographed around 1905.*

One of Australia's most famous poems, Andrew Barton 'Banjo' Paterson's 'The Man from Snowy River' was first published in the Sydney magazine the *Bulletin* in April 1890. In 1895 Paterson drafted a fresh version for a collected edition, *The Man from Snowy River, and Other Verses*, published in Sydney by Angus and Robertson in 1895—a volume that achieved immense popularity in Australia. The 1895 manuscript version, now held in the Mitchell Collection, State Library of New South Wales, is presented here.

In the heady years of the 1890s when Australia was moving to a new identity as a federation and when a new sense of national consciousness was in the ascendant, Paterson's poem was an immediate success. It has remained in the hearts and affections of Australians ever since. Generations of children learned the poem at school, and it was for long a favourite recitation piece in homes around the country. Paterson's epic tale of the chase and capture of 'the colt from old Regret' has been filmed four times, first as a silent version in 1920. In 1982 the poem was given new life in another film version starring Jack Thompson, Tom Burlinson and Sigrid Thornton, with spectacular scenes of dare-devil riding shot in the high country of the Snowy Mountains so powerfully evoked in the original poem.

In 2005 Banjo Paterson's 1895 manuscript was included in the national touring exhibition *National Treasures from Australia's Great Libraries*—the first time that the document was shared with a wider audience around the country. Its inclusion in that exhibition reinforced the iconic status of Paterson's poem while introducing the work to a new generation.

The Man from Snowy River

There was movement at the station for
    the word had passed around
That the colt from old Regret had
    got away
And had joined the wild bush horses
    — he was worth a thousand pound
So all the cracks had gathered to the fray
All the tried and noted riders from
    the stations near and far
Had mustered at the homestedd overnight
For the bushmen love hard-riding where the
    wild bush horses are
And the stock-horse snuffs the battle
    with delight.

There was Harrison who made his pile
    when Pardon won the cup
The old man with his hair as white as snow
But few could ride beside him when his blood
    was fairly up
He would go wherever horse and man could go
And Clancy of the Overflow came down
    to lend a hand
No better horseman ever held the reins
For never horse could throw him while the
    saddlegirths would stand
He learnt to ride while droving on the plains.

And one was there a stripling on a small
    and weedy beast
— He was something like a race-horse undersized
With a touch of Timor pony — three parts
    thorough-bred at least

ABOVE *Paterson's 1895 draft, including his amendments.*

There was movement at the station, for the word had passed around
That the colt from old Regret had got away,
And had joined the wild bush horses—he was worth a thousand pound,
So all the cracks had gathered to the fray.
All the tried and noted riders from the stations near and far
Had mustered at the homestead overnight,
For the bushmen love hard riding where the wild bush horses are,
And the stock-horse snuffs the battle with delight.

There was Harrison, who made his pile when Pardon won the cup,
The old man with his hair as white as snow;
But few could ride beside him when his blood was fairly up—
He would go wherever horse and man could go.
And Clancy of the Overflow came down to lend a hand,
No better horseman ever held the reins;
For never horse could throw him while the saddle-girths would stand—
He learnt to ride while droving on the plains.

And one was there, a stripling on a small and weedy beast;
He was something like a racehorse undersized,
With a touch of Timor pony—three parts thoroughbred at least—
And such as are by mountain horsemen prized.
He was hard and tough and wiry—just the sort that won't say die—
There was courage in his quick impatient tread;
And he bore the badge of gameness in his quick and fiery eye,
And the proud and lofty carriage of his head.

But still so slight and weedy, one would doubt his power to stay,
And the old man said, "That horse will never do
For a long and tiring gallop—lad, you'd better stop away,
These hills are far too rough for such as you."
So he waited, sad and wistful—only Clancy stood his friend—
"I think we ought to let him come," he said;
"I warrant he'll be with us when he's wanted at the end,
For both his horse and he are mountain bred.

"He hails from Snowy River, up by Kosciusko's side,
Where the hills are twice as steep and twice as rough;
Where a horse's hooves strike firelight from the flint stones every stride,
The man that holds his own is good enough.
And the Snowy River riders on the mountains make their home,
Where the river runs those giant hills between;
I have seen full many horsemen since I first commenced to roam,
But nowhere yet such horsemen have I seen."

So he went: they found the horses by the big mimosa clump,
They raced away towards the mountain's brow,
And the old man gave his orders, "Boys, go at them from the jump,

No use to try for fancy riding now.
And, Clancy, you must wheel them, try and wheel them to the right.
Ride boldly lad, and never fear the spills,
For never yet was rider that could keep the mob in sight,
If once they gain the shelter of those hills."

So Clancy rode to wheel them—he was racing on the wing
Where the best and boldest riders take their place,
And he raced his stock-horse past them and he made the ranges ring
With the stockwhip, as he met them face to face.
Then they halted for a moment, while he swung the dreaded lash,
But they saw their well-loved mountain full in view,
And they charged beneath the stockwhip with a sharp and sudden dash,
And off into the mountain scrub they flew.

Then fast the horsemen followed, where the gorges deep and black,
Resounded to the thunder of their tread,
And the stockwhips woke the echoes, and they fiercely answered back
From cliffs and crags that beetled overhead.
And upward, ever upward, the wild horses held their way,
Where mountain ash and kurrajong grew wide;
And the old man muttered fiercely, "We may bid the mob good day,
NO man can hold them down the other side."

When they reached the mountain's summit, even Clancy took a pull—
It well might make the boldest hold their breath;
The wild hop scrub grew thickly, and the hidden ground was full
Of wombat holes, and any slip was death.
But the man from Snowy River let the pony have his head,
And he swung his stockwhip round and gave a cheer,
And he raced him down the mountain like a torrent down its bed,
While the others stood and watched in very fear.

He sent the flint-stones flying, but the pony kept his feet,
He cleared the fallen timber in his stride,
And the man from Snowy River never shifted in his seat
It was grand to see that mountain horseman ride.
Through the stringybarks and saplings, on the rough and broken ground,
Down the hillside at a racing pace he went;
And he never drew the bridle till he landed safe and sound
At the bottom of that terrible descent.

He was right among the horses as they climbed the farther hill,
And the watchers on the mountain, standing mute,
Saw him ply the stockwhip fiercely; he was right among them still,
As he raced across the clearing in pursuit.
Then they lost him for a moment, where two mountain gullies met
In the ranges—but a final glimpse reveals

On a dim and distant hillside the wild horses racing yet,
With the man from Snowy River at their heels.

And he ran them single-handed till their sides were white with foam;
He followed like a bloodhound on their track,
Till they halted, cowed and beaten; then he turned their heads for home,
And alone and unassisted brought them back.
But his hardy mountain pony he could scarcely raise a trot,
He was blood from hip to shoulder from the spur;
But his pluck was still undaunted, and his courage fiery hot,
For never yet was mountain horse a cur.

And down by Kosciusko, where the pine-clad ridges raise
Their torn and rugged battlements on high,
Where the air is clear as crystal, and the white stars fairly blaze
At midnight in the cold and frosty sky,
And where around the Overflow the reed-beds sweep and sway
To the breezes, and the rolling plains are wide,
The Man from Snowy River is a household word today,
And the stockmen tell the story of his ride.

The birth of the Australian labour movement

BUSHMEN'S OFFICIAL PROCLAMATION

In January 1891 the Queensland Shearers' Union pursued and lost a bitter dispute with the Pastoralists' Union over terms and conditions of employment. The confrontation erupted during a period of economic depression in Australia, when profits were in serious decline.

Flexing their muscle, the pastoralists sought to reduce the wages of their workers, while also introducing a range of measures designed to improve productivity and efficiency in their industry and to break the back of the union movement itself. Central to the dispute was the refusal by the Pastoralists' Union to concede the union demand that only union labour should be employed. Instead, the pastoralists insisted on imposing a so-called 'freedom of contract' that would allow men to be engaged in shearing sheds free of union rules. In response, the Queensland Shearers' Union and the Queensland Labourers' Union called on their members to strike and by so doing to 'frustrate the attempts of organised Capitalism to crush unionism' and to reduce wages.

The conservative Queensland government gave the pastoralists its full support. More than 1000 armed soldiers and special constables were sent to the strikers' camps in central Queensland. So-called 'scab' or 'black leg' labourers hired by the pastoralists were given military escorts. Twenty-one strikers' camps had been established at various locations, but the largest was at the town of Barcaldine in central Queensland, where around 4500 protestors had gathered. There the Eureka Flag was flown and the strikers sang Henry Lawson's anthem of radical protest, 'Freedom on the Wallaby', with its threat that if the shearers were denied justice, then 'They needn't say the fault is ours/If blood should stain the wattle'. For a time, indeed, violence threatened, but it was averted as the strikers exercised remarkable discipline in the face of provocation. The strike itself began to lose its momentum in March 1891, with the arrest of a number of its leaders at Barcaldine and Clermont. A protracted and controversial trial resulted in severe penal sentences for thirteen strikers. With their resources depleted, the unions declared the strike at an end on 20 June 1891.

On the strikers' side of the confrontation, the Bushmen's Official Proclamation stands as the official manifesto of the dispute and as a landmark statement of the rights of labour to organise and to negotiate conditions of employment with employers. The proclamation was issued to members of the Queensland Shearers' Union and the Queensland Labourers' Union. Also published in the Worker on 7 February 1891, the proclamation is today honoured as one of the 'birth certificates' of the Australian labour movement. While the shearers' strike fractured social consensus, its ideals have lived on to find a constructive expression in parliamentary politics and in the formation of the Australian Labor Party.

ABOVE *Wood engraving from 1891 depicting the unionists' camp, and 'scab' labour hired by the pastoralists working under military escort.*

Fellow unionists,

An unprovoked and unjustifiable attack has been made upon the above unions by the squatters' associations. It therefore becomes our duty to take such action as will best conserve our interests and frustrate the attempts of organised Capitalism to crush unionism and reduce wages in this district.

The terms which the capitalists are attempting to enforce are known to you all. The agreements, which apply to both shearers and shed hands, deny us the right to resist any insidious undermining of our unions, even though such undermining should take the form of the introduction of that "cheap and reliable" labour which so many squatters seem to prefer to their own flesh and blood. In other ways the squatter—whose treatment of the bushman first brought the bush unions into resistance—is made the sole arbiter of the working conditions of those whom Capitalism can force to sign away their rights as men. Even the Eight Hour Day is not conserved. Even the wages which have been so hardly earned may be forfeited without appeal to law under this unrighteous agreement, particularly at the option of the squatter. On top of this, it is demanded that shearers pay for combs and cutters broken in the squatters' "labour saving machinery" and that labourers submit to reductions on the scale of wages established for years past, the reductions in some items being as high as 33 per cent.

So sweeping and unreasonable are these attempted changes that some importance has been attached to a malicious statement which asserts that the squatters' associations submitted their proposals to the annual meetings of these unions. It has seemed absurd that such an attack should be made without even the appearance of consulting us beforehand. We have to inform you, therefore, that our unions have been insultingly ignored in this matter, that no official information concerning agreements or reductions has been received from the squatters and that the first heard of the affair was from advertisements in the newspapers and from the managers at sheds at which our members expected to work in due course. It is very evident from the whole circumstance that the squatters' intention is to endeavour to wipe unionism out of existence and to make a bold bid for the unqualified mastership of the wage earners of the District. They evidently imagine that because our comrades, the maritime men, went down before shipping companies that therefore the bush workers must go down before the squatting companies.

Fellow unionists! We call upon you all, individually and unitedly, to pull the unions through this fight let the cost be what it may. You all know what the squatter was and what he is and what we shall be if we let him get the whip hand over us. Here in the bush we have no voice in the making of the laws and no share in the Government, we are disfranchised and denied our rights as citizens, we have only our unions to which we can look for justice and if our unions go down we are totally enslaved.

Fellow unionists, the squatters expect the Queensland bush unions will fight hard but they do not know how hard. We call upon you to show them, not underestimating the difficulties that confront us or the power of organised Capitalism that backs the squatters, but relying with confidence upon the devotion of the bushmen of Queensland to their unions and to the Labour

Bushmen's Official Proclamation.

cause. For it is not ourselves alone we fight for—though we ourselves have much at stake. The Queensland bush is to be a battleground whereon is to be decided whether Capitalism can crush Australian unionism altogether into the dust. Remembering this we ask each one and all together to resolve come what may we will not be beaten, that when the battle is over our unions shall still live. We have a right to resolve this, for disfranchised though we are, we are the men whose labour mainly upholds Queensland. It is our toil that brings rich dividends to banks and fat incomes to squatters and profitable trade to great cities. Yet we have no votes by which we can secure laws to protect us even in our earnings and the squatting companies dream of dragooning us into submission with hordes of police-protected blacklegs when we refuse to work under any conditions which the profit-mongers who fleece us choose to draw up in some bank-parlour.

Fellow unionists, our cause is just as every man knows. We have found the verbal agreement works more smoothly and satisfactorily than any other. It was last year worked by the great majority of stations in Queensland without complaint or cause for complaint. The Darling Downs was satisfactorily worked under an agreement which we are willing to work under there for the ensuing year also. The wages of the QLU scale are not in excess of the last three years' rates. If the squatters had meant fairly they would have asked us to a conference to consider any points they wished to improve or any better conditions they desired to make, in exactly the same way we asked them to meet us when our unions were first formed. That they did not do so indicates to us that they did not want a conference but deliberately planned an attack on us. Nevertheless, we have requested the General Executive ALF to ask for an open conference from the Federated Employers' Union and we are prepared to show at such a conference, if it is agreed to by the squatters, that these unions desire nothing but what is just and right.

Should a conference be held we still hope that the struggle may be averted, but should an unprovoked fight still be forced upon us we consider that those who force it should help pay for it, particularly as many of our bitterest enemies are sheltering themselves behind earlier sheds, expecting that the battle will be decided one way or another before it reaches them. The Central District Council has therefore unanimously resolved:

"That any employer or member of the Pastoralists' Association in the Colony of Queensland who does not before the first of March accept through this office the agreements of the Queensland Shearers' Union and the scale of wages of the Queensland Labourers' Union, shall pay for every week or portion of a week after that date an extra sixpence per hundred for shearing, wages of the QLU to be increased pro rata."

Those squatters who have bound themselves by bond to break down our scale of wages, our agreements and our organisation can thank nobody but themselves if they find it expensive to get work done by competent union hands, when the blacklegs they rely on do not come to time. If they want conference, we still offer it to them, but if they want fight, we offer that also.

Fellow unionists! From time to time it may be again necessary to address you but for the present there is only this to add: If the worst comes to the worst we can always ride down to Brisbane and ask the Government that swamps in surplus labour to help Capitalism degrade wage-earners what it is going to do with 10,000 able-bodied bushmen unemployed because they hung out for a fair thing.

By order of the Central DC: W.J. Bennett, W. Fothergill, J.R. Risley (Strike Committee), M. Murphy, A.J. Brown.

Central DC Office, Barcaldine, February 1, 1891.

Bushmen's Official Proclamation.

> 254
>
> To the Honorable the Speaker, and Members of the Legislative Assembly of the Colony of Victoria, in Parliament assembled.
>
> The Humble Petition of the undersigned Women of Victoria respectfully sheweth:—
>
> That your Petitioners believe:—
>
> That Government of the People by the People, and for the People should mean all the People, and not one-half.—
>
> That Taxation and Representation should go together without regard to the sex of the Taxed.———
>
> That all Adult Persons should have a voice in Making the Laws which they are required to obey.—
>
> That, in short, Women should Vote on Equal Terms with Men.———
>
> Your Petitioners, therefore, humbly pray your Honorable House to pass a Measure for conferring the Parliamentary Franchise upon Women, regarding this as a right which they most earnestly desire.——
>
> And your Petitioners will ever Pray.
>
> | Name | Address |
> |---|---|
> | Mrs William McLean | East Melbourne |
> | Mrs James Munro | Armadale |
> | Marie E. Hirt | Camberwell |
> | E. A. Mather | Lidiard St Marguerite |
> | Margaret Higinbotham | South Yarra |
> | Rosie Lee | Madison St Richmond |

ABOVE *Top section of the Monster petition. The second signature, 'Mrs James Munro', is that of Jane Munro, the premier's wife.*

Door-knocking for women's right to vote

THE MONSTER PETITION IN VICTORIA

Victoria's constitution of 1855 did not confer on women the right to vote. That right would be hard won, though without the extraordinary bitterness that marked the protracted campaign fought by suffragettes in Britain.

In 1891, Victorian Premier James Munro (1832–1908) said he would introduce a bill for women's suffrage if it were demonstrated that ordinary women wanted this right. Certainly there was a lively interest in the female suffrage question, not only in Victoria but also in the neighbouring colonies and in New Zealand, but Munro's sympathy for the cause was not without political self-interest linked to another cause. Committed all his public life to the temperance movement, Munro's support for female suffrage was due in part to his belief (possibly well-founded) that women voters would be natural supporters of abstinence and that his own standing and advantage would be enhanced as a result.

With Munro's bill in the offing, the Victorian Christian Temperance Union and the Women's Suffrage Society joined forces to organise a petition. They embarked on a door-knocking campaign across Victoria and in six weeks collected almost 30,000 signatures. The second signature on the petition belonged to Jane Munro. As the wife of the premier, she had presumably conducted a campaign of her own at home. Owing to its size—the document measured 260 metres—the petition was called the 'Monster Petition': several attendants were required to carry it into the Parliament for tabling in the Legislative Assembly in September 1891.

Although women in Victoria did not gain the right to vote in state elections until 1908, the 1891 petition helped raise the profile of the women's suffrage movement and to galvanise a large constituency of support. Today it has a high symbolic value as a singular relic of the Australian campaigns fought by women for equality of rights and opportunity. The petition is preserved in the Public Record Office of Victoria.

ABOVE *The petition is 260 metres long and 20 centimetres wide.*

The Humble Petition of the undersigned *Women of Victoria* respectfully sheweth:

That your Petitioners believe:

That Government of the People by the People, and for the People should mean all the People, and not one-half.

That Taxation and Representation should go together without regard to the sex of the Taxed.

That all Adult Persons should have a voice in Making the Laws which they are required to obey.

That, in short, Women should Vote on equal terms with men.

Your petitioners therefore humbly pray your Honourable House to press a Measure for conferring the Parliamentary Franchise upon Women, regarding this as a right which they most earnestly desire.

And your Petitioners will ever Pray.

Australia's national song

'WALTZING MATILDA'

'Waltzing Matilda' is the name of what was for many years Australia's most famous song and, indeed, was regarded as the country's unofficial national anthem. The song won an especially strong following among Australian troops in the First World War. While it has been today perhaps somewhat eclipsed in its appeal to younger generations, it still ranks high in the affections of Australians, especially for its irreverence, its disdain for authority and its sympathy for the underdog. Oddly, it was these very qualities that worked against the song in 1977 when a national plebiscite placed 'Advance Australia Fair' in first place, with 43 per cent of the vote, as the preferred Australian national anthem. 'Waltzing Matilda' polled in second place, with 28 per cent of the vote

While much of the appeal of 'Waltzing Matilda' lies in its distillation of what Australians like to think of as their spirit of national rebelliousness, the song came into existence in the genteel surrounds of a drawing room at Dagworth Station, a 100,000 hectare property near the township of Winton, in central Queensland, in January 1895. The poet and balladist A.B. 'Banjo' Paterson, one of the guests of the household, was much taken with a melody played on the piano by Christina Rutherford Macpherson (1864–1936), the sister of Dagworth's owner and a friend of Paterson's fiancée, Sarah Riley. The melody was 'Craigielea', a march adapted from the Scottish song 'Thou Bonnie Wood of Craigielea' which Macpherson had first heard at the Warrnambool races in Victoria the previous April.

Paterson began drafting the verses and chorus on that first evening and completed them over the following days. As he wrote, he drew on several experiences of his stay at Dagworth: the discovery of a dead sheep (the jumbuck of the song) with a forequarter missing; a picnic held at a local waterhole where a suicide had taken place; and finally the casual references in conversation to the bush phrase 'waltzing Matilda' or 'to waltz Matilda', meaning to carry a swag on the road. Paterson is also thought to have been influenced by the protests and defiance of the Dagworth Station shearers, who had played a role in the Queensland shearers' strike of 1891.

'Waltzing Matilda' was performed publicly for the first time at Winton in April 1895 and soon won a popular following in the district. In 1903 the song was rearranged by Marie Cowan for use in an advertisement for Billy Tea. That version, with different words and a variation of the old 'Craigielea' melody, was eventually accepted as the standard popular version of the song. But 'Waltzing Matilda' survives in its earliest version (the document reproduced here) in Christina Macpherson's original notated version, which she wrote down later at the request of A.B. Paterson. That version, which had been retained by the family of Christina Macpherson, came to light in 1970 and was later presented to the National Library of Australia in Canberra.

ABOVE *Christina Macpherson around 1900.*

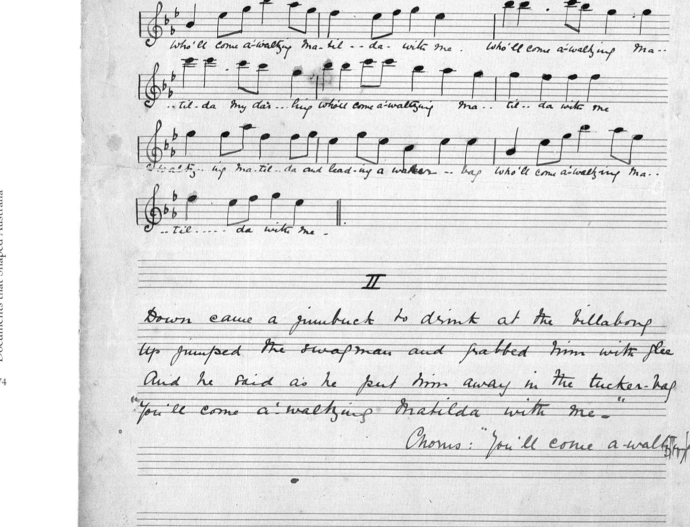

III

Down came the squatter a-riding his thoroughbred.
Down came policemen one, two, and three:
"Whose is the jumbuck you've got in the tucker-bag?
You'll come a-waltzing Matilda with we."
    Chorus: "You'll come a-waltzing" etc.

IV

But the swagman he up and he jumped in the water-hole
Drowning himself by the Coolibah tree;
And his ghost may be heard as it sings by the billabong
"Who'll come a-waltzing Matilda with me?"
    Chorus: "Who'll come a-waltzing" etc.

ABOVE *'Waltzing Matilda' manuscript from around 1895, notated by Christina Macpherson.*

"Waltzing Matilda"

Oh there once was a swag-man camped in the billabong,
Under the shade of a coolibah tree,
And he sang as he looked at the old billy boiling,
Who'll come a-waltzing Matilda with me
Who'll come a-waltzing Matilda my darling,
Who'll come a-waltzing Matilda with me
Waltzing Matilda and leading a waterbag,
Who'll come a-waltzing Matilda with me.

2nd Verse
Down came a jumbuck to drink at the billabong.
Up jumped the swagman and grabbed him with glee,
And he said as he put him away in the tucker bag
"You'll come a-waltzing Matilda with me!"—
CHORUS: "You'll come …"

3rd Verse
Down came the squatter a-riding his thoroughbred.
Down came policemen, one, two and three,
"Whose is the jumbuck you've got in the tucker bag?
You'll come a-waltzing Matilda with me"
CHORUS: "You'll come …"

4th Verse
But the swagman he up & he jumped in the water-hole
Drowning himself by the coolibah tree,
And his ghost may be heard as it sings by the billabong
Who'll come a-waltzing Matilda with me —
CHORUS: "Who'll come …"

The first Australian women to win the vote

FEMALE SUFFRAGE IN SOUTH AUSTRALIA

A bill to grant women the right to vote and stand for election in the colony's Parliament was passed in South Australia in 1894, and was enacted when Queen Victoria signed her assent at Osborne House on the Isle of Wight on 2 February 1895. The South Australian legislation was an Australian first, though women in New Zealand had secured the right to vote (but not the right to stand for parliament) in 1893. South Australia had granted voting rights in local government elections to women property owners in 1861, but it had taken eight attempts and another thirty years before the parliamentary franchise was extended to all adult females, including Aboriginal women, the first Aboriginal people to get the vote in Australia. Even so, the bill was hard fought, with a difficult debate in the Parliament.

Historian Susan Magarey has noted that South Australia's achievement of female suffrage was critical to the nation's enfranchisement of women in 1902. Lobbied by the suffragists, South Australian delegates to the Federal Convention of 1897 had threatened to forgo federation rather than see the disenfranchisement of South Australian women in the federal arena. The South Australian example and its successful impact on voting rights in the new Commonwealth of Australia gave what Magarey has called 'heart and hope' to suffrage campaigners in the other Australian states. Western Australia passed female suffrage legislation in 1899; New South Wales, in 1902 (following the ruling in the Commonwealth Parliament); Tasmania in 1903; and Queensland in 1905. Only in Victoria was there continued opposition, but that was finally overcome in 1908.

The right of women to stand for parliament was not achieved so easily: Queensland conceded this right in 1915; New South Wales in 1918; Western Australia in 1920; Tasmania in 1921; and Victoria in 1923. The relative ease of the successes in South Australia and in the new Commonwealth placed Australia on the cutting edge of democracy and well ahead of Britain, where a long and bitter campaign of civil disobedience was fought from 1872 until January 1918, when women finally won the right to vote.

The first polling day in Australia to include women was held in South Australia on 25 April 1896. The *Adelaide Observer* of 2 May 1896 noted the event with a mixture of pride and condescension. 'Memorable in the history of the southern continent must be the general election in South Australia ... as the first in which women took part ... And the women have polled remarkably well as to both numbers and the intelligence displayed in fulfilling the requirements of the Act.'

No. 613

An Act to amend the Constitution.

Be it Enacted by the Governor of the Province of South Australia, with the advice and consent of the Legislative Council and House of Assembly of the said province, in this Parliament assembled as follows:

1. The right to vote for persons to sit in Parliament as members of the Legislative Council, and the right to vote for persons to sit in Parliament as members of the House of Assembly, are hereby extended to women.

2. Women shall possess and may exercise the rights hereby granted, subject to the same qualifications and in the same manner as men.

3. All Constitution and Electoral Acts and all other laws are hereby amended, so far as may be necessary to give effect to this Act.

4. (1) Every female voter, whether she has reason to believe she will be absent from the electoral district or not, shall be entitled at any time after the issuing of the writ to apply for a certificate in one of the forms, as the case may be, of the Schedule A to "The Absent Voters Electoral Act, 1890," from the Returning Officer that she is registered as a voter upon the electoral roll and entitled to vote at the forthcoming elections.

(2) The application hereinbefore mentioned need not contain the matters set forth in paragraph 3 of the application in Schedules A and B of the Act No. 577 of 1893; but in lieu thereof the applicant shall declare that she is resident more than three miles from the nearest polling-place, or that by reason of the state of her health she will probably be unable to vote at the polling-place on polling day.

(3) The provisions of "The Absent Voters Electoral Act, 1890," and the said Act No. 577 of 1893 shall, except so far as inconsistent with the provisions in sub-sections (1) and (2) of this clause, apply to every female voter.

5. This Act may be cited as "The Constitution Amendment, 1894."

OPPOSITE *A Bill for an Act to amend the Constitution (Female Suffrage).*

ANNO QUINQUAGESIMO SEPTIMO ET QUINQUA-
GESIMO OCTAVO

VICTORIÆ REGINÆ.

A.D. 1894.

****

No. 613.

An Act to amend the Constitution.

[Reserved 21st December 1894]

BE it Enacted by the Governor of the Province of South Australia, with the advice and consent of the Legislative Council and House of Assembly of the said province, in this present Parliament assembled, as follows:

1. The right to vote for persons to sit in Parliament as members of the Legislative Council, and the right to vote for persons to sit in Parliament as members of the House of Assembly, are hereby extended to women. <small>Extension of franchise</small>

2. Women shall possess and may exercise the rights hereby granted, subject to the same qualifications and in the same manner as men. <small>Qualifications.</small>

3. All Constitution and Electoral Acts and all other laws are hereby amended, so far as may be necessary to give effect to this Act. <small>Acts amended to give effect to this Act.</small>

4. (1) Every female voter, whether she has reason to believe she will be absent from the electoral district or not, shall be entitled at any time after the issuing of the writ to apply for a certificate in one of the forms, as the case may be, of the Schedule A to "The Absent Voters Electoral Act, 1890," from the Returning Officer that she is registered as a voter upon the electoral roll and entitled to vote at the forthcoming elections. <small>Mode of voting.</small>

(2) The

Certified that this Bill originated in the Legislative Council, and has finally passed both Houses.

E. G. Blackmore

Clerk of the Legislative Council and Clerk of the Parliaments.

President.

I reserve this Act for the signification of Her Majesty's pleasure. Victor, Governor

'a complete collection for Australian books will be curious'

CREATING THE MITCHELL LIBRARY

Independently wealthy and free of the constraints of earning a living, the reclusive David Scott Mitchell (1836–1907) was Australia's greatest book collector. At his death, he bequeathed his collection of books, manuscripts, maps and pictures relating to Australia and the Pacific to the Public (now State) Library of New South Wales. The bequest specified that the collection should be housed separately and that it should be known as the Mitchell Library. In addition to the collection itself, Mitchell provided an endowment of £70,000 to support the future growth of a collection he had built assiduously and held tenaciously in his home in Sydney's Darlinghurst over many years. Today Mitchell is honoured as one of Australia's most significant cultural benefactors though, in truth, benefaction in the expansive sense seems to have been the least part of his motives for giving his collection to the public. Certainly he hoped that, in using his collection, future historians might have the means to 'write the history of Australia in general and New South Wales in particular', but we may speculate that this sat also with a narrower ambition to create his own monument.

While Mitchell collected books in other fields of interest, including Elizabethan drama, eighteenth-century literature, nineteenth-century poetry and erotica, it was eventually the range of Australian materials—books, original manuscripts, pictures, maps, coins, medals and tokens—that became the focus of his interest. In July 1868 he wrote to his cousin Rose Scott (1847–1925), the noted feminist and campaigner who was probably also his favourite relative, 'I generally get all the Australian literature I come across.' He valued it, he said, 'less for its intrinsic merit' than because some day 'anything like a complete collection for Australian books will be curious'.

In January 1899 Mitchell had handed to the Trustees of the Public Library of New South Wales more than 10,000 non-Australian books from his collection. This gift, acknowledged in the document that follows, allowed Mitchell to make room at home for his expanding Australian holdings. The letter also foreshadows the great Mitchell Library bequest of Australiana and reveals something of the care taken by the library trustees to secure the inestimable prize that was David Scott Mitchell's Australian library.

The historian Brian Fletcher has remarked that Mitchell's bequest was more than a very generous cultural gift. It created a substantial public research collection in an area where none had existed before. That area—the study of Australia itself—has been crucial in defining the country to its own people. Elizabeth Ellis, a former Mitchell Librarian, has commented that since its foundation in 1910, 'the Mitchell Library has been linked to almost every major historical venture in Australia'. For many years the Mitchell collection was the indispensable tool for scholars writing about Australia and the Pacific. Today, while other great Australian libraries share the responsibility of serving the nation and nourishing a distinctive scholarship in Australian studies, the Mitchell collection remains a formidable cultural asset, not only of New South Wales but also of the nation as a whole.

19th. September, 1899

Sir,

I have the honour to inform you that at the last meeting of the Trustees of this Library the following resolution was passed, and it was resolved that a copy of the same should be forwarded to you.—

"The Trustees of the Public Library of New South Wales having carefully examined the donation of 10,025 books, and 50 pictures and engravings presented to this Library by Mr. David Scott Mitchell, M.A., desire to place on record their high appreciation of this splendid gift to the people of New South Wales. They recognise that these books are especially useful as supplementing the present Collection, and will be of inestimable value to future Students of Literature, History, Language and Fine Arts.

This public-spirited generosity being unprecedented in Australia will probably stimulate other Australians to follow the example set them by Mr. Mitchell to the enrichment of our public libraries and a marked increase of the appreciation in which the Colony is already held by lovers of literature.

The Trustees in making this record have been unable to ignore the fact that the present donation is only an earnest of Mr. Mitchell's intention to bequeath to this Library the whole of his unequalled Collection of Australian books, pictures and engravings, and to make provision for its future maintenance and growth, and that by these means the Public Library of New South Wales must necessarily become pre-eminently the greatest Library in Australia, and must take its place as one of the remarkable National Collections of the World.

The Trustees, recognising the full importance of the present munificent donation and of Mr. Mitchell's generous intentions for the future, desire to convey to him their best thanks for his gift, and to assure him of their cordial appreciation of his efforts, and of their determination to their utmost ability to care for and treat his Collection in accordance with his wishes."

In conveying this resolution to you, I beg to express the great personal pleasure I feel in expressing the Board's feelings in this matter

I have the honour to be,

Sir,
Your obedient servant
James Norton
President.

David Scott Mitchell, Esq., M.A.,
17 Darlinghurst Road,
Sydney.

A model of democracy

COMMONWEALTH OF AUSTRALIA CONSTITUTION ACT

Of the myriad documents that influence the lives of Australians, the constitution of the Commonwealth of Australia is of overriding importance. It is the supreme law and foundation of our political and legal system. Historically, it is the expression of Australia's view of itself as a democratically self-governing nation. The movement towards self-government and nationhood evolved incrementally throughout the nineteenth century, with the *Australian Colonies Government Act 1850* being the major landmark before the federation of the Australian colonies in 1901. That act established elected legislative councils in each colony, which in turn had the power to set up local legislatures and to regulate the franchise and qualifications for membership of those legislatures. The act of 1850 also conferred on the new colonial legislatures the general power to make laws for the 'peace, welfare and good government' of the respective colonies, including the power to vary their own constitutions.

During the second half of the nineteenth century the Australian colonies asserted their new and separate independence from both Britain and each other. Growing slowly at first, but assuming greater urgency as the century advanced, was a movement to unite the Australian colonies into some form of federal union that might deal in a unified way with matters such as defence and immigration policy. And there were those who took the larger view that Australia should stand as a democratic, united and independent nation. Those aspirations coalesced into the campaign for federation that preoccupied colonial politicians throughout the 1890s and saw the drafting of the Constitution at a series of conventions and meetings held in 1891, 1897–98 and 1899. The federal issue was also pursued in conferences held at Corowa, Hobart and Bathurst, and in campaigns conducted by organisations such as the Australasian Federation League and the Australian Natives' Association. Following this complex process a series of referendums was held: South Australia was first in June 1898 and Western Australia the last in July 1900. In some colonies, two referendums were held, with sufficient numbers supporting the proposal being achieved only in a second vote; for a time a 'yes' vote in Western Australia had seemed uncertain. As it was, that affirmation came only three weeks after the *Commonwealth of Australia Constitution Act 1900* had passed through the British Parliament.

The British act took the form of a modest preamble (the document published here) to which the Constitution was attached in clause 9. The Constitution proper is divided into eight chapters with sections consecutively numbered from 1 to 128. The constitution was inaugurated at a jubilant public ceremony held in Centennial Park in Sydney on 1 January 1901.

The Constitution has continued to operate since that time, substantially in the form in which it was enacted in 1900. Thirty-seven proposals for amendment have been taken to referendum—including the unsuccessful proposal in 1999 that Australia should become a republic—but only eight have been carried.

By world standards in 1900, the Australian Constitution was a model of democracy. But in the first decade of the twenty-first century, measured against contemporary expectations, it seems old-fashioned. Some Australians would like to see it amended to carry a bill of rights; others argue for a definition of Australian citizenship; others see an acknowledgment of the original Indigenous peoples as an essential step to national maturity and reconciliation; republicanism remains an issue of passionate concern to many; and overriding these matters of substance is the view that the constitution lacks an aspirational or expressive preamble.

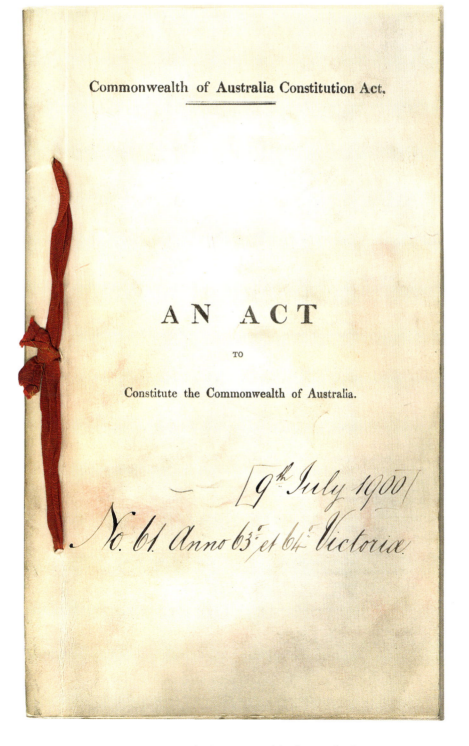

ABOVE *The Commonwealth of Australia Constitution Act 1900 was presented to Australia by Queen Victoria on 9 July 1900.*

An Act to constitute the Commonwealth of Australia.

[9th July 1900]

WHEREAS the people of New South Wales, Victoria, South Australia, Queensland, and Tasmania, humbly relying on the blessing of Almighty God, have agreed to unite in one indissoluble Federal Commonwealth under the Crown of the United Kingdom of Great Britain and Ireland, and under the Constitution hereby established:

And whereas it is expedient to provide for the admission into the Commonwealth of other Australasian Colonies and possessions of the Queen:

Be it therefore enacted by the Queen's most Excellent Majesty, by and with the advice and consent of the Lords Spiritual and Temporal, and Commons, in this present Parliament assembled, and by the authority of the same, as follows:—

1. This Act may be cited as the Commonwealth of Australia Constitution Act.
2. The provisions of this Act referring to the Queen shall extend to Her Majesty's heirs and successors in the sovereignty of the United Kingdom.
3. It shall be lawful for the Queen, with the advice of the Privy Council, to declare by proclamation that, on and after a day herein appointed, not being later than one year after the passing of this Act, the people of New South Wales, Victoria, South Australia, Queensland, and Tasmania, and also, if Her Majesty is satisfied that the people of Western Australia have agreed thereto, of Western Australia, shall be united in a Federal Commonwealth under the name of the Commonwealth of Australia. But the Queen may, at any time after the proclamation, appoint a Governor-General for the Commonwealth.
4. The Commonwealth shall be established, and the Constitution shall take effect, on and after the day so appointed. But the Parliaments of the several colonies may at any time after the passing of this Act make any such laws, to come into operation on the day so appointed, as they might have made if the Constitution had taken effect at the passing of this Act.
5. This Act, and all laws made by the Parliament of the Commonwealth under the Constitution, shall be binding on the courts, judges and people of every State and of every part of the Commonwealth, notwithstanding anything in the laws of any State; and the laws of the Commonwealth shall be in force on all British ships, the Queen's ships of war excepted, whose port of first clearance and whose port of destination are in the Commonwealth.
6. "The Commonwealth" shall mean the Commonwealth of Australia established under this Act.

    "The States" shall mean such of the colonies of New South Wales, New Zealand, Queensland, Tasmania, Victoria, Western Australia, and South Australia, including the northern territory of South Australia, as for the time being are parts of the Commonwealth, and such colonies or territories as may be admitted into or established by the Commonwealth as States; and each of such parts of the Commonwealth shall be called "a State." "Original States" shall mean such States as are parts of the Commonwealth at its establishment.

7. The Federal Council of Australasia Act, 1885, is hereby repealed, but so as not to affect any laws passed by the Federal Council of Australasia and in force at the establishment of the Commonwealth.

Any such law may be repealed as to any State by the Parliament of the Commonwealth, or as to any colony not being a State by the Parliament thereof.

8. After the passing of this Act the Colonial Boundaries Act, 1895, shall not apply to any colony which becomes a State of the Commonwealth; but the Commonwealth shall be taken to be a self-governing colony for the purposes of that Act.

9. The Constitution of the Commonwealth shall be as follows:—

THE CONSTITUTION

The Constitution is divided as follows:—

Chapter I.—The Parliament:
    Part I.—General:
    Part II.—The Senate:
    Part III.—The House of Representatives:
    Part IV.—Both Houses of Parliament:
    Part V.—Powers of the Parliament:
Chapter II.—The Executive Government:
Chapter III.—The Judicature:
Chapter IV.—Finance and Trade:
Chapter V.—The States:
Chapter VI.—New States:
Chapter VII.—Miscellaneous:
Chapter VIII.—Alteration of the Constitution.
The Schedule.

A birth certificate for the Australian nation

INSTRUCTIONS FOR THE INAUGURATION OF THE COMMONWEALTH OF AUSTRALIA

One of a suite of documents concerned with establishing the machinery of the new Commonwealth of Australia, these royal instructions from Queen Victoria to the first governor-general were intended to set in motion the government of a federated Australia. Under section 2 of the Australia Constitution, a governor-general, serving as the monarch's representative, was to be appointed to hold what was symbolically the pre-eminent position in the governance of an Australian Commonwealth, established as a constitutional monarchy under the British Crown.

The instructions required the governor-general to execute a number of specific powers and responsibilities, including the power to grant pardons. At the public ceremony to inaugurate the Commonwealth (set down for 1 January 1901), arrangements were to be made for the reading of the letters patent establishing the office of governor-general. After this public reading of the key instrument of his appointment, the governor-general was to take the various oaths of office in the presence of the governors of the six colonies, together with members of the Executive Council, judges and parliamentary representatives. In addition, the instructions provided for the governor-general himself to administer the oaths of office to the principal office-holders of the Commonwealth. Thus were laid down the components of the public ceremony that would confirm the delegation of constitutional authority from the monarch to her representative in Australia and to those he would commission to exercise authority as ministers or other officials. For later appointments to the vice-regal office in Australia, the instructions also provided the requisite oaths to be administered by the chief justice of the High Court of Australia or, in his absence, another member of the court.

Curiously, the original document containing Queen Victoria's instructions to her first Australian governor-general is at present known only in the form of a photocopy held by the National Archives of Australia. This copy shows that the original document was of five foolscap pages, with the signature of Queen Victoria inscribed on the first page and her initials on the last. It is thought that the copy was made in 1946 from the original then in the possession of the office of the governor-general. Subsequently, however, efforts to locate the original have been unsuccessful. The National Archives of Australia maintains a watching brief to locate the original and to see it reinstated to a place of honour among that group of documents celebrated today as the 'birth certificates' of the Australian nation.

INSTRUCTIONS to Our Governor-General and Commander-in-Chief in and over Our Commonwealth of Australia, or in his absence, to Our Lieutenant-Governor or the officer for the time being administering the Government of Our said Commonwealth.

Given at Our Court at Saint James's this [Twenty-ninth] day of [October] 1900 in the Sixty-fourth year of Our Reign.

WHEREAS by certain Letters Patent ... We have constituted, ordered, and declared that there shall be a Governor-General and Commander-in Chief ... in and over Our Commonwealth of Australia ... And We have thereby authorized and commanded Our said Governor-General to do and execute in due manner all things that shall belong to his said command, and to the trust We have reposed in him, according to the several powers and authorities granted or appointed him by virtue of the said Letters Patent ... Now, therefore, We do, by these Our Instructions under our Sign Manual and Signet, declare Our pleasure to be as follows:—

I. Our first appointed Governor-General shall, with all due solemnity, cause our Commission under Our Sign Manual and Signet, appointing Our said Governor-General, to be read and published in the presence of Our Governors ... of Our Colonies of New South Wales, Victoria, South Australia, Queensland, Tasmania and Western Australia and such of the members of the Executive Council, Judges, and members of the Legislatures of Our said Colonies as are able to attend.

II. Our said Governor-General of Our said Commonwealth shall take the Oath of Allegiance in the form provided by an Act passed in the Session holden in the thirty-first and thirty-second years of Our Reign ... and likewise the usual Oath for the due execution of the Office of Our Governor-General in and over Our said Commonwealth, and for the due and impartial administration of justice; which Oaths Our said Governor and Commander-in Chief of Our Colony of New South Wales [or delegate] shall and he is hereby required to tender and administer unto him.

III. Every Governor-General, and every other officer appointed to administer the Government of Our said Commonwealth after Our said first appointed Governor-General, shall, with all due solemnity, cause Our Commission, under Our Sign Manual and Signet, appointing Our said Governor-General, to be read and published in the presence of the Chief Justice of the High Court of Australia, or some other Judge of the said Court.

IV. Every Governor-General, and every other officer appointed to administer the Government of Our said Commonwealth after Our said first appointed Governor-General, shall take the Oath of allegiance in the form provided by an Act passed in the Session holden in the thirty-first and thirty-second years of Our Reign ... and likewise the usual Oath for the due execution of the Office of Our Governor-General in and over Our said Commonwealth, and for the due and impartial administration of justice; which Oaths the Chief Justice of the High Court of Australia or some other Judge of the said Court shall and he is hereby required to tender and administer unto him or them.

V. And We do authorize and require Our said Governor-General from time to time, by himself or by any other person to be authorized by him in that behalf, to administer to all and to every persons or person, ... who shall hold any office or place of trust or profit in Our said Commonwealth, the said Oath of Allegiance, together with such other Oath or Oaths as may ... be prescribed by any laws or statutes in that behalf made and provided.

VI. And We do require Our said Governor-General to communicate forthwith to the Members of the Executive Council for Our said Commonwealth these Our Instructions, and likewise all such others, from time to time as he shall find convenient for Our service to be imparted to them.

VII. Our said Governor-General is to take care that all laws assented to by him in Our name, or reserved for the signification of Our pleasure thereon, shall ... be fairly abstracted in the margins, and be accompanied, in such cases as may seem to him to be necessary, with such explanatory observations as may be required to exhibit the reasons and occasions for proposing such laws; and he shall transmit fair copies of the Journals and Minutes of the proceedings of the Parliament of Our said Commonwealth ... of the said Parliament.

VIII. And We do further authorize and empower Our said Governor-General, ... in Our name and on Our behalf, when any crime or offence against the laws of Our Commonwealth has been committed for which the offender may be tried within Our said Commonwealth, to grant pardon to any accomplice in such crime or offence who shall give such information as shall lead to the conviction of the principal offender, or of any one of such offenders if more than one; and further to grant to any offender convicted of any such crime or offence in any Court, or before any Judge, Justice, or Magistrate, within Our said Commonwealth, a pardon, either free or subject to lawful conditions, or any respite of the execution of the sentence of any such offender, for such period as to Our said Governor-General may seem fit, and to remit any fines, penalties, or forfeitures which may become due and payable to Us. Provided always, that Our said Governor-General shall not in any case, except where the offence has been of a political nature, make it a condition of any pardon or remission of sentence that the offender shall be banished from or shall absent himself from Our said Commonwealth. And we do hereby direct and enjoin that Our said Governor-General shall not pardon or reprieve any such offender without first receiving in capital cases the advice of the Executive Council of Our said Commonwealth, and in other cases the advice of one, at least, of his Ministers; and in any case in which such pardon or reprieve might directly affect the interests of Our Empire, or of any country or place beyond the jurisdiction of the Government of Our said Commonwealth, Our said Governor-General shall, take those interests specially into his own personal consideration in conjunction with such advice as aforesaid.

IX. And whereas great prejudice may happen to Our service and to the security of Our said Commonwealth by the absence of Our said Governor-General, he shall not, upon any pretence whatever, quit Our said Commonwealth without having first obtained leave from Us for so doing under Our Sign Manual and Signet, or through one of Our Principal Secretaries of State.

VICTORIA

ABOVE *The inauguration ceremony at Centennial Park, Sydney, on 1 January 1901.*

ABOVE *Second page of the letters patent constituting the office of governor-general.*

The queen's representative

THE OFFICE OF GOVERNOR-GENERAL AND COMMANDER-IN-CHIEF OF THE COMMONWEALTH OF AUSTRALIA

The first governor-general of Australia, John Adrian Louis Hope (1860–1908), 7th Earl of Hopetoun and later 1st Marquess of Linlithgow, was appointed to the office by Queen Victoria. With the public reading of the letters patent quoted here, Lord Hopetoun formally assumed the responsibilities of the vice-regal office at the grand celebration to inaugurate the new Commonwealth of Australia at Centennial Park in Sydney on 1 January 1901. The letters patent were then published in the first issue of the *Commonwealth of Australia Gazette*. Lord Hopetoun relinquished the role of governor-general on 9 January 1903.

The broad formal powers of the governor-general as declared in the letters patent signed by the Queen at Westminster, on 29 October 1900, were specified (and remain so to the present) in section 61 of the Australian Constitution. This section vested the executive power of the Commonwealth in the queen but noted that it was to be exercised by the governor-general as the queen's representative in Australia. That power given to the governor-general by the founders of Federation 'extends to the execution and maintenance of the Constitution, and of the laws of the Commonwealth'. Such powers of the governor-general were either ceremonial or formal duties to be undertaken on the advice of ministers.

Also vested in the office of governor-general under section 64 of the Constitution were the so-called 'reserve powers', by which the incumbent was given the discretion to remove or to suspend any office holder of the Commonwealth. Since this section provided for the governor-general appointing 'Ministers of State for the Commonwealth', the complementary discretionary power of dismissal—'upon sufficient cause to him appearing', in the words of the document of 1900—ensured that the office of governor-general had an independent capacity to exercise a singular power. The strength of that power, long thought to be dormant, was not tested until the events of November 1975, when the then governor-general, Sir John Kerr, terminated the commissions of Prime Minister Gough Whitlam and members of his ministry in order to break a deadlock between the two Houses of Parliament, to ensure the passage of the budget and to force a general election (see page 314). That later traumatic event in Australia's history provides an additional layer of interest to the document that ceremonially and publicly proclaimed the powers of the governor-general at the commencement of the twentieth century.

VICTORIA, by the Grace of God of the United Kingdom of Great Britain and Ireland, Queen, Defender of the Faith, Empress of India: To all to whom these Presents shall come, Greeting.

WHEREAS, by an Act of Parliament passed on the ninth day of July One thousand nine hundred, in the Sixty fourth year of Our reign, intituled "An Act to constitute the Commonwealth of Australia," it is enacted that "it shall be lawful for the Queen, with the advice of the Privy Council, to declare by Proclamation that, on and after a day therein appointed, not being later than one year after the passing of this ACT, the people of New South Wales, Victoria, South Australia, Queensland, and Tasmania, and also, if Her Majesty is satisfied that the people of Western Australia have agreed thereto, of Western Australia, shall be united in a Federal Commonwealth under the name of the Commonwealth of Australia. But the Queen may, at any time after Proclamation, appoint a Governor General for the Commonwealth:" ...

Now know ye that We have thought fit to constitute, order, and declare ... that there shall be a Governor General and Commander in Chief ... in and over Our Commonwealth of Australia ... and that the person who shall fill the said Office of Governor General shall be from time to time appointed by Commission under Our Sign Manual and Signet. And we do hereby authorize and command Our said Governor General to do and execute, in due manner, all things that shall belong to his said command, and to the trust We have reposed in him, according to the several powers and authorities granted or appointed him by virtue of "The Commonwealth of Australia Constitution Act, 1900", and of these present Letters Patent and of such Commission as may be issued to him under Our Sign Manual and Signet, and according to such Instructions as may from time to time be given to him under Our Sign Manual and Signet, or by Our Order in Our Privy Council, or by Us through one of our Principal Secretaries of State, and to such laws as shall hereafter be in force in Our said Commonwealth.

II. There shall be a Great Seal of and for Our said Commonwealth which Our said Governor General shall keep and use for sealing all things whatsoever that shall pass the said Great Seal. Provided that until a Great Seal shall be provided, the Private Seal of our said Governor General may be used as the Great Seal of the Commonwealth of Australia.

III. The Governor General may constitute and appoint, in Our name and on Our behalf, all such Judges, Commissioners, Justices of the Peace, and other necessary Officers and Ministers of Our said Commonwealth, as may be lawfully constituted or appointed by Us.

IV. The Governor General, so far as We Ourselves lawfully may, upon sufficient cause to him appearing, may remove from his office, or suspend from the exercise of the same, any person exercising any office of Our said Commonwealth, under or by virtue of any—Commission or Warrant granted, or which may be granted, by Us in Our name or under Our authority.

V. The Governor General may on Our behalf exercise all powers under the Commonwealth of Australia Constitution Act, 1900, or otherwise in respect of the summoning, proroguing, or dissolving the Parliament of Our said Commonwealth.

VI. And whereas by "The Commonwealth of Australia Constitution Act, 1900," it is amongst other things enacted, that we may authorise the Governor General to appoint any person or persons, jointly or severally, to be his Deputy or Deputies within any part of Our Commonwealth, and in that capacity to exercise, during the pleasure of the Governor General, such powers and functions of the said Governor General as he thinks fit to assign ... subject to any limitations expressed or directions given by Us: Now We do hereby authorise and empower Our said Governor General ... to appoint any person or persons, jointly or severally, to be his Deputy or Deputies within any part of Our said Commonwealth of Australia, and in that capacity to exercise, during his pleasure, such of his powers and functions, as he may deem it necessary or expedient to assign ...

VII. And we do hereby declare Our pleasure to be that, in the event of the death, incapacity, removal, or absence of Our said Governor General out of Our said Commonwealth, all and every the powers and authorities herein granted to him shall, until Our further pleasure is signified therein, be vested in such person as may be appointed by Us under Our Sign Manual and Signet to be Our Lieutenant Governor of Our said Commonwealth: or if there shall be no such Lieutenant Governor in Our said Commonwealth, then in such person or persons as may be appointed by Us ... to administer the Government of the same. No such powers or authorities shall vest in such Lieutenant Governor, or such other person or persons, until he or they shall have taken the oaths appointed to be taken by the Governor General of Our said Commonwealth, and in the manner provided by the Instructions accompanying these Our Letters Patent.

VIII. And We do hereby require and command all Our Officers and Ministers, Civil and Military, and all other the inhabitants of Our said Commonwealth to be obedient, aiding, and assisting unto Our said Governor General, or ... to such person or persons as may, from time to time ... administer the Government of Our said Commonwealth.

IX. And We do hereby reserve to Ourselves, Our heirs and successors, full power and authority from time to time to revoke, alter, or amend these Our Letters Patent as to Us or them shall seem meet.

X. And We do further direct and enjoin that these Our Letters Patent shall be read and proclaimed at such place or places as Our said Governor General shall think fit within Our said Commonwealth of Australia

In Witness whereof We have caused these Our Letters to be made Patent.

Witness Ourself at Westminster the twenty ninth day of October, in the sixty-fourth year of Our reign

By Warrant under the Queen's Sign Manual

Muir Mackenzie

Australia 'will act as one'

EDMUND BARTON'S SPEECH ON A NEW AUSTRALIAN COMMONWEALTH

With the great and laborious work of the campaign for federation over and with only three weeks to go before the inauguration of the new Commonwealth of Australia, one of the principal architects of the new Australian polity delivered this reflective speech to an audience in Sydney. Its author was Edmund Barton (1849–1920), who would serve as the first Australian prime minister and later as a foundation judge of the High Court. The occasion of the speech is not recorded, but it provides a powerful sense of the conservative vision that informed the new Commonwealth and the prevailing sense of Australia at the close of the nineteenth century as a bastion of British stock—the 'purest example' of the parent stock to be found outside the British Isles.

On 17 January 1901 Barton would return to this theme in a speech he delivered at West Maitland in New South Wales to open his campaign for the first Commonwealth election. More explicitly on that occasion, Barton moved from the broad sweep of his imperial rhetoric to promote the cause of a 'White Australia', which would become an early priority of his term in government.

ABOVE *Portrait of Edmund Barton, dated 1902.*

On this day three weeks, Australia will begin her new career. In affairs which are national in their Australian range, she will act as one. In affairs which are national in the Imperial sense, she will act as a powerful unit of a mighty empire. In reality, she will take a new departure in each of these capacities; and in each, she must march with her responsibilities at the heels of her great opportunities. Let us then consider her advantages and her duties, first, as she stands in these seas by herself; and next, as she holds herself towards the Empire, with new strength and, as we all know, with unlessened loyalty. First then, take the primary effects of Federation upon the great group of Australian Colonies which includes Tasmania. Wholly or almost wholly British in blood (and for convenience I use the word "British" to denote our kinship with the inhabitants of both the British Isles), she is the purest example of the parent stock to be found outside those isles, albeit she is separated further from them by thousands of miles than any other great community of the same stock. Thus she is furthest in distance, yet closest in kinship. In times past, the distance has unfortunately made full appreciation on both sides difficult at least until certain happenings quite recent but very great. Yet the closeness of relationship has kept, and still keeps, the principles of British self-government as fully (if not more fully) alive in Australia as in any other part of the world.

In the Conventions of 1891 and of 1897–1898 and in the campaigns of the two successive referendums, nothing was more apparent than the repugnance of the Australian people to any form of government which tended to depart from the ideals of British statesmanship. Strongly as they desired a true Federation, and reluctant as they were to make any rash provision which should make their Federation less true, they were resolute to preserve the principle of ministerial responsibility which, in its every day application, has been found in British communities a buttress of popular common sense, however often in people of opposite instincts it may have been experimentally used, and misapplied as a vehicle to carry caprice to mischievous ends. And if it is true that our Constitution is a "Monument of legislative capacity", it is only because we are of the stock which insists on equal opportunity, and uses it boldly, but wisely, under the feeling of responsibility; or, in other words, keeps its balance by the equipoise of freedom and duty. As a new and free nation, what then are our duties to each other? Half a dozen communities, varying in numbers, varying but little in our pursuits, but differing often in our mere opinions as to particular methods of advancing the public good, diverging in our land laws and our systems of taxation, but equally aglow with the same instinct of popular freedom, we have decided to make a legislative declaration of the racial identity which was always ours; and, feeling our oneness, to act as one in our internal national affairs. As one people in one country, we cannot long continue to tax each other as if we had no national government; therefore, intercolonial taxes are to cease as soon as a national system of customs and excise can reasonably be thought out; and one tariff will then be substituted for half a dozen, we may all hope without unnecessary loss and destruction. We are to defend ourselves as one. We do not mean to be aggressive invaders, but I trust we shall ever remember that the true place of self-defence is not always to be found within artificial limits. The British American Colonies were defended, and the war carried on to the conquest of French Canada: French aggression in India was repelled and British power in India was established:—both these things quite as much on German battlefields where British soldiers were led by Prince Ferdinand of Brunswick, as on the heights of Quebec or through the marshes of Masulipatum. Our fleet, if we ever have one, may be better employed in assisting to destroy a powerful naval combination thousands of miles away, than it could be if distributed in the defence of separated ports, and so left in detail at the mercy of strong attacking squadrons. If concentration is powerful for aggression, it would be foolhardy to neglect it when defence is the only object.

Soon, too, our Federation will have to unite the six differing postal and telegraph systems in existence, and the instinct of equal self-government will be rather prompt in levelling off these systems. Much may be done towards equalising rates and facilities throughout the Federation. We are not likely ever to have the uniform twopenny rate so often marshalled among the "bogeys," but we are drawing at least one stage nearer to a universal penny post. Next, it cannot be long before the immigration of persons and races not wanted in Australia will be regulated by one equable law. Marriage will be as sacred a tie in one State as in another, and its dissolution must be made subject to the same just conditions in all of them. Nor will Australia hesitate, after she has found that her finance will bear the strain, to legislate humanely for the comfort of her aged poor and their freedom from humiliation. Here are a few examples of the strength of unity and the call of duty to Australia self-contained. But what of the other outlook? I mean the Imperial forecast. There are those, though happily they are now few, who repel the idea of Imperial cohesion. Some of them there are who honestly think that we should be not only safer but better alone; but there are others—indeed a very small band—who hate the mother of us all, and gird at *us* when we stand at her side. But the men of Australia as well as of Canada and New Zealand are of better mettle than this. The British Empire may not in our day, or ever indeed, be federated by any written bond, but it is already federated by two living facts; one is that the blood of citizen soldiers from all parts of the Empire has often in the last fifteen months flowed in one stream, shed for the protection of the soil of that Empire, and to prevent a recurrence of its rash invasion. The other great fact is that the equality of British citizenship, and with it the equality of self-government, is recognised from end to end of the Queen's dominions, whether you call the citizen Englishman or Australian, Irishman or Canadian, Scotchman or New Zealander. The mother land has always been ready to defend, even in earth's furthest corner, the sons of the Empire struggling to hold their own, whether to her the place of strife seemed profitable or useless; and we others have not been slow to discover that, as we expect every part of the Empire to stand by us when our day of need arrives, so we must in all conscience admit and fulfill our reciprocal duty to every part when invaded. We shall keep the right of considering whether duty calls: but if we hear its call, I hope we shall always be swift to respond, as we have lately been. There is no aggressive militarism here, for the case is one of the commonest duty, if once the principle which binds us together is attacked.

> "There dwells a wife by the Northern Gate,
> And a wealthy wife is she;
> She breeds a breed of rovin' men
> And casts them over sea".

Speaking in London on the 24th of October, the honorary freedom of one of the great City Companies having just been conferred upon him, the remarkable statesman who at the head of the Colonial Office has been so greatly concerned in South African questions which have led to the present war, made special reference to what he called "The greatest feature of all in this eventful modern history." "Look," he said, "at the action of the colonies, the self-governing colonies, in the period of trouble and trial which came upon the mother land. What sympathy they have shown! How practically they have shewn it! How universal has been the sentiment! ... At the first threat of war, they hastened spontaneously—it was not our suggestion, it was their own good thought—they hastened spontaneously to offer their aid, and they have given us of their best and bravest ... They have done something more; they have given us their moral support—the moral support of great, free, independent nations proud of their own liberty and *able to take an impartial and judicial view of the merits of the struggle in which we are engaged*. I do not think that anything could have been more grateful to the people of this country, more useful in regard to our position with other nations, than the sight of the colonies of Great Britain—the sons of Great Britain — hastening freely to give their support to the mother land in a cause which *they themselves have considered, and believe to be just*. In view of all this, is it too much to say that in this last twelve months the Empire has been born anew? The Empire now is undoubtedly not the Empire of England alone, but the Empire almost of the world—of all our possessions—of all our dependencies. It must be borne in mind in future that *we recognise in them absolute equality of right and possession in all that we claim in regard to ourselves* ... Shall we ever forget? Will anyone ever again say that the Colonies are an encumbrance to the Empire which they have done so much to maintain and support? ... This is the new Imperialism ... I do not think that there is any fear now that we shall not hand down those great possessions unimpaired and strengthened as we received them from our ancestors, and I am sanguine enough to look forward to a future even brighter than the present. I cannot but believe that when this progress has been made in so short a time, in the future still greater progress will be made. I think I am not wrong in seeing in the federation of Canada and in the 'indissoluble union' of the Commonwealth of Australia, a sign and an example to our possessions in South Africa, and a foreshadowing of that greater federation—that federation of kindred nations, which will realise the dream of every patriotic man and will strengthen the foundations of our Empire that in the good providence of God, it will continue long into the future to fulfil its mission—its destined mission—justice, civilisation and peace".

Well did the Lord Chief Justice say of this utterance that it was seldom a speech had been conceived in the same noble tone; that it was a speech which would be echoed through the years, and perhaps generations.

I venture to think that the federation which Mr Chamberlain saw foreshadowed has in fact arrived—, a federation of kindred nations, whose common defence is assured without the aid of ink, for its duty is imprinted on their brains, cemented with their blood, and sacred by every memory of the rivalry of heroism.

Ladies and Gentlemen, the expansion of this Empire by cruelty or aggression is no more the desire of its rulers or its citizens now than it has been in the past. Every nation has its crimes to repent; but none has fewer than the freest of Empires, because freedom and cruelty do not stand together, however often license and barbarity may elsewhere have been synonymous ...

The recent expansion of the Empire by way of territory was the result of an unjustified and preconcerted aggression from without—an aggression so designed that to allow its repetition were not mercy but folly. [Chamberlain's scheme of administration.] On these hitherto peaceful shores, the Empire is expanding in another way. The self-government of the Island Continent which is the home of one of its many nations, is about to be extended in a way which gives expansion to the strength, and tenacity to the cohesion, of the whole of that Empire. In the United Kingdom, from the highest statesman of all parties to the humblest citizen, there is for you and the Commonwealth but one great voice of welcome and one great heart of love. Your recognition that a just partnership in empire carries with it some perils to set against its priceless benefits, has evoked from across the seas a gratitude which we here, who view our conduct as a mere act of duty, may find it hard to understand. I who have so lately seen it evidenced, find it impossible to describe. [Visit.]

When the Commonwealth sets out on her stately march, she will carry with her hopes and prayers and paeans of pride from the "Wife that dwells by the Northern Gate", quite as fervent as any that will resound here, and she will be blessed by the gratitude and trust which the "men from over sea" can never do more and must not do less than repay. May

"The Good Wife's sons come home again
For her blessing on their head!"

The star of justice, prudence, temperance and fortitude

A NATIONAL FLAG FOR AUSTRALIA

Curiously, when Australia was inaugurated as an independent nation, or Commonwealth, on 1 January 1901, no official national flag and no official national emblem had been put in place. At the various celebrations held to mark the inauguration of the new Commonwealth of Australia, including the principal celebration in Sydney's Centennial Park, the United Kingdom's union flag was universally flown. The Union Jack remained in use for several months at other national ceremonies, including the opening of the first Australian federal Parliament in Melbourne on 9 May 1901.

With the pressure of other business, the matter of choosing a new and distinctive Australian flag was given a low priority by the new legislators, whose dual loyalty was to both Britain and Australia and who saw no slight to the nation in flying the Union Jack. Officially, Australia relished its new independence at home, but was also proud to acknowledge its membership of a great and powerful empire, standing shoulder to shoulder under the Grand Old Flag of the United Kingdom.

Nevertheless, led by an enthusiastic press, there was a growing swell of popular interest in a new flag for Australia. Two unofficial competitions were announced, which between them yielded a large number of entries and an amazing plethora of designs. But it was as a result of promptings by the Colonial Office in London that the Commonwealth government finally moved to embrace the quest for a new national flag. In the *Commonwealth of Australia Gazette* of 29 April 1901 the government announced its own competition for a 'Commonwealth Flag', the successful design to be submitted for approval to 'the Imperial authorities'. More than 32,823 entries were evaluated by the judging panel and five similar designs selected as being of equal merit. The Commonwealth government eventually submitted two designs—one representing the winners of the national competition and the other the so-called Australian Federation Flag, colours that had been used unofficially for nearly seventy years and had assumed prominence during the campaign for federation. The first of these was approved as Australia's national flag and was proclaimed by King Edward VII on 20 February 1903.

One of the winning designers, 14-year-old Melbourne schoolboy Ivor Evans, later wrote of his thoughts on the flag. He believed that the Southern Cross, the brightest constellation in the southern hemisphere, signified Australia's bright future as a leading nation of the world. He drew also on Dante's vision of four bright stars symbolising the moral virtues of justice, prudence, temperance and fortitude—symbols that might guide the new nation.

Apart from the historic salute to the Union Jack, the Commonwealth Star was the other symbol of special importance. Its six points represented the newly federated states. In 1908 a seventh point was added to represent the federal territories, which today include the Northern Territory, the Australian Capital Territory, the Cocos Islands and the Australian Antarctic Territory.

In this document, two of the judges of the design competition frame the official report to Edmund Barton, prime minister of Australia, on 2 September 1901.

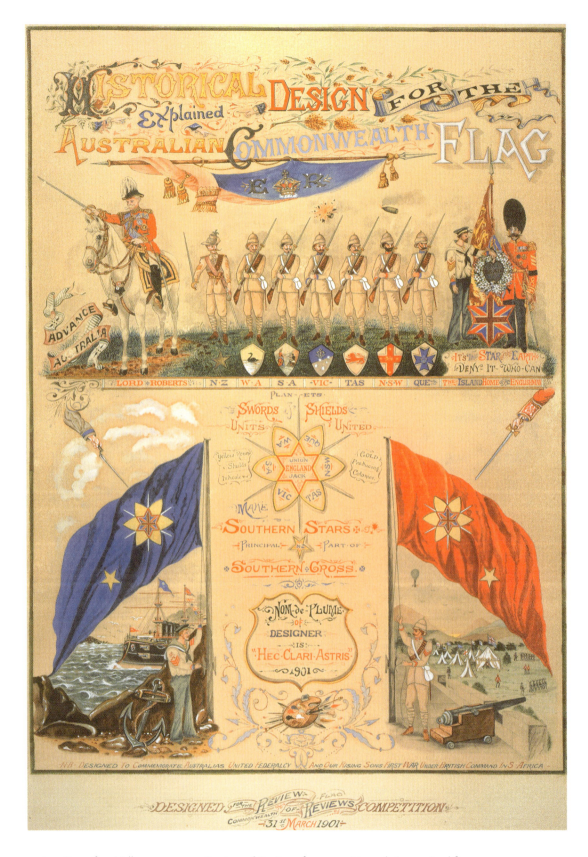

ABOVE *Poster from Melbourne newspaper* Review of Reviews *for a competition to design a national flag.*

Sir,

Attracted by the loyalty and sentiment of the Australian people, as represented by 30,000 designs for a national flag (the great majority of which contained the Union Jack and the Southern Cross), it was felt that the only additional emblem required was one representing the federation of the six states. This was supplied by various forms, such as coloured bars, shields, devices, stars, figures, letters, animals &c, introduced in various forms, colours and positions on the several designs. Having carefully examined every exhibit and with due regard to the history, heraldry, blazonry, distinctiveness, utility, and cost of making up in bunting, it was apparent that a Commonwealth flag, to be representative, should contain:—

1. The Union Jack on a blue or red ground.
2. A six-pointed star, representing the six federated States of Australia, immediately underneath the Union Jack and pointing direct to the centre of the St George's Cross, of a size to occupy the major portion of one quarter of the flag.
3. The "Southern Cross" in the fly as indicative of the sentiment of the Australian nation.

Such a combination should be easily distinguished as a signal of distress, is original in character, and should be agreeable to the home authorities, as they have already given their sanction to the "Southern Cross" being shown in some of the State flags, such as New Zealand, Victoria, &c, and exception should not be taken to the one star under the Jack. Many designs somewhat similar were rejected as not being in accord with heraldry, borders round the Union Jack, contrary to the heraldry and blazonry of flags, crosses, coloured stars, stars too small to be seen at a distance, and otherwise faulty in design.

In conclusion we may state that our task was not an easy one, but our desire was to give to the people of our new-born nation a symbol that would be endearing and lasting in its effect, and with that end in view, we hope we have been successful.

We have the honour to be, sir, your obedient servants, on behalf of the judges,

J.W. Evans
J.A. Mitchell

To the Right Honourable E. Barton, MHR, Prime Minister.

A national flag for Australia.

'the truest I ever read'

MILES FRANKLIN'S
MY BRILLIANT CAREER

ABOVE *Miles Franklin, photographed in 1901.*

Miles Franklin (1879–1954) was a precocious talent when her first novel *My Brilliant Career* was published in 1901. At only 19 years of age she had written and revised the novel in the period from September 1898 to November 1899. With its setting in her native Monaro district of New South Wales, *My Brilliant Career* poignantly assessed the barren existence of bush life for a sensitive woman. At the same time it expressed a deep love of the Australian landscape. In giving his imprimatur to the work, Henry Lawson declared it 'true to Australia—the truest I ever read'. His praise warmed Franklin's heart.

While it was not written as a public document, Franklin's letter to the great J.F. Archibald, editor of the famously nationalistic Sydney paper the *Bulletin*, announces her novel to one of the leading supporters of Australian literature and declares her commitment to her country. The egotistical letter is the clear voice of a young writer full of justifiable pride and ambition in the immediate triumph of publication. While noting its rawness and a lack of cultivation, the English critics of the day admired the novel's passion and power. In Australia, especially, *My Brilliant Career* has endured as a classic of its time. In 1979, with the actor Judy Davis as a memorable Sybylla Melvyn, Franklin's fictional heroine made her film debut, winning a new generation of admirers.

Bangalora,
Goulburn,
Sept. 5th, 1901.

J.F. Archibald, Esq.

My dear Sir,

Per same post I send you a copy of a self-written yarn entitled, "My Brilliant Career" if you would kindly do me the honor of accepting same you will afford me much gratification. Don't for a moment imagine me so unsophisticatedly green as to think the ignorance and inexperience of a bush 18 yrs. (most unadulterated bush too) could produce anything to a litterateur of yr. experience, but spare me a moment and I will 's explain. In '99 I sent you an M.S.: you, or Alex Montgomery for you—wrote to me and said you hadn't time to read the ch's. but from occasional glances you considered it fairly well written, and gave me some good information—advice. It was the first honest letter I received from anyone in the ink & paper business and I shall always remember it. The scribblings submitted to you was this yarn. I re-wrote it and appealed to our poet Lawson for help. You must know him as Yr. name is in the front of his book, so you will know he didn't hum or haw but came to my rescue oh! so kindly and sympathetically as only Henry Lawson could, or would. This book is the result. The title should be "My Brilliant (?) Career", also any passages not orthodox and have been toned to a correct girly-girlishness. To the discretion or prejudice or something of Blackwood I am indebted, but without gratitude, for this.

Thanking you for that letter
Respectfully,
Sir,

Name:—Miles Franklin.
Occupation:—Bush whacker.
Residence:—"The Land o' lots o' time".

My sex, brain & mind etc. preclude me from being great or wise but the common of us can be true & that has been my careful endeavor. I am glad he made that remark.

A uniquely British people

IMMIGRATION RESTRICTION ACT

When the Australian colonies joined into a federation in January 1901, they did so with the belief that the country stood united as a uniquely 'British' people. Its population was a mix of the transplanted elements of English, Scottish, Irish and Welsh cultures and peoples that had shaped Australia's formation and development from the time of European settlement and throughout the nineteenth century. As it entered the twentieth century, Australia boasted that its stock was 98 per cent British; its people 'Independent Australian Britons', in the phrase later used by historian Keith Hancock in his seminal study of 1930 entitled *Australia*. The corollary of this British Australian nationhood was the preservation of so-called racial purity in a White Australia (see page 194).

One of the earliest legislative enactments of the new Commonwealth of Australia was the *Immigration Restriction Act 1901* (No. 17). Although the restrictions on entry enumerated in the crucial defining section of the act (section 3) made no reference to race, the legislation was fundamentally conceived to restrict the entry of persons of colour into Australia. However, the test of exclusion was not to be colour itself, but rather the capacity of a person to pass a dictation test of fifty words in any unspecified European language: in practice, this meant a language unlikely to be understood by the applicant to whom the test was administered. In fact, fifty-two people successfully completed the test in the years 1902–08, but after 1909 the test served as it was conceived—an effective means of exclusion. The dictation test remained a requirement for immigration into Australia until 1958, by which time its racial character had marred the country's reputation, especially among its Asian neighbours.

AN ACT

To place certain restrictions on Immigration and to provide for the removal from the Commonwealth of prohibited Immigrants. [Assented to 23rd December 1901]

BE it enacted by the King's Most Excellent Majesty the Senate and the House of Representatives of the Commonwealth of Australia as follows:— ...

3. The immigration into the Commonwealth of the persons described in any of the following paragraphs of this section (hereinafter called "prohibited immigrants") is prohibited, namely:—

(a) Any person who when asked to do so by an officer fails to write out at dictation and sign in the presence of the officer a passage of fifty words in length in an European language directed by the officer;

(b) any person likely in the opinion of the Minister or of an officer to become a charge upon the public or upon any public or charitable institution;

(c) any idiot or insane person;

(d) any person suffering from an infectious or contagious disease of a loathsome or dangerous character;

(e) any person who has within three years been convicted of an offence, not being a mere political offence, and has been sentenced to imprisonment for one year or longer therefor, and has not received a pardon;

(f) any prostitute or person living on the prostitution of others;

(g) any persons under a contract to perform manual labour within the Commonwealth: Provided that this paragraph shall not apply to workmen exempted by the Minister for special skill required in Australia or to persons under contract or agreement to serve as part of the crew of a vessel engaged in the coasting trade in Australian waters if the rates of wages specified therein are not lower than the rates ruling in the Commonwealth ...

5. (1) Any immigrant who evades an officer or who enters the Commonwealth at any place where no officer is stationed may if at any time thereafter he is found within the Commonwealth be asked to comply with the requirements of paragraph *(a)* of section three, and shall if he fails to do so be deemed to be a prohibited immigrant offending against this Act.

5. (2) Any immigrant may at any time within one year after he has entered the Commonwealth be asked to comply with the requirements of paragraph *(a)* of section three, and shall if he fails to do so be deemed to be a prohibited immigrant offending against this Act.

'to raise or improve the public taste'

ALFRED FELTON'S BEQUEST

Announcements in the Melbourne newspapers of 13 January 1904 carried the surprising news of the bequest to charities and to the Melbourne National Art Gallery (later the National Gallery of Victoria) made under the will of the businessman Alfred Felton (1831–1904), who had died a few days earlier. The estate that would support this bequest was valued at £500,000 sterling, a sum estimated in the year 2008 at $64 million. The scale of Felton's generosity was extraordinary in the Australia of its day, and the bequest has been of enormous benefit both to the charities it has supported and to the National Gallery of Victoria. The first press reports spoke of the benefits the bequest offered to the people of Victoria, but in the support given to the National Gallery of Victoria, the beneficiaries of Felton's gift have been the Australian people as a whole. The accumulation of artworks acquired under what is known as the Felton Bequest has ranged widely over many different forms of art and in fields that have not, except occasionally, been accessible to other Australian art galleries.

Alfred Felton was born in England but arrived in Australia in 1853, where his first money was earned in the carting of goods on the goldfields. Later he became a merchant in Melbourne before establishing himself as a wholesale druggist in the city. In 1867, in partnership with F.S. Grimwade he purchased a wholesale drug house that was soon renamed Felton, Grimwade & Co. Under the direction of the partners, the firm expanded profitably, while also diversifying its interests; both partners built substantial personal wealth from their shared enterprise.

Felton, who never married, accumulated over the last twenty years of his life a personal collection of books, pictures and art objects, but the specific inspiration of his endowment of the Melbourne National Art Gallery remains uncertain. His biographer, John Poynter, noted in 2003 that, while nothing is known of the processes by which he formed his intentions, Felton had, during the 1880s, visited New York's Metropolitan Museum of Art, founded in 1870 and charged with a mission to elevate public taste, and that he knew of other, similar instances of benefaction in both Australia and in England.

Over the years, much has been written of the Felton Bequest, of both its triumphs and its occasional disappointments. While many undeniably great acquisitions have been made, it is true also that there have been lost opportunities, some wilful but some fully understood only with the benefit of hindsight and with the growth of artistic reputations and standing. Sometimes works originally acquired with much fanfare as acclaimed masterpieces have been assigned a more modest status. Occasionally, too, advances in scholarship have seen some Felton ugly ducklings turned into handsome swans. These are the variables of taste, judgment, knowledge, vision and prejudice. But in the grand scheme of the building of public collections of art in Australia, and in the elevation and refinement of public taste and understanding, the Felton Bequest has abundantly fulfilled the quietly stated hopes and expectations that were first announced to Melbournians in the summer of 1904.

Mr. Alfred Felton's Estate.

MUNIFICENT PUBLIC BEQUEST.

CHARITIES AND ART GALLERIES ENDOWED.

One of the largest public bequests ever made in Australia has been left for benefit of the people of Victoria by the late Mr. Alfred Felton, who died at St. Kilda on Friday last. By the terms of a will dated August, 1900, nearly the whole of Mr. Felton's fortune, amounting to close on half a million sterling, is to be invested and the income derived will be divided between the Melbourne National Art Gallery and the charitable institutions of this State. The Trustees, Executors and Agency Company, of 412 Collins-street, which is sole executor of the estate, estimates its total value at from £450,000 to £500,000. Out of this a sum of £50,000 will be paid away in various legacies, and £150,000 will be set aside for a period of years to provide from the interest earned by the money life incomes for other legatees. As these legatees die the capital from which they drew their life incomes will revert to the bequest, till ultimately the whole £150,000 thus set aside, in addition to the residue of the estate, will be available for the charitable and educational purposes designed by the donor. Eventually this will mean the utilisation of the income arising from £400,000 to £450,000.

The residue, amounting to about £300,000, and the £150,000 as it falls in under the will, is to be held in perpetuity, and to be invested. The income arising from the investments is to be divided into two parts. One moiety will be devoted to charitable purposes, and the other half is to be applied, according to the donor's direction, "to the purchase of works of ancient or modern art, antiquities, or other works or objects of artistic or educational value, calculated to raise or improve the public taste." These will be placed in the Melbourne Art Gallery.

In order that the bequest may be properly carried out, the giver directs that the management of the estate shall be vested in a committee of five, consisting of his late partner (Mr. F.S. Grimwade, M.L.C.), with succession to that gentleman's two sons, Professor Morris—[since the date of the will Professor Morris has died]—Dr. Charles Bage, one of the trustees of the Melbourne Public Gallery, and one of the directors of the Trustees, Executors and Agency Company. The will makes provision for the filling up of any vacancy on this committee that will from time to time occur on similar lines—for instance, should the trustee representing the Gallery die, his place will be taken by another trustee—the whole of the members being thus provided for, so that, though its personnel may change, the committee will always remain in existence. This committee is vested with absolute power regarding the allocation and distribution of the charitable bequest, and is not hampered with any stipulation regarding its art purchases for the gallery. Although it is left to the discretion of the committee to decide what charitable institutions shall participate in the amount to be yearly dispersed amongst them, Mr. Felton indicates in a general way in the will how he should like it divided. "Without in any way fettering the absolute discretion of the said committee," he states, "I hereby indicate to them my hope that in the application of such income they will favorably consider, firstly, charities for children; for example, children's hospitals and orphanages; secondly, charities for women, such as women's hospitals; thirdly such institutions or societies as general hospitals, societies for the relief of the educated poor, and other charitable institutions of a general character."

The trustees of the Melbourne National Art Gallery, by the will, are also given the right to make a selection from the deceased gentleman's magnificent collection of pictures and articles of virtu, and whatever they select are a bequest to them for the gallery. The pictures chosen and the pictures purchased out of the income from the estate are, by direction of the will, to be labelled "The Felton Bequest."

Establishing a 'fair and reasonable' wage

THE HARVESTER JUDGMENT

The Harvester judgment of Mr Justice Henry Bournes Higgins (1851–1929) in the Commonwealth Court of Conciliation and Arbitration on 8 November 1907 was a landmark in the first decade after Federation and of long-term significance in Australia. It enunciated a principle by which future wages would be determined. From this was derived the concept of the living wage, or basic wage, which became the central plank of Australian wage fixing until late in the twentieth century.

Higgins succeeded R.E. O'Connor as president of the Commonwealth Court of Conciliation and Arbitration in 1907. In his first case he had to decide whether the manufacturer H.V. McKay of Sunshine Harvesters in Victoria was paying the 'fair and reasonable' wages to his employees required by the Commonwealth government's new protection legislation as embodied in the *Excise Act 1906*. Under the provisions of this act, manufacturers of harvesters who wanted to receive the full benefit of the protective import duty on harvester machinery were required to pay so-called, but undefined, 'fair and reasonable' wages. Higgins delivered a rebuke to the Parliament for its failure to define what it meant by 'fair and reasonable', but he seized the initiative himself to spell out the rights of the worker to live 'as a human being in a civilized community' with an entitlement to marry and raise a family. Having calculated a family budget for a household of 'about five persons', Higgins declared that the minimum wage for an unskilled labourer should be seven shillings per day for a six-day working week. The legislation that gave rise to the Harvester judgment was later invalidated in the High Court, but the concept of a minimum wage remained for many years a sacrosanct principle of fairness in the Commonwealth jurisdiction.

When Higgins died in Melbourne in 1929, the Victorian Trades Hall flew the Australian flag at half-mast as a tribute to a judge who had conferred dignity on the rights of working men in Australia.

ABOVE *Undated photograph of Justice Henry Bournes Higgins.*

The President, after hearing witnesses on all sides, delivered the following JUDGMENT:—

Application of H.V. McKay under section 2 (d) of the Excise Tariff 1906. The Commonwealth Parliament has by this Act imposed certain Excise duties on agricultural implements; but it has provided that the Act shall not apply to goods manufactured in Australia under conditions as to the remuneration of labour which are declared by the President of the Court to be fair and reasonable. My sole duty is to ascertain whether the conditions of remuneration submitted to me "are fair and reasonable." I have not the function of finding out whether the rates of wages have, or have not, been in fact paid since the 1st of January, 1907, when this Act came into force.

I select Mr. McKay's application out of some 112 applications made by Victorian manufacturers because I found that the factory was one of the largest, and had the greatest number and variety of employees; and because his application was to be keenly fought ...

The provision for fair and reasonable remuneration is obviously designed for the benefit of employees in the industry; and it must be meant to secure to them something which they cannot get by the ordinary system of individual bargaining with employers. If Parliament meant that the conditions shall be such as they can get by individual bargaining—if it meant that those conditions are to be fair and reasonable, which employees will accept and employers will give, in contracts of service—there would have been no need for this provision. The remuneration could safely have been left to the usual, but unequal contest, the "higgling of the market" for labour with the pressure for bread on one side, and the pressure for profits on the other. The standard of "fair and reasonable" must, therefore, be something else; and I cannot think of any other standard appropriate than the normal needs of the average employee, regarded as a human being living in a civilized community. I have invited counsel and all concerned to suggest any other standard; and they have been unable to do so. If, instead of individual bargaining, one can conceive of a collective agreement—an agreement between all the employers in a given trade on the one side, and all the employees on the other—it seems to me that the framers of the agreement would have to take, as the first and dominant factor, the cost of living of a civilized being. If A lets B have the use of his horses, on the terms that he give them fair and reasonable treatment, I have no doubt that it is B's duty to give them proper food and water, and such shelter and rest as they need; and, as wages are the means of obtaining commodities, surely the State, in stipulating for fair and reasonable remuneration for the employees, means that the wages shall be sufficient to provide these things, and clothing, and a condition of frugal comfort estimated by current human standards. This, then, is the primary test, the test which I shall apply in ascertaining the minimum wage that can be treated as "fair and reasonable" in the case of unskilled labourers. Those who have acquired a skilled handicraft have to be paid more than the unskilled labourer's minimum; and in ascertaining how much more, in the case of each of the numerous trades concerned in this factory, I have been invited to make myself expert in a large number of technical details, and familiar with the mysteries of many mechanical appliances ...

It was strongly urged before me that I should compel the applicant to disclose his books, so as to enable the objectors to see what are his profits; and that if the profits are large the wages should be large also. The applicant objected to such disclosure, and I declined to compel him. I cannot find anything in the Act to suggest a scheme of profit sharing. The *Customs Tariff* 1906 imposes a heavy import duty as to stripper harvesters—£12 each. Then the Excise Tariff imposes on Australian harvesters an Excise duty of £6 each; but even this Excise duty is not to apply if the goods are manufactured under conditions as to remuneration which I (or some other of the Authorities mentioned in the Act) declare to be fair and reasonable. That is all. Fair and reasonable remuneration is a condition precedent to exemption from the duty; and the remuneration of the employee is not made to depend on the profits of the employer. If the profits are nil, the fair and reasonable remuneration must be paid; and if the profits are 100 per cent., it must be paid. There is far more ground for the view that, under this section, the fair and reasonable remuneration has to be paid before the profits are ascertained—that it stands on the same level as the cost of the raw material of the manufacture. In this case, moreover, Mr. McKay relieved me of all doubt by admitting, through his counsel, that he is able to pay fair and reasonable wages—whatever may be declared to be fair and reasonable. As at present advised, I shall certainly refuse to pry, or allow others to pry, into the financial affairs of the manufacturers, or to expose their financial affairs to their competitors in business. If it is to be cards on the table, it ought to be all cards on the table. But having regard to the Tariff protection given, the Excise exemption offered, and the admission which I have mentioned, I shall ignore any consideration that the business will not stand what I would otherwise regard as fair and reasonable remuneration.

I come now to consider the remuneration of the employees mentioned in this application. I propose to take unskilled labourers first. The standard wage—the wage paid to the most of the labourers by the applicant—is 6s. per day of eight hours, with no extra allowance for overtime; but there is one man receiving only 5s. 6d. There is no constancy of employment, as the employer has to put a considerable number of men off in the intervals between the seasons. The seed-drill and plough season, I am told, is in the earlier part of the year, about April; but the busiest time is in the harvester season, about August to November. But even if the employment were constant and uninterrupted, is a wage of 36s. per week fair and reasonable, in view of the cost of living in Victoria? I have tried to ascertain the cost of living—the amount which has to be paid for food, shelter, clothing, for an average labourer with normal wants, and under normal conditions. Some very interesting evidence has been given, by working men's wives and others; and the evidence has been absolutely undisputed ... One witness, the wife of one who formerly a vatman in a candle works, says that in the days when her husband was working at the vat at 36s. a week, she was unable to provide meat for him on about three days in the week. The inability to procure sustaining food—whatever kind may be selected—is certainly not conducive to the maintenance of the worker in industrial efficiency.

Core of my Heart.

The love of field and coppice
Of green and shaded lanes
Of ordered woods and gardens
Is running in your veins —
Strong love of grey-blue distance
Brown streams and soft dim skies — — —
I know but cannot share it,
My love is otherwise.

I love a sunburnt country,
A land of sweeping plains
Of ragged mountain-ranges
Of droughts and flooding rains.
I love her far horizons
I love her jewel-sea,
Her beauty and her terror —
The wide brown land for me!

ABOVE 'Core of My Heart' from Dorothea Mackellar's 139-page notebook, held in the State Library of New South Wales.

'I love a sunburnt country'

DOROTHEA MACKELLAR'S AUSTRALIA

In 1908 in the *Spectator* in London, the young Australian Dorothea Mackellar (1885–1968) published a poem she called 'Core of My Heart'. It was destined to bring her enduring fame. The poem itself, renamed 'My Country' in 1911, went on to become what writer Peter Luck has called 'Australia's unofficial spoken national anthem'. Learning Mackellar's poem by heart and reciting it was an essential part of the education of many generations of young Australians until the 1960s. The poem gained renewed attention in 2008 with the celebration of the centenary of its first publication.

Although the poem does not survive in Mackellar's earliest drafts, it does exist in a manuscript held in the Mitchell Library collection in the State Library of New South Wales. There, in a modest notebook inscribed by Mackellar as 'Verses 1907–1908', is an early version of the poem that was later revised and polished to become the much-loved Australian classic. After its debut in London, the poem was published in the *Sydney Morning Herald* in October 1908. It also appeared later as 'My Country' in Mackellar's first book *The Closed Door* (1911), and it is as 'My Country' that it has been known ever since. Written in Mackellar's robust and determined hand, the manuscript is a document of a very special kind. It has an urgency that expresses the irritation and anger she felt for Australians of her generation who gave their primary allegiance to a distant 'Mother Country' in the northern hemisphere.

ABOVE *Dorothea Mackellar, pictured in an undated photograph.*

'Core of My Heart'

The love of field and coppice,
Of green and shaded lanes,
Of ordered woods and gardens
Is running in your veins,
Strong love of grey-blue distance,
Brown streams and soft, dim skies—
I know but cannot share it,
My love is otherwise.

I love a sunburnt country,
A land of sweeping plains,
Of ragged mountain ranges,
Of droughts and flooding rains.
I love her far horizons,
I love her jewel-sea,
Her beauty and her terror—
The wide brown land for me!

The tragic ringbarked forests
Stark white beneath the moon,
The sapphire-misted mountains,
The hot gold hush of noon,
Green tangle of the brushes,
Where lithe lianas coil
And orchids deck the tree tops
And ferns the crimson soil.

Core of my heart, my country!
Her pitiless blue sky,
When sick at heart around us,
We see the cattle die—
And then the grey clouds gather,
And we can bless again
The drumming of an army,
The steady, soaking rain.

Core of my heart, my country!
Young land of Rainbow Gold,
For flood and fire and famine,
She pays us back threefold—
Over the thirsty paddocks,
Watch, after many days,
A filmy veil of greenness
That thickens as we gaze …

An opal-hearted country,
A wilful lavish land—
All you who have not loved her,
You will not understand—
Though earth holds many
splendours,
Wherever I may die,
I know to what brown country
My homing thoughts will fly!

A national capital for Australia

AN ACT TO DETERMINE THE SEAT OF GOVERNMENT OF THE COMMONWEALTH

When plans were being formulated for the new Australian Commonwealth in the 1890s, one of the potential points of conflict—the selection and location of a seat of government—was avoided by a compromise defined within the Constitution itself. Since neither New South Wales nor Victoria was willing for the other to have the national capital in the cities of Sydney or Melbourne, politicians provided an arrangement determined as much by expediency as by the idealism that later informed the building of Canberra as a model city. Section 125 of the Constitution provided for the placement of a new federal capital within territory to be granted or acquired within New South Wales but sited not less than 100 miles from Sydney. This section of the act also provided for the Commonwealth to conduct its affairs in Melbourne until such time as Parliament could meet at the new seat of government.

While the Commonwealth soon turned its attention to the question of choosing a site for the new capital, the issue would not be resolved until 1909. In 1902 a Capital Sites Enquiry Board inspected several potential sites, which led in 1903 to the tabling of the first Seat of Government Bill that resulted in a vote for the Snowy Mountains town of Tumut. This aroused strong public criticism, and also led to a deadlock in Parliament, with the Senate favouring Bombala on the south coast and the House of Representatives continuing to support the choice of Tumut. With the lapse of the 1903 bill, the matter was brought forward again in 1904. On this occasion the bill was passed into law as the *Seat of Government Act 1904*, with the town of Dalgety named as the chosen site.

Subsequently, negotiations with New South Wales were impeded by a disagreement concerning the size of the proposed federal territory. The Commonwealth then removed Dalgety from the list of acceptable sites and agreed to review other choices, including Yass–Canberra in the Monaro district of New South Wales. Further delays occurred in protracted negotiations with New South Wales, in the difficult process of evaluating other sites and in strategies for advancing the matter within the uncertain political flux of the early Commonwealth Parliament, where governments were short-lived. The matter finally reached its legislative resolution in 1908, though work was still to be done on the best siting of the new capital city within the Yass–Canberra district that was now specified in the act as the location of the future capital. Viewed with the knowledge of history and of fulfilment, founding documents can surprise with their modesty. So it is with the Act to determine the Seat of Government of the Commonwealth: in Australian fashion, it is prosaic—a piece of legislative machinery. It does its business in workmanlike style without any flourishes and without any statement of ambition or aspiration.

The question of a name for Australia's new city was not resolved until 1913, when Lady Denman, the wife of the governor-general, declared: 'I name the capital of Australia Canberra'. For years Canberra was derided as 'the bush capital'. Visitors remain bemused by the lack of a discernible metropolitan presence and the mix of national monuments against a backdrop of dormitory suburbs and car parks, pockets of bushland and remnant pastures surviving from the days when Canberra was little more than a sheep run. And yet, as urban historian Graeme Davison has commented, Canberra is the most affluent, best-planned and best-educated city in Australia. These are the inevitable consequences of the power Canberra has come to exercise over the lives of all Australians. In Davison's observation, 'no other Australian city is visited more religiously, admired more grudgingly, or reviled more unreasoningly. Once a symbol of national ideals, it is also, for some, a symbol of national disenchantment.'

An Act to determine the Seat of Government of the Commonwealth.

[Assented to 14th August 1908]

Be it enacted by the King's Most Excellent Majesty, the Senate and the House of Representatives of the Commonwealth of Australia, as follows:—

1. This Act may be cited as the *Seat of Government Act* 1908.
2. The *Seat of Government Act* 1904 is hereby repealed.
3. It is hereby determined that the Seat of Government of the Commonwealth shall be in the district of Yass–Canberra in the State of New South Wales.
4. The territory to be granted to or acquired by the Commonwealth for the Seat of Government shall contain an area not less that nine hundred square miles, and have access to the sea.
5. — (1.) Any person thereto authorized in writing by the Minister may, for the purposes of any survey of land with a view to ascertaining the territory proper to be granted to or acquired by the Commonwealth for the Seat of Government, enter upon and remain on any lands whether Crown lands of the State of New South Wales or not, and do thereon all things for the purposes of the survey, and shall do no more damage than is necessary.

(2.) The Commonwealth shall, out of moneys appropriated for the purpose, make compensation for any damage done to the property of any person in the exercise of powers conferred by this section.

6. The amount of compensation to be paid by the Commonwealth for any land to be acquired by the Commonwealth within the territory granted to or acquired by the Commonwealth for the Seat of Government shall not exceed the value of the land on the eighth day of October One thousand nine hundred and eight, and in other respects the provisions of the *Lands Acquisition Act* 1906 shall apply to the acquisition of the land.

ABOVE *Charles Coulter's 1901 watercolour,* An ideal federal city, Lake George, NSW, *features Lake George filled with water.*

An Act to determine the Seat of Government of the Commonwealth

Australia in Antarctica

DOUGLAS MAWSON'S AMBITIONS FOR THE ANTARCTIC EXPEDITION OF 1911–14

The Australasian Antarctic Expedition of 1911–14 falls within what is known as the heroic age of Antarctic exploration and stands as a landmark in Australia's efforts to explore the sub-Antarctic and Antarctic regions, to claim new lands for the British Empire and to establish a significant Australian presence on the Antarctic mainland.

The expedition was vigorously promoted by its leader, the young Australian scientist Douglas Mawson (1882–1958), as both an imperial and an Australasian venture. Mawson personally conducted a campaign of letter writing, meetings with political leaders and public addresses to raise funds for the expedition in England, throughout Australia and in New Zealand. In a stream of letters to scientific leaders, press barons and politicians, Mawson conveyed a persuasive enthusiasm for his enterprise; he was adept in constructing arguments to appeal to the sometimes different interests of those from whom he sought financial backing. Even so, some of his appeals for funds were unsuccessful. Queensland, Western Australia and New Zealand were unmoved by his eloquence, but private backers included such figures as Australian businessmen Samuel Hordern and Robert Barr Smith, Governor-General Lord Denman and opera singer Nellie Melba.

Mawson's passion for the Antarctic had begun during his first visit to the continent with the British expedition led by Ernest Shackleton in 1907–09, when he had been among the first to scale Mt Erebus and to sledge to the South Magnetic Pole. Thereafter he became not only a powerful advocate for his own great enterprise of 1911–14, but also a driving force for the rest of his life in the expansion and consolidation of Australia's interests in Antarctica. In this document Mawson lists his key points in making the case for Australian support for the expedition of 1911–14. This summary—urgent, visionary and patriotic—was the basis of Mawson's many fundraising addresses and also informed the many long letters he wrote to advance his cause.

Mawson's expedition was a feat of human endeavour carried out in the harshest physical conditions and marked by the tragic loss of some of its participants. The survival of Mawson himself was nothing short of remarkable. It is that human record that stands as the most accessible story of the expedition. But the achievements, too, are significant. The new regions explored and claimed formed the precedents for the establishment of the Australian Antarctic Territory, which was formally proclaimed in 1936, and much valuable scientific data was accumulated. Honouring the venture, Mawson's leadership, and the achievements of Mawson and his party, the original expedition base camp and its immediate surrounds have been placed on the Australian Heritage Commission's Register of the National Estate. And, remarkably, as Mawson predicted, Antarctica has become a destination for tourists.

ABOVE *Douglas Mawson sitting on the rail of the Aurora, 1911.*

I   The Expedition is an Australasian scientific effort.

II   It will advance & stimulate science throughout Australasia.

III   It has National and Imperial aspects advancing Australia in the world's estimation.

IV   It will stimulate enterprise in young Australians reviving the spirit of discovery which laid the foundations of the British Empire and to which the State of Queensland certainly owes everything.

V   We ask to take possession of the new Land for the Empire—the Empire has for all time helped us—now surely it will be a fair return for us to help the Empire.

VI   There is a considerable prospect of a commercial future for the Australian Quadrant of the Antarctic Continent—sealing, whaling, fisheries, minerals etc. The whole of the food supplies and equipment for such Antarctic settlement will come from Australasia and will therefore be a source of wealth to Australia.

VII   A meteorological station on the Antarctic coastline adjacent to Australia will certainly be of value in weather predictions in Australia.

VIII The Antarctic shores are sure to be the scene of summer tourist visits & sanitoria before long.

IX   An unknown sea and an unknown land lies at our very doors. Surely this stigma on an enlightened 20th century is sufficient for us to unite in clearing away reproach.

X   Our magnetic observations will complete the South Magnetic Pole problem and earmark that as an Australian achievement.

XI   The oceanographic and magnetic survey will be of direct practical benefit to shipping in Australasian waters.

XII   The development of an Antarctic whaling & sealing industry will lead to the building of a hardy class of seamen to whom may be looked recruits to the Australian navy.

XIII Our collections will be of practical benefit to our museums.

Douglas Mawson's ambitions for the Antarctic expedition of 1911–14

The birth of the Anzac legend

THE FIRST PUBLISHED ACCOUNT OF THE ANZAC LANDING

The news of the landing on Gallipoli by men of the Australian and New Zealand Army Corps (Anzac) on 25 April 1915 was delayed by the censors for four days for security reasons. But as soon as the objectives of the operation became known—the capture of the Dardanelles and the intimidation of Germany's ally Turkey—and as soon as the casualty lists began to appear in the press, praise began to flow from political leaders in Australia, New Zealand and Britain for the gallantry and skill of the troops in their first encounter with a brave and tenacious enemy. It quickly became apparent that in their 'baptism of fire', the Australians and New Zealanders had performed with exceptional valour and courage. For all the tragedy and waste caused by the larger strategic failure of the Gallipoli campaign, it has long been accepted that the feats of the Australians and New Zealanders in April 1915 brought credit and distinction to both their countries and marked for each a national coming of age.

As it turned out, the first comprehensive report in Australia of the Anzac landing was made, not by the nation's own correspondent C.E.W. Bean (1879–1968), but by an Englishman, the experienced journalist Ellis Ashmead-Bartlett (1881–1931). Bean's report had been held up pending his formal accreditation to report from Gallipoli, and his account of the landing did not appear in the Australian press until some time later. At the time of Ashmead-Bartlett's death in 1931, Bean wrote in tribute that 'the tradition of the Anzac landing is probably more influenced by that first story than by all the other accounts that have since been written'.

Ashmead-Bartlett's account was reported in England before it appeared in Australia on 8 May 1915, when the story was published in the *Sydney Morning Herald* and in the two Melbourne dailies, the *Age* and the *Argus*. The story carried immense authority. Ashmead-Bartlett was a senior journalist with experience of several other conflicts, including the Boer War in South Africa in 1901 and the Russo-Japanese war of 1904. In 1912–13 he covered the Balkan wars for the *Daily Telegraph* in London, and it was through that assignment that he obtained his official accreditation for the campaign in the Dardanelles. For the rest of his life, Ashmead-Bartlett continued to pay honour to the courage and skill of the Anzac troops he had observed at close quarters in 1915. His written account of the landing is complemented by a film he made, which provides the only moving picture of the campaign.

The Australian press gave generous space to Ashmead-Bartlett's account, immediately recognising that the Australian and New Zealand soldiers had indeed made a remarkable debut. On the morning of 8 May the *Sydney Morning Herald* announced the 'Glorious Entry into War' by the Australasians, while drawing the attention of its readers to the praise expressed by Ashmead-Bartlett that 'there has been no finer feat of arms in this war than that of the Colonial troops'. On 12 May, when the *Hobart Mercury* published Ashmead-Bartlett's account (the version printed here), its praise for the Australian achievement was absolute. Its headline reported that the Australians had covered themselves with glory. The account by Ellis Ashmead-Bartlett marks the beginning of the shared Australian and New Zealand veneration of the Anzacs that continues to be expressed in both countries in their respective national Anzac Day commemorations.

At 2 o'clock on April 24 the flagship of the division conveying the Australians and New Zealanders passed down the long line of slowly-moving transports, amid tremendous cheering and was played out of the bay by the French warship.

At 4 o'clock the ship's company and troops on board assembled to hear the admiral's proclamation to the combined force. This was followed by the last service before the battle, in which the chaplain uttered a prayer for victory, and besought the Divine blessing for the expedition, all the men standing with uncovered, bowed heads.

At dark all the lights were put out, and the troops rested for their ordeal at dawn. It was a beautiful calm night, with a bright half-moon.

By 1 o'clock in the morning the ships reached their rendezvous, five miles from the intended landing place. The soldiers were aroused, and served with their last hot meal before landing. The Australians, who were about to go into action for the first time under trying circumstances, were cheerful, quiet, and confident, and there was no sign of nerves or excitement.

As the moon waned, the boats were swung out. The Australians received their last instructions, and these men who only six months ago were living peaceful, civilian lives, began to disembark on a strange, unknown shore, and in a strange land to attack an enemy of a different race …

At 3 o'clock it was quite dark, and a start was made towards the shore with suppressed excitement. Would the enemy be surprised or be on the alert?

At 4 o'clock three battleships, line abreast and four cables apart, arrived 2,500 yards from the shore, with their guns manned and their searchlights in readiness. Very slowly, the boats in tow, like twelve great snakes, moved towards the shore. Each edged towards each other in order to reach the beach four cables apart. The battleships moved in after them until the water shallowed. Every eye was fixed on the grim line of hills in front, menacing in the gloom, and the mysteries of which those in the boats were about to solve.

Not a sound was heard, not a light seen, and it appeared as if the enemy had been surprised. In our nervy state the stars often were mistaken for lights ashore.

The progress of the boats was slow, and dawn was rapidly breaking at 4.50 when the enemy showed alarm for a light which had flashed for ten minutes and then disappeared. The boats appeared almost like one on the beach. Seven torpedo-boat destroyers then glided noiselessly towards the shore.

At 4.53 came a sharp burst of rifle fire from the beach. The sound relieved the prolonged suspense which had become almost intolerable. The rifle fire lasted a few minutes, and a faint British cheer came over the waters, telling that the first position was won.

At three minutes past 5 the fire was intensified. By the sound of the reports we could tell our men were in action. The firing lasted for twenty three minutes, and then died down somewhat …

The Australians rose to the occasion. They did not wait for orders, or for the boats to reach the beach, but sprang into the sea, formed a sort of rough line, and rushed at the enemy's trenches. Their magazines were not charged, so they just went in with the cold steel, and it was over in a minute for the Turks in the first trench had either been bayoneted or had run away, and the Maxim guns were captured.

Then the Australians found themselves facing an almost perpendicular cliff of loose sandstone covered with thick shrubbery. Somewhere half-way up the enemy had a second trench, strongly held, from which there poured a terrible fire on the troops below and on those pulling back to the torpedo-boat destroyers for a second landing party.

Here was a tough proposition to tackle in the darkness, but these Colonials are practical above all else, and went about it in a practical way. They stopped for a few minutes to pull themselves together, got rid of their packs, and charged the magazines of their rifles. Then this race of athletes proceeded to scale the cliffs, without responding to the enemy's fire. They lost some men, but did not worry. In less than a quarter of an hour the Turks had been hurled out of their second position, all either bayoneted or fled.

As daylight came it was seen that the landing had been effected rather further north of Gaba Tepe than had originally been intended, and at a point where the cliffs rise very sheer. The error was a blessing in disguise, for there were no places down which the enemy could fire, and the broken ground afforded good cover once the Australians had passed the forty yards of the flat beach.

The country in the vicinity of the landing looked formidable and forbidding. To the sea it presents a steep front, broken into innumerable ridges, bluffs, valleys, and sandpits, rising to a height of several hundred feet. The surface is bare, crumbly sandstone, covered with shrubbery about six feet in height.

It is an ideal place for snipers, as the Australians and New Zealanders soon found to their cost. On the other hand, the Colonials proved themselves adept at this kind of warfare ...

When the sun had fully risen we could see that the Australians and New Zealanders had actually established themselves on the ridge, and were trying to work their way northward along it. The fighting was so confused and occurred on such broken ground that it was difficult to follow exactly what had happened on the 25th April, but the task of the covering forces had been so splendidly carried out that the Turks allowed the disembarkation of the remainder to proceed uninterruptedly, except for the never-ceasing sniping. But then the Australians, whose blood was up, instead of entrenching, rushed to the northwards and to the eastwards searching for fresh enemies to bayonet. It was very difficult country in which to entrench, and they therefore preferred to advance.

The Turks only had a weak force actually holding the beach, and relied on the difficult ground and the snipers to delay the advance until reinforcement came. Some of the Australians and New Zealanders who pushed inland were counter-attacked and almost outflanked by oncoming reserves, and had to fall back after suffering heavy losses.

The Turks continued to counter-attack the whole of the afternoon, but the Colonials did not yield a foot on the main ridge.

Reinforcements poured up from the beach, but the Turks enfiladed the beach with two field guns from Gaba Tepe. This shrapnel fire was incessant and deadly, and the warships vainly for some hours tried to silence it.

The majority of the heavy casualties received during the day were from shrapnel which swept the beach and ridge where the Australians had established themselves. Later in the day the Turkish guns were silenced or forced to withdraw, and a cruiser, moving close in shore plastered Gaba Tepe with a hail of shell.

Towards dusk the attacks became more vigorous. The enemy were supported by powerful artillery inland which the ships' guns were powerless to deal with. The pressure on the Australians became heavier, and their lines had been contracted ...

Some idea of the difficulties in the way can be gathered when it is remembered that every round of ammunition and all the water and stores had to be landed on a narrow beach, and carried up pathless hills and valleys several hundred feet high to the firing line. The whole of the troops were concentrated upon a very small area, and were unable to reply, though exposed to a relentless and incessant shrapnel fire, which swept every yard of ground ...

The most serious problem was the getting of the wounded to the shore for all those unable to hobble had to be carried from the hills on stretchers; then their wounds were hastily dressed, and they were carried to the boats.

The boat parties worked unceasingly the entire day and night.

The courage displayed by these wounded Australians and New Zealanders will never be forgotten. Hastily placed in trawlers, lighters or boats, they were towed to the ships, and, in spite of their sufferings, they cheered the ship from which they had set out in the morning.

In fact, I have never seen anything like these wounded Colonials in war before.

Though many were shot to bits, and without hope of recovery, their cheers resounded throughout the night and you could see in the midst of a mass of suffering humanity arms waving in greeting to the crews of the warships. They were happy because they knew they had been tried for the first time, and had not been found wanting.

For 15 mortal hours the Australians and New Zealanders occupied the heights under an incessant shell fire, and without the moral and material support of a single gun from the shore. They were subjected the whole time to violent counter-attacks from a brave enemy, skillfully led, and with snipers deliberately picking off every officer who endeavoured to give the command or to lead his men. No finer feat has happened in this war than this sudden landing in the dark, and the storming of the heights, and, above all, the holding on whilst the reinforcements were landing. These raw colonial troops, in these desperate hours, proved worthy to fight side by side with the heroes of the battles of Mons, the Aisne, Ypres, and Neuve Chapelle.

Early on the morning of April 26 the Turks repeatedly tried to drive the Colonials from their position. The latter made local counter-attacks, and drove off the enemy with the bayonet, which the Turks will never face ...

The first published account of the Anzac landing

ABOVE *Captain Leslie Morehead of the 2nd Battalion surveys the bodies of Australian and Turkish soldiers on the parapet of a trench at Lone Pine.*

'one of the most terrible chapters in our history'

KEITH MURDOCH'S LETTER TO PRIME MINISTER ANDREW FISHER

While the experience of the Australian soldiers at Gallipoli in 1915 has been invested with almost mystical significance and is honoured in the national commemoration of Anzac Day, the landing itself foundered and ended in the evacuation of the peninsula after an occupation of eight months. Although the Anzacs had performed heroically in establishing a toehold on the ridges above Anzac Cove, they were unable to make much progress towards the strategic objective of winning the summit and capturing the Turkish gun emplacements protecting the Dardanelles: some remarkable gains were made but there were some terrible losses. Defending home soil, the Turks were tenacious and had the advantage in managing an unfavourable terrain, but the campaign was also handicapped by failings in the British High Command and the lack of resources—both men and equipment.

Influential in exposing the flawed campaign in the Dardanelles was a long letter written by the Australian journalist Keith Murdoch (1885–1952) to the Australian prime minister, Andrew Fisher, on 23 September 1915. Murdoch—later a newspaper proprietor and founder of a media dynasty—was a correspondent with the Melbourne *Sun* when he was narrowly defeated by C.E.W. Bean in an Australian Journalists' Association ballot to be appointed an official Australian war correspondent. But when he travelled to London in 1915, he agreed to a request by Andrew Fisher and the minister of defence, George Pearce, to investigate Australian Imperial Force mail services and other matters.

On his journey, Murdoch visited Gallipoli where, over the course of four days, he was gravely disturbed by what he saw and heard about the management and direction of the campaign. In this he was much influenced by the views of the British journalist Ellis Ashmead-Bartlett, who had asked him to carry a secret letter addressed to the British prime minister setting out detailed criticisms of the incompetence and amateurism of the British command. Before it could be delivered, however, the letter was seized at Marseilles by a British army officer. Continuing his journey, Murdoch composed his own 8000-word letter with an account of 'the unfortunate Dardanelles expedition ... undoubtedly one of the most terrible chapters in our history', though he lavished praise on the Australian soldiers for their spirit and their triumph in adversity.

Murdoch's letter was not without its errors of fact and exaggeration, and nor was it the only criticism then being made of General Sir Ian Hamilton, the British commander-in-chief. In London, however, Murdoch's views gained considerable attention and were taken seriously. He was able to present his criticisms in person to several cabinet ministers and his letter was printed as a secret state paper and circulated to the members of the Committee of Imperial Defence.

In a private reflection in 1933 Murdoch admitted and regretted the mistakes he had made in the letter, but he stood by the essence of his account. In this he was vindicated by the consensus that the British command had failed on the ground and that, notwithstanding the larger strategic ambitions of the campaign in the Dardanelles, the investment of resources had been inadequate to the task at hand. It was this situation that Murdoch addressed and in this he was both persuasive and effective. In the letter itself he made no direct case for an evacuation, though he put this view forward in his meetings with British cabinet ministers. The criticisms in his letter, though sometimes impressionistic and anecdotal, have overall the force of witness, and on the failings of the command they are damning. In his official Australian history of the 1914–18 war, C.E.W. Bean later judged the letter as containing 'important truths'.

High Commissioner's Office,
London.
September 23, 1915.
Dear Mr. Fisher,

... I now write of the unfortunate Dardanelles expedition, in the light of the knowledge I could gain on the spot, on the lines of communication, and in Egypt.

It is undoubtedly one of the most terrible chapters in our history. Your fears have been justified. I have not military knowledge to be able to say whether the enterprise ever had a chance of succeeding. Certainly there has been a series of disastrous underestimations, and I think our Australian generals are right when they say, that had any one of these been luckily so unEnglish a thing as an overestimation, we should have been through to Constantinople at much less cost than we have paid for our slender perch on the cliffs of the Peninsula ...

I visited most parts of Anzac and Suvla Bay positions, walked many miles through the trenches, conversed with the leaders and what senior and junior officers I could reach, and was favoured in all parts with full and frank confidence. I could not visit Helles, where we have about 25,000 men and many animals and cars ... We have abandoned our intentions of taking Achi Baba by frontal assault. This was always a hopeless scheme, after early May, and no one can understand why Hamilton persisted with it. Achi Baba is a gradual, bare slope, a mass of trenches and gun emplacements, but so little did the General Staff know of its task that it expected to storm it with ease ...

A strong advance inland from Anzac has never been attempted. It is broken, rough, scrubby country, full of gullies and sharp ridges, and it is all within easy range of the guns of the Turkish forts at the Narrows, and their artillery on Achi Baba and round about. No serious advance could be made direct inland from this quarter. Our men I found immensely proud of their little progress on the plateau on our right—Lone Pine Plateau ... But I found that we had paid 2500 men for this advance, on a short front, of 300 yards! That is the only sort of advance we can make from Anzac proper.

Suvla Bay is a shallow, open indentation in the thickest part of the peninsula, about two miles and a half to the left of Anzac. The flat country leading from the beach consists mostly of a marsh called Bitter Lake, which in winter becomes a great morass. After heavy rains the flat is inundated.

On this flat in August nearly 90,000 men were landed. They were New Army and Territorial divisions. They had spent a fortnight on the water in transports which even the most careful arrangements could not make wholesome. I was on the lower deck on one of these, and the place was putrid. The men could not be allowed on shore at ports of call.

You can imagine, then, that these fresh, raw, untried troops, under amateur officers, homesick and apprehensive, were under normal in morale when the day of the landing approached. They had to be packed like sardines on the trawlers and small destroyers and vessels for the actual landing, and were kept like this for most of an afternoon and the whole of a night. Before this embarkation, they had each received three days' supply of iron rations—

biscuits and bully beef—and had filled their water bottles—one bottle to each man ...

I do not say that better arrangements could have been made. But I do say that in the first place to send raw, young recruits on the perilous enterprise was to court disaster ...

The landing was unopposed; the Turks were taken completely by surprise. But with great celerity they galloped their artillery round, and opened fire also from their forts. Before the new troops had advanced any distance they were being racked with shell fire.

I am informed by many officers that one division went ashore without any orders whatsoever. Another division, to which had been allotted the essential work of occupying the Anafarta Hills, were marched far to the left before the mistake in direction was noticed. It was then recalled, and reformed, and sent off towards the ridge. As a practical man, how much water do you think would be left in these thirsty English boys' bottles by this time—after the night on the seas, and the hot march out, march back and advance? Of course, not a drop. And yet the staff professes surprise that before noon the men were weak for want of water. The whole army suffered intensely from thirst during the next three days. There were many deaths from thirst ...

I am of course only repeating what I have been told on all hands. But you will trust me when I say that the work of the general staff in Gallipoli has been deplorable ...

Perhaps this awful defeat of August 6–10, in which our Imperial armies lost 35 per cent. of their strength—fully 33,000 men—was due as much to inferior troops as to any other cause. But that cannot be said of the desperate effort made on August 21, after the Turks had had plenty of time in which to bring up strong reinforcements and to increase the natural strength of their positions, to take their positions by frontal assault. Some of the finest forces on the Peninsula were used in this bloody battle ... They and other troops were dashed against the Turkish lines, and broken. They never had a chance of holding their positions when for one brief hour they pierced the Turks' first line: and the slaughter of fine youth was appalling. My criticism is that, as these troops were available, they should undoubtedly have been used in early August; and to fling them, without even the element of surprise, against such trenches as the Turks make, was murder ...

We have to face ... the frightful weakening effect of sickness. Already the flies are spreading dysentery to an alarming extent, and the sick rate would astonish you. It cannot be less than 600 a day. We must be evacuating fully 1000 sick and wounded men every day. When the autumn rains come and unbury our dead, now lying under a light soil in our trenches, sickness must increase. Even now the stench in many of our trenches is sickening. Alas, the good human stuff that there lies buried, the brave hearts still, the sorrow in our hard-hit Australian households.

Supposing we lose only 30,000 during winter from sickness. That means that when spring comes we shall have about 60,000 men left. But they will not be an army. They will be a broken force spent. A winter in Gallipoli will be a winter under severe strain, under shell fire, under the expectation of attack, and in the anguish which is inescapable on this shell-torn spot. The troops will in reality be on guard throughout the winter. They will stand to arms throughout long and bitter nights. Nothing can be expected from them when at last the normal fighting days come again. The new offensive must then be made with a huge army of new troops. Can we get them? Already the complaint in France is that we cannot fill the gaps, that after an advance our thinned ranks cannot be replenished.

But I am not a pessimist, and if there is really a military necessity for this awful ordeal, then I am sure the Australian troops will face it. Indeed, anxious as they are to leave the dreary and sombre scene of their wreckage, the Australian divisions would strongly resent the confession of failure that a withdrawal would entail. They are dispirited, they have been through such warfare as no army has yet seen in any part of the world, but they are game to the end.

On the high political question of whether good is to be served by keeping the armies in Gallipoli, I can say little, for I am uninformed. Cabinet Ministers here impress me with the fact that a failure in the Dardanelles would have most serious results in India. Persia is giving endless trouble, and there seems to be little doubt that India is ripe for trouble. Nor do I know whether the appalling outlay in money on the Dardanelles expedition, with its huge and costly line of communications, can be allowed to continue without endangering those financial resources on which we rely to so great an extent in the wearing down of Germany's strength …

You would have wept with Hughes and myself if you had gone with us over the ground where two of our finest Light Horse regiments were wiped out in ten minutes in a brave effort to advance to Dead Man's Ridge. We lost five hundred men, squatter's sons and farmer's sons, on that terrible spot. Such is the cost of so much as looking out over the top of our trenches.

And now one word about the troops. No one who sees them at work in trenches and on beaches and in saps can doubt their morale is very severely shaken indeed. It is far worse at Suvla, although the men there are only two months from home, than anywhere else. The spirit at Suvla is simply deplorable. The men have no confidence in the staff, and to tell the truth they have little confidence in London … All the new army is still clothed in tropical uniforms, and when I left, London was still sending out drafts in thin "shorts". Everywhere one encountered the same fear that the armies would be left to their fate, and that the many shipments of materials, food and clothing required for winter would not be despatched until the weather made their landing impossible. This lack of confidence in the authorities arises principally from the fact that every man knows that the last operations were grossly bungled by the general staff, and that Hamilton has led a series of armies into a series of cul-de-sacs. You would hardly believe the evidence of your own eyes at Suvla. You would refuse to believe that these men were really British soldiers. So badly shaken are they by their miserable defeats and by their surroundings, so physically affected are they by the lack of water and the monotony of a salt beef and rice diet, that they show an atrophy of mind and body that is appalling. I must confess that in our own trenches, where our men have been kept on guard for abnormally long periods, I saw the same terrible atrophy. You can understand how it arises. It is like the look of a tortured dumb animal. Men living in trenches with no movement except when they are digging, and with nothing to look at except a narrow strip of sky and the blank walls of their prisons, cannot remain cheerful or even thoughtful. Perhaps some efforts could have been made by the War Office to provide them with cinemas, or entertainments, but of course Gallipoli is at the end of a long and costly, not to say dangerous, line of communications ...

At Anzac the morale is good. The men are thoroughly dispirited, except the new arrivals. They are weakened sadly by dysentery and illness. They have been overworked, through lack of reinforcements. And as an army of offence they are done. Not one step can be made with the First Australian division until it has been completely rested and refitted ...

But I could pour into your ears so much truth about the grandeur of our Australian army, and the wonderful affection of these fine young soldiers for each other and their homeland, that your Australianism would become a more powerful sentiment than before. It is stirring to see them, magnificent manhood, swinging their fine limbs as they walk about Anzac. They have the noble faces of men who have endured. Oh, if you could picture Anzac as I have seen it, you would find that to be an Australian is the greatest privilege the world has to offer ...

We are lucky in these men. But for the general staff, and I fear for Hamilton, officers and men have nothing but contempt. They express it fearlessly. That however is not peculiar to Anzac. Sedition is talked round every tin of bully beef on the peninsula, and it is only loyalty that holds the forces together. Every returning troopship, every section of the line of communications, is full of the same talk. I like General Hamilton, and found him exceedingly kindly ... But as a strategist he has completely failed. Undoubtedly, the essential and first step to restore morale of the shaken forces is to recall him and his Chief of Staff ...

What I want to say to you now very seriously is that the continuous and ghastly bungling over the Dardanelles enterprise was to be expected from such a General Staff as the British Army possesses, so far as I have seen it. The conceit and complacency of the red feather men are equalled only by their incapacity. Along the lines of communications ... are countless high officers and conceited young cubs who are plainly only playing at war. What can you expect of men who have never worked seriously, who have lived for their appearance and for social distinction and selfsatisfaction, and who are now called on to conduct a gigantic war? ...

You will think that all this is a very sorry picture, but do not forget that the enemy has his troubles, and that we have certain signs that his morale is deteriorating. From what I saw of the Turk I am convinced that he is a brave and generous foe, and he is fighting now for dear home, with a feeling that he is winning, and that he is a better man than those opposed to him. The Turks by the way are as generous in their praise of our men as the British and the French are. Certainly the Turks are positively afraid of our men, and one of their trenches—that opposite Quinn's Post—is such a place of fear, owing to the indomitable way in which our snipers and bomb-throwers have got their men down, that Turks will not go into it unless they are made corporals ...

I hope I have not made the picture too gloomy. I have great faith still in the Englishman ... But this unfortunate expedition has never been given a chance. It required large bodies of seasoned troops. It required a great leader. It required self-sacrifice on the part of the staff as well as that sacrifice so wonderfully and liberally made on the part of the soldiers. It has none of these things. Its troops have been second class, because untried before their awful battles and privations of the peninsula. And behind it all is a gross selfishness and complacency on the part of the staff.

Much more I could tell you, but my task is done ... This of course is a private letter ... so I shall say nothing more than the plain goodbye of a friend.

Sincerely yours

Keith Murdoch

From small beginnings to a mighty solemnisation

JOHN MONASH DESCRIBES THE FIRST ANZAC DAY

Anzac Day is celebrated in Australia as the nation's most emotionally charged public holiday. As it has evolved over the years, its purpose is to commemorate the country's war dead and to pay homage to the veterans of war. The origin of this national observance was the heroic but strategically doomed landing by the men of the Australian and New Zealand Army Corps at Gallipoli, in Turkey, on 25 April 1915. It has often been said that Australia 'came of age' as a nation at Gallipoli.

The first anniversary of the landing, in 1916, was widely observed in Australia, where the grief from the nation's losses was keenly felt and compounded by the absence of those still serving abroad. From the outset, the commemoration was officially designated as Anzac Day, but neither the Commonwealth nor state governments played a direct part in the commemorations of the early years or in the first observance on home soil. Instead, the first Anzac Day at home was spontaneously marked by the people themselves, as large crowds turned out for church services and public ceremonies. In Sydney alone 60,000 to 100,000 people were estimated to have assembled in the Domain. The mood of the day there mixed commemoration with celebration. Some worried that this blending of elements struck the wrong note—so much so that Sydney's *Truth* newspaper asked whether it was appropriate 'to hold a picnic o'er Australia's war dead'.

No such agonising took place in the Australian encampment at Serapeum in Egypt, where many of the survivors of the Gallipoli landing joined in a lively commemoration of the first Anzac Day. As Brigadier-General John Monash (1865–1931) testified in a letter written home to his wife in Melbourne, the first celebration of 'Anzac day' was indeed a gala occasion. Without effort or pomposity, it assumed a character of its own, complete with a comic skit 'on the memorable landing'. Monash himself was one of the select company of those who had survived the Dardanelles campaign, and it is clear that he took a special pride in the distinctive unfolding of the celebration he called 'Our Day'. In civilian life at home, he would later remark on the growth of Anzac Day 'year by year from small beginnings to a mighty solemnisation'. But as in the first observation in 1916, Australians have carried forward into their Anzac Days a unique mixture of solemnity, celebration and festiveness that is very much a reflection of the national character.

ABOVE *Brigadier-General John Monash, photographed on 13 August 1916.*

Now I must tell you about the celebration of "Anzac day" yesterday.—I turned out the whole Brigade, with all attached Units, at 6.45 in the morning.—Every man who had served on Gallipoli wore a blue ribbon on the right breast, & every man, who, in addition had taken part in the historic landing on April 25/15 wore a red ribbon also.—I am enclosing mine to you, as a Keepsake.— Alas, how few of us are left who were entitled to wear both!—We then had a short but very dignified Service, ending with a fine stirring address by Chaplain Lt. Col. Wray, (who landed with us).—Then the massed bands of the Brigade played "The Dead March in Saul" while the parade stood to attention, & then the massed buglers blew the "Last Post"—For the rest of the day, everyone was given a whole holiday.—We spent the morning in cricket matches & other amusements, & in the afternoon, the whole Division went down to the Canal to swim & take part in a great Aquatic Carnival. I enclose the programme.—From the Serapeum pontoon bridge, both sloping banks of the Suez Canal for fully a mile north, was one teeming mass of naked humanity—at times there were over 15,000 men in the water, & whenever the judges' launch tooted to notify that the course must be cleared, the scamper to the banks was a sight worth seeing & remembering. Of course we had many comic items not on the programme, including a skit on the memorable landing—by a freak destroyer manned by a lot of cork blackfellows hauling ashore a number of tiny tin boats full of tiny tin soldiers. It was screamingly funny.—The judges had a busy, splashy, time & the contests were fine.— Godley & his staff came down from Ismailia, & about 5, HRH came up in his little pinnace from Suez where he had been spending the day, & stayed an hour with us, heartily enjoying the fun, & the afternoon tea, & the ovation of cheers the men gave him wherever he went.—The whole thing was a very unique spectacle under very unique circumstances, & many of us wished our folks at home could have seen it.—We also sent cables to 5th Division, to Birdwood, & to 1st Anzac in France.—In the evening we had mess dinners everywhere, & finished up with band contests, and wished each other the opportunity of enjoying many happy returns of the famous Day—*Our Day*.

'the burden falls as equally as possible on everyone'

THE PREMIERS' PLAN

By the late autumn of 1931, with the world financial depression tightening its grip on the country, the leaders of the Commonwealth and state governments met in conference at Parliament House in Melbourne to consider the latest in a series of plans to solve the financial crisis. Like governments everywhere, Australia was suffering the flow-on effects of the American share market crash of October 1929. But Australia was also carrying the liabilities of a substantial trade deficit and heavy overseas borrowings, so the country was not well placed to withstand the ravages of the world-wide economic catastrophe.

With pressure mounting on the Labor prime minister, James Scullin (1876–1953), to default on overseas short-term debt—a solution he opposed—and with unemployment rising, the country was in a state of near panic. Riots had broken out in Western Australia, while across the country some 200,000 men employed on public works had lost their jobs as the flow of loan moneys from London ceased. Historian Erik Eklund wrote in 2009 of 'the growing fears, real and imagined, of social and political breakdown'.

In May–June 1931 Prime Minister Scullin and the state premiers gathered in Melbourne to negotiate a nationally coordinated solution to the crisis. The result was the so-called Premiers' Plan, developed on the basis of recommendations made by a cohort of Australian economists led by economist Douglas Copland (1894–1971), whose overriding aim was the restoration of financial stability. Details of the plan were published in newspapers on 11 June 1931.

The prescription offered by the economists was draconian, involving reductions in interest rates and heavy cuts to expenditure, to be achieved through slashing public sector salaries and wages, together with matching reductions in age and war pensions. With an economist's logic, Copland claimed the plan offered 'a judicious mixture of inflation and deflation', but it was left to the politicians to undertake the difficult task of selling the plan through the slogan 'equality of sacrifice'.

While mainstream political opinion gathered in its support, the Premiers' Plan was bitterly opposed by radical groups on both the left and right. The left saw those most vulnerable cruelly exposed to the machinations of the capitalist system. The right resented a perceived threat to the sanctity of private property. At the extreme, movements such as the New Guard and the All for Australia League saw a brief flirtation with fascism. These extremes opened an ugly divide in Australian politics that was slow to heal and to reconcile, while the Depression itself cast its own long shadow on the lives of Australians. As a prescription for illness, the Premiers' Plan offered much pain of its own, relying—perhaps over-heavily—on deflationary policies, which slowed recovery and impeded confidence. Nevertheless, the plan was endorsed at the election of 1931, though seven ministers were defeated in their own seats.

The Governments of Australia have met in conference to consider what measures are possible to restore solvency and to avoid default. The national income was £650,000,000 in 1927–28. It fell to £564,000,000 in 1929–30, and a further fall to £450,000,000 in 1931–32 is estimated. This has re-acted on Government finance.

The total deficit of the seven Australian Governments will be £31,000,000 for the present financial year. The Governments are now going behind at the rate of £40,000,000 a year, in spite of reduction of expenditure amounting to £11,000,000 per annum since 1929–30. The deficits have been met hitherto by bank overdraft. The Commonwealth Bank has notified the Governments that the limit to the process has been reached. Early in July Governments will have insufficient means to meet their obligations. Unless the drift be stopped, public service salaries and wages, pensions and interest could not be paid in full. Public default would be followed by a partial breakdown in public utilities such as railways, and in private industry and trade. Revenue would come toppling down, and even half payment might become impossible. With this prospect everything that can be got from Government economy, from taxation, and from reduction of interest must be called on to bring the debit balance within manageable limits that can safely and practically be covered for a time by borrowing.

The Conference has therefore adopted a plan which combines all possible remedies in such a way that the burden falls as equally as possible on everyone, and no considerable section of the people is left in a privileged position. This sharing of the burden is necessary to make the load more tolerable; it is still more necessary because only on this condition will it be possible to get the combined effort required.

The plan has been adopted by the Conference as a whole, each part of which is accepted on the understanding that all other parts are equally and simultaneously put into operation. It embraces the following measures:—

(a) A reduction of 20 per cent in all adjustable Government expenditure, as compared with the year ending 30th June, 1930, including all emoluments, wages, salaries and pensions paid by the Governments, whether fixed by statute or otherwise, such reduction to be equitably effected.

(b) Conversion of the internal debts of the Governments on the basis of a 22½ per cent reduction of interest.

(c) The securing of additional revenue by taxation, both Commonwealth and State.

(d) A reduction of bank and savings bank rates of interest on deposits and advances.

(e) Relief in respect of private mortgages.

These proposals require the greatest effort in economy and taxation which the Conference considers it safe to attempt. The effect will be still to have a gap of from £13,000,000 to £15,000,000 to be covered for a time by borrowing ...

To the bondholder the plan involves a reduction of interest by 22½ per cent, but it safeguards the capital of the investor.

To the Government employee the plan involves a reduction which, with reductions already effected, represents an average of 20 per cent, but it makes his position and future emoluments much more secure.

To the war pensioner the plan involves a reduction of 20 per cent (in some cases less), but it removes the danger of any sudden stoppage, and provides security for future payments.

To the invalid and old-age pensioner the plan involves a reduction in most cases of 12½ per cent, but it removes the danger of any sudden stoppage, and provides security for future payments.

To all of these a large part of the reduction is counterbalanced by the fall in prices and in the cost of living.

To the unemployed the plan provides for a restoration of employment, and in the meantime makes more secure the continuation of sustenance and relief.

With the sacrifice distributed over the whole community in this manner, with the lead of Governments followed by all citizens, with the revival of business confidence and activity, a sure foundation will have been laid for the restoration of general prosperity in Australia.

ABOVE *Waiting for a free lunch in Fortitude Valley, Brisbane, December 1933.*

Beyond cricket

THE BODYLINE TESTS

Since its inception, the Test cricket series played between Australia and England have always been hard fought. But no contest between the two arch foes has occasioned such acrimony and high drama as the 1932–33 English tour of Australia, which came to be known as Bodyline, and which survives now in legend and folklore. Ric Sissons and Brian Stodart, two of the leading historians of the circumstances surrounding Bodyline, have remarked that the events of one hot Australian summer 'went far beyond the cricket ground fences and into the collective memory of an Anglo-Australian generation for whom cricket was a major cultural bond'. Fifty years later, feelings on the matter still ran high. The anniversary, in 1982–83, was seen to be no occasion for celebration, though of course it was dissected by historians and aficionados of the game. But as an indicator of the continuing depth of feeling, there were those who took the view that a controversy that had so rocked the Anglo-Australian connection should be quietly left to rest.

At the level of the game itself, what came to be called bodyline bowling was an application of leg-side theory devised by the English captain Douglas Jardine (1900–1958) to restrict scoring opportunities for the Australian batsmen, especially Donald Bradman (1908–2001). The English fast bowlers were to aim at leg stump and outside, supported by a net of catchers close in-field. By bowling short balls, they forced the batsman either to hit out or defend, and so risk being caught in the field or take blows to the body. As an attack strategy, this worked brilliantly for England: scoring opportunities for the Australian batsmen were greatly reduced, the home side was intimidated, and England regained the Ashes—lost in 1930—by four Tests to one. But there was a question over the means by which this victory had been achieved. Australian opinion held that England had betrayed the best traditions of the game. The counter charge was that, in defeat, the Australians were 'whingers'.

Applied with such apparent ruthlessness by Jardine, the aggressive bowling strategy aroused much anger in Australia and some dissension (as it was later revealed) even among the English players. In the arena of public opinion, the tourists were despised, especially Jardine, who was depicted as the devil incarnate.

Throughout the series, but especially in Adelaide, the Australian batsmen took some terrible body blows, to the great disapproval of the crowds and to the growing consternation of the Australian Board of Control for International Cricket, which sent a famous telegram to the Marylebone Cricket Club, accusing the English side of unsportsmanlike behaviour. That charge was firmly denied, and in the series of carefully worded telegrams that followed, both sides managed to draw back from the looming possibility of an open rupture. In England and Australia, wise counsel was sought beyond the confines of cricket administration with the sensitivities of the matter—the relationship between the two countries—an issue of diplomacy that was even discussed at the cabinet tables in Downing Street and in Canberra.

ABOVE *Captain Bill Woodfull is struck by the ball at Adelaide Oval.*

AUSTRALIAN BOARD OF CONTROL TO MCC, January 18, 1933
Bodyline bowling assumed such proportions as to menace best interests of game, making protection of body by batsmen the main consideration. Causing intensely bitter feeling between players as well as injury. In our opinion is unsportsmanlike. Unless stopped at once likely to upset friendly relations existing between England and Australia

MCC TO AUSTRALIAN BOARD OF CONTROL, January 23, 1933:
We, Marylebone Cricket Club deplore your cable. We deprecate your opinion that there has been unsportsmanlike play. We have fullest confidence in captain, team and managers, and are convinced that they would do nothing to infringe either the Laws of Cricket or the spirit of the game. We have no evidence that our confidence has been misplaced. Much as we regret accidents to Woodfull and Oldfield, we understand that in neither case was the bowler to blame. If the Australian Board of Control wish to propose a new law or rule it shall receive our careful consideration in due course. We hope the situation is not now as serious as your cable would seem to indicate, but if it is such as to jeopardize the good relations between English and Australian cricketers, and you consider it desirable to cancel remainder of programme, we would consent with great reluctance.

AUSTRALIAN BOARD OF CONTROL TO MCC, January 30, 1933
We, Australian Board of Control, appreciate your difficulty in dealing with matter raised in our cable without having seen the actual play. We unanimously regard bodyline bowling as adopted in some of the games in the present tour as being opposed to the spirit of cricket and unnecessarily dangerous to players. We are deeply concerned that the ideals of the game shall be protected, and have therefore appointed a committee to report on the action necessary to eliminate such bowling from all cricket in Australia as from beginning 1933–34 season. Will forward copy of committee's recommendation for your consideration, and, it is hoped, co-operation, as to its application in all cricket. We do not consider it necessary to cancel remainder of programme.

MCC TO AUSTRALIAN BOARD OF CONTROL, February 2, 1933
We, the Committee of the Marylebone Cricket Club note with pleasure that you do not consider it necessary to cancel the remainder of programme, and that you are postponing the whole issue involved until after the present tour is completed. May we accept this as a clear indication that the good sportsmanship of our team is not in question? We are sure you will appreciate how impossible it would be to play any Test match in the spirit we all desire unless both sides were satisfied there was no reflection upon their sportsmanship. When your recommendation reaches us it shall receive our most careful consideration and will be submitted to the Imperial Cricket Conference.

ABOVE *Supporters outside the hall where President J.T. Patten gave his address.*

Our historic day of mourning and protest

AUSTRALIA DAY CONFERENCE OF AUSTRALIAN ABORIGINAL PEOPLE

In January 1938 white Australians celebrated the one hundred and fiftieth anniversary of the landing of the First Fleet and the beginnings of European settlement. While this was cast as a national celebration, it was inevitable that the anniversary was marked more strongly and enthusiastically in Sydney and New South Wales than anywhere else in Australia. Events planned for 26 January itself included a re-enactment of Governor Phillip's landing, tactlessly complete with a party of Aboriginal people brought to Sydney from Menindee and Brewarrina to perform a contrived role in the ceremony. The efforts of Aboriginal protesters to meet with and dissuade the country visitors from taking part were impeded by white officials, and the re-enactment proceeded as planned.

But in Sydney that day another event brought into focus the distress about Australia Day that continues to be felt by Aboriginal people. About one hundred Aboriginal men and women assembled at Australian Hall, in Elizabeth Street in the city, to confer and to observe a Day of Mourning and Protest. The meeting was well organised and there was a powerful and specific agenda of concerns. It came as the culmination of years of protest and agitation by Aboriginal people in New South Wales against the stultifying and paternalistic policies of the Aborigines Protection Board. Plans had been made to seek agreement to demands for national citizenship and equal status with white Australians, which were to be presented to the state premiers and to the prime minister, J.A. Lyons.

Aboriginal leaders from many parts of New South Wales and Victoria attended. Notable in the Melbourne delegation was William Cooper (1861?–1941) from Cummeroogunja, an Aboriginal community in the Riverina district. Cooper was a seasoned campaigner in the Aboriginal cause, and it was he who had conceived the anniversary as a Day of Mourning and Protest.

The proceedings were opened by the conference president, J.T. Patten, with a fervent address that encapsulated the grievances of Aboriginal Australians not only about the sesquicentenary but also about their conditions of life and work, and their lack of equality with 'the white people of Australia'. Several other delegates spoke in support of the president's address. At 3.15 pm, the president read a resolution as it appeared on the notice paper by which the conference had been convened. Again, several speakers—from Dubbo, the South Coast, Batemans Bay, Nowra, La Perouse and Brewarrina—offered their support for the resolution. At 4.20 pm the resolution was put to the vote and carried unanimously.

A few days later, on 31 January, a deputation of twenty Aboriginal men and women was received by the prime minister and Mrs Enid Lyons, and the interior minister, John McEwen, who had responsibility, on behalf of the Commonwealth, for Aboriginal people in the Northern Territory. The deputation presented a ten-point plan setting out a long-range policy for Aboriginal people, including Commonwealth control of Aboriginal affairs; equality in education, employment, benefits, land ownership and housing; and the right to manage their own money. The deputation was given a polite hearing but little more.

It was apparent that no gains could be achieved until the Commonwealth had the constitutional powers it needed to legislate for Aborigines across the country as a whole. That change would not be made for another thirty years (see 'A symbolic victory', page 299).

The grievances articulated so eloquently at the meeting of 1938 and in the formal resolution of protest brought little immediate change, but they stand as landmarks in a sustained movement of Aboriginal activism that has gained in strength with the years.

PRESIDENT'S ADDRESS

1.30 p.m.

Mr. J.T. Patten, President, said: On this day the white people are rejoicing, but we, as Aborigines, have no reason to rejoice on Australia's 150th birthday. Our purpose in meeting today is to bring home to the white people of Australia the frightful conditions in which the native Aborigines of this continent live. This land belonged to our forefathers 150 years ago, but today we are pushed further and further into the background. The Aborigines Progressive Association has been formed to put before the white people the fact that Aborigines throughout Australia are literally being starved to death. We refuse to be pushed into the background. We have decided to make ourselves heard. White men pretend that the Australian Aboriginal is a low type, who cannot be bettered. Our reply to that is, "Give us the chance!" We do not wish to be left behind in Australia's march to progress. We ask for full citizen rights, including old-age pensions, maternity bonus, relief work when unemployed, and the right to a full Australian education for our children. We do not wish to be herded like cattle, and treated as a special class. As regards the Aborigines Protection Board of New South Wales, white people in the cities do not realise the terrible conditions of slavery under which our people live in the outback districts. I have unanswerable evidence that women of our race are forced to work in return for rations, without other payment. Is this not slavery? Do white Australians realise that there is actual slavery in this fair progressive Commonwealth? Yet such is the case. We are looking in vain to white people to help us by charity. We must do something ourselves to draw public attention to our plight. That is why this Conference is held, to discuss ways and means of arousing the conscience of White Australians, who have us in their power, but have hitherto refused to help us. Our children on the Government Stations are badly fed and poorly educated. The result is that when they go out into life, they feel inferior to white people. This is not a matter of race, it is a matter of education and opportunity. That is why we ask for a better education and better opportunity for our people. We say that it is a disgrace to Australia's name that our people should be handicapped by undernourishment and poor education, and then be blamed for being backward. We do not trust the present Aborigines Protection Board, and that is why we ask for its abolition. (Applause.) Incompetent teachers are provided on the Aboriginal Stations. That is the greatest handicap put on us. We have had 150 years of the white men looking after us, and the result is, our people are being exterminated. The reason why this conference is called today is so that the Aborigines themselves may discuss their problems and to try to bring before the notice of the public and of parliament what our grievance is, and how it may be remedied. We ask for ordinary citizen rights, and full equality with other Australians. (*Moved resolutions.*) ...

3.15 p.m.
The President, (Mr. Patten): **I will read 'the resolution' as on the notice-paper convening this Conference:**

"We, representing the Aborigines of Australia, assembled in conference at the Australian Hall, Sydney, on the 26th day of January, 1938, this being the 150th anniversary of the Whiteman's seizure of our country, hereby make protest against the callous treatment of our people by the whiteman during the past 150 years, and we appeal to the Australian nation of today to make new laws for the education and care of Aborigines, and we ask for a new policy which will raise our people to full citizen status and equality within the community." ...

4.20 p.m.
The resolution was put to the vote and carried unanimously.

The scourge of bushfire in Australia

ROYAL COMMISSION INTO THE VICTORIAN BUSHFIRES

In the long hot summer of 1939, Victoria suffered terrible bushfires, as the state had done in the past and as it would again in the future. At their peak on Friday 13 January 1939, 'in a devastating confluence of flame', townships and vast tracts of countryside were laid to waste; industries were destroyed; stock and wildlife were burned; and seventy-one human lives were lost. Inevitably, the day came to be known as Black Friday; before and since, that same designation has marked too many other Australian Wednesdays, Thursdays and Fridays and other days that have suffered the scarifying burden of fire, the destruction of homes and the heartbreaking loss of human life. Certainly though, as historian Tom Griffiths has remarked, the events of January 1939 reminded Australians of the enduring power of fire on their continent. Another historian, Stephen J. Pyne, has drawn on Australia's experience of war to register the devastating impact of the Victorian fires: 'What the fall of Singapore was to Australian political history, Black Friday was to its environmental history.'

In the immediate aftermath of the fires, the state of Victoria appointed a *Royal Commission to Inquire into The Causes of and Measures Taken to Prevent the Bush Fires of January, 1939, and to Protect Life and Property and The Measures to be Taken to Prevent Bush Fires and to Protect Life in the Event of Future Bush Fires*. The Royal Commissioner, Mr Justice L.E.B. Stretton (1893–1967), brought an unusual descriptive power to bear in the writing of his official report. In particular, his Introduction—the document published here—is a masterly literary evocation of the terrifying power of the fire itself. The report was later anthologised in a collection of Australian nature writing, *Land of Wonder*, edited by A.H. Chisholm, and senior students of English in Victoria were asked to read passages from the report as a prescribed study text. Stretton's recommendations led directly to improvements in fire management practices in Victoria and more widely in Australia but, as experience has shown, to no lasting effect. The work done by Stretton as royal commissioner recently provided the basis for Tom Griffiths' own potent work of 2001, *Forests of Ash: An Environmental History*. In the aftermath of the Victorian bushfires of 2009, Stretton's words were again widely quoted as Australians sought once more to comprehend the scourge of bushfire in their country.

To His Excellency The Right Honourable **FREDERICK WOLLASTON MANN,**
K.C.M.G., Lieutenant-Governor of the State of Victoria and its Dependencies in the Commonwealth of Australia, &c., &c., &c.

MAY IT PLEASE YOUR EXCELLENCY:

INTRODUCTION.—PART I.

In the State of Victoria, the month of January of the year 1939 came towards the end of a long drought which had been aggravated by a severe hot, dry summer season. For more than twenty years the State of Victoria had not seen its countryside and forests in such travail. Creeks and springs ceased to run. Water storages were depleted. Provincial towns were facing the probability of cessation of water supply. In Melbourne, more than a million inhabitants were subjected to restrictions upon the use of water. Throughout the countryside, the farmers were carting water, if such was available, for their stock and themselves. The rich plains, denied their beneficent rains, lay bare and baking; and the forests, from the foothills to the alpine heights, were tinder. The soft carpet of the forest floor was gone; the bone-dry litter crackled underfoot; dry heat and hot dry winds worked upon a land already dry, to suck from it the last, least drop of moisture. Men who had lived their lives in the bush went their ways in the shadow of dread expectancy. But though they felt the imminence of danger they could not tell that it was to be far greater than they could imagine. They had not lived long enough. The experience of the past could not guide them to an understanding of what might, and did, happen. And so it was that, when millions of acres of the forest were invaded by the bushfires which were almost State-wide, there happened, because of great loss of life and property, the most disastrous forest calamity the State of Victoria has known.

These fires were lit by the hand of man.

Seventy-one lives were lost. Sixty-nine mills were burned. Millions of acres of fine forest, of almost incalculable value, were destroyed or badly damaged. Townships were obliterated in a few minutes. Mills, houses, bridges, tramways, machinery, were burned to the ground; men, cattle, horses, sheep, were devoured by the fires or asphyxiated by the scorching debilitated air. Generally, the numerous fires which during December, in many parts of Victoria, had been burning separately, as they do in any summer, either "under control" as it is falsely and dangerously called, or entirely untended, reached the climax of their intensity and joined forces in a devastating confluence of flame on Friday, the 1st of January.

On that day it appeared that the whole State was alight. At midday, in many places, it was dark as night. Men carrying hurricane lamps, worked to make safe their families and belongings. Travellers on the highways were trapped by fires or blazing fallen trees, and perished. Throughout the land there was daytime darkness. At one mill, desperate but futile efforts were made to clear of inflammable scrub the borders of the mill and mill settlement. All but one person, at that mill, were burned to death, many of them while trying to burrow to imagined safety in the sawdust heap. Horses were found,

ABOVE *The 1839 bushfire raced through the Gippsland forests, destroying homes and resulting in the deaths of seventy-one people.*

still harnessed, in their stalls, dead, their limbs fantastically distorted. The full story of the killing of this small community is one of unpreparedness, because of apathy and ignorance and perhaps of something worse.

Steel girders and machinery were twisted by heat as if they had been of fine wire. Sleepers of heavy durable timber, set in the soil, their upper surfaces flush with the ground, were burnt through. Other heavy wood work disappeared, leaving no trace. Where the fires was most intense the soil was burnt and destroyed to such a depth that it may be many years before it shall have been restored by the slow chemistry of Nature. Acres upon acres of the soil itself can be retained only by the effort of man in a fight against natural erosive forces.

The speed of the fires was appalling. They leaped from mountain peak to mountain peak, or far out into the lower country, lighting the forests 6 or 7 miles in advance of the main fires. Blown by a wind of great force, they roared as they travelled. Balls of crackling fire sped at a great pace in advance of the fires, consuming with a roaring, explosive noise, all that they touched. Houses of brick were seen and heard to leap into a roar of flame before the fires had reached them. Some men of science hold the view that the fires generated and were preceded by inflammable gases which became alight. Great pieces of burning bark were carried by the wind to set in raging flame regions not yet touched by the fires. Such was the force of the wind that, in many places, hundreds of trees of great size were blown clear of the earth, tons of soil, with embedded masses of rock still adhering to the roots; for mile upon mile the former forest monarchs were laid in confusion, burnt, torn from the earth, and piled one upon another as matches strewn by a giant hand.

There had been no fires to equal these in destructiveness or intensity in the history of settlement in this State, except perhaps the fires of 1851, which, too, came at summer culmination of a long drought.

Some impression, then, of the unusual antecedents of the fires and of their extreme and unexpected severity may be gained. It will, it is hoped, be apparent that the experience of men in Victoria was such as to leave them unprepared for disaster on such a scale. It is with such facts in mind and with the belief that the facile wisdom which comes after an event is not wisdom, but foolishness, that your Commissioner proceeds to report upon matters into which, to his great honour, he has been appointed by Royal Commission, to inquire.

Australia is at war

ROBERT MENZIES DECLARES WAR AGAINST GERMANY

In the last days of August 1939, with tensions rising in Europe over Germany's policy of aggression, Australians watched anxiously as events moved relentlessly towards war. From 10 Downing Street on 23 August, Britain's prime minister, Neville Chamberlain, warned that if Poland's independence were threatened, Britain stood ready to resist: the policy of appeasement had run its bitter course. On the same day the Australian prime minister, Robert Menzies (1894–1978), announced that if Britain was forced to go to war to defend the territorial integrity of Poland, 'it will not go alone'. A week later, on 31 August, he outlined in a radio broadcast the precautionary steps taken by the federal government 'to prepare Australia for an emergency'. On 1 September Germany breached the frontier and began bombing Polish cities. In Berlin the British ambassador delivered a final note to the German government calling for the withdrawal of all troops from Poland and imposing a deadline. With no response to that last appeal, Britain made a formal declaration of war against Germany on 3 September 1939. Within seconds—at around 8 pm local time—the British announcement was heard throughout Australia by short-wave radio listeners.

In Melbourne, without other formal advice from Britain, members of federal cabinet decided to accept the wireless broadcast in Chamberlain's voice as confirmation of the British action, though this was soon followed by a telegram from the Admiralty in London formally announcing the commencement of hostilities against Germany. The Executive Council then approved a proclamation declaring a state of war. At 9.15 pm, in a national broadcast from the Commonwealth offices in Treasury Place, Melbourne, Menzies delivered the announcement that Australia was also at war. The message went out through every national and commercial broadcasting station across the country.

The declaration of war followed from two things: the first was Germany's persistence in the invasion of Poland, which the prime minister explained both in terms of high principle in international law and in the homely metaphor of a dispute between two neighbours; and the second was Australia's status as a self-governing British dominion. If Britain was at war, the consequence was that Australia was also at war.

Menzies' biographer A.W. Martin described the declaration as a 'clear and succinct speech' that effectively explained the genesis and development of the crisis. Well-crafted and delivered with appropriate sadness and solemnity, Robert Menzies' declaration of war is one of the most famous Australian documents. On the one hand, it is a momentous commitment of Australians to a just cause and an international conflict that would extend for six years; on the other, it is a practical and loyal assertion of commitment by the Australian nation to the shared ideals of British people throughout the world.

ABOVE *Prime Minister Menzies broadcasts news of the outbreak of war.*

Fellow Australians. It is my melancholy duty to inform you officially that, in consequence of a persistence by Germany in her invasion of Poland, Great Britain has declared war upon her, and that, as a result, Australia is also at war.

No harder task can fall to the lot of a democratic leader than to make such an announcement. Great Britain and France, with the cooperation of the British dominions, have struggled to avoid this tragedy. They have ... been patient; they have kept the door of negotiations open; they have given no cause for aggression. But, in the result, their efforts have failed, and we are therefore, as a great family of nations, involved in a struggle which we must at all costs win, and which we believe in our hearts we will win.

What I want to do tonight is to put before you ... a short account of how this crisis has developed. The history of recent months in Europe has been an eventful one. It will exhibit to the eyes of the future student some of the most remarkable instances of a ruthlessness and indifference to common humanity which the darkest centuries of European history can scarcely parallel. Moreover, it will, I believe, demonstrate that the leader of Germany has for a long time steadily pursued a policy which was deliberately designed to produce either war or a subjugation of one non-German country after another by the threat of war. We all have vivid recollections of September of last year. Speaking in Berlin on September 26, 1938, Herr Hitler said, referring to the Sudeten–German problem, which was then approaching its acutest stage: 'And now the last problem which must be solved, and which will be solved, concerns us. It is the last territorial claim which I have to make in Europe.'

Four days later, at Munich, when the problem had been settled on terms which provided for the absorption of the Sudeten country into Germany, and which otherwise professed to respect the integrity of the remainder of the Czechoslovak state, Hitler participated with the Prime Minister of Great Britain in a statement which went out to all the world. Its most important sentence was this:

> We are resolved that the method of consultation shall be the method adopted to deal with any other question that may concern our two countries, and we are determined to continue our efforts to remove possible causes of difference and thus to contribute to assure the peace of Europe.

What a strange piece of irony that seems today, only twelve months later. In those twelve months, what has happened? In cold-blooded breach of the solemn obligations implied in both the statements I have quoted, Herr Hitler has annexed the whole of the Czechoslovak state; has, without flickering an eyelid, made a pact with Russia, a country the denouncing and reviling of which has been his chief stock-in-trade ever since he became Chancellor; and has now, in circumstances which I shall describe to you, invaded with armed force, and in defiance of civilised opinion, the independent nation of Poland. Your own comments on this dreadful history will need no re-inforcement by me. All I need to say is that whatever the inflamed ambitions of the German

Fuhrer may be, he will undoubtedly learn, as other great enemies of freedom have learned before, that no empire, no dominion can be soundly established upon a basis of broken promises or dishonoured agreements.

Let me say something about the events of the last few days. The facts are not really in dispute, they are for the most part contained in documents which are now a matter of record. On Friday, August 25—that is, nine days ago—Herr Hitler asked the British ambassador to call on him, and had a long interview with him. Herr Hitler said he wished to make a move towards England as decisive as his recent Russian move, but that first, the problem of Danzig and the Corridor must be solved. He went on to indicate that he was looking forward to a general European settlement, and that if this could be achieved he would be willing to accept a reasonable limitation of armaments. On Saturday, August 26, the British ambassador flew to London to give a detailed account of his conversation to the British government. On Sunday, August 27, the British cabinet fully considered the whole matter, and, incidentally, was appraised by me of the views of the Australian Government. On Monday, August 28, the British reply—which I may say was entirely in line with our own views—was taken back to Berlin, and was delivered to Herr Hitler in the evening. That reply stated that the British government desired a complete and lasting understanding between the two countries, and agreed that a prerequisite to such a state of affairs was a settlement of German–Polish differences. It emphasised the obligations which Great Britain had to Poland, and made it clear that Great Britain could not acquiesce in a settlement which would put in jeopardy the independence of a state to which it had given its guarantee. The government said, however, that it would be prepared to participate in an international guarantee of any settlement reached by direct negotiation between Germany and Poland which did not prejudice Poland's essential interests.

The note pointed out that the Polish government was ready to enter into discussions, and that it was hoped that the German government would do the same. On the night of Tuesday, August 29, Herr Hitler communicated to Sir Nevile Henderson his reply to the British note. In it he reiterated his demands, but agreed to accept the British government's offer of its good offices in securing the dispatch to Berlin of a Polish emissary. In the meantime, it was stated, the German government would draw up proposals acceptable to itself, and would, if possible, place these at the disposal of the British government before the arrival of the Polish negotiator. Astonishingly enough—for the German proposals were not then even drafted—the note went on to say that the German government counted on the arrival of the Polish emissary on Wednesday, August 30, which was the very next day. Sir Nevile Henderson pointed out at once that this was an impossible condition, but Herr Hitler assured him that it was only intended to stress the urgency of the matter. On the Wednesday Herr Hitler's communication was received by the British government, and their reply was handed by Sir Nevile Henderson to von Ribbentrop, the German Foreign Minister, at midnight. At the same time the British ambassador asked whether the German proposals which were to be drawn up were ready, and suggested that von Ribbentrop should invite the Polish ambassador to call, and should hand to him the proposals for transmission to his government. I would have thought this a very sensible suggestion, but von Ribbentrop rejected it in violent terms. Von Ribbentrop then produced a lengthy document containing the German proposals, which you subsequently saw in the newspapers, and read it aloud in German at top speed. Sir Nevile Henderson naturally asked for a copy of the document, but the reply was that it was now too late as the Polish representative had not arrived in Berlin by midnight.

You see what a travesty the whole thing was. The German government was treating Poland as in default, because she had not by Wednesday night offered an opinion upon or discussed with Germany a set of proposals of which, in fact, she had at that time never heard. Indeed, apart from the hurried reading to which I have referred, the British government had no proper account of these proposals until they were broadcast from Germany on Thursday, August 31.

On the night of August 31 the Polish ambassador at Berlin saw von Ribbentrop, and told him that the Polish government was willing to negotiate with Germany about their disputes on an equal basis. The only reply was that German troops passed the Polish frontier and began war on the Poles on the morning of Friday, September 1.

One further fact should be mentioned and it is this: in the British government's communication of August 30 it informed the German Chancellor that it recognised the need for speed and that it was also recognised the dangers which arose from the fact that two mobilised armies were facing each other on opposite sides of the Polish frontier, and that accordingly, it strongly urged that both Germany and Poland should undertake that during the negotiations no aggressive military movements would take place. That being communicated to Poland, the Polish government on Thursday, August 31, categorically stated that it was prepared to give a formal guarantee that, during negotiations, Polish troops would not violate the frontiers, provided a corresponding guarantee was given by Germany. The German government made no reply whatever.

My comments on these events need not be very long. The matter was admirably stated by the British Prime Minister to the House of Commons ...

> It is plain, therefore, that Germany claims to treat Poland as in the wrong because she had not by Wednesday night entered upon discussions with Germany about a set of proposals of which she had never heard.

Let me elaborate this a little. You can make an offer of settlement for two entirely different purposes. You may make your offer genuinely and hoping to have it accepted or discussed with a view to avoiding war. On the other hand, you may make it hoping to use it as 'window dressing' and with no intention or desire to have it accepted. If I were to make an offer to my neighbour about a piece of land in dispute between us and before he had the faintest opportunity of dealing with my offer I violently assaulted him, my offer would stand revealed as a fraud. If Germany had really desired a peaceful settlement of questions relating to Danzig and the Corridor she would have taken every step to see that her proposals were adequately considered by

Poland and that there was proper opportunity for discussion. In other words, if Germany had wanted peace, does anybody believe that there would be today fighting on the Polish frontier, or that Europe would be plunged into war? Who wanted war? Poland? Great Britain? France?

A review of all these circumstances makes it clear that the German Chancellor has, throughout this week of tension, been set upon war, and that the publication of his proposals for settlement was destined merely as a bid for world opinion before he set his armies on the move.

We have, of course, been deluged with propaganda from Berlin. We have been told harrowing stories of the oppression of Germans; we have been told that Poland invaded Germany; we have even been told—somewhat contradictorily—that Germany was forced to invade Poland to defend herself against aggression. The technique of German propaganda, of carefully fomented agitations in neighbouring countries; the constant talk of persecution and injustice; these are all nauseatingly familiar to us. We made the acquaintance of all of them during the dispute over Czechoslovakia and we may well ask what has become of the Czech minority and the Slovak minority since the forced absorption of their country into the German state.

It is plain—indeed it is brutally plain—that the Herr Hitler ambition has been, not as he once said, to unite the German peoples under one rule, but to bring under that rule as many European countries, even of alien race, as can be subdued by force. If such a policy were allowed to go unchecked, there could be no just peace for the world.

A halt has been called. Force has had to be resorted to to check the march of force. Honest dealing, the peaceful adjustment of differences, the rights of independent peoples to live their own lives, the honouring of international obligations and promises—all these things are at stake.

There never was any doubt as to where Great Britain stood in relation to them. There can be no doubt that where Great Britain stands, there stand the people of the entire British world. Bitter as we all feel at this wanton crime, this is not a moment for rhetoric, prompt as the action of many thousands must be, it is for the rest a moment for quiet thinking, for that calm fortitude, which rests not upon the beating of drums, but upon the unconquerable spirit of man created by God in His own image.

What may be before us, we do not know; nor how long the journey. But this we do know; that Truth is our companion on that journey, that Truth is with us in the battle and that Truth must win.

Before I end may I say this to you? In the bitter months that are to come, calmness, resoluteness, confidence and hard work will be required as never before. This war will involve not only soldiers and sailors and airmen, but supplies, foodstuffs, money.

Our staying power, and particularly the staying power of the Mother Country, will be best assisted by keeping our production going; by continuing our avocations and our business as fully as we can; by maintaining employment, and with it our strength. I know that in spite of the emotions that we are all feeling, you will show that Australia is ready to see it through.

May God in His mercy and compassion grant that the world may soon be delivered from this agony.

'The thread of peace has snapped'

JOHN CURTIN DECLARES WAR AGAINST JAPAN

John Curtin (1885–1945) was sworn in as prime minister of Australia on 7 October 1941. Two months later he faced the dreadful responsibility of taking the nation into war against Japan at a time when the greater part of Australia's military forces were engaged in the war in western Europe, the Middle East and the Mediterranean.

Curtin's declaration was made in a radio broadcast to the nation from Melbourne on the evening of 8 December 1941. The formal proclamation of a state of war was signed by the governor-general, Lord Gowrie, and published in the *Commonwealth Gazette* (no. 252) on 9 December 1941. Although there was no effective choice of whether to go to war against Japan, it is noteworthy that Curtin made the Australian declaration unilaterally and independently. In this, Curtin's declaration differed from the announcement made by Robert Menzies in September 1939 when Australia's commitment to the war in Europe was explicitly acknowledged as a consequence of the British declaration of war against Germany (see page 246).

Since about 5 December, Australian officials had been alerted to a dangerous build-up of Japanese naval forces in the Pacific: it was clear that a crisis was imminent. The first news of an attack was heard in Australia early on the morning of 8 December from short-wave radio news services. At 5.45 am came the news of the bombing of Pearl Harbor. Later both Singapore and Thailand were attacked.

Woken with the news in his Melbourne hotel room, Curtin was stoical: 'Well, it has come', he said. The war cabinet met later in the day and agreed that the situation now put Australia in a state of war against Japan. That evening Curtin made his forthright declaration to the Australian people, making it clear that the nation faced its darkest hour. The next morning, the *Age* newspaper in Melbourne commented that the prime minister's latest speeches, made under the strain of greatly increased responsibilities, had been 'nobly inspirational' and 'soundly practical': 'In these first hours, when our eyes are opening on fresh vistas of war, there is reassurance in his frankness, foresight and fearlessness.' Throughout the war Curtin gave the country exemplary leadership. He died in office just one month before the war came to its end.

ABOVE *Prime Minister Curtin watches Lord Gowrie sign the declaration of war against Japan.*

Men and Women of Australia:

We are at war with Japan. That has happened because, in the first instance, Japanese naval and air forces launched an unprovoked attack on British and United States territory.

Because our vital interests are imperilled and because the rights of free people in the whole Pacific are assailed, the Australian Government, this afternoon, took the necessary steps which will mean that a state of war exists between Australia and Japan.

Tomorrow, in common with the United Kingdom, the United States, and the Netherlands East Indies, the Australian Government will solemnly declare a state of war it has tried so sincerely and strenuously to avoid. Throughout the whole affair, and despite discouragement, the Australian Government has struggled hard to prevent a breakdown of discussions.

We did not want war in the Pacific. The Australian Government has repeatedly made it clear, as have the Governments of the United Kingdom, the United States, and the Netherlands East Indies that if war came to the Pacific, it would be of Japan's making.

Japan has now made war. I point out that the hands of the Democracies are clean. The discussions and negotiations which have taken place between Japan and the Democracies were not merely the bandying of words on the Democracies' part. Since last February it has been the constant aim and endeavour of the Democracies to keep peace in the Pacific. It has been a problem fraught with difficulties but, in the view of the Democracies, it was a problem capable of being overcome.

Accordingly, the best brains of the Democracies were brought to bear on the problem. It will stand on record that the President of the United States, the United States Secretary of State, Mr. Cordell Hull, and the British and Dominion Governments worked untiringly and unceasingly.

Yet, when the President of the United States had decided to communicate to the Japanese Emperor a personal appeal for an Imperial intervention on the side of peace, the war Government of Japan struck.

That war Government set on aggression, and lusting for power in the same fashion as its Axis partners, anticipated the undoubted weight of the President's plea, and shattered the century-old friendship between the two countries.

For the first time in the history of the Pacific, armed conflict stalks abroad.

No other country but Japan desires war in the Pacific. The guilt for plunging this hemisphere into actual warfare is therefore on Japan.

By so doing Japan chose the Hitler method. While its diplomatic representatives were actually at the White House; while all the Democratic Powers regarded the conversations as continuing, Japan ignored the convention of a formal declaration of war and struck like an assassin in the night.

As the dawn broke this morning at places as far apart as Honolulu, Nauru, Ocean Island, Guam, Singapore, and British Malaya shells from Japanese warships, bombs from Japanese aircraft, and shots from Japanese military forces struck death to United States citizens and members of its defence forces, to the peaceful subjects of Great Britain and to our men on ships and on the land. The Pacific Ocean was reddened with the blood of Japan's victims.

These wanton killings will be followed by attacks on the Netherlands East Indies, on the Commonwealth of Australia, and on the Dominion of New Zealand, if Japan can get its brutal way.

Australia, therefore, being a nation which believes in a way of life which has freedom and liberty as its corner stones, goes to battle stations in defence of the free way of living.

Our course is clear; our cause is just, as has been the case ever since September, 1939, when we stood in the path of Hitlerism and declared that we would stand up to the end, against ruthlessness and wanton aggression.

I say, then, to the people of Australia, give of your best in the service of the nation. There is a place and part for all of us. Each must take his or her place in the service of the nation for the nation itself is imperilled.

This is our darkest hour. Let that be fully realised. Our efforts in the past two years must be as nothing compared with the efforts we must now put forward. I can give you the assurance that the Australian Government is fully prepared ...

One thing remains, and on it depends our very lives. That thing is the co-operation, the strength and the will power of you the people of the Commonwealth.

Without it we are lost indeed.

Men and women of Australia, the call is to you for your courage, your physical and mental ability, your inflexible determination that we as a nation of free people shall survive.

My appeal to you is in the name of Australia, for Australia is the stake in this conflict.

The thread of peace has snapped. Only the valour of our fighting forces backed to the very utmost of what we are capable in factory and workshop can knit that thread again into security.

Let there be no idle hand. The road of service is ahead. Let us all tread it firmly, victoriously. We here in this spacious land, where for more than 150 years peace and security have prevailed, are now called upon to meet the external aggressor.

The enemy presses from without. I have said that our forces are at their battle stations. They are not alone. It is true also that Japan is not alone. As I speak to you to-night the United States, Great Britain, and her Colonies and Dominions (which include Australia and New Zealand), the great Federation of Russian Republics, and the Netherlands East Indies, and China are associated in the common cause of preserving for free men and free women, not only their inheritance, but every hope they have of decency and dignity and liberty.

We Australians have imperishable traditions. We shall maintain and vindicate them. We shall hold this country, and keep it as a citadel for the British-speaking race and as a place where civilisation will persist.

Looking to America

JOHN CURTIN'S NEW YEAR MESSAGE

With the waning of 1941, and just three weeks after Japan's entry into the war, Prime Minister John Curtin accepted the invitation of the *Herald* newspaper in Melbourne to deliver a New Year message to the Australian people. The message—largely written by Curtin's press secretary Don Rodgers—caused controversy in Australia and also in the distant capitals of London and Washington. With the statement that Australia 'looks to America, free of any pangs as to our traditional links or kinship with the United Kingdom', Curtin roused the anger of Australian conservatives, who had always been doubtful of the loyalty of the Australian Labor Party to Britain. Anger was also felt in London and Washington, since Curtin's statement seemed to blunder across the agreed Anglo-American strategy that the first priority was to defeat Germany. But Curtin was acutely aware of Australia's vulnerability and that Japan had initiated a new and different war. His purpose was twofold: to define a new foreign policy imperative for the nation, and to give his own people a more certain understanding of the country's peril and so stimulate their commitment to the struggle now before them.

Curtin's message, headlined by the *Herald* as 'The Task Ahead', has been hailed as a defining moment in Australian history, when the country turned away from Britain and embraced a new reality that saw the United States as its new protector. But as recent revisions have shown, most notably work by Curtin's biographer David Day, the reality was more complex and more problematic. It is clear, however, that Curtin's statement was prescient, alert to a potential realignment of powers and responsibilities that would profoundly alter Australia's orientation in the post-war world. David Day accepts that the message of 27 December 1941 was at the least iconic and certainly crucial in the framing of a gradual reworking of Australia's place in the world, both during the war itself and later, in 1951, when the post-war Liberal–Country Party coalition government negotiated the ANZUS Treaty to help defend Australia's interests in what eventually came to be called the Asia–Pacific region.

In the days that followed, Curtin robustly defended his and Australia's commitment to a place in the British Commonwealth of Nations, and he continued to support the war effort in Europe, including keeping the Australian 9th Division in the Middle East until after the victory at El Alamein late in 1942. But he would also have found some comfort in the sympathetic response to his New Year message in the editorial in *The Times* of London published the following day. While *The Times* insisted on the indivisibility of the war effort by the Allies, including Australia, it acknowledged that the reality of geography made it natural for Japan to be seen as Australia's more immediately dangerous enemy. The stern realism of Curtin's message to his own people at home and the courage of his stance in beginning to move his country in a new and more independent direction were vindicated as events unfolded.

The year that begins next Thursday will be the most critical in the history of Australia.

Here the Prime Minister (Mr Curtin) in a special message, tells the Australian people of the job that has to be done in 1942.

The Task Ahead
By John Curtin

> That reddish veil which o'er the face
> Of night-hag East is drawn ...
> Flames new disaster for the race?
> Or can it be the Dawn?

So wrote Bernard O'Dowd. I see 1942 as a year in which we shall know the answer.

I would, however, that we would provide the answer. We can and we will. Therefore I see 1942 as a year of immense change in Australian life.

The Australian Government's policy has been grounded on two facts. One is that the war with Japan is not a phase of the struggle with the Axis powers, but is a new war.

The second is that Australia must go on to a war footing.

Those two facts involve two lines of action—one in the direction of external policy as to our dealings with Britain, the United States, Russia, the Netherlands East Indies and China in the higher direction of the war in the Pacific.

The second is the reshaping, in fact the revolutionising, of the Australian way of life until a war footing is attained quickly, efficiently and without question.

As the Australian Government enters 1942, it has behind it a record of realism in respect of foreign affairs. I point to the forthright declaration in respect of Finland, Hungary and Rumania which was followed with little delay in a declaration of war by the Democracies.

We felt that there could be no half-measures in our dealings with the Soviet when that nation was being assailed by the three countries mentioned.

Similarly we put forward that a reciprocal agreement between Russia and Britain should be negotiated to meet an event of aggression by Japan. Our suggestion was then regarded, wrongly as it proved, as premature.

Now with equal realism, we take the view that while the determination of military policy is the Soviet's business, we should be able to look forward with reason to aid from Russia against Japan.

We look for a solid and impregnable barrier of the democracies against the three Axis powers, and we refuse to accept the dictum that the Pacific struggle must be treated as a subordinate segment of the general conflict. By that it is not meant that any one of the other theatres of war is of less importance than the Pacific, but that Australia asks for a concerted plan evoking the greatest strength at the Democracies' disposal, determined upon hurling Japan back.

The Australian Government therefore regards the Pacific struggle as primarily one in which the United States and Australia must have the fullest say in the direction of the Democracies' fighting plan.

> Without any inhibitions of any kind, I make it quite clear that Australia looks to America, free of any pangs as to our traditional links or kinship with the United Kingdom.

We know the problems that the United Kingdom faces. We know the constant threat of invasion. We know the dangers of dispersal of strength. But we know too that Australia can go, and Britain can still hold on.

We are therefore determined that Australia shall not go, and we shall exert all our energies toward the shaping of a plan, with the United States as its keystone, which will give to our country some confidence of being able to hold out until the tide of battle swings against the enemy.

> Summed up, Australian external policy will be shaped toward obtaining Russian aid, and working out, with the United States as the major factor, a plan of Pacific strategy, along with British, Chinese and Dutch forces.

Australian internal policy has undergone striking changes in the past few weeks. These, and those that will inevitably come before 1942 is far advanced, have been prompted by several reasons.

In the first place the Commonwealth Government found it exceedingly difficult to bring the Australian people to a realisation of what, after two years of war, our position had become. Even the entry of Japan, bringing a direct threat in our own waters, was met with a subconscious view that the Americans would deal with the short-sighted, underfed and fanatical Japanese.

The announcement that no further appeals would be made to the Australian people, and the decisions that followed, were motivated by psychological factors. They had an arresting effect. They awakened in the somewhat lackadaisical Australian mind the attitude that was imperative if we were to save ourselves, to enter an all-in effort in the only possible manner.

> That experiment in psychology was eminently successful, and we commence 1942 with a better realisation, by a greater number of Australians, of what the war means than in the whole preceding two years.

The decisions were prompted by other reasons, all related to the necessity of getting onto a war footing, and the results so far achieved have been most heartening, especially in respect of production and conservation of stocks.

I make it clear that the experiment undertaken was never intended as one to awaken Australian patriotism or sense of duty. Those qualities have been over-present, but the response to leadership and direction had never been requested of the people, and desirable talents and untapped resources had lain dormant.

Our task for 1942 is stern. The Government is under no illusions as to "something cropping up" in the future.

The nadir of our fortunes in this struggle as compared with 1914–1918 has yet to be reached.

Let there be no mistake about that. The position Australia faces internally far exceeds in potential and sweeping dangers anything that confronted us in 1914–1918.

> The year 1942 will impose supreme tests. These range from resistance to invasion to deprivation of more and more amenities, not only the amenities of peacetime but those enjoyed in time of war.

Australians must realise that to place the nation on a war footing every citizen must place himself, his private and business affairs, his entire mode of living, on a war footing. The civilian way of life cannot be any less rigorous, can contribute no less than that which the fighting men have to follow.

I demand that Australians everywhere realise that Australia is now inside the fighting lines.

Australian governmental policy will be directed strictly on those lines. We have to regard our country and its 7,000,000 people as though we were a nation and a people with the enemy hammering at our frontier.

Australians must be perpetually on guard; against the possibility, at any hour without warning, of raid or invasion; on guard against spending money, or doing anything that cannot be justified; on guard against hampering by disputation or idle, irresponsible chatter, the decisions of the Government taken for the welfare of all.

All Australia is the stake in this war. All Australia must stand together to hold that stake. We face a powerful, ably led and unbelievably courageous foe.

We must watch the enemy accordingly. We shall watch him accordingly.

John Curtin's New Year message

Modest, decent, hard-working Australians: 'the forgotten people'

ROBERT MENZIES' APPEAL TO THE MIDDLE CLASS

On 22 May 1942, Robert Menzies—only nine months previously the prime minister of Australia, but now a backbench member in a dispirited Opposition—delivered a radio broadcast. It was addressed to those Menzies called 'the forgotten people'. These were members of the Australian middle class who yet did not see themselves in class terms, but as individuals: modest, decent, hard-working Australians—clerks, accountants, salaried officers, white-collar workers, small farmers and home-making wives with a commitment to family life and to the good works of church and community service.

Menzies' broadcast was one of a series of twenty-three on international and domestic affairs presented on national radio over two years. In the political wilderness, this was for him a time of reflection and of reinvention. The broadcasts were soon published under the collective title *The Forgotten People* and offered to readers as the views of a 'true patriot' speaking simply but eloquently 'man to man'. Looking to Australia's future in the post-war world, Menzies articulated the responsibilities of citizenship, and the meaning and achievements of democracy, while throughout upholding the dignity and rights of the middle classes—'the forgotten people'—whom he described as 'the backbone of the country'. Something of the voice of a headmaster or parson is present in these homilies, but Menzies' voice was the voice of its time and part of the appeal that sustained him on his return to office in 1949.

In her detailed and perceptive analysis of Menzies' address to 'the forgotten people', political biographer Judith Brett summed it up as one of the richest, most creative and most influential in the long career of this master politician. Not only was the address a persuasive appeal to a constituency that Menzies came to make his own through the long years of his second prime ministership from 1949 to 1966, but it also marked a turning point in the larger fortunes of the conservative side of Australian politics. Now, too, that side had the images it needed to re-create itself as a political force and the means to extend its reach into Australian life. For the Liberal Party in particular, the ideas embodied in Menzies' address would serve as a source of inspiration and nourishment for years to come—so much so that even in the very different Australia of the late twentieth century and into the new millennium, they could be reworked and revitalised with similar success by another political master, John Winston Howard (b. 1939), who held office as prime minister from 1996 to 2008, a tenure exceeded only by that of Menzies.

The Forgotten People

Quite recently, a bishop wrote a letter to a great daily newspaper. His theme was the importance of doing justice to the workers. His belief, apparently, was that the workers are those who work with their hands. He sought to divide the people of Australia into classes. He was obviously suffering from what has for years seemed to me to be our greatest political disease—the disease of thinking that the community is divided into the rich and relatively idle, and the laborious poor, and that every social and political controversy can be resolved into the question: What side are you on?

Now, the last thing I want to do is to commence or take part in a false war of this kind. In a country like Australia the class war must always be a false war. But if we are to talk of classes, then the time has come to say something of the forgotten class—the middle class—those people who are constantly in danger of being ground between the upper and the nether millstones of the false class war; the middle class who, properly regarded, represent the backbone of this country.

We do not have classes here as in England, and therefore the terms do not mean the same; so I must define what I mean when I use the expression "middle class".

Let me first define it by exclusion. I exclude at one end of the scale the rich and powerful: those who control great funds and enterprises, and are as a rule able to protect themselves—though it must be said that in a political sense they have as a rule shown neither comprehension nor competence. But I exclude them because, in most material difficulties, the rich can look after themselves.

I exclude at the other end of the scale the mass of unskilled people, almost invariably well-organized, and with their wages and conditions safeguarded by popular law. What I am excluding them from is my definition of the middle class. We cannot exclude them from the problem of social progress, for one of the prime objects of modern social and political policy is to give to them a proper measure of security, and provide the conditions which will enable them to acquire skill and knowledge and individuality.

These exclusions being made, I include the intervening range—the kind of people I myself represent in Parliament—salary-earners, shopkeepers, skilled artisans, professional men and women, farmers, and so on. These are, in the political and economic sense, the middle class. They are for the most part unorganized and unself-conscious. They are envied by those whose social benefits are largely obtained by taxing them. They are not rich enough to have individual power. They are taken for granted by each political party in turn. They are not sufficiently lacking in individualism to be organized for what in these days we call "pressure politics". And yet, as I have said, they are the backbone of the nation.

The communist has always hated what he called the "bourgeoisie", because he sees clearly that the existence of one has kept British countries from revolution, while the substantial absence of one in feudal France at the end of the eighteenth century and in Tsarist Russia at the end of the last war made revolution easy and indeed inevitable.

You may say to me, "Why bring this matter up at this stage, when we are fighting a war in the result of which we are all equally concerned?" My answer is that I am bringing it up because under the pressures of war we may, if we are not careful—if we are not as thoughtful as the times will permit us to be—inflict a fatal injury upon our own backbone.

In point of political, industrial and social theory and practice there are great delays in times of war. But there are also great accelerations. We must watch each, remembering always that whether we know it or not, and whether we like it or not, the foundations of whatever new order is to come after the war are inevitably being laid down now. We cannot go wrong right up to the peace treaty and expect suddenly thereafter to go right.

Now, what is the value of this middle class, so defined and described? First, it has "a stake in the country". It has responsibility for homes—homes material, homes human, homes spiritual.

I do not believe that the real life of this nation is to be found either in great luxury hotels and the petty gossip of so-called fashionable suburbs, or in the officialdom of organized masses. It is to be found in the homes of people who are nameless and unadvertised, and who, whatever their individual religious conviction or dogma, see in their children their greatest contribution to the immortality of their race. The home is the foundation of sanity and sobriety; it is the indispensable condition of continuity; its health determines the health of society as a whole.

I have mentioned homes material, homes human, and homes spiritual. Let me take them in their order. What do I mean by "homes material"?

The material home represents the concrete expression of the habits of frugality and saving "for a home of our own". Your advanced socialist may rage against private property even while he acquires it; but one of the best instincts in us is that which induces us to have one little piece of earth with a house and a garden which is ours: to which we can withdraw, in which we can be among our friends, into which no stranger may come against our will.

If you consider it, you will see that if, as in the old saying, "the Englishman's home is his castle", it is this very fact that leads on to the conclusion that he who seeks to violate that law by violating the soil of England must be repelled and defeated.

National patriotism, in other words, inevitably springs from the instinct to defend and preserve our own homes.

Then we have homes human. A great house, full of loneliness, is not a home. "Stone walls do not a prison make", nor do they make a house. They may equally make a stable or a piggery. Brick walls, dormer windows and central heating need not make more than a hotel. My home is where my wife and children are. The instinct to be with them is the great instinct of civilized man; the instinct to give them a chance in life—to make them not leaners but lifters—is a noble instinct.

If Scotland has made a great contribution to the theory and practice of education, it is because of the tradition of Scottish homes. The Scottish ploughman, walking behind his team, cons ways and means of making his son a farmer, and so he sends him to the village school. The Scottish farmer ponders upon the future of his son, and sees it most assured not by the inheritance of money but by the acquisition of that knowledge which will give him power; and so the sons of many Scottish farmers find their way to Edinburgh and a university degree.

The great question is, "How can I qualify my son to help society?" Not, as we have so frequently thought, "How can I qualify society to help my son?" If human homes are to fulfil their destiny, then we must have frugality and saving for education and progress.

And finally, we have homes spiritual. This is a notion which finds its simplest and most moving expression in "The Cotter's Saturday Night" of Burns. Human nature is at its greatest when it combines dependence upon God with independence of man.

We offer no affront—on the contrary we have nothing but the warmest human compassion—toward those whom fate has compelled to live upon the bounty of the State, when we say that the greatest element in a strong people is a fierce independence of spirit. This is the only *real* freedom, and it has as its corollary a brave acceptance of unclouded individual responsibility. The moment a man seeks moral and intellectual refuge in the emotions of a crowd, he ceases to be a human being and becomes a cipher. The home spiritual so understood is not produced by lassitude or by dependence; it is produced by self-sacrifice, by frugality and saving.

In a war, as indeed at most times, we become the ready victims of phrases. We speak glibly of many things without pausing to consider what they signify. We speak of "financial power", forgetting that the financial power of 1942 is based upon the savings of generations which have preceded it. We speak of "morale" as if it were a quality induced from without—created by others for our benefit—when in truth there can be no national morale which is not based upon the individual courage of men and women. We speak of "man power" as if it were a mere matter of arithmetic: as if it were made up of a multiplication of men and muscles without spirit.

Second, the middle class, more than any other, provides the intelligent ambition which is the motive power of human progress. The idea entertained by many people that, in a well-constituted world, we shall all live on the State is the quintessence of madness, for what is the State but *us*? We collectively must provide what we individually receive.

The great vice of democracy—a vice which is exacting a bitter retribution from it at this moment—is that for a generation we have been busy getting ourselves on to the list of beneficiaries and removing ourselves from the list of contributors, as if somewhere there was somebody else's wealth and somebody else's effort on which we could thrive.

To discourage ambition, to envy success, to hate achieved superiority, to distrust independent thought, to sneer at and impute false motives to public services—these are the maladies of modern democracy, and of Australian democracy in particular. Yet ambition, effort, thinking, and readiness to serve are not only the design and objectives of self-government but are the essential conditions of its success. If this is not so, then we had better put back the clock, and search for a benevolent autocracy once more.

Where do we find these great elements most commonly? Among the defensive and comfortable rich, among the unthinking and unskilled mass, or among what I have called the "middle class"?

Third, the middle class provides more than perhaps any other the intellectual life which marks us off from the beast: the life which finds room for literature, for the arts, for science, for medicine and the law.

Consider the case of literature and art. Could these survive as a department of State? Are we to publish our poets according to their political colour? Is the State to decree surrealism because surrealism gets a heavy vote in a key electorate? The truth is that no great book was ever written and no great picture ever painted by the clock or according to civil service rules. These things are done by man, not men. You cannot regiment them. They require opportunity, and sometimes leisure. The artist, if he is to live, must have a buyer; the writer an audience. He finds them among frugal people to whom the margin above bare living means a chance to reach out a little towards that heaven which is just beyond our grasp. It has always seemed to me, for example, that an artist is better helped by the man who sacrifices something to buy a picture he loves than by a rich patron who follows the fashion.

Fourth, this middle class maintains and fills the higher schools and universities, and so feeds the lamps of learning.

What are schools for? To train people for examinations, to enable people to comply with the law, or to produce developed men and women?

Are the universities mere technical schools, or have they as one of their functions the preservation of pure learning, bringing in its train not merely riches for the imagination but a comparative sense for the mind, and leading to what we need so badly — the recognition of values which are other than pecuniary?

One of the great blots on our modern living is the cult of false values, a repeated application of the test of money, notoriety, applause. A world in which a comedian or a beautiful half-wit on the screen can be paid fabulous sums, whilst scientific researchers and discoverers can suffer neglect and starvation, is a world which needs to have its sense of values violently set right.

Now, have we realized and recognized these things, or is most of our policy designed to discourage or penalize thrift, to encourage dependence on the State, to bring about a dull equality on the fantastic idea that all men are equal in mind and needs and deserts: to level down by taking the mountains out of the landscape, to weigh men according to their political organizations and power—as votes and not as human beings? These are formidable questions, and we cannot escape from answering them if there is really to be a new order for the world.

I have been actively engaged in politics for fourteen years in the Sate of Victoria and in the Commonwealth of Australia. In that period I cannot readily recall many occasions upon which any policy was pursued which was designed to help the thrifty, to encourage independence, to recognize the divine and valuable variations of men's minds. On the contrary, there have been many instances in which the votes of the thriftless have been used to defeat the thrifty. On occasions of emergency, as in the depression and during the present war, we have hastened to make it clear that the provision made by man for his own retirement and old age is not half as sacrosanct as the provision the State would have made for him had he never saved at all.

We have talked of income from savings as if it possessed a somewhat discreditable character. We have taxed it more and more heavily. We have spoken slightingly of the earning of interest at the very moment when we have advocated new pensions and social schemes. I have myself heard a minister of power and influence declare that no deprivation is suffered by a man if he still has the means to fill his stomach, clothe his body and keep a roof over his head. And yet the truth is, as I have endeavoured to show, that frugal people who strive for and obtain the margin above these materially necessary things are the whole foundation of a really active and developing national life.

The case for the middle class is the case for a dynamic democracy as against a stagnant one. Stagnant waters are level, and in them the scum rises. Active waters are never level: they toss and tumble and have crests and troughs; but the scientists tell us that they purify themselves in a few hundred yards.

That we are all, as human souls, of like value cannot be denied. That each of us should have his chance is and must be the great objective of political and social policy. But to say that the industrious and intelligent son of self-sacrificing and saving and forward-looking parents has the same social deserts and even material needs as the dull offspring of stupid and improvident parents is absurd.

If the motto is to be, "Eat, drink and be merry, for to-morrow you will die, and if it chances you don't die, the State will look after you; but if you don't eat, drink and be merry, and save, we shall take your savings from you", then the whole business of life will become foundationless.

Are you looking forward to a breed of men after the war who will have become boneless wonders? Leaners grow flabby; lifters grow muscles. Men without ambition readily become slaves. Indeed, there is much more slavery in Australia than most people imagine. How many hundreds of thousands of us are slaves to greed, to fear, to newspapers, to public opinion—represented by the accumulated views of our neighbours! Landless men smell the vapours of the street corner. Landed men smell the brown earth, and plant their feet upon it and know that it is good.

To all of this many of my friends will retort, "Ah, that's all very well, but when this war is over the levellers will have won the day." My answer is that, on the contrary, men will come out of this war as gloriously unequal in many things as when they entered it. Much wealth will have been destroyed; inherited riches will be suspect; a fellowship of suffering, if we really experience it, will have opened many hearts and perhaps closed many mouths. Many great edifices will have fallen, and we shall be able to study foundations as never before, because war will have exposed them.

But I do not believe that we shall come out into the over-lordship of an all-powerful State on whose benevolence we shall live, spineless and effortless—a State which will dole out bread and ideas with neatly regulated accuracy;

where we shall all have our dividend without subscribing our capital; where the Government, that almost deity, will nurse us and rear us and maintain us and pension us and bury us; where we shall all be civil servants, and all presumably, since we are equal, heads of departments.

If the new world is to be a world of men, we must be not pallid and bloodless ghosts, but a community of people whose motto shall be, "To strive, to seek, to find, and not to yield". Individual enterprise must drive us forward. That does not mean that we are to return to the old and selfish notions of laissez-faire. The functions of the State will be much more than merely keeping the ring within which the competitors will fight. Our social and industrial obligations will be increased. There will be more law, not less; more control, not less.

But what really happens to us will depend on how many people we have who are of the great and sober and dynamic middle-class—the strivers, the planners, the ambitious ones. We shall destroy them at our peril.

22 May, 1942.

'on my shoulders rests a great weight of responsibility'

ENID LYONS DELIVERS HER MAIDEN SPEECH IN FEDERAL PARLIAMENT

Dame Enid Lyons (1897–1981) was the first woman elected to the House of Representatives in Australia's federal Parliament. She won her seat as the United Australia Party's candidate for the Tasmanian electorate of Darwin at the election held on 21 August 1943. The result was a personal triumph, as well as a triumph for the conservative side of Australian politics, though the election itself was won resoundingly by the Australian Labor Party led by John Curtin. Enid Lyons was widely known and respected as the widow of Prime Minister J.A. Lyons, who had died in 1939. The mother of twelve children, her paramount interest during the years of her parliamentary career were family life and women

Delivering her maiden speech on 29 September 1939, Enid Lyons admitted later that she had felt extremely nervous. She had not eaten and recalled that 'my lips were stiff when I started but all the men were wishing me well'. She held six small cards of handwritten notes each with three or four key phrases that provided the themes for her speech. Those cards are preserved in Dame Enid's papers in the National Library of Australia in Canberra.

As a 'first' for Australian women, the speech she delivered was by definition a historic occasion, but as her biographer Anne Henderson remarked in 2008, the speech was also notable for its breadth and its quality: it 'was eloquent, richly written, and delivered in [Lyons'] long-practised and well-trained lilting voice. It surprised then and still remains one of the classic speeches in Australian political life.' Both in the Parliament itself and outside, the speech was highly praised. Curtin honoured it as a 'historic episode', commenting further that 'the struggle for the enfranchisement of women belongs ... to the great struggle for freedom and free institutions which have marked the evolution of our race'.

ABOVE *Dame Enid Lyons, photographed in the 1940s.*

It would be strange indeed were I not tonight deeply conscious of the fact, if not a little awed by the knowledge, that on my shoulders rests a great weight of responsibility; because this is the first occasion upon which a woman has addressed this House. For that reason, it is an occasion which, for every woman in the Commonwealth, marks in some degree a turning point in history. I am well aware that, as I acquit myself in the work that I have undertaken for the next three years, so shall I either prejudice or enhance the prospects of those who wish to follow me in public service in the years to come. I know that many honourable members have viewed the advent of women to the legislative halls with something approaching alarm; they have feared, I have no doubt, the somewhat too vigorous use of a new broom. I wish to reassure them. I hold very sound views on brooms, and sweeping. Although I quite realise that a new broom is a very useful adjunct to the work of the housewife, I also know that it undoubtedly is very unpopular in the broom cupboard; and this particular new broom knows that she has a very great deal to learn from the occupants of—I dare not say this particular cupboard. At all events, she hopes to conduct herself with sufficient modesty and sufficient sense of her lack of knowledge at least to earn the desire of honourable members to give her whatever help they may be able to give. I believe, very sincerely, that any woman entering the public arena must be prepared to work as men work; she must justify herself not as a woman, but as a citizen; she must attack the same problems, and be prepared to shoulder the same burdens. But because I am a woman, and cannot divest myself of those qualities that are inherent in my sex, and because every one of us speaks broadly in the terms of one's own experience, honourable members will have to become accustomed to the application of the homely metaphors of the kitchen rather than those of the operating theatre, the workshop or the farm. They must also become accustomed to the application of all kinds of measures of the touchstone of their effect upon the home and the family life. I hope that no one will imagine that that implies in any way a limitation of my political interests. Rather, it implies an ever-widening outlook on every problem that faces the world today. Every subject, from high finance to international relations, from social security to the winning of the war, touches very closely the home and the family. The late King George V, as he neared the end of a great reign and a good life, made a statement upon which any one may base the whole of one's political philosophy when he said, "The foundation of a nation's greatness is in the homes of its people." Therefore, honourable members will not, I know, be surprised when I say that I am likely to be even more concerned with national character than with national effort.

Somewhere about the year 1830 there began a period in Australian history which for me has always held a peculiar fascination. I should like to have been born at about that time. I should like to have been alive in the days when bushrangers flourished, when life was hard and even raw, when gold was discovered, when the colonies became states, and when all of the great social and political movements were born which so coloured the fabric of Australian life; because, during all those years very much of what we now know as the Australian character was formed. It was during those years that we learned those things which still characterise the great bulk of our people—hatred of oppression, love of "a fair go", a passion for justice. It was in those years that we developed those qualities of initiative and daring that have marked our men in every war in which they have fought—qualities which, I hope, will never be allowed to die. We are not on the threshold of such another era, when further formative measures will have to be taken; because we are today an organised community which no longer exists purely upon the initiative of its individual members, and if we would serve Australia well we must preserve those characteristics that were formed during that early period of our history.

I have been delighted, since I came here, to find the almost unanimity that exists in respect of the need for social service and in respect of many of the other problems that have been discussed in this chamber. In the matter of social security one thing stands out clearly in my mind. Such things are necessary in order that the weak shall not go to the wall, that the strong may be supported, that all may have justice. But we must never so blanket ourselves that those fine national qualities of which I have spoken shall no longer have play. I know so well that fear, want and idleness can kill the spirit of any people. But I know, too, that security can be bought at too great a cost—the cost of spiritual freedom. How, then, may we strike a balance? That, it seems to me, is the big question for us to decide today. There is one answer. We know perfectly well that any system of social security devised today must be financed largely from general taxation. Yet I would insist that every person in the community in receipt of any income whatsoever must make some contribution to the fund for social security. I want it to be an act of conscious citizenship. I want every child to be taught that when he begins to earn, then, for the first time, he will have the first privilege and right of citizenship—to begin to contribute to the great scheme that has been designed to serve him when he is no longer able to work and to help all of those who at any period of their lives may meet with distress or trouble. In such a scheme, I believe, there should be pensions for all; there should be no means test; those who have should contribute according to their means. But every one, however little he or she earns, should contribute something, be it only a three-penny stamp, as a sort of token payment for the advantage of being of Australian citizenship ...

I thought then, as I think now, that we should not fail occasionally to pause and look back upon the great moments of our past. We go along, thinking always that we progress, but sometimes we have to pause and take stock. I think that every Australian should pause now and again and say to himself, "Only 150 years ago this land was wilderness. Now we have great cities, wonderful feats of engineering and beautiful buildings everywhere. And this is still a land of promise." We cannot afford to neglect some recognition of our past, even though we gaze into the future.

Now, honourable members will forgive me, I know, when I say that I bear the name of one of whom it was said in this chamber that to him the problems of government were not problems of blue books, not problems of statistics, but problems of human values and human hearts and human feelings. That, it seems to me, is a concept of government that we might well cherish.

It is certainly one that I hold very dear. I hope that I shall never forget that everything that takes place in this chamber goes out somewhere to strike a human heart, to influence the life of some fellow being, and I believe this, too, with all my heart, that the duty of every government, whether in this country or any other, is to see that no man, because of the condition of his life, shall ever need lose his vision of the city of God.

'Fellow citizens, the war is over'

BEN CHIFLEY'S RADIO ADDRESS

ABOVE *Prime Minister Ben Chifley photographed giving a radio address.*

At 9.30 am on 15 August 1945, the Australian prime minister, Ben Chifley, in a broadcast to the nation advised his fellow citizens that the war was over. He was speaking of the Pacific War. Only a short time before, in May, in a similar broadcast to the people and in Parliament, he had brought news of peace in Europe. But for Chifley and his fellow Australians, that announcement had been overshadowed by the continuing struggle for victory in the Pacific.

Arguably more poignant than his speech in May, because Japan had posed a more immediate threat to the Australian homeland, Chifley's address in August is a document of quiet eloquence and dignity. His words are simple, direct, honest and sober, with occasional shades of poetic beauty. The prime minister acknowledged the nation's terrible losses while also offering grateful thanks for all those who had served in the front lines and at home. Other cruel losses in the Allied enterprise were noted: the deaths, only a short time before victory was won, of US President Franklin Delano Roosevelt on 12 April, and of Australia's Prime Minister John Curtin on 5 July. While Chifley looked back to the struggle and to the high honours won by Australians in the conflicts, he also looked forward to a new future when the nation's citizens must join together in the building of the peace: 'Here in Australia, there is much to be done.'

Fellow citizens, the war is over.

The Japanese Government has accepted the terms of surrender imposed by the Allied Nations and hostilities will now cease. The reply by the Japanese Government to the Note sent by Britain, the United States, the U.S.S.R. and China has been received and accepted by the Allied Nations.

At this moment, let us offer thanks to God.

Let us remember those whose lives were given that we may enjoy this glorious moment and may look forward to a peace which they have won for us. Let us remember those whose thoughts, with proud sorrow, turn towards gallant, loved ones who will not come back. On behalf of the people and Government of Australia, I offer humble thanks to the fighting men of the United Nations, whose gallantry, sacrifice and devotion to duty have brought us the victory. Nothing can fully repay the debt we owe them, nor can history record in adequate terms their deeds from the black days that followed September 1939 and December 1941 until this moment.

We owe, too, a great debt to those men and women who performed miracles of production, in secondary and primary industries, so that the battle of supply could be won and a massive effort achieved. Materials, money and resources have been poured out so that the fighting men would not go short. Australia's part, comparatively, in terms of fighting forces and supplies, ranks high and the Australian people may be justly proud of everything they have done.

I am sure that you would like me to convey to the commanders of the fighting forces the warmest thanks for their skill, efficiency and great devotion. Especially do I mention General Douglas MacArthur, with whom we had so much in common and with whom we shared the dangers when Australia was threatened with invasion.

In your name, I offer to the leaders of the United Nations our congratulations and thanks. We join with the United States in a common regret that their own inspiring leader, the late Mr Roosevelt, did not live to see this day. We thank his successor, President Truman, for the work he has done. Australians, too, will feel their happiness tinged with sorrow that another man who gave his all, was not spared to be with us today. That man was John Curtin. To Mr Churchill, Generalissimo Stalin and Generalissimo Chiang Kai-shek go the unstinted thanks of free people everywhere for what they have done for the common cause. Especially do we honour Mr Churchill, with whom in the dark days—to use his own words—we had the honour to stand alone against aggression.

And now our men and women will come home; our fighting men with battle honours thick upon them from every theatre of war. Australians stopped the Japanese in their drive south, just as they helped start the first match towards ultimate victory in North Africa. Australians fought in the battles of the air everywhere and Australian seamen covered every ocean. They are coming home to a peace which has yet to be won. The United Nations Charter for a World Organization is the hope of the world and Australia has pledged the same activity in making it successful as she showed in the framing of it. Here in Australia, there is much to be done. The Australian Government, which stood steadfast during the dread days of war, will give all that it has to working and planning to ensure that the peace will be a real thing. I ask that the State governments and all sections of the community should cooperate in facing the tasks and solving the problems that are ahead. Let us join together in the march of our nation to future greatness.

You are aware of what has been arranged for the celebration of this great victory and deliverance. In the name of the Commonwealth Government, I invite you to join in the thanksgiving services arranged for, truly, this is a time to give thanks to God and to those men against whose sacrifice for us there is no comparison.

'the light on the hill'

BEN CHIFLEY'S ADDRESS TO THE LABOR PARTY

In his memorable phrase 'the light on the hill', Prime Minister Ben Chifley created one of the Australian Labor Party's most powerful and inspirational catchcries. The phrase was embedded in an otherwise gentle and modest address to the New South Wales State Conference of the Australian Labor Party, delivered on 12 June 1949, just six months before a general election. The ALP would be swept from office, to be replaced by a triumphant Liberal–Country Party coalition led by Robert Gordon Menzies. The defeat when it came was crushing: losing 3.7 per cent of the total vote, the ALP was reduced to forty-seven seats in the House of Representatives, compared with seventy-four seats won by the coalition. The ALP would remain in opposition for twenty-three years, and for seventeen of those years Menzies would hold power as prime minister.

A former engine driver and later a union official, Chifley re-entered federal Parliament in 1940, where he had sat briefly a decade earlier. He served as treasurer in Curtin's wartime cabinet and became prime minister when John Curtin died in office in 1945. With the cessation of hostilities in Europe and later in the Pacific, it fell to Chifley to implement a program of postwar reconstruction—a program informed by his vision of a just social order. It was in that context—perhaps even as a valediction—that Chifley coined the phrase 'the light on the hill', though others have seen him cloaking the political ideals of socialism in homely comfort. Nonetheless, Chifley stands undiminished as one of the heroes of the ALP and of the nation itself. Perhaps because of the defeat of 1949 and the ALP's long period in the wilderness, Chifley's phrase has acquired a deeper resonance over the years since then. It was revived in the title of Ross McMullin's 1991 history of the Labor Party and was also invoked as an ideal by Prime Minister Paul Keating.

I have had the privilege of leading the Labor Party for nearly four years. They have not been easy times and it has not been an easy job. It is a man-killing job and would be impossible if it were not for the help of my colleagues and members of the movement.

No Labor Minister or leader ever has an easy job. The urgency that rests behind the Labor movement, pushing it on to do things, to create new conditions, to reorganise the economy of the country, always means that the people who work within the Labor movement, people who lead, can never have an easy job. The job of the evangelist is never easy.

Because of the turn of fortune's wheel your Premier (Mr McGirr) and I have gained some prominence in the Labor movement. But the strength of the movement cannot come from us. We make plans and pass legislation to help and direct the economy of the country. But the job of getting the things the people of the country want comes from the roots of the Labor movement—the people who support it.

When I sat at a Labor meeting in the country with only ten or fifteen men there, I found a man sitting beside me who had been working in the Labor movement for fifty-four years. I have no doubt that many of you have been doing the same, not hoping for any advantage of the movement, not hoping for any personal gain, but because you believe in a movement that has been built up to bring better conditions to the people. Therefore, the success of the Labor party at the next election depends entirely, as it always has done, on the people who work.

I try to think of the Labor movement, not as putting an extra sixpence into somebody's pocket, or making somebody Prime Minister or Premier, but as a movement bringing something better to the people, better standards of living, greater happiness to the mass of the people. We have a great objective—the light on the hill—which we aim to reach by working for the betterment of mankind not only here but anywhere we may give a helping hand. If it were not for that, the Labor movement would not be worth fighting for.

If the movement can make someone more comfortable, give to some father or mother a greater feeling of security for their children, a feeling that if a depression comes there will be work, that the government is striving its hardest to do its best, then the Labor movement will be completely justified.

It does not matter about persons like me who have our limitations. I only hope that the generosity, kindliness and friendliness shown to me by thousands of my colleagues in the Labor movement will continue to be given to the movement and add zest to its work.

The Hon. J.B. Chifley
Prime Minister of Australia

ABOVE *Military representatives of Australia, New Zealand and the United States meet at Pearl Harbor, Hawaii in 1952.*

Making an alliance with the United States

THE ANZUS TREATY

What has come to be called, 'the American alliance' is the first and most fundamental plank of Australian foreign policy. The alliance is embodied in the form of a regional defence agreement, known as the ANZUS Treaty, negotiated between Australia, New Zealand and the United States in 1951. The treaty was a response to shared fears of communist expansion in southeast Asia, and concerns in Australia and New Zealand over the terms of the peace treaty the United States had entered into with Japan. By means of the ANZUS Treaty, the Australian and New Zealand governments sought to gain the protection of a powerful ally and to ensure that their countries would sit firmly within America's strategic orbit. So much was this the direction in which Australia began to move after it had entered into war with Japan in 1941 that the new treaty gave form and substance to what legal historian J.G. Starke called 'a political reality of long standing—the *de facto* alliance between [the parties] in regard to defence matters in the Pacific'.

While the three signatories affirmed their desire 'to declare publicly and formally their sense of unity, so that no potential aggressor could be under the illusion that any one of them would stand alone in the Pacific area', the treaty itself is marked by ambiguities that have never been tested, and popular understanding of it has given rise to a number of misconceptions and misapprehensions. Certainly the treaty does not bind the United States to unconditional military support of its allies in all circumstances. Nor does it establish any mechanism or structure equivalent to that established in western Europe by the North Atlantic Security Treaty of 4 April 1949, which gave birth to the NATO alliance.

In 1984 the ANZUS Treaty came under pressure when New Zealand declared its country a nuclear-free zone and refused to allow US nuclear-powered submarines to visit its ports. Two years later the United States and Australia concluded a series of bilateral talks confirming that the two countries would continue to honour their obligations to one another under the ANZUS Treaty, in spite of the fact that the treaty's trilateral aspect had been compromised by New Zealand's stance on the nuclear question. On 17 September 1986, the US suspended its treaty obligations to New Zealand. This suspension remains in force although Australia and New Zealand continue their own bilateral defence relationship as defined by the treaty.

Prompted partly by the rhetoric of politicians, there is an exaggerated understanding of the power and obligations of the ANZUS Treaty and a trusting faith in the protection it offers. Nevertheless great sentiment attaches to it, and it still stands as the symbol and expression of the shared values and ideals of two committed democracies. That sentiment was tested in the immediate aftermath of the terrorist attacks on the World Trade Center in New York and the Pentagon in Washington on 11 September 2001. In making its commitment to join the United States in its declared 'war on terror', the Australian government under Prime Minister John Howard invoked the articles of the treaty for the first time in its history.

The conservative side of politics has suggested the Australian Labor Party is careless of the treaty and the relationship with the United States. But both the treaty and the alliance have strong bipartisan support, a position backed by the wider Australian electorate. As one-time Labor leader Mark Latham found to his cost, politicians who scorn the alliance do so at their peril. The electorate is, however, less comfortable with sycophancy in the management of the relationship with the United States and with incumbents of the presidency.

SECURITY TREATY BETWEEN AUSTRALIA, NEW ZEALAND, AND THE UNITED STATES OF AMERICA

THE PARTIES TO THIS TREATY,

REAFFIRMING their faith in the purposes and principles of the Charter of the United Nations and their desire to live in peace with all peoples and all Governments, and desiring to strengthen the fabric of peace in the Pacific Area,

NOTING that the United States already has arrangements pursuant to which its armed forces are stationed in the Philippines, and has armed forces and administrative responsibilities in the Ryukyus, and upon the coming into force of the Japanese Peace Treaty may also station armed forces in and about Japan to assist in the preservation of peace and security in the Japan area,

RECOGNIZING that Australia and New Zealand as members of the British Commonwealth of Nations have military obligations outside as well as within the Pacific Area,

DESIRING to declare publicly and formally their sense of unity, so that no potential aggressor could be under the illusion that any of them stand alone in the Pacific area, and

DESIRING further to coordinate their efforts for collective defense for the preservation of peace and security pending the development of a more comprehensive system of regional security in the Pacific Area,

THEREFORE DECLARE AND AGREE as follows:

Article I
The Parties undertake, as set forth in the Charter of the United Nations, to settle any international disputes in which they may be involved by peaceful means in such a manner that international peace and security and justice are not endangered and to refrain in their international relations from the threat or use of force in any manner inconsistent with the purposes of the United Nations.

Article II
In order more effectively to achieve the objective of this Treaty the Parties separately and jointly by means of effective self-help and mutual aid will maintain and develop their individual and collective capacity to resist armed attack.

Article III
The Parties will consult together whenever in the opinion of any of them the territorial integrity, political independence or security of any of the Parties is threatened in the Pacific.

Article IV
Each party recognizes that an armed attack in the Pacific Area on any of the Parties would be dangerous to its own peace and safety and declares that it

would act to meet the common danger in accordance with its constitutional processes.

Any such armed attack and all measures taken as a result shall be immediately reported to the Security Council of the United Nations. Such measures shall be terminated when the Security Council has taken the measures necessary to restore and maintain international peace and security.

Article V

For the purpose of Article IV, an armed attack on any of the parties is deemed to include an armed attack on the metropolitan territory of any of the Parties, or on the island territories under its jurisdiction in the Pacific or on its armed forces, public vessels or aircraft in the Pacific.

Article VI

This Treaty does not affect and shall not be interpreted as affecting in any way the rights and obligations of the Parties under the Charter of the United Nations or the responsibility of the United Nations for the maintenance of international peace and security.

Article VII

The Parties hereby establish a Council, consisting of their Foreign Ministers or their Deputies, to consider matters concerning the implementation of this Treaty. The Council should be so organized as to be able to meet at any time.

Article VIII

Pending the development of a more comprehensive system of regional security in the Pacific Area and the development by the United Nations of more effective means to maintain international peace and security, the Council, established by Article VII, is authorized to maintain a consultative relationship with States, Regional Organizations, Associations of States or other authorities in the Pacific Area in a position to further the purposes of this Treaty and to contribute to the security of that Area.

Article IX

This Treaty shall be ratified by the Parties in accordance with their respective constitutional processes. The instruments of ratification shall be deposited as soon as possible with the Government of Australia, which will notify each of the other signatories of such deposit. The Treaty shall enter into force as soon as the ratifications of the signatories have been deposited.

Article X

The Treaty shall remain in force indefinitely. Any Party may cease to be a member of the Council established by Article VII one year after notice has been given to the Government of Australia, which will inform the Governments of the other Parties of the deposit of such notice

Article XI

This Treaty in the English language shall be deposited in the archives of the Government of Australia. Duly certified copies thereof will be transmitted by that Government to the Governments of each of the other signatories.

IN WITNESS WHEREOF the undersigned Plenipotentiaries have signed this Treaty.

DONE at the city of San Francisco this first day of September, 1951,

FOR AUSTRALIA:
PERCY C. SPENDER

FOR NEW ZEALAND:
C.A. BERENDSEN

FOR THE UNITED STATES OF AMERICA:
DEAN ACHESON
JOHN FOSTER DULLES
ALEXANDER WILEY
JOHN J. SPARKMAN

'present Australian Life in any of its phases'

THE MILES FRANKLIN AWARD FOR AUSTRALIAN LITERATURE

The reading of the will of Australian writer Miles Franklin, who died on 19 September 1954, revealed a surprise in its direction for the establishment of an award for Australian literature. In other respects the will—signed by Franklin on 9 July 1948—was conventional. Various small treasures and items of sentimental value were distributed to family and friends; modest financial support was provided for two nephews; and personal, literary and other family records were divided between the Public (State) Library of New South Wales (for the Mitchell Library) and the National Library of Australia in Canberra. The major clause of the will (Clause 6) provided for the consolidation of the residue of the estate and for the money to be dedicated to the Franklin Fund, from which prizes might be awarded to a novel 'of the highest literary merit and which must present Australian Life in any of its phases'. At least three judges were to be appointed, with the award—to be called the Franklin Award—to be determined by a majority, or not at all if there were no novel of sufficient merit in a given year. The will also empowered the judges to award the prize to a play written for the stage, radio, television 'or such medium as may develop'. Franklin's assets were modest, but her intent was forward looking, ambitious and generous.

It is not known when the idea of funding such a literary award occurred to Miles Franklin, but as both a writer and a passionate supporter of Australian literature, she knew the struggle writers faced to find time and opportunity to create. She herself had been twice awarded the S.H. Prior Memorial Prize, and perhaps its demise in 1947 had been a prompt. Possibly, too, she was moved by the example of the Pulitzer Prize in the United States. But it is the view of Jill Roe, her recent biographer, that the award encapsulated the two great hopes of Miles Franklin's later life: that Australian writers be encouraged and supported, and that Australian writing 'would become a significant field in world literature'. In this ambitious vision, the award she created was for excellence.

The first decision of the inaugural judges was to ensure that the award be named the Miles Franklin Award. The prize was awarded for the first time in 1957 to Patrick White for *Voss*. White won the prize again in 1961 for *Riders in the Chariot*, before his ultimate success as winner of the Nobel Prize for Literature in 1973. Other Miles Franklin Award winners have included Glenda Adams, Jessica Anderson, Thea Astley, Peter Carey, Elizabeth Jolley, David Malouf, Randolph Stow and Tim Winton. No longer the most valuable literary prize offered in Australia, the Miles Franklin Award is, however, the country's most prestigious recognition of literary achievement. In Jill Roe's opinion, it has the standing of an antipodean Booker or Pulitzer. The author of *My Brilliant Career* would surely have been well pleased with the results of her bequest.

6. I DIRECT my Trustee to stand possessed of the balance of my Estate ... and to hold the same Upon Trust to establish a fund to be called the Franklin Fund and to invest the same in or upon any of the securities authorised by this my Will with power from time to time to transpose any such securities into any other authorised security or securities and out of the income arising therefrom or any part thereof as my Trustee may think fit to provide prizes to be known as the Franklin Awards such prizes to be awarded annually or at such times as my Trustee may think fit with full power to postpone such award or awards for such time as my Trustee may deem proper such prizes to be awarded to authors for the advancement improvement and betterment of Australian Literature to improve the educational style of such authors and to provide them with additional monetary amounts and thus enable them to improve their literary efforts and work and in connection with such Awards I request my Trustee to appoint [three or more Judges] ... I REQUEST my Trustee to be guided in making the award by the decision of the majority of the judges for the time being and such prize shall be awarded for the Novel for the year which is of the highest literary merit and which must present Australian Life in any of its phases and if there be no Novel worthy of the prize in the opinion of the said Judges then such Award may be given as such judges may advise to the Author of a play for either stage, radio or Television or such medium as may develop but not for farce or musical comedy and so that my Trustee may at any time suspend the awarding of such prize or prizes for such time as it may think proper and my Trustee shall be the sole Judge as to such prize not being awarded ...

'it is always the few who have to pioneer the way'

PREMIER J.J. CAHILL PLANS AN OPERA HOUSE FOR AUSTRALIA

The Sydney Opera House, designed by the Danish architect Jørn Utzon (1918–2008), has become an icon not only for its home city but also for Australia. On 28 June 2007 it was added to the UNESCO World Heritage List with a commendation that noted: 'Sydney Opera House stands by itself as one of the indisputable masterpieces of human creativity, not only in the twentieth century but in the history of humankind'. But the story of the design and building of the Sydney Opera House is one charged with high drama, emotion and deep controversy, not least for the effective dismissal of Utzon from the project in 1966. Compounding this, the opera house was completed in ways that compromised its functionality.

As a symbol, however, the structure itself is transcendent. Architectural historian Philip Drew has seen it as 'one of the truly great buildings of the world: two out of three readers of *The Times* Britain and the *Australian* placed it in their list of the Seven Wonders of the Modern World in 1992, and it is the leading tourist attraction in New South Wales. A symbol, not only of Sydney but Australia, its distinctive zig-zag roof was adopted for the successful 2000 Olympic logo.'

Sydney's ambitions for an acoustically perfect performing space to serve a symphony orchestra and an opera company, together with a smaller venue for chamber music, owe much to the vision of the English composer and conductor Eugene Goossens (1893–1962). In July 1947 Goossens took up his appointment as chief conductor of the Sydney Symphony Orchestra and soon began campaigning to elevate the place of music in the city's cultural life. His large artistic vision found a political ally in the Australian Labor Party's John Joseph Cahill (1891–1959), who became premier of New South Wales in 1952.

Two years later, on 30 November 1954, Cahill called a public meeting at the State Library of New South Wales. There, in a display of political leadership and cultural commitment rarely seen in Australian public life, he articulated plans for an opera house that might adorn both Sydney and Australia. Cahill's modest opening remarks at that public meeting have an enduring significance as one of the landmark documents in the evolution of the arts in Australia and as the imprimatur that gave substance to the project that would emerge as the Sydney Opera House.

ABOVE *Premier Cahill signs the contract for the building of the Sydney Opera House, 1959.*

Ladies and Gentlemen ... I express my sincere thanks for your presence at this conference ... As you are aware, the Government has decided that an Opera House shall be established in Sydney and that it will be worthy of this city ... The people who have gathered here this morning are interested in opera and other forms of art to which perhaps many in the community might not give a second thought. Experience has proved that it is always the few who have to pioneer the way, and the Government has decided to go ahead with this project. We are appreciative of your willingness to help us place it on a proper footing.

The purpose of this conference is not to decide the form the building will take or the site on which it will be erected. That would obviously be impossible in so short a time. This meeting has been called to enable the Government to hear the views of as many interested people as possible, and draw on the experience of people who are interested in opera, drama and ballet, and may possibly have investigated or been associated with opera both here and overseas. Sydney's Opera House will be the first in Australia. It is probably many years since a similar project was undertaken anywhere in the world, therefore, we want to adopt the best features and discard the worst, of existing opera houses, both as to site and architecture.

The Government has no preconceived ideas as to site or design, but we hope that from this conference will emerge a broad pattern which will be of assistance to the small working committee whose job it will be to examine such matters in detail on the Government's behalf and submit recommendations ...

I should like to touch briefly on the reasons for the Government's decision to build an Opera House, but before I do so, it is appropriate that I should pay tribute to the body which has done so much to make opera a permanent feature of the musical life of New South Wales, namely the National Opera of Australia ...

By their enthusiasm and hard work they have stimulated and fostered an ever-widening interest in opera. They have brought it to the man in the street and made him more conscious of an art in which the natural talents of many Australians, such as singing, can find expression. I pay tribute also to those other bodies ... which form the basis of our cultural life. I refer to those musical and dramatic societies, choirs and ballet organisations which encourage artistic talent and provide facilities for training singers, actors and dancers.

The Government considers that the best incentive and encouragement it can give to these artists and to the development of talent is to provide an Opera House in which the best singers, actors and dancers might aspire to perform.

In Sydney a wonderful opportunity is offered to build a musical tradition which, in time, can equal anything the older countries can produce. The basis for that tradition is already firmly established by the Sydney Symphony Orchestra under the able direction of Mr. Eugene Goossens. Australian singers have made and are making a name for themselves in London and we, the people of New South Wales, would be recreant to our trust if we did not provide the facilities for those talents to flourish and bring lustre to Australia.

Some will say that the time is not opportune to build an Opera House here in Sydney, and that we could apply our resources to better advantage. I have been in public life for thirty years and there was never a time when a similar criticism would not have been offered against any great national venture of this nature. If such a criticism were valid one wonders how London ever got its Covent Garden, Paris, New York and Vienna their fine opera houses and Milan its La Scala, which was destroyed during the war and has since been rebuilt. This State cannot go on without proper facilities for the expression of talent and the staging of the highest forms of artistic entertainment which add grace and charm to living and which help to develop and mould a better, more enlightened community. The Opera House should not be regarded as the special preserve of Sydney people. It should be regarded as something which belongs to the people of New South Wales as a whole—or, for that matter to the people of Australia ...

ABOVE *Aerial view of Sydney Harbour before the Opera House was built.*

Premier J.J. Cahill plans an opera house for Australia.

'the existence of painting as an independent art is in danger'

THE ANTIPODEAN MANIFESTO

In August 1959 the Australian art world erupted into a dispute that saw battle lines drawn between adherents of figurative painting and converts to abstract expressionism. The focal points of the brouhaha were the state capitals of Melbourne and Sydney, the two as usual standing in opposition to each other, each seeming to speak a different language. Art historian, teacher and critic Bernard Smith (b. 1916)—the key draftsman of the manifesto—noted in 2001 that the conversion of the Sydney artists and critics to abstract expressionism was accomplished with 'the enthusiasm, speed and efficiency of a modern evangelical crusade'. That conversion brought with it a fanatical devotion to the principles of abstract art and a disdain for figurative painting. For a time, the long-standing rivalry between the two cities came to express itself in an argument about these two forms of painting.

The initiative in the dispute was taken earnestly by a group of Melbourne artists—the self-styled Antipodeans—who issued a polemical statement or manifesto. The Antipodean Manifesto was written to accompany an exhibition at the Victorian Artists' Society, held between 4–15 August 1959. Those taking part were the painters Charles Blackman (b. 1928), Arthur Boyd (1920–1999), David Boyd (b. 1924), John Brack (1920–1999), Robert Dickerson (b. 1924) and Clifton Pugh (1924–1990). Significant also was Bernard Smith (b. 1916) who, although not a painter himself, was the principal author of the statement. Other leading Melbourne painters were invited to join the group but refused.

As the unnamed targets of the Melbourne criticisms of abstract art, several Sydney artists were happy to satirise the serious tone of the Antipodean Manifesto. John Coburn (1925–2006), Oscar Edwards (1905–1996), Roy Fluke (b. 1921), Elwyn Lynn (1917–1997), John Ogburn (b. 1925) and Henry Salkauskas (1925–1979) came together briefly as a collective to protest that most 'art is too solemn ... and duller than television'. But it was in Adelaide that Ross Luck (b. 1918), an office-bearer in the Contemporary Art Society (SA), made one of the most considered criticisms of the Melbourne manifesto. Luck saw the Antipodeans as latter-day King Canutes trying to push back the rolling tide of abstract expressionism, and he derided the manifesto as 'anti-climactic, irrelevant, childish—a professor's attempt to categorise and control his recalcitrant charges'.

While critical of its content and its failure to define its terms, art critic Robert Hughes in 1970 described the manifesto as 'a widely heard shot [that] proved in the end to be the most controversial document in recent Australian painting'. But he also noted that it had generated 'a great deal of dust'. Perhaps elevating the purpose of the manifesto, Bernard Smith suggested that the concerns of the Antipodeans might be seen as part of the uneasiness among Australian intellectuals about the insidious undermining of the national culture by Americanisation.

Let it be said in the first place that we have all played a part in that movement which has sought for a better understanding of the work of contemporary artists both here and abroad. Indeed, we are, in no uncertain sense, members of the modern movement in art. We take cognisance of all that has happened in art during the past fifty years—not to do so would be folly.

But today we believe, like many others, that the existence of painting as an independent art is in danger. Today *tachistes*, action painters, geometric abstractionists, abstract expressionists and their innumerable band of camp followers threaten to benumb the intellect and wit of art with their bland and pretentious mysteries. The art which they champion is not an art sufficient for our time, it is not an art for living men. It reveals, it seems to us, a death of the mind and spirit.

And yet wherever we look, New York, Paris, London, San Francisco or Sydney, we see young artists dazzled by the luxurious pageantry and colour of non-figuration. It has become necessary therefore for us to point out, as clearly and as unmistakably as we can, that the great Tachiste Emperor has no clothes—nor has he a body. He is only a blot—a most colourful, elegant and shapely blot.

Modern art has liberated the artist from his bondage to the world of natural appearances, it has not imposed on him the need to withdraw from life. The widespread desire, as it is claimed, to 'purify' painting has led many artists to claim they have invented a new language. We see no evidence at all of the emergence of such a new language nor any likelihood of its appearance. Painting for us is more than paint. Certainly the non-figurative arts can express moods and attitudes, but they are not capable of producing a new artistic language. We are not, it seems to us, witnessing in non-figuration the emergence of an utterly new form of art. We are witnessing yet another attempt by puritan and iconoclast to reduce the living speech of art to the silence of decoration.

Art is, for the artist, his speech, his way of communication. And the image, the recognisable shape, the meaningful symbol, is the basic unit of his language. Lines, shapes and colours though they may be beautiful and expressive are by no means images. For us the image is a figured shape or symbol fashioned by the artist from his perceptions and imaginative experience. It is born of experience and refers back to past experience—and it communicates. It communicates because it has the capacity to refer to experiences the artist shares with his audience.

Art is willed. No matter how much the artist may draw upon the instinctive and unconscious levels of his experience, a work of art remains a purposive act, a humanisation of nature. The artist's purpose achieves vitality and power in his images. Take the great black bull of Lascaux, for example, an old beast and a powerful one, who has watched over the birth of many arts and many mythologies. He is endowed with a vitality which is an emblem of life itself. Destroy the living power of the image and you have humbled and humiliated the artist, have made him a blind and powerless Samson fit only to grind the corn of Philistines.

As Antipodeans we accept the image as representing some form of acceptance of, and involvement in life. For the image has always been concerned with life, whether of the flesh or the spirit. Art cannot live much longer feeding upon the disillusions of the generation of 1914. Today Dada is as dead as the dodo and it is time we buried this antique hobby-horse of our fathers.

When we look about us there still seems much to be done in art worth doing. People, their surroundings and the past that made them are still subjects, we should like to point out, worthy of the consideration of the artist. We are not, of course, seeking to create a national style. But we do seek to draw inspiration from our own lives and the lives of those about us. Life here in this country has similarities to life elsewhere and also significant differences. Our experience of this life must be our material. We believe that we have both a right and a duty to draw upon our experience both of society and nature in Australia for the materials of our art. For Europeans this country has always been a primordial and curious land. To the ancients the antipodes was a kind of nether world, to the peoples of the Middle Ages its forms of life were monstrous, and for us, Europeans by heritage (but not by birth) much of this strangeness lingers. It is natural therefore that we should see and experience nature differently in some degree from the artists of the northern hemisphere.

We live in a young society still making myths. The emergence of myth is a continuous social activity. In the growth and transformation of its myths a society achieves its own sense of identity. In this process the artist may play a creative and liberating role. The ways in which a society images its own feelings and attitudes in myth provides him with one of the deepest sources of art.

Nevertheless our final obligation is neither to place nor nation. So far as we are concerned the society of man is indivisible and we are in it. When we think of all that has happened to people like ourselves during the last fifty years we know that we do not fully understand them—and we want to. How can they bear living? But they do. So we want to ask questions. If such an aim is impure then we should say that purism leads to puritanism, puritanism to image-smashing, and image-smashing, after an Indian summer of decorative luxury, to the death of art.

If the triumph of non-figurative art in the West fills us with concern so, too, does the dominance of socialist realism in the East. Socialist realism, as we understand it, places too many restraints upon the independent creative activity of the artist for it to produce work of vitality and power. We wish to stress that in defending the image we are not seeking to return to naturalistic forms of painting and sculpture but are defending something which is vital to the life of art itself.

We want to say, finally, that we are more directly concerned with our own art, more involved in it, than in anything else. This is not escapism. It is simply a recognition that the first loyalty of an artist is to his art. Today that loyalty requires, beyond all else, the defence of the image.

Hear the views of the people of Yirrkala

THE BARK PETITION OF THE YOLNGU PEOPLE

Troubled by the encroachment of bauxite mining on the Gove Peninsula in northeast Arnhem Land, the area's Yolngu people drew up a petition in 1963 seeking the Commonwealth Parliament's recognition of their rights to the traditional lands used for hunting and food gathering 'from time immemorial'. The inspiration for the petition, and advice on its formulation and content, came from two senior Labor members of Parliament, Kim Beazley senior (1917–2007) and Gordon Bryant (1914–1991), both of whom had a long-standing interest in Aboriginal affairs. However, the petition is accepted as an independent expression of Yolngu concerns and aspirations.

The petition was remarkable both in its physical form and in its requests. It was drawn on two separate panels, the first from the Dhuwa moiety of the Yolngu and the second from the Yirritaj moiety. Written in Gumatj, an Indigenous dialect known only to a handful of Europeans, and with an English translation, the two parts of the typed petition are attached to bark, each with a decorative border—goannas, snakes, dugongs, turtles and birds—painted in black, white, and shades of brown and ochre on a finely drawn ground of overlapping lines and geometric shapes. The explicit clan symbols form an integral part of the petition: their purpose was to depict the Yolngu relationship with the land. While the text and signatures of each petition are identical, the decorative elements differ in detail. At the time of their presentation, the panels were certified by the Clerk of the House of Representatives as being in conformity with Standing Orders, the first on 14 August and the second on 28 August 1963.

The two-part Yolngu petition is the first officially recognised document in Australia asserting the Indigenous claims of land use, occupation and ownership. The protest, however, was specific in its intent, prompted not by the larger issue of land ownership but by the lack of consultation and secrecy of the government's agreement with the bauxite miner Nabalco. Following the receipt of the petition, a parliamentary committee of inquiry heard evidence at Yirrkala and Darwin, and subsequently it recommended the payment of compensation to the Yolngu for the loss of livelihood, protection for sacred sites and parliamentary oversight of the mining project.

These recommendations addressed the immediate concerns of the Yolngu people, but they did not deal with the question of land rights, which were pursued in the first instance—and without success—in the Supreme Court of the Northern Territory in 1968. Yolngu ownership rights were eventually recognised in the Northern Territory *Land Rights Act 1976*.

Historian Julie Fenwick, writing in 2001, has cautioned that the Yirrkala petition did not in itself initiate fundamental change—its plea was particular and, within its limits, successful. But, Fenwick argues, the petition sits within a larger and more complex environment, where a consciousness of Yolngu notions of ownership fed into a growing understanding of the history of Aboriginal dispossession more generally. In time this created a climate of opinion that was sympathetic to the recognition of Aboriginal land ownership and to a correction, however unevenly, of an historical injustice. The notion of Aboriginal rights to land developed tentatively and in stages, before it eventually became the key goal of the Aboriginal political movement. But, as a first step, the Yirrkala petition is recognised and honoured as a symbolic landmark and as a document that contributed to the shaping of Australian opinion and the raising of awareness on the question of Indigenous rights.

TO THE HONOURABLE SPEAKER AND MEMBERS OF THE HOUSE OF REPRESENTATIVES

IN PARLIAMENT ASSEMBLED.

The Humble Petition of the Undersigned aboriginal people of Yirrkala, being members of the Balamumu, Narrkala, Gapiny, Miliwurrwurr people and Djapu, Mangalili, Madarrpa, Magarrwanalmirri, Djambarrpuynu, Gumaitj, Marrakulu, Galpu, Dhaluangu, Wangurri, Warramirri, Naymil, Riritjingu, tribes respectfully showeth.

1. That nearly 500 people of the above tribes are residents of the land excised from the Aboriginal Reserve in Arnhem Land.
2. That the procedures of the excision of this land and the fate of the people on it were never explained to them beforehand, and were kept secret from them.
3. That when Welfare Officers and Government officials came to inform them of decisions taken without them and against them, they did not undertake to convey to the Government in Canberra the views and feelings of the Yirrkala aboriginal people.
4. That the land in question has been hunting and food gathering land for the Yirrkala tribes from time immemorial: we were all born here.
5. That places sacred to the Yirrkala people, as well as vital to their livelihood are in the excised land, especially Melville Bay.
6. That the people of this area fear that their needs and interests will be completely ignored as they have been ignored in the past, and they fear that the fate which has overtaken the Larrakeah tribe will overtake them.
7. And they humbly pray that the Honourable the House of Representatives will appoint a Committee, accompanied by competent interpreters, to hear the views of the people of Yirrkala before permitting excision of this land.
8. They humbly pray that no arrangements be entered into with any company which will destroy the livelihood and independence of the Yirrkala people.

And your petitioners as in duty bound will ever pray God to help you and us.
(English language translation.)

ABOVE *The decorated borders on the petition depict the Yolngu relationship with the land.*

ABOVE *First edition of the Australian, published on 15 July 1964.*

A national newspaper for Australia

RUPERT MURDOCH LAUNCHES THE *AUSTRALIAN*

Australia's national newspaper, the *Australian*, was founded in 1964 by Melbourne-born Rupert Murdoch (b. 1931), who was later to go on to build a vast global communications and publishing empire. The *Australian* was the first newspaper he had created, rather than merely bought. On 15 July 1964 the first issue rolled off a second-hand press in Canberra. The aims of the paper and the expectations of its proprietor were sketched briefly in an editorial statement published on the first page and reproduced here. The first editor of the new broadsheet was the mercurial Maxwell Newton (1929–1990), a man said to have 'rolled dice with governments and redirected the careers of Prime Ministers'.

Murdoch's aim for his editor and the paper was ambitious: 'to report the nation to Canberra and Canberra to the nation'. Later, the *Sydney Morning Herald*, one of the great rivals of the *Australian*, acknowledged the launch of the new paper as 'the most significant event in post-war Australian journalism. It was a force in opening up Australian society and preparing the ground for great changes in Australia after 1972'. In covering national and international news in greater depth and in better economic and technological reporting, the *Australian* forced improvements on its rivals in the state capitals.

As Australia's first national daily, Murdoch's venture was more than just a newspaper. Its resonance was both symbolic and emotional, and its purpose was, and has remained, serious. Murdoch later described his creation as 'an idealistic effort ... a way to ... have a national debate'. But financially the paper was a gamble: funds were borrowed; the country was scoured for advertisers willing to support a brave but highly uncertain venture. Circulation flagged and losses accumulated. Newspaper readers in Australia were parochial by habit and by circumstance—in a vast country, loyalties were to state-based papers and to local news. Physically the challenges of running and distributing a national newspaper out of Canberra were immense. In the days before easy long-distance communication, and later still computer typesetting, paper matrices had to be flown to printing plants in Melbourne and Sydney. Closure of Canberra's airport because of fog during the winter months played havoc with production schedules and distribution.

In the pioneering days of the new paper, Rupert Murdoch was in his element. One of his biographers, William Shawcross, has given a vivid account of the proprietor actively engaged in every stage and aspect of the paper's production and of his determination to conquer Australia's 'tyranny of distance'. The *Australian* survives, more conservative now than at its beginning, but having maintained a remarkable adherence to its first vision of itself.

GOOD DAY

Here is Australia's first truly national newspaper. It is produced today because you want it; because the nation needs it.

In these pages you will find the impartial information and the independent thinking that are essential to the further advance of our country.

This paper is tied to no party, to no state, and has no chains of any kind. Its guide is faith in Australia and the country's future.

SPEAK OUT

It will be our duty to inform Australians everywhere of what is really happening in their country; of what is really happening in the rest of the world; and how this affects our prosperity, our prospects, our national conscience and our public image.

We shall not hesitate to speak fearlessly. We shall criticise.

We will not be influenced when there is public need for us to be outspoken.

We shall praise. We shall encourage those feelings and movements in public and private life which elevate the individual and advance the nation's welfare.

WORLD NEWS

The world news service which appears in The Australian surpasses any yet assembled in the pages of one newspaper anywhere in the world.

The authoritative writers who will contribute regularly on topics ranging from the arts to aviation are acknowledged leaders in the subjects they will discuss. The business and financial section is organised and written by the shrewdest and best-informed commercial journalists in the nation.

FRIENDS

Vigor, truth and information without dullness will be found day by day in these columns. We believe the people of Australia will welcome this new approach to national journalism.

This morning, we believe, we shall make thousands of friends, who as the thinking men and women of Australia will have a profound influence on the future. You are welcome to this company of progress.

'we're at war, don't let's make any mistake about it'

AUSTRALIA ENTERS THE WAR IN VIETNAM

On the evening of 29 April 1965, Prime Minister Sir Robert Menzies stepped to the dispatch box to deliver a ministerial statement to a depleted House of Representatives. Neither the leader of the Opposition, A.A. Calwell, nor his deputy, Gough Whitlam, was present in the chamber, and many other members were also absent. In his statement, the prime minister announced that the government, being 'in receipt of a request from the Government of South Vietnam', had resolved to send a battalion of infantry soldiers for service in that country. The prime minister made it clear that this new contribution would build on a small presence of Australian military advisers and other personnel who had been sent to Vietnam as early as 1962. Less clear—because the prime minister did not spell out the facts—was that by sending a combat battalion, the government was committing Australia to a war in a foreign country. That war was, for the present, undeclared, just as the enemy was not defined. In private, however, Menzies had no doubts. In a speech at an Australia Club dinner at London's Savoy Hotel on 28 June, he spoke of a 'communist tide' that had the potential to engulf Australia itself. With grave emphasis, he told his audience: 'Gentlemen, we're at war, don't let's make any mistake about it'.

Historically, it remains a point of contention whether the South Vietnamese government—faced with powerful domestic sensitivities—ever formally tendered a request to Australia for a military presence in its country. Certainly no request was ever made in writing, though Phan Huy Quat, the prime minister, was persuaded to make an oral acceptance of the offer of troops, and he immediately confirmed this in a letter to the Australian ambassador in South Vietnam. The oral acceptance was notified by cable to Canberra late in the afternoon of the day Menzies was to deliver his ministerial statement.

In lieu of a formal South Vietnamese request—and probably altogether more powerful and persuasive to his constituency at home—was a letter to Menzies from the president of the United States, Lyndon Baines Johnson (1908–1973), expressing delight in the decision of the Australian government to commit an infantry battalion to service in South Vietnam. From a public relations point of view, it was helpful that the American president noted that Australia was acting 'at the request of the Government of South Vietnam'. As historian Paul Ham has noted, the letter certainly bolstered Menzies' position and it must have reinforced his belief that the 'request', however it had been formulated and made, was indeed genuine and sincere. In the end, however, President Johnson's letter establishes that Australia, in serving its own geopolitical interests, was also nourishing the traditional US–Australian alliance. So clear and unequivocal was Johnson's letter that Menzies read it in full in his statement to the House. And Australia entered a bitter and protracted war that led eventually to defeat, and which both divided and changed the nation.

Dear Mr. Prime Minister:

I am delighted at the decision of your Government to provide an infantry battalion for service in South Vietnam at the request of the Government of South Vietnam.

This action simply underscores the full co-operation and understanding that has existed between our two Governments, and between both and the Government of South Vietnam, in assisting South Vietnam to maintain its independence. Like you, we have no desire to maintain military forces in Vietnam any longer than necessary to ensure the security of South Vietnam. But we share your belief that we must respond to the needs brought about by the aggression being carried on from North Vietnam.

More broadly, this action proves again the deep ties between our two countries in the cause of world peace and security. As you know, my personal experiences in association with Australians during World War II have made this a particularly deep and abiding feeling for me. I am confident that our two nations, working together, can continue to make great contributions to checking the spread of aggression and to bringing about the peace that South Vietnam and South-East Asia deserve.

Sincerely yours,
Lyndon B. Johnson

ABOVE *Australian troops bound for Vietnam board HMAS Sydney in April 1966.*

The campaign against capital punishment

THE CASE OF RONALD RYAN

When the death sentence by hanging of the convicted murderer Ronald Joseph Ryan was carried out at Melbourne's Pentridge Prison in 1967, it followed a strong campaign against capital punishment. In Victoria, especially, the hanging was opposed by lawyers, the press, the churches, social welfare organisations, Opposition members of state parliament, the union movement, student groups and several of the jury members who had delivered the guilty verdict. Letters to the editor in Melbourne's *Age* and *Herald* newspapers were substantially opposed to the hanging, while street demonstrations and vigils organised by the Anti-Hanging Committee ensured the highest visibility for the campaign opposing the death penalty. The Victorian government, led by Premier Henry Bolte (1908–1990), took the view that the murder of people in positions of authority warranted more severe punishment than the murder of ordinary citizens. The premier was determined to have his way. He demeaned the opposition campaign as one run by a few church leaders, the press, some academics 'who think they've got to object about something' and a rabble of political thugs.

On 19 December 1965, Ronald Ryan and Peter Walker broke out of Melbourne's Pentridge Prison. In the melee of the escape, a warder was shot dead. The two felons were recaptured in January 1966. Shortly afterward, at the trial conducted by Justice Sir John Starke (1913–1994), Ryan was given the then mandatory sentence of death for murder, despite doubts that he had fired the fatal shot. It was assumed that the sentence would be commuted—the practice in Victoria since 1951. Late in the year, however, state cabinet announced its intention to implement the death penalty. The execution was delayed by appeals, including a final appeal for clemency, but was carried out early in the morning of 3 February 1967.

Capital punishment was abolished in Victoria in 1975. The last Australian state to abolish the death penalty was Western Australia in 1984. Ronald Ryan (1925–1967) was the last man to be hanged in Australia. Historian Mike Richards' 2002 book, *The Hanged Man: The Life and Death of Ronald Ryan*, details the campaign against his execution.

The court record of the appeal hearing on 30 January 1967 is presented here. It captures a dramatic moment when, with the execution due at 8.00 am the next morning, Sir John Starke agreed to an application for a stay of proceedings to allow Ryan's lawyer, P.J. Brusey, to present previously unheard (though possibly tainted) testimony. The application to stay the execution was based on a sworn statement of John Henry Tolmie, who claimed to have witnessed a warder aim and fire a rifle from one of the prison watch-posts at about the time the warder was killed. If true, this cast doubt on who had fired the fatal shot and raised the possibility of an accidental death. Starke took the view that had the new testimony been presented at the trial, it may have had a bearing on the determination of the prisoner's guilt. While noting the possibility of a tainted statement, Starke granted the stay, pointing to the larger interests of justice, commenting that 'in these circumstances one must not make a mistake'.

The statement was quickly discredited, and its author charged with perjury. In the highly charged atmosphere of the powerful public campaign against capital punishment, the Victorian cabinet reviewed other possibly contentious claims about the shooting, but satisfied itself there were no grounds to order a fresh trial. On the evening of 2 February, acting on the advice of the premier, the Executive Council formally declined an appeal for clemency. The execution was carried out the next morning.

P.J. Brusey, for the applicant.
B.J. Shaw, for the Crown.

Starke, J.: This is an application by Ronald Joseph Ryan for an order staying the carrying out of the sentence of death imposed upon him on 30 March 1966, and for a further order of an injunctive nature. The question of whether at this stage, that is, after the time and place of execution has been fixed by the Governor in Council, I have power to grant a stay of execution, is a matter which has been debated in this Court before and which is the subject of a difference of opinion. I think it is clear that if any single judge has the power at this stage, it is only the trial judge. I think I would do little service to the jurisprudence relating to criminal law in this State if I were to endeavour, without the opportunity of collecting the authorities, to express my views in detail at this time ... I hold, accordingly, that I have the power to grant a stay in proper circumstances. It is quite clear, however, that this power should only be exercised sparingly and on clear material. The trial judge has not power to decide whether or not the death penalty should be carried out. The Executive and the Executive alone is charged with this decision and this Court should not interfere with such a decision except in exceptional and rare circumstances. It can in any event only intervene as a temporary measure. However, there can be no doubt that in the long run, if the Court senses that there is a real possibility of a miscarriage of justice, then the Court must not hesitate to intervene. In regard to that matter, I refer to the case of *Ras Behari Lal* v. *King-Emperor* (1933) ... which is a Privy Council decision. The judgment of the Judicial Committee was delivered by Lord Aitkin [saying] "It would be remarkable indeed, if what may be 'a scandal and perversion of justice' may be prevented during the trial, but after it has taken effect the Courts are powerless to interfere. Finality is a good thing, but justice is better."

The cases in which a judge has interfered in the past [cites cases outside the criminal law jurisdiction to which the *Crimes Act 1958* does not apply] are referred to by Smith, J., in *Tait* v. *R.*, ... He says this: "It was a power to suspend the operation of the sentence pronounced, so that it ceased temporarily to be an authority which could be acted upon. If cases of reprieves granted pursuant to royal command are disregarded, the exercise of the power would appear to have been confined to the following situations and purposes:—

"(a) The judge had a discretion to grant a reprieve whenever the interests of justice appeared to require that the sentence should be suspended for some temporary purpose, e.g. to enable him to consult the other judges upon a point of law, or to enable him to submit a recommendation for mercy and obtain the Sovereign's decision thereon."

The last words, I think, are of importance in this matter in view of the way Mr. Brusey has put his submission. Mr. Brusey concedes that at this stage he cannot ask for a stay so that he may seek from the Court of Criminal Appeal a new trial on the ground of fresh evidence. But Mr. Brusey does contend that new material has just become available which the Executive has not considered, and which there is no time for it to consider prior to the time set for execution, and that the Executive has acted in this case without the assistance of such material which he submits might cause it to act differently to the way it has acted. It seems to me that if at common law a judge could grant a stay to enable him to submit a recommendation for mercy and obtain the Sovereign's decision thereon, it is consistent that the power would have been used in proper circumstances if material had come before the judge after conviction which the legal representatives of the prisoner desired to bring before the Executive, but for lack of time could not, for the purpose of obtaining, if possible, an exercise of the prerogative of mercy. Now the question in this case is really this: does the affidavit of John Henry Tolmie provide further information which was not considered by the Executive which might cause the Executive to alter its opinion? I am very clearly of the opinion that unless it does satisfy that test, I would be acting quite wrongly to accede to this application. The deponent Tolmie says that he saw Mr. Patterson, the warder on No. 1 Post, aim and fire a rifle ... Assuming that is true, having presided at the trial I believe that this evidence would necessarily have weighed heavily with the jury. Of course one cannot, in the long run, say for certain whether it would have made a decisive difference or not. The whole contest at the trial was whether Ryan fired a shot at all, or whether only one shot was fired and that by a witness also named Patterson, who was also a warder and who admitted he fired from outside the walls of the gaol. If ... there had been introduced into the conflict of evidence which [arose] during the trial, the fact that a further shot was fired at about the same time, obviously no one can say that the verdict must have been the same, and, accordingly, I think it is not possible to say what view the Executive would have taken of this new material. In those circumstances I am put in a position in which I suppose no judge would wish to be put. If there were time I might adjourn the proceedings and allow the Crown to file further affidavits and cross-examine Mr. Tolmie if the Crown so wished so that I might form a view as to whether there was material which would or might cause the Executive to alter its view. But there is, of course, not time. The time element is one of the necessary concomitants flowing from the death penalty, and, therefore, I am in this position. Can I say sitting in the judicial seat, that this affidavit must be untruthful? I can clearly see that there are criticisms to be made of the affidavit, perhaps weighty, perhaps not. The less I say about those matters probably the better. But there is the oath of an individual that he saw a man fire a rifle from No.1 Post ... But to disbelieve an affidavit simply because there are matters of criticisms relating to it, and perhaps of weighty criticism, is, I think, quite beyond the judicial function. If one had the opportunity of hearing the deponent cross-examined, if one had the advantage of other affidavits, one might disbelieve it and that is the course I might normally have taken ... to ascertain if there were material worthy of consideration by the Executive which might affect its decision. But there is no time, and in these circumstances one must not make a mistake, and consequently I propose to accede to the application and suspend the operation of the sentence which I pronounced, solely so that the weight, if any, of this material may be considered by the Executive ...

The order that I propose to make is this. Upon the undertaking of the solicitor for the prisoner to place the material which is before me, and any other material as to which he may be advised, before the Executive within 48 hours, I order that the execution of the prisoner fixed for eight o'clock tomorrow morning, Tuesday, 31 January 1967, be not carried out but be stayed until the further pleasure of His Excellency the Governor is known. I further order that the Chief Secretary and the Sheriff and his deputy or deputies be restrained accordingly.

Orders accordingly.

A symbolic victory

THE REFERENDUM ON ALTERING THE AUSTRALIAN CONSTITUTION

On 27 May 1967 the Australian people passed at referendum a proposal to alter in the Australian Constitution two clauses relating to Aboriginal people. The referendum victory was emphatic. The 'yes' vote passed in all states and won 90.77 per cent support nationally. In no electorate was the affirmative vote less than 70 per cent. This was a remarkable result in a country that has shown great reluctance to allow changes to the Constitution: since the time of Federation, of twenty-four proposed constitutional alterations, only four had passed and none with such acclamation. The two constitutional amendments were embodied in the *Constitution Alteration Act (Aboriginals) 1967*, which, after being approved at the referendum, became law on 10 August 1967.

Subsequent history and folklore together have seen large and erroneous claims made for the referendum result, in part because of the decisive vote by the electors. In fact, the amendments, though cosmetically important, were not in themselves of overwhelming significance in advancing the cause of Aboriginal rights in Australia. The amendment of section 51 (xxvi) empowered the Commonwealth (concurrently with the states) to enact 'special laws' in respect of Aborigines, as it already could in respect to any other race, but there was no requirement on the Commonwealth to exercise these powers, and nor were there any plans for the government to move in a new direction. Deletion of section 127 mandated the inclusion of Aborigines in national census counts, a change that eliminated an overtly discriminatory clause of the Australian constitution conceived in the years of high racism in which the document had been drafted.

The outcome of the 1967 referendum and the benefits it conferred on Aboriginal Australians have been widely misunderstood and misinterpreted—in the media, in politics, in schools and universities, in the wider community, and in the hearts and minds of many Aboriginal people themselves. Notwithstanding careful rebuttals by historians such as Bain Attwood and Andrew Markus and, in 2009, by Russell McGregor, the belief persists that the referendum conferred on Aborigines the right to vote, the status of citizenship, and equality under the law, and brought Aboriginal affairs under federal control. None of these is true: but as McGregor has emphasised, the referendum 'was a crucial moment in Australian history for its public affirmation of the principle of national inclusiveness'. McGregor also points out that between the affirmation of that principle and the achievement of real change there was—and remains—a wide gulf. For a range of reasons though, over time, popular memory has construed the symbolic victory of 1967 as a legal breakthrough, even though in its immediate aftermath there was much disillusionment about the practical value of the change that had been won. In 2007 activist Garry Foley noted that, for the generation of emerging black leaders, the referendum brought anger, not celebration. For them, a symbolic victory on its own was not enough. That led, in its turn, to an examination of more confrontational methods, including the politics of the international Black Power movement.

THIS is a copy of the Proposed Law as presented to the Governor-General, and, according to the Constitution, in pursuance of a Writ of His Excellency the Administrator of the Government of the Commonwealth of Australia, submitted to a Referendum of the Electors. The period allowed by law for disputing the Referendum has expired, and no petition disputing the Referendum, or disputing any return or statement showing the voting on the Referendum, has been filed. The said Proposed Law was approved in a majority of the States by a majority of the Electors voting, and also approved by a majority of all the Electors voting.

The Bill is now presented to the Governor-General for the Queen's Assent.

Clerk of the House of Representatives
9 August 1967

Speaker

COMMONWEALTH OF AUSTRALIA

Constitution Alteration (Aboriginals) 1967

No. 55 of 1967

AN ACT

To alter the Constitution so as to omit certain words relating to the People of the Aboriginal Race in any State and so that Aboriginals are to be counted in reckoning the Population.

BE it enacted by the Queen's Most Excellent Majesty, the Senate, and the House of Representatives of the Commonwealth of Australia, with the approval of the electors, as required by the Constitution, as follows:—

1. This Act may be cited as the *Constitution Alteration (Aboriginals) 1967*.   Short title.

2. The Constitution is altered by omitting from paragraph (xxvi.) of section 51 the words ", other than the aboriginal race in any State,".   Alteration of section 51 (xxvi.).

3. The Constitution is altered by repealing section 127.   Repeal of section 127.

IN THE NAME OF HER MAJESTY, I assent to this Act.

Casey
Governor-General
10th August 1967

By Authority: A. J. ARTHUR, Commonwealth Government Printer, Canberra

ABOVE Constitution Alteration Act (Aboriginals) 1967.

Constitution Alteration (Aboriginals) 1967
Act No. 55 of 1967

An Act to alter the Constitution so as to omit certain words relating to the People of the Aboriginal Race in any State and so that Aboriginals are to be counted in reckoning the Population.

BE it enacted by the Queen's Most Excellent Majesty, the Senate, and the House of Representatives of the Commonwealth of Australia, with the approval of the electors, as required by the Constitution, as follows:—

1. This Act may be cited as the *Constitution Alteration (Aboriginals) 1967*. (Short title.)

2. The Constitution is altered by omitting from paragraph (xxvi.) of section 51 the words " , other than the aboriginal race in any State,". (Alteration of section 51 (xxvi).)

3 The Constitution is altered by repealing section 127. (Repeal of section 127.)

Act No. 55 of 1967; *Assented to 10 August 1967*

'It's time!'

GOUGH WHITLAM LAUNCHES THE ALP ELECTION CAMPAIGN

ABOVE *Labor Party leader Gough Whitlam the day before the election.*

With the election of E.G. 'Gough' Whitlam (*b*. 1916) as prime minister of Australia, and the defeat of the Liberal–Country Party coalition led by William McMahon, the year 1972 was a momentous one in federal politics. The coalition had maintained its hold on government since 1949, due in part to a weak, divided and poorly led Australian Labor Party, but also to the preference votes flowing to it from the conservative Democratic Labor Party, the staunchly anti-communist party formed after ideological dissent had split the ALP in 1956. But as the 1960s advanced, there were signs of change and restlessness in the electorate. The deeply unpopular Vietnam War, and the divisive and discriminatory conscription of young Australian men to fight in it, had seen an inexorable decline in the moral and political authority of the incumbent government. The energetic and commanding leadership of Gough Whitlam had also restored credibility to the ALP. At the elections held in October 1969, Whitlam achieved a 7.1 per cent swing, reducing the Liberal–Country Party majority from thirty-nine seats to seven, though the government had survived on conservative preferences. The result placed Whitlam in striking distance of government at the next election.

So it was with a sense of destiny that Whitlam rose to deliver the Labor Party policy speech at the Blacktown Civic Centre in suburban Sydney on 13 November 1972. 'It's been a long road, comrade', he remarked to his speech writer Graham Freudenberg as he moved to the podium, 'but we're there'. He then delivered his statement with his usual brilliant eloquence and bravura. In his egalitarian salutation 'Men and women of Australia!', he offered first an invocation of Curtin's wartime broadcasts and messages, and then he called on the country to renew and to revitalise itself. In this timely call for change, Whitlam made his demand for a new chance for the Australian nation. His victory in December ushered in an extraordinary period of change and high achievement, much of which was delivered in haste and compromised by hubris and ineptitude.

Men and women of Australia!

The decision we will make for our country on 2 December is a choice between the past and the future, between the habits and the fears of the past, and the demands and opportunities of the future. There are moments in history when the whole fate and future of nations can be decided by a single decision. For Australia this is such a time. It's time for a new team, a new program, a new drive for equality of opportunities; it's time to create new opportunities for Australians, time for a new vision of what we can achieve in this generation for our nation and the region in which we live.

It's time for a new government—a Labor government.

My fellow citizens, I put these questions to you:

Do you believe that Australia can afford another three years like the last twenty months? Are you prepared to maintain at the head of your affairs a coalition which has lurched into crisis after crisis, embarrassment piled on embarrassment week after week? Will you accept another three years of waiting for next week's crisis, next week's blunder? Will you again trust the nation's economy to the men who deliberately, but needlessly, created Australia's worst unemployment for ten years? Or to the same men who have presided over the worst inflation for twenty years?

Can you trust the last-minute promises of men who stood against these very same proposals for twenty-three years? Would you trust your international affairs again to the men who gave you Vietnam? Will you trust your defences to the men who haven't even yet given you the F-111?

We have a new chance for our nation. We can recreate this nation. We have a new chance for our region. We can help recreate this region.

The war of intervention in Vietnam is ending. The great powers are rethinking and remoulding their relationships and their obligations. Australia cannot stand still at such a time. We cannot afford to limp along with men whose attitudes are rooted in the slogans of the 1950s—the slogans of fear and hate. If we made such a mistake, we would make Australia a backwater in our region and a back number in history. The Australian Labor Party—vindicated as we have been on all the great issues of the past—stands ready to take Australia forward to her rightful, proud, secure and independent place in the future of our region.

Our program has three great aims. They are:
- to promote equality
- to involve the people of Australia in the decision-making processes of our land
- and to liberate the talents and uplift the horizons of the Australian people.

We want to give a new life and meaning in this new nation to the touchstone of modern democracy—to liberty, equality, fraternity.

Gough Whitlam launches the ALP election campaign

'a change of government'

A LETTER TO THE *AGE*

Possibly no other election in Australian federal history ushered in so great or concentrated a period of political, cultural and social change as the election of 1972, when Gough Whitlam took the Australian Labor Party to victory, bringing to an end twenty-three years of conservative rule. Whitlam's campaign was running on the theme of 'It's time'—time for a change of government and time for the reinvigoration of the Australian nation. It was a most persuasive call. Whitlam's impressive personal authority made him an attractive candidate against a coalition that had grown stale and weary over a long term in government. But there remained a fear that once again a conservative Australian electorate might withhold its mandate.

It was in this context that a group of distinguished business, academic and cultural names came together as signatories to a letter written to Melbourne's *Age* newspaper on 23 November 1972, calling for a change of government. The letter was not so much an endorsement of the Australian Labor Party and its platform as a plea for Australian democracy to renew and refresh itself. So striking was the letter and so remarkable its coalition of writers—among them scientist Sir Macfarlane Burnet, historian Manning Clark, artist Leonard French, historian Sir Keith Hancock, businessman Kenneth Myer, novelist Patrick White and poet Judith Wright—that it received attention well beyond the readership of the *Age*. It was a powerful indicator that a decisive shift was taking place in the electorate, and in the days before a later generation of conservatives derided the so-called elite as the 'chattering class', the standing of the signatories brought a persuasive appeal to their plea.

Sir,—

We, the undersigned, who are not members of any political party, believe that Australia's interests will be best served by a change of Government as a result of this election.

Our democratic system works properly only when each of the major parties has the chance to govern. Each benefits from the responsibilities of office. Each gains from the freedom of opposition.

Some of us think the Liberal–Country Party coalition has had a productive, as well as long period in office. Others of us are less enthusiastic about its record, especially in recent years.

But we all agree that today, after 23 years in office, it needs new ideas and has problems of long-term leadership which can best be worked out in opposition.

Although we do not subscribe to all the Australian Labor Party's policies, we see no over-riding reason for continuing to exclude it from office.

It is Australia's oldest and biggest party. It represents aspirations in our society which cannot be ignored. It has prepared itself for office and needs only a moderate swing in its favor at this election to take power.

If denied office any longer, the Labor Party is in danger of disintegrating as a force in Australia's political life.

We believe a change of Government will benefit both the major parties, on which the vitality of our political system depends.

The ultimate beneficiary will be the Australian nation and its people.

Professor R.R. Andrew
Sir Macfarlane Burnet
David Campbell
Manning Clark
Sir Walter Crocker
Professor R.I. Downing
Dr Frank Fenner
Leonard French
Bruce Grant
Sir Keith Hancock
Professor Hedley Bull
Rev Dr J.D. McCaughey
Professor Macmahon Ball
Kenneth Myer
Patrick White
Judith Wright

A letter to the Age

Promoting excellence in the arts

THE AUSTRALIA COUNCIL CHARTER

Public funding for the arts in Australia has a relatively short history, notwithstanding the early support offered to writers under the Commonwealth Literary Fund from 1908. But it was not until the 1950s that support began to build for a national policy for the arts in a movement substantially influenced by the leadership and advocacy of economist H.C. 'Nugget' Coombs (1906–1997), who used his powerful position within the Commonwealth bureaucracy to persuade politicians that the arts mattered. Coombs' first major achievement was to secure the establishment of the Australian Elizabethan Theatre Trust, in 1954, to provide assistance to theatre and later to other performing arts. This trust was funded initially by private sources but later also gained government aid, eventually becoming the agency through which the federal government supported the performing arts.

Through the continuing advocacy of Coombs during the 1960s and 1970s, both major political parties can claim credit for enlarging the federal government's role and participation in arts funding. The first landmark was the formation of the Australian Council for the Arts in 1968 under a Liberal prime minister, J.G. Gorton (1911–2002), whose larrikin qualities sat comfortably with a keen appreciation for the possibilities of a creative Australian culture. Coombs served as the council's first chairman.

In 1974 Labor's Gough Whitlam further expanded the Commonwealth government's role in arts funding with the establishment of the Australia Council as a statutory authority operating under the *Australia Council Act 1975* and with Coombs retaining office as the new council's inaugural chairman. The council operated through a number of specialised boards offering targeted support to specific arts sectors, such a literature, the visual arts, Aboriginal and Torres Strait Islander arts, and the performing arts. The council's work enshrines two principles: 'arm's length' funding, which aims to ensure that funding is maintained at a distance from political interest or interference; and 'peer review', in which policy decisions about funding support are informed by the views of practising artists.

As a creation of the late twentieth century, the *Australia Council Act 1975* included in section 5 the now almost mandatory charter, which was both a statement of the council's formal responsibilities to the government of the Commonwealth and of its commitment to excellence in the arts, together with associated roles of advocacy and education to raise community appreciation and enjoyment of the arts. Another important element of the charter is the council's responsibility for fostering the expression of national identity by means of the arts.

Admirable as they are in their intent and sweep, such statements can seem too broad to be anything other than tokens, which are in any case difficult to define and hard to measure. Some will worry that the stock formula of numbered points is suggestive less of a creative national vision for the arts than an expression of the bureaucratic mindset to which the arts can potentially be held to ransom. For all its implicit idealism, the Australia Council Charter is not a highly visible document and, surprisingly, cannot be found on the Australia Council's own website.

Under the *Australia Council Act 1975*, the council has substantial independence from government in its policy-making and funding roles. It provides advice on cultural matters to the Commonwealth Government through its minister for the arts.

The functions of the Australia Council
(a) to formulate and carry out policies designed:
   (i) to promote excellence in the arts;
   (ii) to provide, and encourage the provision of, opportunities to persons to practice the arts;
   (iii) to promote the appreciation, understanding and enjoyment of the arts;
   (iv) to promote the general application of the arts in the community;
   (v) to foster the expression of a national identity by means of the arts;
   (vi) to uphold and promote the right of persons to freedom in the practice of the arts
   (vii) to promote knowledge and appreciation of Australian arts by persons in other countries;
   (viii) to promote incentives for, and recognition of, achievement in the practice of the arts; and
   (ix) to encourage the support of the arts by the States, local governing bodies and other persons and organizations;
(b) to furnish advice to the Government of the Commonwealth, either of its own motion or upon request made to it by the Minister, on matters connected with the promotion of the arts or otherwise relating to the performance of its functions; and
(c) to do anything incidental or conducive to the performance of any of the foregoing functions.

The Australia Council Charter

'We will be mates. White and black ...'

GOUGH WHITLAM AND VINCENT LINGIARI MEET AT DAGURAGU

Reviewing the achievements of his short period in government 1972–75, former Labor Prime Minister Gough Whitlam was proud to point to the advances made in Aboriginal affairs across a wide policy spectrum. He noted significant improvements in social conditions, the quality of administration and representation, the development of land rights and the ratification of international conventions. Putting this program into a larger context, Whitlam noted that, at the time of its election in 1972, the new Labor government was 'fortified by a Party organisation and platform which had for many years been committed to Aboriginal reform'.

From the new government's first week in office Aboriginal land rights were placed at the top of the agenda for change and reform. Within days Whitlam announced the establishment of a royal commission to inquire into and report on arrangements for granting title to land to Aboriginal groups, and procedures for examining Aboriginal claims to land in the Northern Territory, where the federal government had full jurisdiction to apply the recommendations and could thereby exercise national leadership on the land rights question. At the same time, negotiations commenced to issue a lease to the Gurindji people of the Victoria River district in the Northern Territory. Their land had been occupied since the 1850s, first by the Wave Hill pastoral station and later by Vestey Limited, a British pastoral company. Those occupations had, at best, reduced the Gurindji people to the role of cheap or even unpaid labour on their own land.

In August 1966 Gurindji elder Vincent Lingiari (1908–1988) had led about two hundred Aboriginal stockmen and their families in a walk-off from Wave Hill in a protest against working and living conditions that had been a source of contention since the 1930s: inadequate wages compared with those paid to non-Indigenous employees; meagre rations; makeshift housing; and poor sanitation. Subsequently, in a significant enlargement of their protest, the Gurindji sought rights to their ancestral lands. Rebuffed by the conservative federal government then in power, Lingiari and other elders mounted a well-organised and determined national campaign to build support for their cause with politicians, lawyers and the wider Australian public. The Gurindji struggle and the strike action that accompanied it through the years 1966–75 was assisted by prominent non-Indigenous campaigners including the author Frank Hardy (1917–1994) whose book *The Unlucky Australians* (1968) exposed for many Australians details of the exploitation of the Aboriginal workforce at Wave Hill and elsewhere.

On 16 August 1975 Gough Whitlam led a bipartisan delegation to Wattie Creek, then bearing its historic name Daguragu, to officiate at a ceremony to grant to the Gurindji people a land lease comprising 3250 square kilometres of the old Wave Hill Station, including sacred sites. In his speech the prime minister formally handed over the new lease. In a ceremonial gesture, he then picked up a handful of red earth and poured it into the outstretched hand of Vincent Lingiari. In response Lingiari gracefully acknowledged the return of the disputed lands while also voicing a plea for reconciliation between black and white Australians. The victory at Wave Hill saw Daguragu established as the first Aboriginal community-owned and managed cattle station in Australia and is a landmark in the evolution of Aboriginal land rights.

ABOVE *Prime Minister Gough Whitlam pours soil into the hand of Gurindji elder Vincent Lingiari as a symbolic gesture of the return of the land to the Gurindji people.*

Prime Minister Gough Whitlam

On this great day, I, Prime Minister of Australia, speak to you on behalf of the people of Australia—all Australians who honour and love this land we live in.

For them I want:

First, to congratulate you, and those who have shared your struggle, on the victory you have won in that fight for justice begun nine years ago when in protest you walked off Wave Hill Station;

Secondly, to acknowledge that we Australians have still much to do to redress the injustice and oppression that has for so long been the lot of black Australians;

Thirdly, to promise you that this act of restitution which we perform today will not stand alone—your fight was not for yourselves alone and we are determined that Aboriginal Australians everywhere will be helped by it;

Fourthly, to promise that, through their government, the people of Australia will help you in your plans to use this place fruitfully for the Gurindji;

Finally to give back to you formally in Aboriginal and Australian law ownership of this land of your fathers.

Vincent Lingiari, I solemnly hand to you these deeds as proof, in Australian law, that these lands belong to the Gurindji people and I put into your hands this piece of earth itself as a sign that we restore them to you and your children forever.

Vincent Lingiari

1. The important white men are giving us this land ceremonially, ceremonially they are giving it to us.
2. It belonged to the whites, but today it is in the hands of us Aboriginals all around here.
3. Let us live happily together as mates, let us not make it hard for each other.
4. The important white men have come here, and they are giving our country back to us now.
5. They will give us cattle, they will give us horses, then we will be happy.
6. They came from different places away, we do not know them, but they are glad for us.
7. We want to live in a better way together, Aboriginals and white men, let us not fight over anything, let us be mates.
8. He [the Prime Minister] will give us cattle and horses ceremonially; we have not seen them yet; they will give us bores, axes, wire, all that sort of thing.
9. These important white men have come here to our ceremonial ground and they are welcome, because they have not come for any other reason, just for this [handover].
10. We will be mates. White and black, you [Gurindji] must keep this land safe for yourselves, it does not belong to any different 'welfare' man.
11. They took our country away from us, now they have brought it back Ceremonially.

Note: Vincent Lingiari's speech translated into English by Patrick McConvell

Building a truly multicultural nation

RACIAL DISCRIMINATION ACT

At a modest ceremony held in Canberra on 31 October 1975 to launch the new Office of the Commissioner for Community Relations, Prime Minister Gough Whitlam spelled out the high objectives of the *Racial Discrimination Act* that had passed both houses of the Australian Parliament earlier in the year. In robustly eliminating race as a basis for discrimination in Australia, the new act also provided for the appointment of a Commissioner for Community Relations charged with specific responsibilities to inquire into infringements and to develop programs by which Australia might realise its full potential as a multicultural society. In welcoming the appointment of the inaugural commissioner, Albert Jaime Grassby (1926–2005)—who had himself experienced slurs in a racially fought election campaign in the Riverina in 1974—Whitlam remarked of the legislation that had created the post:

> The new Act writes it firmly into our laws that Australia is in reality a multicultural nation, in which the linguistic and cultural heritage of the Aboriginal people and of peoples from all parts of the world can find an honoured place. Programs of community education and development flowing from that Act will ensure this reality is translated into practical measures affecting all areas of our national life.

Writing in 1985 in his grand survey of his government's term in office, the former prime minister placed his statement of October 1975 into the larger context of Australia's poor history in matters concerning race. He recalled that it had been a particular ambition of his government that Australia should show a 'clean face' to the world in racial matters. While the Australian Commonwealth had been conceived during a period when it was possible to implement the notion of a 'White Australia', by the 1970s the world had changed. By then the country's racial discrimination in migration policy and in the internal administration of government, business and the trade unions had become a cause of concern, both at home and internationally, particularly in Asia. Whitlam noted his personal concern that at the time of his election as prime minister, Australia had failed to ratify the UN Convention on the Elimination of All Forms of Racial Discrimination, which had come into force in January 1969. This convention outlawed all forms of racial discrimination on the grounds of race, colour, ethnic background, place of birth or descent. By 1972 it had been ratified by eighty-seven countries, but not by Australia. That situation changed with the passage of the *Racial Discrimination Act*, key passages of which are published here. The act provided for the ratification of the convention and established the basis upon which Australia has since flourished as a thriving multi-ethnic and multicultural society.

RACIAL DISCRIMINATION ACT 1975
No. 52 of 1975

An Act relating to the Elimination of Racial and other Discrimination.

WHEREAS a Convention entitled the "International Convention on the Elimination of All Forms of Racial Discrimination" ... was opened for signature on 21 December 1965: ...

AND WHEREAS it is desirable, in pursuance of all relevant powers of the Parliament, including, but not limited to, its power to make laws with respect to external affairs, with respect to the people of any race for whom it is deemed necessary to make special laws and with respect to immigration, to make the provisions contained in this Act for the prohibition of racial discrimination and certain other forms of discrimination and, in particular, to make provision for giving effect to the Convention:

BE IT THEREFORE ENACTED by the Queen, the Senate and the House of Representatives of Australia, as follows:—

PART I—PRELIMINARY

1. This Act may be cited as the *Racial Discrimination Act* 1975 ...

6. This Act binds Australia and each State, but nothing in this Act renders Australia or a State liable to be prosecuted for an offence.

7. Approval is given to ratification by Australia of the Convention ...

PART II—PROHIBITION OF RACIAL DISCRIMINATION

...

9. (1) It is unlawful for a person to do any act involving a distinction, exclusion, restriction or preference based on race, colour, descent or national or ethnic origin which has the purpose or effect of nullifying or impairing the recognition, enjoyment or exercise, of an equal footing, of any human right or fundamental freedom in the political, economic, social, cultural or any other field of public life ...

10. (1) If, by reason of, or of a provision of, a law of Australia or of a State or Territory, persons of a particular race, colour or national or ethnic origin do not enjoy a right that is enjoyed by persons of another race, colour or national or ethnic origin, or enjoy a right to a more limited extent than persons of another race, colour or national or ethnic origin, then, notwithstanding anything in that law, persons of the first-mentioned race, colour or national or ethnic origin shall, by force of this section, enjoy that right to the same extent as persons of that other race, colour or national or ethnic origin ...

11. It is unlawful for a person—
(a) to refuse to allow another person access to or use of any place or vehicle that members of the public are, or a section of the public is, entitled or allowed to enter or use, or to refuse to allow another person access to or use of any such place or vehicle except on less favourable terms or

conditions than those upon or subject to which he would otherwise allow access to or use of that place or vehicle;

(b) to refuse to allow another person use of any facilities in any such place or vehicle that are available to members of the public or to a section of the public, or to refuse to allow another person use of any such facilities except on less favourable terms or conditions than those upon or subject to which he would otherwise allow use of those facilities; or

(c) to require another person to leave or cease to use any such place or vehicle or any such facilities, by reason of the race, colour or national or ethnic origin of that other person or of any relative or associate of that person.

Then follow specific prohibitions of racial discrimination in matters such as land, housing and other accommodation, the provision of goods and services, in the right to join trade unions, in employment, in advertising and in incitement.

PART III—INQUIRIES AND CIVIL PROCEEDINGS

19. For the purposes of this Act there shall be a Commissioner for Community Relations.

20. The functions of the Commissioner are—

(a) to inquire into alleged infringements of Part II, and endeavour to effect a settlement of the matters alleged to constitute those infringements, ...

(b) to promote an understanding and acceptance of, and compliance with, this Act; and

(c) to develop, conduct and foster research and educational programs for the purpose of—

　(i) combating racial discrimination and prejudices that lead to racial discrimination;

　(ii) promoting understanding, tolerance and friendship among racial and ethnic groups; and

　(iii) propagating the purposes and principles of the Convention ...

PART V—COMMUNITY RELATIONS COUNCIL

28. (1) For the purposes of this Act there is established a Community Relations Council.

(2) It is the function of the Council to advise, and make recommendations to, the Attorney-General and the Commissioner ... as the case may be concerning—

(a) the observance and the implementation of the Convention;

(b) the promotion of educational programs with respect to the observance of the Convention;

(c) the promotion of studies and research programs with respect to the observance and implementation of the Convention;

(d) the publication and dissemination of material to assist in the observance and implementation of the Convention;

(e) the promotion of understanding, tolerance and friendship among racial and ethnic groups; and

(f) any other matter related to the observance and implementation of the Convention.

'nothing will save the governor-general'

THE DISMISSAL OF GOUGH WHITLAM'S LABOR GOVERNMENT

In his 1976 Australia Day address, shortly after his dismissal of Gough Whitlam's Labor government, the governor-general, Sir John Kerr (1914–1991), commented that the events of 11 November 1975 were 'now a part of our history'. If these banal words were intended to soothe those Australians who had been shocked and disturbed by the governor-general's unprecedented dismissal of an elected government, they failed to show comprehension of community feeling about the issue or of the legitimacy of concerns about the way in which a constitutional impasse had been resolved. What is now known as 'the dismissal' has generated continuing debate, while also provoking a discussion about Australia's republican options.

Sir John Kerr's dramatic dismissal of the Whitlam government followed a twenty-seven day deadlock, beginning on 15 October, when the Opposition parties in control of the Senate deferred supply. They aimed to force the prime minister to call an election for the House of Representatives. While there was widespread unease about a lack of discipline in Whitlam's government, and its unconventional approach to economic management and social reform, the prime minister maintained that the party with a majority in the lower house was entitled to govern. He refused to countenance the calls for an election made by opponents who had never adjusted to their loss of power, after governing continuously from 1949 until their defeat in 1972.

In the stand-off that followed the deferral of supply, neither Whitlam nor Opposition leader Malcolm Fraser was prepared to concede ground. Sir John Kerr resolved to end the crisis by invoking the so-called 'reserve powers' provided to the governor-general in section 64 of the Australian constitution (see page 190). Kerr had sought an opinion, in confidence and without the prime minister's knowledge, from Sir Garfield Barwick, chief justice of the High Court and himself a former senior minister on the conservative side of politics. Kerr chose neither to mediate the crisis nor to offer any warning that he was prepared to use the reserve powers. Having come to a view of Whitlam as recalcitrant and untrustworthy, Kerr acted without warning or discussion with his prime minister. In the letter of dismissal he handed to Whitlam at an interview at Government House in Canberra in the afternoon of 11 November 1975, Kerr presented the prime minister with a *fait accompli*. For his part, Whitlam misjudged Kerr's resolve, while also denying the credibility of the reserve powers provided under the constitution.

In one sense Sir John Kerr was vindicated. He could claim rightly that his intervention had forced an immediate resolution of the impasse (the supply bills were passed on the day of the dismissal) and that it had provided an opportunity for the people to make their own judgment at a general election. Voters were presented with a choice between an enraged Gough Whitlam, fighting now as leader of the Opposition, and Malcolm Fraser (b. 1930) who went to the polls as caretaker prime minister and won a clear mandate to govern in his own right.

But Kerr paid a terrible price for his actions, and so did the country. Vilified and resented, he resigned as governor-general in 1977 before moving to Europe. He left behind a country divided and one that has, as yet, achieved no resolution of understandings or expectations of constitutional review and reform, including the question of whether Australia should become a republic. As a spur to that larger debate, Sir John Kerr's letter of dismissal, together with its accompanying statement of reasons, stands as one of the most crucial documents framed in the arena of national and constitutional politics.

Government House,
Canberra. 2600.

11 November 1975

Dear Mr Whitlam,

In accordance with section 64 of the Constitution I hereby determine your appointment as my Chief Adviser and Head of the Government. It follows that I also hereby determine the appointments of all of the Ministers in your Government.

You have previously told me that you would never resign or advise an election of the House of Representatives or a double dissolution and that the only way in which such an election could be obtained would be by my dismissal of you and your ministerial colleagues. As it appeared likely that you would today persist in this attitude I decided that, if you did, I would determine your commission and state my reasons for doing so. You have persisted in your attitude and I have accordingly acted as indicated. I attach a statement of my reasons which I intend to publish immediately.

It is with a great deal of regret that I have taken this step both in respect of yourself and your colleagues.

I propose to send for the Leader of the Opposition and to commission him to form a new caretaker Government until an election can be held.

Yours sincerely,

John Kerr

The Honourable E.G. Whitlam, Q.C., M.P.

ABOVE *Sir John Kerr's dismissal letter to Gough Whitlam.*

Dear Mr Whitlam

In accordance with section 64 of the Constitution I hereby determine your appointment as my Chief Adviser and Head of the Government. It follows that I also hereby determine the appointments of all the Ministers in your Government.

You have previously told me that you would never resign or advise an election of the House of Representatives or a double dissolution and that the only way in which such an election could be obtained would be by dismissal of you and your ministerial colleagues. As it appeared likely that you would today persist in this attitude I decided that, if you did, I would determine your commission and state my reasons for doing so. You have persisted in your attitude and I have accordingly acted as indicated. I attach a statement of my reasons which I intend to publish immediately.

It is with a great deal of regret that I have taken this step both in respect of yourself and your colleagues.

I propose to send for the Leader of the Opposition and to commission him to form a new caretaker government until an election can be held.

Yours sincerely,
John R. Kerr

The Honourable E.G. Whitlam, Q.C., M.P.
11 November 1975

Statement by the Governor-General

I have today given careful consideration to the constitutional crisis and have made some decisions which I wish to explain.

Summary

It has been necessary for me to find a democratic and constitutional solution to the current crisis which will permit the people of Australia to decide as soon as possible what should be the outcome of the deadlock which developed over supply between the two Houses of Parliament and between the Government and Opposition parties. The only solution consistent with the Constitution and with my oath of office and my responsibilities, authority and duty as Governor-General is to terminate the commission as Prime Minister of Mr Whitlam and to arrange for a caretaker government able to secure supply and willing to let the issue go to the people.

I shall summarise the elements of the problem and the reasons for my decision which places the matter before the people of Australia for prompt determination.

Because of the federal nature of our Constitution and because of its provisions the Senate undoubtedly has constitutional power to refuse or defer supply to the Government. Because of the principles of responsible government a Prime Minister who cannot obtain supply, including money for carrying on the ordinary services of government, must either advise a general election or resign. If he refuses to do this I have the authority and indeed the duty under the Constitution to withdraw his commission as Prime Minister. The position in Australia is quite different from the position in the United Kingdom. Here the confidence of both Houses on supply is necessary to ensure its provision. In the United Kingdom the confidence of the House of Commons alone is necessary. But both here and in the United Kingdom the duty of the Prime Minister is the same in a most important respect—if he cannot get supply he must resign or advise an election.

If a Prime Minister refuses to resign or to advise an election, and this is the case with Mr Whitlam, my constitutional authority and duty require me to do what I have now done—to withdraw his commission—and to invite the Leader of the Opposition to form a caretaker government—that is one that makes no appointments or dismissals and initiates no policies until a general election is held. It is most desirable that he should guarantee supply. Mr Fraser will be asked to give the necessary undertakings and advise whether he is prepared to recommend a double dissolution. He will also be asked to guarantee supply.

The decisions I have made were made after I was satisfied that Mr Whitlam could not obtain supply. No other decision open to me would enable the Australian people to decide for themselves what should be done.

Once I had made up my mind, for my own part, what I must do if Mr Whitlam persisted in his stated intentions I consulted the Chief Justice of Australia, Sir Garfield Barwick. I have his permission to say that I consulted him in this way.

The result is that there will be an early general election for both Houses and the people can do what, in a democracy such as ours, is their responsibility and duty and theirs alone. It is for the people now to decide the issue which the two leaders have failed to settle.

A declaration of innocence

LINDY CHAMBERLAIN PLEADS FOR JUSTICE

The disappearance and presumed death of infant Azaria Chantel Loren Chamberlain (born and died 1980) on 17 August 1980, during a family holiday at Ayers Rock (Uluru) in the Northern Territory, led to one of the best-known and most controversial cases in Australian legal history. When the baby disappeared from the family's tent, her mother, Alice Lynne (Lindy) Chamberlain (b. 1948), immediately reported that a dingo had taken her child. An extensive search failed to locate the baby, though a week later her blood-stained clothes were found. A coronial inquest commencing in December 1980 delivered a finding in February 1981 that a dingo had indeed removed the child.

A year later, however, a second inquest relying on new forensic evidence overturned that finding, and Lindy Chamberlain and her husband Michael Leigh Chamberlain (b. 1943), a pastor in the Seventh-day Adventist Church, were committed to stand trial. Lindy Chamberlain was convicted and sentenced to life imprisonment for murder; her husband was found guilty as an accessory after the fact. Appeals in the Federal Court and in the High Court both failed.

After the verdict, Lindy Chamberlain was confined in Darwin Prison while her husband served a suspended sentence. From the first report of the baby's disappearance, the case attracted extraordinary and sustained interest. Sensational reporting by the media fuelled intense public speculation about Azaria's fate and the guilt or innocence of her parents: across the nation, the case was widely discussed at dinner parties, barbecues and work places, often in the most brutal and insensitive terms. It seemed that every Australian had an opinion, and for a time many were hostile. Dingo jokes proliferated, and there was frequent and generally ill-informed comment about Seventh-day Adventism. Increasingly, however, opinion began to shift in favour of the Chamberlains as support groups formed in various parts of the country began a sustained campaign to have the case re-examined and the forensic evidence scrutinised afresh.

In February 1986, a matinee jacket worn by Azaria Chamberlain was discovered less than 200 metres from the site where blood-stained clothing had been found one week after her disappearance. Soon afterward, Lindy Chamberlain's sentence was remitted and she was released from prison.

But as the press release published here indicates, she had been fighting her own campaign for a fair hearing. Written late in 1985 and smuggled out of Darwin Prison with the help of supporters, Chamberlain's statement is a clear assertion of her innocence and a protest about her incarceration: in it she declared her intention of going on 'strike' and refusing to continue to cooperate with prison authorities. With the remission of her sentence, the 'strike' action did not proceed.

A royal commission was appointed to review the case. Reporting on 2 June 1987, the commissioner, Mr Justice Trevor Morling (b. 1927), concluded that there were 'serious doubts and questions as to the Chamberlains' guilt'. On 15 September 1988 the two Chamberlain convictions were quashed, and in 1992 compensation was paid. A third coronial inquest was finalised in 1995; it returned an open finding as to the cause and manner of Azaria Chamberlain's death.

As historian Chris Cunneen has noted, the Azaria Chamberlain case has assumed the status of an Australian myth. Several books have been published, including *Through My Eyes*, a long and robust account written by Lindy Chamberlain herself. A film starring the American actor Meryl Streep was released in 1987. Based on John Bryson's book *Evil Angels*, the film was alert to the many ambiguities of the case and to the crass public hysteria it had generated. An opera by Moya Henderson was produced by Opera Australia at the Sydney Opera House in 2002. Nothing quite like the Chamberlain case has been seen in Australia before or since.

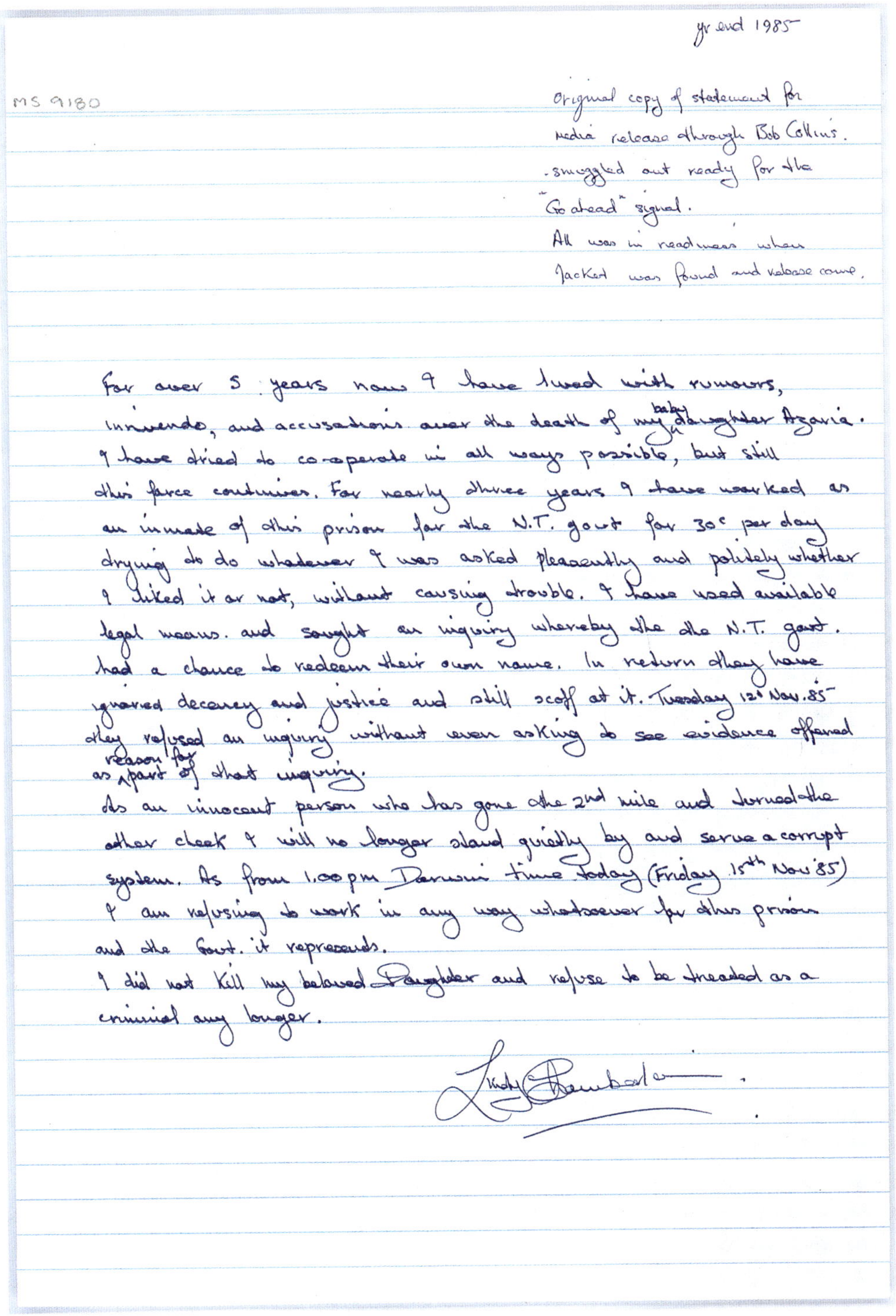

yr end 1985

MS 9180

Original copy of statement for media release through Bob Collins. smuggled out ready for the "Go ahead" signal. All was in readiness when Jacket was found and release came.

For over 5 years now I have lived with rumours, innuendo, and accusations over the death of my baby daughter Azaria. I have tried to co-operate in all ways possible, but still this farce continues. For nearly three years I have worked as an inmate of this prison for the N.T. govt for 30c per day trying to do whatever I was asked pleasantly and politely whether I liked it or not, without causing trouble. I have used available legal means. and sought an inquiry whereby the the N.T. govt. had a chance to redeem their own name. In return they have ignored decency and justice and still scoff at it. Tuesday 12th Nov. 85 they refused an inquiry without even asking to see evidence offered as reason for part of that inquiry.

As an innocent person who has gone the 2nd mile and turned the other cheek I will no longer stand quietly by and serve a corrupt system. As from 1.00 pm Darwin time today (Friday 15th Nov '85) I am refusing to work in any way whatsoever for this prison and the Govt. it represents.

I did not Kill my beloved Daughter and refuse to be treated as a criminal any longer.

Lindy Chamberlain

Lindy Chamberlain pleads for justice

ABOVE *Lindy Chamberlain's letter declaring she will no longer cooperate with prison authorities.*

Yr end 1985
Original copy of statement for
media release through Bob Collins
smuggled out ready for the
"Go ahead" signal
All was in readiness when
Jacket was found and release came.

For over 5 years now I have lived with rumours, innuendo and accusations over the death of my baby daughter Azaria. I have tried to co-operate in all ways possible, but still this farce continues. For nearly three years I have worked as an inmate of this prison for the N.T. govt for 30c per day trying to do whatever I was asked pleasantly and politely whether I liked it or not, without causing trouble. I have used available legal means, and sought an inquiry whereby the N.T. govt. had a chance to redeem their own name. In return they have ignored decency and justice and still scoff at it. Tuesday 12th Nov 85 they refused an inquiry without even asking to see evidence offered as reason for part of that inquiry.

As an innocent person who has gone the 2nd mile and turned the other cheek I will no longer stand quietly by and serve a corrupt system. As from 1.00 pm Darwin time today (Friday 15th Nov '85) I am refusing to work in any way whatsoever for this prison and the Govt. it represents.

I did not kill my beloved Daughter and refuse to be treated as a criminal any longer.

Lindy Chamberlain

'a sovereign, independent and federal nation'

AUSTRALIA ACT

Almost two hundred years after the beginning of European settlement in Australia, the last remaining ties between the country's legislature and judiciary and their counterparts in the United Kingdom were finally eliminated in the *Australia Act 1986*. The severing of these ties was made in a pair of separate, but related, pieces of legislation, one an act of the Australian Parliament (No. 142 of 1985) and the other an act of the Parliament of the United Kingdom (c.2 1986). Extracts of the Australian legislation are published here.

The two complementary acts resolved the anomalous power of the United Kingdom's Parliament to legislate over the individual Australian states. This power had been exercised since colonial times and had not been affected by the *Statute of Westminster 1931* under which legislative equality had been established between the self-governing dominions of the British Empire and the United Kingdom.

One of the most significant effects of the *Australia Act 1986* was the removal of the possibility of appeals from Australian courts to the United Kingdom's Privy Council. In 1968 the Australian Parliament had terminated such appeals in relation to matters involving federal legislation. In 1975, with the passage of the *Privy Council (Appeals from the High Court) Act 1975*, it had closed off almost all routes of appeal from the High Court of Australia. However, appeals to the Privy Council from the supreme courts of the Australian states had remained open, the last vestige of the long Australian legal subservience to Britain.

Another function of the *Australia Act 1986* was to recognise the sovereign independence of the Australian states consistent with the standing of the Commonwealth of Australia in its role as the entity of national government. Over time, various imperial acts, including the *Statute of Westminster 1931*, had incrementally granted degrees of nationhood to the Commonwealth of Australia. However, this had created an anomaly where—at least in a technical sense and even so long after Federation—the states remained colonies under the British Crown.

In addition to the Australian and United Kingdom acts, the modernisation of the constitutional arrangements at both federal and state levels required that each state parliament pass its own enabling legislation. Collectively, the suite of federal, state and British acts are known as the 'Australia acts'. In Australia, the *Australia Act 1986* received vice-regal assent on 4 December 1985; it came into effect with a proclamation signed by Queen Elizabeth II in a ceremony at Government House in Canberra on 3 March 1986 in the presence of the Australian prime minister, R.J.L. 'Bob' Hawke.

ABOVE *Queen Elizabeth II signs her assent to the Australia Act, with Secretary to the Executive Council David Reid and Prime Minister Bob Hawke looking on.*

An Act to bring constitutional arrangements affecting the Commonwealth and the States into conformity with the status of the Commonwealth of Australia as a sovereign, independent and federal nation

WHEREAS the Prime Minister of the Commonwealth and the Premiers of the States at conferences held in Canberra on 24 and 25 June 1982 and 21 June 1984 agreed on the taking of certain measures to bring constitutional arrangements affecting the Commonwealth and the States into conformity with the status of the Commonwealth as a sovereign, independent and federal nation: ...

BE IT THEREFORE ENACTED by the Queen, and the Senate and the House of Representatives of the Commonwealth of Australia, as follows:

1. Termination of power of United Kingdom to legislate for Australia

    No Act of the Parliament of the United Kingdom passed after the commencement of this Act shall extend, or be deemed to extend, to the Commonwealth, to a State or to a Territory as part of the law of the Commonwealth, of the State or of the Territory.

2. Legislative powers of Parliaments of States

    (1) It is hereby declared and enacted that the legislative powers of the Parliament of each State include full power to make laws for the peace, order and good government of that State that have extraterritorial operation.
    (2) It is hereby further declared and enacted that the legislative powers of the Parliament of each State include all legislative powers that the Parliament of the United Kingdom might have exercised before the commencement of this Act for the peace, order and good government of that State but nothing in this subsection confers on a State any capacity that the State did not have immediately before the commencement of this Act to engage in relations with countries outside Australia.

3. Termination of restrictions on legislative powers of Parliaments of States

    (1) The Act of the Parliament of the United Kingdom known as the Colonial Laws Validity Act 1865 shall not apply to any law made after the commencement of this Act by the Parliament of a State.
    (2) No law and no provision of any law made after the commencement of this Act by the parliament of a State shall be void or inoperative on the ground that it is repugnant to the law of England, or to the provisions of any existing or future Act of the Parliament of the United Kingdom, or to any order, rule or regulation made under any such Act, and the powers of the Parliament of a State shall include the power to repeal

or amend any such Act, order, rule or regulation in so far as it is part of the law of the State ...

7. **Powers and functions of Her Majesty and Governors in respect of States**

    (1) Her Majesty's representative in each State shall be the Governor ...
    (5) The advice to Her Majesty in relation to the exercise of the powers and functions of Her Majesty in respect of a State shall be tendered by the Premier of the State.

8. **State laws not subject to disallowance or suspension of operation**

    An Act of the Parliament of a State that has been assented to by the Governor of the State shall not, after commencement of this Act, be subject to disallowance by Her Majesty, nor shall its operation be suspended pending the signification of Her Majesty's pleasure thereon.

9. **State laws not subject to withholding of assent or reservation**

    (1) No law or instrument shall be of any force or effect in so far as it purports to require the Governor of a State to withhold assent from any Bill for an Act of the State that has been passed in such manner and form as may from time to time be required by a law made by the Parliament of the State.
    (2) No law or instrument shall be of any force or effect in so far as it purports to require the reservation of any Bill for an Act of a State for the signification of Her Majesty's pleasure thereon.

10. **Termination of responsibility of United Kingdom Government in relation to State matters**

    After the commencement of this Act Her Majesty's Government in the United Kingdom shall have no responsibility for the government of any State.

11. **Termination of appeals to Her Majesty in Council**

    (1) ... no appeal to Her Majesty in Council lies or shall be brought, whether by leave of any court or of Her Majesty in Council or otherwise, and whether by virtue of any Act of the Parliament of the United Kingdom, the Royal Prerogative or otherwise, from or in respect of any decision of an Australian court ...

Reflecting Australian diversity

A CHARTER FOR THE SPECIAL BROADCASTING SERVICE (SBS)

One of the creative and practical manifestations of Australia's more confident acceptance of its cultural diversity in the post-Whitlam years was the establishment of the Special Broadcasting Service (SBS), on 1 January 1978, by Prime Minister Malcolm Fraser's government.

During the 1950s, security restrictions had imposed strict controls on the use of languages other than English in both the print media and broadcasting. But with the lifting of these restrictions in 1956, a lively ethnic press quickly emerged in Australia. In turn, as radio frequencies expanded and with the substantial postwar growth in immigration, there was a growing demand for the broadcast of minority language programs. Initially that demand was met by services provided by two community radio stations, 2EA in Sydney and 3EA in Melbourne, which both began broadcasting in 1975. With its establishment in 1978, SBS Radio assumed responsibility for the Sydney and Melbourne stations as the foundation of its new network. By 1980 SBS had moved into television broadcasting.

In 1986 an attempt to force an amalgamation of SBS with the Australian Broadcasting Corporation (ABC) was overturned by the intervention of Prime Minister Bob Hawke in response to strong protests by ethnic communities. It is a sign of national maturity that an independent SBS attracts strong bipartisan support and is encouraged to offer services that reach out to Australia's ethnic minorities. SBS Radio broadcasts in sixty-eight languages in all Australian states, while SBS TV devotes a significant part of its morning television schedule to news bulletins in languages other than English. It also offers high-quality evening news and documentaries with a higher concentration on international affairs than either the ABC or the commercial news networks; its sports coverage places a strong emphasis on international sports, especially soccer and cycling. SBS is also one of the world's largest subtitling organisations, producing subtitles both for its own television channel and for foreign film and documentary producers around the world.

With the passage of the *Special Broadcasting Service Act 1991*, SBS entered a new phase of maturity and consolidation. The act established SBS as a corporation and gave the organisation a charter defining government and community expectations of SBS as a national broadcaster charged with special obligations of outreach to inform, educate and entertain. If the charter is workmanlike rather than inspirational, it nevertheless stands as a clear expression of Australia's new ease with the diversity created by its immigration and educational programs, and a sense of its own place in the world.

As historian James Jupp has noted, SBS has generally avoided the public criticism sometimes directed at the ABC for perceived bias against incumbent governments, especially conservative ones. However, particular communities have sometimes been critical. The Jewish community has expressed criticism of SBS's treatment of issues relating to the Israel–Palestine conflict, and in 2003 Australian Vietnamese communities protested about the station's failure to consult before it established a news program from Hanoi. While the charter offers little guidance on matters of this kind, SBS has established other mechanisms for consulting with the many ethnic communities that are the beneficiaries of its services.

Reflecting fashion and other managerial models, the SBS Corporation has also embraced the all-encompassing vision statement as a means of declaring its aims: 'Uniting and enriching our society by creatively communicating the values, the voices and the visions of multicultural Australia and the contemporary world'. As with most statements of this kind, the SBS example is an affirmation that motherhood is a good thing.

(1) The principal function of SBS is to provide multilingual and multicultural radio and television services that inform, educate and entertain all Australians and, in doing so, reflect Australia's multicultural society.

(2) SBS, in performing its principal functions must:

   (a) contribute to meeting the communications needs of Australia's multicultural society, including ethnic, Aboriginal and Torres Strait Islander communities; and
   (b) increase awareness of the contribution of a diversity of cultures to the continuing development of Australian society; and
   (c) promote understanding and acceptance of the cultural, linguistic and ethnic diversity of the Australian people; and
   (d) contribute to the retention and continuing development of language and other cultural skills; and
   (e) as far as practicable, inform, educate and entertain Australians in their preferred languages; and
   (f) make use of Australia's diverse creative resources; and
   (g) contribute to the overall diversity of Australian television and radio services, particularly taking into account the contribution of the Australian Broadcasting Corporation and the public broadcasting sector; and
   (h) contribute to extending the range of Australian television and radio services, and reflect the changing nature of Australian society, by presenting many points of view and using innovative terms of expression.

One of the darkest chapters in Australia's history

TERRA NULLIUS, LAND RIGHTS AND MABO

On 3 June 1992, after litigation extending for ten years, the High Court of Australia brought down its decision in the land rights case brought by Eddie Koiki Mabo (1936–1992) and others against the state of Queensland and the Commonwealth of Australia. The plaintiffs had sought declarations that they held a traditional native title to lands and waters in the Murray Islands group in the Torres Strait—title that had not been extinguished by Queensland's annexation of the islands in 1879 or by any subsequent government actions.

In a landmark finding, the High Court, led by Chief Justice Sir Anthony Mason (b. 1925), held that Australian common law, like the laws of other lands colonised by the British, recognises the pre-existing land rights of Indigenous peoples. One of the High Court's most controversial judgments, *Mabo* generated an intense debate about the objectivity and impartiality of judges, as well as discussion of the role of the court itself. For critics, both of the court and of a perceived new judicial activism, the decision reached in the *Mabo* case represented an unwelcome intrusion by the court into the political process. Supporters believed the court had corrected a great historical wrong.

A triumph for the Murray Islanders, *Mabo*, as the court's decision came to be called, had fundamental implications for the nation itself. In recognising the legitimacy of an Indigenous legal order predating the arrival of Europeans, the decision challenged the traditional understanding of Australian history and nationhood—that before white settlement the continent and its adjacent islands had been a *terra nullius* or a territory inhabited by a people who did not have a recognised social or political organisation. For more than two hundred years that assumption had prevailed as a state of mind in settler Australia. Overcoming that state of mind in ways that would give due recognition to Aboriginal and Torres Strait Islander people as Australia's first population and original proprietors was a task of no small order—politically, legally, constitutionally, and in ways that would persuade and reassure the nation.

In exercising leadership, Prime Minister Paul Keating acknowledged that *Mabo* represented 'an historic turning point ... for a new relationship between indigenous and non-Aboriginal Australians'. It was an honourable and principled acceptance of a new reality that would test the understanding and generosity of the nation as it struggled to achieve a reconciliation with its past and to forge a compact of trust with Aboriginal Australia as the means by which the nation could advance itself. If *Mabo* divided—and in legislative terms, in the *Native Title Act 1993* that followed, the results were hard fought but disappointing—the decision empowered new voices of an Aboriginal leadership that could now claim a legitimate, permanent place in the larger forums of Australian political life.

When the High Court decision was handed down, six of the judges (one dissenting) agreed that there was a concept of native title at common law and that the source of native title was the traditional connection to or occupation of the land. The majority judges agreed that, of itself, native title had not been eliminated by the act of British settlement. The *Mabo* judgment is a long and complex document in which the several judges offer their reasons for the determination of their findings. The first extract published here is drawn from the majority judgment of Sir Gerard Brennan (b. 1928); the second is from the supporting judgment of Sir William Deane (b. 1931) and Mary Gaudron (b. 1943); these are followed by the formal order of the court.

(Brennan, J.) ...
28. The proposition that, when the Crown assumed sovereignty over an Australian colony, it became the universal and absolute beneficial owner of all the land therein, invites critical examination. If the conclusion at which Stephen C.J. arrived in *Attorney-General* v. *Brown* be right, the interests of indigenous inhabitants in colonial land were extinguished so soon as British subjects settled in a colony, though the indigenous inhabitants had neither ceded their lands to the Crown nor suffered them to be taken as spoils of conquest. According to the cases, the common law itself took from indigenous inhabitants any right to occupy their traditional land, exposed them to deprivation of the religious, cultural and economic sustenance which the land provides, vested the land effectively in the control of the Imperial authorities without any right to compensation and made the indigenous inhabitants intruders in their own homes and mendicants for a place to live. Judged by any civilised standard, such a law is unjust and its claim to be a part of the common law to be applied in contemporary Australia must be questioned. This Court must now determine whether, by the common law of this country, the rights and interests of the Meriam people of today are to be determined on the footing that their ancestors lost their traditional rights and interests in the land of the Murray Islands on 1 August 1879 [when they were annexed by the Colony of Queensland] ...

(Deane and Gaudron JJ): ...
56. If this were any ordinary case, the Court would not be justified in reopening the validity of fundamental propositions which have been endorsed by long-established authority and which have been accepted as a basis of the real property law of the country for more than one hundred and fifty years. And that would be so notwithstanding that the combined effect of Crown grants, of assumed acquiescence in reservations and dedications and of statutes of limitations would be that, as a practical matter, the consequences of re-examination and rejection of the two propositions would be largely, and probably completely, confined to lands which remain under Aboriginal occupation or use. Far from being ordinary, however, the circumstances of the present case make it unique. As has been seen, the two propositions in question provided the legal basis for the dispossession of the Aboriginal peoples of most of their traditional lands. The acts and events by which that dispossession in legal theory was carried into practical effect constitute the darkest aspect of the history of this nation. The nation as a whole must remain diminished unless and until there is an acknowledgment of, and retreat from, these past injustices. In these circumstances, the Court is under a clear duty to re-examine the two propositions. For the reasons which we have explained, that re-examination compels their rejection. The lands of this continent were not terra nullius or "practically unoccupied" in 1788. The Crown's property in the lands of the Colony of New South Wales was, under the common law which became applicable upon the establishment of the Colony in 1788, reduced or qualified by the burden of the common law native title of the Aboriginal tribes and clans to the particular areas of land on which they lived or which they used for traditional purposes ...

Order

In lieu of answering the questions reserved for the consideration of the Full Court,

(1) declare that the land in the Murray Islands is not Crown land within the meaning of that term in s. 5 of the *Land Act 1962* (Q);
(2) putting to one side the Islands of Dauer and Waier and the parcel of land leased to the Trustees of the Australian Board of Missions and those parcels of land (if any) which have been validly appropriated for use for administrative purposes the use of which is inconsistent with the continued enjoyment of the rights and privileges of the Meriam people under native title, declare that the Meriam people are entitled as against the whole world to possession, occupation, use and enjoyment of the lands of the Murray Islands;
(3) declare that the title of the Meriam people is subject to the power of the Parliament of Queensland and the power of the Governor in Council of Queensland to extinguish that title by valid exercise of their respective powers, provided any exercise of those powers is not inconsistent with the laws of the Commonwealth.

ABOVE *Eddie Mabo died five months before the High Court judgment was handed down.*

ABOVE **Herald** *clipping from 1934 sent to the minister for the interior, with handwritten note indicating the writer's preferred child.*

'Grief and loss ... Tenacity and survival'

BRINGING THEM HOME REPORT

In 1981 the New South Wales Department of Aboriginal Affairs published a ground-breaking study by historian Peter Read (b. 1945) on the removal of 5625 Aboriginal children from their families in the state between 1883 and 1969. Read used the phrase 'The Stolen Generations' as the title of his study and it quickly became both the means of identifying those who had been removed from their families and an evocation of what historian Tim Rowse has called 'the ... public grief and pain of Aboriginal Australians', now being more publicly exposed and shared.

The problems Read had identified as the experience in one Australian state were examined again on a national basis in two powerful and poignant reports. The first was the 1991 *Report of the Commonwealth Royal Commission into Aboriginal Deaths in Custody*, which raised the awareness of policy-makers and the public generally of what Read referred to as the pervasive psychological morbidity of Indigenous Australians. The second was the 1997 report *Bringing Them Home*, an inquiry into the 'separation' programs of all the various Australian governments. That inquiry, commissioned by the Keating Labor government in August 1995, was carried out by the Human Rights and Equal Opportunity Commission and led by Sir Ronald Wilson (1992–2005), a former judge of the High Court.

Anecdotally based, the *Bringing Them Home* inquiry brought together for the first time, and in their own words, the testimony of some 535 individuals who had been affected by the 'separation' programs that had disrupted their experience of childhood and growing up in Australia. Cathartic as those testimonies were for those who could deliver them to the inquiry, they presented difficulties when read objectively as 'evidence'. Wilson had hoped that the process of storytelling might initiate healing, but some critics of the inquiry were troubled that no test had been made of the truth of testimonies and that there had been no exploration of the intentions, methods and rationales of the authorities charged with responsibility for the management and implementation of programs of Indigenous child removal. Certainly it has proved difficult in legal actions pursued by some individual members of the 'Stolen Generations' to achieve redress for pain and suffering arising from so-called 'illegal' or 'unconstitutional' removals, even though their pain and suffering was manifest. Courts in various Australian jurisdictions, including the High Court, have not been persuaded that programs of separation, however distressing to those affected by them, were either unconstitutional or illegal under the laws that had been in place at the time.

Nevertheless, the *Bringing Them Home* report has been crucial in making the wider community of Australians aware of the source and nature of Aboriginal pain and suffering. It has been valuable in the long and difficult process of negotiating a path to reconciliation between white and black Australians. It is clear, also, that Aboriginal Australians have gained a powerful emotional release in the public telling of so many representative human stories, shared and made vivid after years of private pain and introspection. A larger personal gain flowing both from the *Bringing Them Home* inquiry, and from others, such as Peter Read's pioneering study, has been the reunification of many scattered and broken Aboriginal families—though sadly for others reunions could not always be made.

The *Bringing Them Home* report is represented here in Ronald Wilson's formal introduction to the published findings of his inquiry. It is a document of significance and power, distilling in simple and accessible words the range of the inquiry, while also looking forward with hope to the possibilities of a reconciliation of the kind that had been envisaged by Sir William Deane (b. 1931) early in his term as governor-general of Australia, 1996–2001.

Our life pattern was created by the government policies and are forever with me, as though an invisible anchor around my neck. The moments that should be shared and rejoiced by a family unit, for [my brother] and mum and I are forever lost. The stolen years that are worth more than any treasure are irrecoverable.

Confidential submission 338, Victoria

Grief and loss are the predominant themes of this report. Tenacity and survival are also acknowledged. It is no ordinary report. Much of its subject matter is so personal and intimate that ordinarily it would not be discussed. These matters have only been discussed with the Inquiry with great difficulty and much personal distress. The suffering and the courage of those who have told their stories inspire sensitivity and respect.

The histories we trace are complex and pervasive. Most significantly the actions of the past resonate in the present and will continue to do so in the future. The laws, policies and practices which separated Indigenous children from their families have contributed directly to the alienation of Indigenous societies today.

For individuals, their removal as children and the abuse they experienced at the hands of the authorities or their delegates have permanently scarred their lives. The harm continues in later generations, affecting their children and grandchildren.

In no sense has the Inquiry been 'raking over the past' for its own sake. The truth is that the past is very much with us today, in the continuing devastation of the lives of Indigenous Australians. That devastation cannot be addressed unless the whole community listens with an open heart and mind to the stories of what has happened in the past, and having listened and understood, commits itself to reconciliation. As the Governor-General [Sir William Deane] stated in August 1996,

> It should, I think, be apparent to all well-meaning people that true reconciliation between the Australian nation and its indigenous peoples is not achievable in the absence of an acknowledgement by the nation of the wrongfulness of the past dispossession, oppression and degradation of the Aboriginal peoples. That is not to say that individual Australians who had no part in what was done in the past should feel or acknowledge personal guilt. It is simply to assert our identity as a nation and the basic fact that national shame, as well as national pride, can and should exist in relation to past acts and omissions, at least when done or made in the name of the community or with the authority of government ...
>
> The present plight, in terms of health, employment, education, living conditions and self-esteem, of so many Aborigines must be acknowledged as largely flowing from what happened in the past. The dispossession, the destruction of hunting fields and the devastation of lives were all related. The new diseases, the alcohol and the new pressures of living were all introduced. True acknowledgement cannot stop short of recognition of the extent to which present disadvantage

flows from past injustice and oppression ...

Theoretically, there could be national reconciliation without any redress at all of the dispossession and other wrongs sustained by the Aborigines. As a practical matter, however, it is apparent that recognition of the need for appropriate redress for present disadvantage is a pre-requisite of reconciliation. There is, I believe, widespread acceptance of such a need.

The Inquiry's recommendations are directed to healing and reconciliation for the benefit of all Australians.

'we will decide who comes to this country'

JOHN HOWARD'S ELECTION POLICY SPEECH

In October 2001, in the aftermath of the MV *Tampa* refugee crisis and of the terror attacks on the World Trade Center and the Pentagon in the United States, the Howard government called a federal election. It would be an election fought largely and emotively on the issues of border protection, and national and international security in a world transformed by the audacious scale and ferocity of the attacks on US sovereignty. But while the two issues were linked, the evidence of opinion polling suggested that border protection and the problems posed to Australia by burgeoning numbers of asylum seekers cruelly exploited by people smugglers had created the greatest unease for voters. This issue had gained particular prominence in August 2001 when the Norwegian cargo ship MV *Tampa* had rescued 438 asylum seekers from an overloaded fishing boat sinking in the Indian Ocean. This incident developed into a national crisis as the Australian government moved decisively and with force to prevent the asylum seekers landing in Australia, a position that had wide public support but was also troubling in its moral and ethical dimensions.

With an election called in these circumstances, the battle lines were drawn between the two major political parties. On its side, the government was making the running on an issue that was of clear concern to an electorate that was demonstrably susceptible to fear and anxiety. On its side, the Opposition—no less concerned about the protection of Australia's borders—became an easy target for criticism and scorn if it expressed even the smallest qualification about aspects of the treatment of asylum seekers and, more especially, the methods that might be employed to maintain the integrity of Australia's borders. These issues had been played out on the floor of the Australian Parliament to the disadvantage of the Labor leader Kim Beazley. Having initially supported the government in its early response to the *Tampa* issue, Beazley had subsequently opposed the severe clauses of a hurriedly introduced Border Protection Bill, a position that exposed him to severe criticism by his opponents and the fury of an anxious public.

It was in this context that Prime Minister John Howard delivered his election policy speech in Sydney on 28 October 2001 with its potent—and unscripted—declaration that 'we will decide who comes to this country and the circumstances in which they come'. In an admittedly partisan audience, the prime minister's remark was greeted with uproarious applause. But Howard's unequivocal stand also helped deliver an election victory that earlier in the year had seemed much less certain. On 10 November, the coalition parties retained office with 51 per cent of the vote to Labor's 49 per cent. In an Australia made uneasy by terror and with doubts about the integrity and good intentions of those seeking unauthorised entry into Australia, Howard's appeal to what political commentator Robert Manne has called a 'populist conservatism' was as potent in its own way as Menzies' wartime call to 'the forgotten people' in 1942 (see page 258).

... But I now want to bring my remarks very much to the context of this election campaign. I said in Perth during the week that this campaign and all the individual things that are being said in it, are being fought against the background of two overriding issues. They are the issues of national security and the issue of economic management. We are as you all know in a new and dangerous part of the world's history. The tragic events of the 11th of September have changed our lives, they have caused us to take pause and think about the values we hold in common with the American people and free people around the world. That was an attack on Australia as much as it was an attack on the United States. It not only claimed the lives of Australians but it assaulted the very values that we hold dear and that we take for granted. So therefore a military response and wise diplomacy and a steady hand on the helm are needed to guide Australians through those very difficult circumstances. National security is therefore about a proper response to terrorism. It's also about having a far-sighted, strong well thought out defence policy. It is also about having an uncompromising view about the fundamental right of this country to protect its borders, it's about this nation saying to the world we are a generous open-hearted people taking more refugees on a per capita basis than any other country except Canada, we have a proud record of welcoming people from 140 different nations. But we will decide who comes to this country and the circumstances in which they come ...

What a contrast with the Labor Party. The morning ... I made the announcement that we had to board the motor vessel *Tampa* I was told by the Leader of the Opposition that the last thing I wanted or Australia needed was a negative carping opposition. But in four and a half hours he was accusing me of engaging in wedge politics and fanning Hansonism. He voted against the border protection bill, he ultimately voted for it although it covered a wider area and while the debate was going on in the Senate many of his colleagues were darkly muttering if we win the election campaign, we'll change it. We have had a single irrevocable view on this, and that is that we will defend our borders and we'll decide who comes to this country. But we'll do that within the framework of the decency for which Australians have always been renowned.

I want to place on record my gratitude ... to the men and women of the Royal Australian Navy who have not only been protecting our borders but saving lives in the process of doing it. Now that's the face of Australia to the world. We will be compassionate, we will save lives, we will care for people but we will decide and nobody else who comes to this country ...

A charter of human rights

A CHARTER OF HUMAN RIGHTS AND RESPONSIBILITIES

So far only two Australian jurisdictions have implemented legislation to safeguard and enshrine human rights as a key plank of the democratic system of government. The first to do so was the Australian Capital Territory with its *Human Rights Act 2004*. The state of Victoria followed with its *Charter of Human Rights and Responsibilities Act 2006*, a landmark in Australia's constitutional and political history, as it is the first such instrument in an Australian state. Similar to the legislation enacted in the ACT, the Victorian charter has been described in a detailed commentary by lawyers Alistair Pound and Kylie Evans as 'an innovative, if modest change to the Australian system of government in the form of an entrenched Act of Parliament that protects a range of civil and political rights'. The Victorian charter is primarily based on the UK's *Human Rights Act 1998* and the *New Zealand Bill of Rights Act 1990* rather than the constitutional models offered most famously in the United States Bill of Rights (1791) or the more recent South African Bill of Rights (1997).

The document presented here is an extract from the Victorian charter and comprises the preamble and the statement of purpose and citation. The charter itself formally defines a set of twenty-seven rights, freedoms and responsibilities. These include a recognition that Aboriginal people hold distinct cultural rights and must not be denied the right, with other members of their community, to enjoy their identity and culture, to maintain and use their language, to maintain their kinship ties and to maintain their distinctive spiritual, material and economic relationship with the land, waters and other resources with which they have a connection under traditional laws and customs.

As a national polity Australia is the only democratic country in the world without a codified charter of rights. As a founding member of the United Nations it became a signatory to the Universal Declaration of Human Rights, adopted soon after the Second World War. Later (1976) Australia also ratified the International Covenant on Civil and Political Rights and the International Covenant on Economic, Social and Cultural Rights. In ratifying these covenants, Australia agreed to make them part of its own domestic law. So far, however, this has not occurred, even though laws have been passed in a few areas, such as freedom from discrimination on the basis of race.

In examining the case for a national charter of rights, constitutional lawyer George Williams has pointed to a prevailing conservatism in Australia that has trusted in a belief that the basic freedoms of citizens have been and remain adequately protected by the common law and by the good sense of those elected as the people's representatives in parliament. In this context it should be noted that in 2008, the newly elected government led by Prime Minister Kevin Rudd appointed a committee to undertake an Australia-wide community consultation for protecting and promoting human rights and corresponding responsibilities in Australia, but with the proviso that the sovereignty of Parliament should be preserved and that there should be no constitutionally entrenched bill of rights.

No.43 of 2006

Charter of Human Rights and Responsibilities Act 2006

[Assented to 25 July 2006]
Preamble

On behalf of the people of Victoria the Parliament enacts this Charter, recognising that all people are born free and equal in dignity and rights.

This Charter is founded on the following principles—
- human rights are essential in a democratic and inclusive society that respects the rule of law, human dignity, equality and freedom;
- human rights belong to all people without discrimination, and the diversity of the people of Victoria enhances our community;
- human rights come with responsibilities and must be exercised in a way that respects the human rights of others;
- human rights have a special importance for the Aboriginal people of Victoria, as descendants of Australia's first people, with their diverse spiritual, social, cultural and economic relationship with their traditional lands and waters.

The Parliament of Victoria therefore enacts as follows:

PART 1 PRELIMINARY
Purpose and citation

1. Purpose and citation

(1) This Act may be referred to as the Charter of Human Rights and Responsibilities and is so referred to in this Act.
(2) The main purpose of this Charter is to protect and promote human rights by—
   (a) setting out the human rights that Parliament specifically seeks to protect and promote; and
   (b) ensuring that all statutory provisions, whenever enacted, are interpreted so far as is possible in a way that is compatible with human rights; and
   (c) imposing an obligation on all public authorities to act in a way that is compatible with human rights; and
   (d) requiring statements of compatibility with human rights to be prepared in respect of all Bills introduced into Parliament and enabling the Scrutiny of Acts and Regulations Committee to report on such compatibility; and
   (e) conferring jurisdiction on the Supreme Court to declare that a statutory provision cannot be interpreted consistently with a human right and requiring the relevant Minister to respond to that declaration ...

ABOVE *Thousands of people gathered at Federation Square, Melbourne, to watch the broadcast of Prime Minister Kevin Rudd deliver the apology.*

Saying sorry

A NATIONAL APOLOGY TO THE STOLEN GENERATIONS

It is difficult to pinpoint the precise moment when white Australians began seriously to embrace the idea of a national apology to Aboriginal Australians for the pain and suffering caused in myriad ways since the beginning of European settlement. There had always been cries of conscience, but through the nineteenth and most of the twentieth centuries, these were occasional and too isolated to represent any kind of consensus. But as political commentator Robert Manne noted in 2009, since the 1960s Australia had experienced 'a transformation grounded in the questioning of traditional attitudes to ethnicity and race'. One of the key prompts to this questioning was the 1967 constitutional referendum to end constitutional discrimination against Aboriginal people. Symbolically at least, this had acknowledged Aboriginal Australians as an integral part of the body politic and it won overwhelming public support. Another prompt to conscience and to notions of fairness was the increasingly well-coordinated and articulate Aboriginal land rights movement. Yet another was the intrinsically flawed Australian bicentennial celebration of 1988. While it celebrated European settlement and the achievements of nation building, it was a forceful reminder that the First Australians had paid a terrible price for the gains of the white majority. In 1992 the High Court decision in *Mabo* confronted Aboriginal dispossession as the darkest aspect of the nation's history (see page 327). Later that same year, Paul Keating spoke as no Australian prime minister had done before: at Redfern Park in inner suburban Sydney he called on non-Aboriginal Australians to try to imagine the Aboriginal point of view.

There were sobering prompts of a different kind, including the *Report of the Commonwealth Government's Royal Commission into Aboriginal Deaths in Custody*, 1991. Soon afterward, the *Bringing Them Home* report produced graphic descriptions of the experiences of what became known as the Stolen Generations—Aboriginal families that had been fractured or destroyed through the well-intentioned, but ill-conceived and often brutally executed 'separation programs' administered by governments in Australia to achieve assimilation (see page 330).

European Australians were now better informed than they had ever been that the country had prospered at the expense of its Aboriginal people. Calls grew for a process of reconciliation: at its heart was the growing conviction that the nation itself, through the Commonwealth Parliament, must find a way to apologise and atone for past wrongs and for the mistakes made by successive governments. In conscience, so it was argued, some opposed such an idea, but over time that opposition came to be seen as wilfully stubborn, blind and against the national interest.

On 13 February 2008, in a ceremony unprecedented in the Commonwealth Parliament, Prime Minister Kevin Rudd (b. 1957) rose to present a formal apology to the Stolen Generations. That apology was offered by a new Australian government, elected in December 2007, as its first act of official business in its inaugural session of Parliament. Guests in the chamber and the crowds inside and outside the building cheered and clapped as the prime minister uttered the simple word 'sorry', so long denied to those who had suffered terrible pain. That affirmation was shared around the country as crowds gathered in schools and public places, and at big screens in city squares and streets. It was agreed that, of itself, no apology was sufficient to overcome Aboriginal disadvantage in Australia, but as a formal and public expression of the nation's sorrow offered by the country's elected leader, the words spoken that day offered a chance for the country to move forward in greater harmony and with an agreed purpose to build a better future for all its people.

I move that today we honour the Indigenous peoples of this land, the oldest continuing cultures in human history.

We reflect on their past mistreatment. We reflect in particular on the mistreatment of those who were Stolen Generations—this blemished chapter in our nation's history.

The time has now come for the nation to turn a new page in Australia's history by righting the wrongs of the past and so moving forward with confidence to the future.

We apologise for the laws and policies of successive Parliaments and governments that have inflicted profound grief, suffering and loss on these our fellow Australians. We apologise especially for the removal of Aboriginal and Torres Strait Islander children from their families, their communities and their country.

For the pain, suffering and hurt of these Stolen Generations, their descendants and for their families left behind, we say sorry.

To the mothers and the fathers, the brothers and the sisters, for the breaking up of families and communities, we say sorry.

And for the indignity and degradation thus inflicted on a proud people and a proud culture, we say sorry.

We the Parliament of Australia respectfully request that this apology be received in the spirit in which it is offered as part of the healing of the nation.

For the future we take heart; resolving that this new page in the history of our great continent can now be written.

We today take this first step by acknowledging the past and laying claim to a future that embraces all Australians.

A future where this Parliament resolves that the injustices of the past must never, never happen again. A future where we harness the determination of all Australians, Indigenous and non-Indigenous, to close the gap that lies between us in life expectancy, educational achievement and economic opportunity.

A future where we embrace the possibility of new solutions to enduring problems where old approaches have failed. A future based on mutual respect, mutual resolve and mutual responsibility. A future where all Australians, whatever their origins, are truly equal partners, with equal opportunities and with an equal stake in shaping the next chapter in the history of this great country, Australia.

There comes a time in the history of nations when their peoples must become fully reconciled to their past if they are to go forward with confidence to embrace their future. Our nation, Australia, has reached such a time. That is why the parliament is today here assembled: to deal with this unfinished business of the nation, to remove a great stain from the nation's soul and, in a true spirit of reconciliation, to open a new chapter in the history of this great land, Australia.

Last year I made a commitment to the Australian people that if we formed the next government of the Commonwealth we would in parliament say sorry to the stolen generations. Today I honour that commitment. I said we would do so early in the life of the new parliament.

Again, today I honour that commitment by doing so at the commencement of this the 42nd parliament of the Commonwealth. Because the time has come, well and truly come, for all peoples of our great country, for all citizens of our great Commonwealth, for all Australians—those who are Indigenous and those who are not—to come together to reconcile and together build a new future for our nation.

Some have asked, 'Why apologise?' Let me begin to answer by telling the parliament just a little of one person's story—an elegant, eloquent and wonderful woman in her 80s, full of life, full of funny stories, despite what has happened in her life's journey, a woman who has travelled a long way to be with us today, a member of the stolen generation who shared some of her story with me when I called around to see her just a few days ago.

Nanna Nungala Fejo, as she prefers to be called, was born in the late 1920s. She remembers her earliest childhood days living with her family and her community in a bush camp just outside Tennant Creek. She remembers the love and the warmth and the kinship of those days long ago, including traditional dancing around the camp fire at night. She loved the dancing.

She remembers once getting into strife when, as a four-year-old girl, she insisted on dancing with the male tribal elders rather than just sitting and watching the men, as the girls were supposed to do.

But then, sometime around 1932, when she was about four, she remembers the coming of the welfare men. Her family had feared that day and had dug holes in the creek bank where the children could run and hide. What they had not expected was that the white welfare men did not come alone.

They brought a truck, two white men and an Aboriginal stockman on horseback cracking his stockwhip. The kids were found; they ran for their mothers, screaming, but they could not get away. They were herded and piled onto the back of the truck. Tears flowing, her mum tried clinging to the sides of the truck as her children were taken away to the Bungalow in Alice, all in the name of protection.

A few years later, government policy changed. Now the children would be handed over to the missions to be cared for by the churches. But which church would care for them? The kids were simply told to line up in three lines. Nanna Fejo and her sister stood in the middle line, her older brother and cousin on her left.

Those on the left were told that they had become Catholics, those in the middle Methodists and those on the right Church of England. That is how the complex questions of post-reformation theology were resolved in the Australian outback in the 1930s. It was as crude as that.

She and her sister were sent to a Methodist mission on Goulburn Island and then Croker Island. Her Catholic brother was sent to work at a cattle station and her cousin to a Catholic mission. Nanna Fejo's family had been broken up for a second time.

She stayed at the mission until after the war, when she was allowed to leave for a prearranged job as a domestic in Darwin. She was 16. Nanna Fejo never saw her mum again. After she left the mission, her brother let her know that her mum had died years before, a broken woman fretting for the children that had literally been ripped away from her.

ABOVE Members of the Stolen Generations listen in Parliament to the prime minister's apology.

I asked Nanna Fejo what she would have me say today about her story. She thought for a few moments then said that what I should say today was that all mothers are important. And she added: 'Families—keeping them together is very important. It's a good thing that you are surrounded by love and that love is passed down the generations. That's what gives you happiness.'

As I left, later on, Nanna Fejo took one of my staff aside, wanting to make sure that I was not too hard on the Aboriginal stockman who had hunted those kids down all those years ago. The stockman had found her again decades later, this time himself to say, 'Sorry.' And remarkably, extraordinarily, she had forgiven him.

Nanna Fejo's is just one story. There are thousands, tens of thousands of them: stories of forced separation of Aboriginal and Torres Strait Islander children from their mums and dads over the better part of a century. Some of these stories are graphically told in *Bringing Them Home*, the report commissioned in 1995 by Prime Minister Keating and received in 1997 by Prime Minister Howard.

There is something terribly primal about these firsthand accounts. The pain is searing; it screams from the pages. The hurt, the humiliation, the degradation and the sheer brutality of the act of physically separating a mother from her children is a deep assault on our senses and on our most elemental humanity.

These stories cry out to be heard; they cry out for an apology. Instead, from the nation's parliament there has been a stony, stubborn and deafening silence for more than a decade; a view that somehow we, the parliament, should suspend our most basic instincts of what is right and what is wrong; a view that, instead, we should look for any pretext to push this great wrong to one side, to leave it languishing with the historians, the academics and the cultural warriors, as if the stolen generations are little more than an interesting sociological phenomenon.

But the stolen generations are not intellectual curiosities. They are human beings, human beings who have been damaged deeply by the decisions of parliaments and governments. But, as of today, the time for denial, the time for delay, has at last come to an end.

The nation is demanding of its political leadership to take us forward. Decency, human decency, universal human decency, demands that the nation now step forward to right an historical wrong. That is what we are doing in this place today.

But should there still be doubts as to why we must now act, let the parliament reflect for a moment on the following facts: that, between 1910 and 1970, between 10 and 30 per cent of Indigenous children were forcibly taken from their mothers and fathers; that, as a result, up to 50,000 children were forcibly taken from their families; that this was the product of the deliberate, calculated policies of the state as reflected in the explicit powers given to them under statute; that this policy was taken to such extremes by some in administrative authority that the forced extractions of children of so-called 'mixed lineage' were seen as part of a broader policy of dealing with 'the problem of the Aboriginal population'.

One of the most notorious examples of this approach was from the Northern Territory Protector of Natives, who stated: 'Generally by the fifth and invariably by the sixth generation, all native characteristics of the Australian aborigine are eradicated.

'The problem of our half-castes—to quote the protector—will quickly be eliminated by the complete disappearance of the black race, and the swift submergence of their progeny in the white ...'

The Western Australian Protector of Natives expressed not dissimilar views, expounding them at length in Canberra in 1937 at the first national conference on Indigenous affairs that brought together the Commonwealth and state protectors of natives.

These are uncomfortable things to be brought out into the light. They are not pleasant. They are profoundly disturbing. But we must acknowledge these facts if we are to deal once and for all with the argument that the policy of generic forced separation was somehow well motivated, justified by its historical context and, as a result, unworthy of any apology today.

Then we come to the argument of intergenerational responsibility, also used by some to argue against giving an apology today. But let us remember the fact that the forced removal of Aboriginal children was happening as late as the early 1970s.

The 1970s is not exactly a point in remote antiquity. There are still serving members of this parliament who were first elected to this place in the early 1970s. It is well within the adult memory span of many of us. The uncomfortable truth for us all is that the parliaments of the nation, individually and collectively, enacted statutes and delegated authority under those statutes that made the forced removal of children on racial grounds fully lawful.

There is a further reason for an apology as well: it is that reconciliation is in fact an expression of a core value of our nation—and that value is a fair go for all. There is a deep and abiding belief in the Australian community that, for the stolen generations, there was no fair go at all. There is a pretty basic Aussie belief that says that it is time to put right this most outrageous of wrongs.

It is for these reasons, quite apart from concerns of fundamental human decency, that the governments and parliaments of this nation must make this apology—because, put simply, the laws that our parliaments enacted made the stolen generations possible.

We, the parliaments of the nation, are ultimately responsible, not those who gave effect to our laws. And the problem lay with the laws themselves. As has been said of settler societies elsewhere, we are the bearers of many blessings from our ancestors; therefore we must also be the bearer of their burdens as well. Therefore, for our nation, the course of action is clear: that is, to deal now with what has become one of the darkest chapters in Australia's history.

In doing so, we are doing more than contending with the facts, the evidence and the often rancorous public debate. In doing so, we are also wrestling with our own soul. This is not, as some would argue, a black-armband view of history; it is just the truth: the cold, confronting, uncomfortable truth—facing it, dealing with it, moving on from it. Until we fully confront that truth, there will always be a shadow hanging over us and our future as a fully united and fully reconciled people. It is time to reconcile. It is time to recognise the injustices of the past. It is time to say sorry. It is time to move forward together.

To the stolen generations, I say the following: as Prime Minister of Australia, I am sorry. On behalf of the government of Australia, I am sorry. On behalf of the parliament of Australia, I am sorry. I offer you this apology without qualification.

We apologise for the hurt, the pain and suffering that we, the parliament, have caused you by the laws that previous parliaments have enacted. We apologise for the indignity, the degradation and the humiliation these laws embodied.

We offer this apology to the mothers, the fathers, the brothers, the sisters, the families and the communities whose lives were ripped apart by the actions of successive governments under successive parliaments. In making this apology, I would also like to speak personally to the members of the stolen generations and their families: to those here today, so many of you; to those listening across the nation—from Yuendumu, in the central west of the Northern Territory, to Yabara, in North Queensland, and to Pitjantjatjara in South Australia.

I know that, in offering this apology on behalf of the government and the parliament, there is nothing I can say today that can take away the pain you have suffered personally. Whatever words I speak today, I cannot undo that. Words alone are not that powerful; grief is a very personal thing. I ask those non-Indigenous Australians listening today who may not fully understand why what we are doing is so important to imagine for a moment that this had happened to you.

I say to honourable members here present: imagine if this had happened to us. Imagine the crippling effect. Imagine how hard it would be to forgive. My proposal is this: if the apology we extend today is accepted in the spirit of reconciliation, in which it is offered, we can today resolve together that there be a new beginning for Australia. And it is to such a new beginning that I believe the nation is now calling us.

Australians are a passionate lot. We are also a very practical lot. For us, symbolism is important but, unless the great symbolism of reconciliation is accompanied by an even greater substance, it is little more than a clanging gong. It is not sentiment that makes history; it is our actions that make history. Today's apology, however inadequate, is aimed at righting past wrongs. It is also aimed at building a bridge between Indigenous and non-Indigenous Australians—a bridge based on a real respect rather than a thinly veiled contempt.

Our challenge for the future is to cross that bridge and, in so doing, to embrace a new partnership between Indigenous and non-Indigenous Australians—to embrace, as part of that partnership, expanded Link-up and other critical services to help the stolen generations to trace their families if at all possible and to provide dignity to their lives.

But the core of this partnership for the future is to close the gap between Indigenous and non-Indigenous Australians on life expectancy, educational achievement and employment opportunities.

This new partnership on closing the gap will set concrete targets for the future: within a decade to halve the widening gap in literacy, numeracy and employment outcomes and opportunities for Indigenous Australians, within a decade to halve the appalling gap in infant mortality rates between Indigenous and non-Indigenous children and, within a generation, to close the equally appalling 17-year life gap between Indigenous and non-Indigenous in overall life expectancy.

The truth is: a business as usual approach towards Indigenous Australians is not working. Most old approaches are not working. We need a new beginning—a new beginning which contains real measures of policy success or policy failure; a new beginning, a new partnership, on closing the gap with sufficient flexibility not to insist on a one-size-fits-all approach for each of the hundreds of remote and regional Indigenous communities across the country but instead allowing flexible, tailored, local approaches to achieve commonly-agreed national objectives that lie at the core of our proposed new partnership; a new beginning that draws intelligently on the experiences of new policy settings across the nation. However, unless we as a parliament set a destination for the nation, we have no clear point to guide our policy, our programs or our purpose; we have no centralised organising principle.

Let us resolve today to begin with the little children—a fitting place to start on this day of apology for the stolen generations. Let us resolve over the next five years to have every Indigenous four-year-old in a remote Aboriginal community enrolled in and attending a proper early childhood education centre or opportunity and engaged in proper preliteracy and prenumeracy programs.

Let us resolve to build new educational opportunities for these little ones, year by year, step by step, following the completion of their crucial preschool year. Let us resolve to use this systematic approach to build future educational opportunities for Indigenous children to provide proper primary and preventive health care for the same children, to begin the task of rolling back the obscenity that we find today in infant mortality rates in remote Indigenous communities—up to four times higher than in other communities.

None of this will be easy. Most of it will be hard—very hard. But none of it is impossible, and all of it is achievable with clear goals, clear thinking, and by placing an absolute premium on respect, cooperation and mutual responsibility as the guiding principles of this new partnership on closing the gap.

The mood of the nation is for reconciliation now, between Indigenous and non-Indigenous Australians. The mood of the nation on Indigenous policy and politics is now very simple. The nation is calling on us, the politicians, to move beyond our infantile bickering, our point-scoring and our mindlessly partisan politics and to elevate this one core area of national responsibility to a rare position beyond the partisan divide. Surely this is the unfulfilled spirit of the 1967 referendum. Surely, at least from this day forward, we should give it a go.

Let me take this one step further and take what some may see as a piece of political posturing and make a practical proposal to the opposition on this day, the first full sitting day of the new parliament. I said before the election that the nation needed a kind of war cabinet on parts of Indigenous policy, because the challenges are too great and the consequences are too great to allow it all to become a political football, as it has been so often in the past.

I therefore propose a joint policy commission, to be led by the Leader of the Opposition and me, with a mandate to develop and implement—to begin with—an effective housing strategy for remote communities over the next five years. It will be consistent with the government's policy framework, a new partnership for closing the gap.

If this commission operates well, I then propose that it work on the further task of constitutional recognition of the first Australians, consistent with the longstanding platform commitments of my party and the pre-election position of the opposition.

This would probably be desirable in any event because, unless such a proposition were absolutely bipartisan, it would fail at a referendum. As I have said before, the time has come for new approaches to enduring problems. Working constructively together on such defined projects would, I believe, meet with the support of the nation. It is time for fresh ideas to fashion the nation's future.

Mr Speaker, today the parliament has come together to right a great wrong. We have come together to deal with the past so that we might fully embrace the future. We have had sufficient audacity of faith to advance a pathway to that future, with arms extended rather than with fists still clenched. So let us seize the day.

Let it not become a moment of mere sentimental reflection. Let us take it with both hands and allow this day, this day of national reconciliation, to become one of those rare moments in which we might just be able to transform the way in which the nation thinks about itself, whereby the injustice administered to the stolen generations in the name of these, our parliaments, causes all of us to reappraise, at the deepest level of our beliefs, the real possibility of reconciliation writ large: reconciliation across all Indigenous Australia; reconciliation across the entire history of the often bloody encounter between those who emerged from the Dreamtime a thousand generations ago and those who, like me, came across the seas only yesterday; reconciliation which opens up whole new possibilities for the future.

It is for the nation to bring the first two centuries of our settled history to a close, as we begin a new chapter. We embrace with pride, admiration and awe these great and ancient cultures we are truly blessed to have among us—cultures that provide a unique, uninterrupted human thread linking our Australian continent to the most ancient prehistory of our planet.

Growing from this new respect, we see our Indigenous brothers and sisters with fresh eyes, with new eyes, and we have our minds wide open as to how we might tackle, together, the great practical challenges that Indigenous Australia faces in the future.

Let us turn this page together: Indigenous and non-Indigenous Australians, government and opposition, Commonwealth and state, and write this new chapter in our nation's story together. First Australians, First Fleeters, and those who first took the oath of allegiance just a few weeks ago. Let's grasp this opportunity to craft a new future for this great land: Australia. I commend the motion to the House.

Acknowledgments

No less than other works of authorship, the compilation of an anthology is a demanding undertaking. Ideas and inspiration come from many people, not least those who have led the way before. In this context, I wish to acknowledge especially the work of earlier anthologists of Australian documents, especially the late C.M.H. (Manning) Clark, whom I knew as a teacher and friend, and whose pioneering two volumes of *Select Documents in Australian History* (published 1950 and 1955) remain a landmark of scholarship and a still-fascinating window onto the broad sweep of Australia's colonial history. A similar debt is owed to Frank Crowley's *Modern Australia in Documents* (1973), which does for a large portion of twentieth century Australian history what Manning Clark did previously for the eighteenth and nineteenth centuries. It is important also to acknowledge Sally Warhaft's editorship of *Well May We Say ... The Speeches That Made Australia* (2004). This rich anthology of Australian speeches was an invaluable source of ideas both in the tasks of editorship and in suggesting material that could not be overlooked for inclusion in this new anthology of Australian documents.

No anthologist can do his or her work without the support, encouragement and help provided by librarians, archivists and curators. The greater part of the work done for this present book was in the State Library of New South Wales, where staff members in the reading rooms of both the General Reference Library and the Mitchell Library were unfailingly polite and generous in their efforts to assist my research, to help in solving problems and in offering skilled practical assistance to use microfilm and microfiche readers, and to prepare usable copies of rare and early materials. Not all the names are known of those who helped me in this way, but I acknowledge here my grateful thanks for all the help I was given in my many visits to one of Australia's great research libraries.

I extend my thanks to a number of specialist staff at the State Library of New South Wales. Paul Brunton was especially helpful in a number of ways, including in his efforts to obtain for me a copy of the will of Miles Franklin. I thank also Martin Beckett, the late Arthur Easton and Stephen Martin.

At the State Library of Victoria I thank especially Dr Kevin Molloy and his colleague Sandra Burt in the Australian Manuscripts Collection for their assistance in providing copies and transcriptions of original documents, in answering queries and in making suggestions of materials that might be considered for inclusion.

At the State Library of Tasmania I thank Tony Marshall for his sterling and willing efforts to guide me to some elusive Tasmanian documents, to answer a number of queries and to provide copies of material I needed urgently.

Similar support was provided by Dr Marie-Louise Ayres, Curator of Manuscripts at the National Library of Australia in Canberra. I thank her warmly for her assistance and for the welcoming hospitality provided by her colleagues in the Manuscripts Reading Room.

In the course of a project of this kind, ideas and support come from many quarters and often in surprising and unexpected ways. Chance encounters and conversations can suddenly suggest new ideas and directions while others offer their expertise in more deliberate and considered ways. I owe much to Nicholas Korner of Hunters Hill in Sydney for the considerable efforts he made to advise me on various Australian legal documents and to suggest possibile material for inclusion. He was especially helpful in explaining to me aspects of the Mabo judgment and in providing me with copies of background and contextual material. Thanks are due also to Nancy Flannery and Mark Pharaoh in Adelaide, to Professor K.S. Inglis, Trevor Ruddell, Douglas Stewart and David Studham in Melbourne, and to Paul Bentley, Matthew Fishburn, Robert Holden, John Immig and Professor R.N. Jose in Sydney, where I also thank Hordern House for providing the illustration of Joseph Banks featured on page 9. I am especially grateful for several suggestions and help with research given to me by my brother Kim Thompson in Melbourne.

I owe much to the lively, constant and generous support given to me throughout this project by my partner Clive Faro. A historian and writer himself, Clive was from the outset a stimulating source of advice and suggestions that led to some useful discoveries and several important inclusions. He offered his practical support throughout and much needed encouragement in times of difficulty and doubt. This book could not have been produced without him.

To my publisher Diana Hill and her colleagues at Murdoch Books, I extend particular thanks. From the outset the Murdoch team was a joy to work with and the smooth execution of this project from start to finish is a tribute to their skills and to their high professionalism. I am especially grateful to project editor Sophia Oravecz and her colleague Paul O'Beirne, to editor Meryl Potter, to picture researcher Amanda McKittrick and to designer Emilia Toia. In the shaping of text and in their deft, practical and shrewd interventions and suggestions, Sophia Oravecz and Meryl Potter have made this a better and richer book than I could have achieved on my own.

Picture credits

Archives Office of Tasmania: page 110

Art Gallery of South Australia: page 102, *The Proclamation of South Australia 1836*, oil on canvas, 133.3 × 274.3 cm by Charles Hill (1824–1915), c. 1856–76. Morgan Thomas Bequest Fund 1936, Adelaide.

Australian War Memorial: pages 224, Negative Number A02025, donated by F.G.H. Schuler; 274, Negative Number 044320

Corbis: pages 3, 231, 283, 330

Douglas Stewart Fine Books: page 153

Getty Images: pages 189, 302, 338, 342

Hordern House Rare Books: page 9

iStockphoto/belterz: cover, page 1; iStockphoto/Bill Noll: endpapers

John Curtin Prime Ministerial Library: page 251

Melbourne Cricket Club: pages 130–131

National Archives of Australia: pages 190 NAA: A10873; 202 NAA: A1200, L32223; 300 NAA: A1559, 1967/55; 315 NAA: A1209/88; 322 NAA: A8746, KN18/3/86/33

National Archives of the UK: pages 37, 78, 97

National Library of Australia: pages vi–vii, 2, 5, 7, 14, 25, 56, 82, 87, 132, 140, 150, 156, 173, 174–175, 194, 209, 217, 246, 265, 269, 281, 319

Newspix: pages 160, 213, 236, 244, 290, 294, 309, 329

Parliamentary Archives, London: pages 44: 27 Geo. III C.2; 183: HL/PO/PU/1/1900/63&64V1n61

Parliament House Canberra: page 289. Reproduced by permission of the Yirrkala community.

Parliament of Victoria: pages 170, 171. Reproduced by permission of the Honourable Speaker of the Legislative Assembly. Photographer: Laura Daniele

Photolibrary/Bridgeman Art Library: page 58

State Library of New South Wales: pages 66, 70, 103, 136, 238

State Library of New South Wales and The Estate of Dorthea Mackellar c/-Curtis Brown (Aust) Pty Ltd: page 212

State Library of Queensland: pages 68 neg no. 78178; 235 neg no. 42835

State Library of South Australia: page 138 SLSA B 16

State Library of Victoria: pages 19, 52, 90–91, 93, 124, 127, 134, 146–147, 148, 166, 200, 218

State Records of New South Wales: pages 50–51 SRNSW: X24; 106 SRNSW: 4/1310; 112 NRS13032/1/10

State Records of South Australia: page 179 GRG 2/55/369

University of Melbourne Archives: page 145

Sources

References are in order of appearance followed by the source for the transcript and are reproduced with kind permission of the copyright holder.

Introduction
Arthur Phillip, *The Voyage of Governor Phillip to Botany Bay*, London: John Stockdale, 1789, p. 64.
Tim Flannery (ed.) *1788 Watkin Tench*, Melbourne: Text Publishing, 1996, p. 46.
Grace Karskens, *The Colony: A History of Early Sydney*, Sydney: Allen & Unwin, 2009, p. 33.
Jon Stallworthy (ed.), *The Oxford Book of War Poetry*, Oxford: Oxford University Press, 2008, p. 209
Patricia Grimshaw, Marilyn Lake, Ann McGrath & Marian Quartly (eds), *Creating a Nation*, Melbourne: McPhee Gribble, 1994, p. 2.
Martin Crotty & David Andrew Roberts, *Turning Points in Australian History*, Sydney: UNSW Press, 2009, p. 4; p. 6.
Nettie Palmer, *Fourteen Years: Extracts from a Private Journal*, Melbourne: Meanjin Press, 1948, pp. 40–1.
K.S. Inglis, *Sacred Places: War Memorials in the Australian Landscape*, Melbourne: Melbourne University Press, 2008.

First report of the Southern Cross
Raffaello Carboni, *The Eureka Stockade*, North Carolina: Hayes Barton Press, 1963.
Andrea Corsali, Letter to Giulano de Medici, 1516.
Transcript: *National Treasures from Australia's Great Libraries*, Canberra: National Library of Australia, 2005, pp. 10–11.

The secret instructions for James Cook
James Cook, *Captain Cook's Journal During the First Voyage Round the World made in H.M. Bark 'Endeavour'*, 1768.
Instructions issued to Lt James Cook by the Admiralty Commissioners, with Additional Instructions.
Transcript: J.C. Beaglehole (ed.), *The Voyage of the Endeavour 1768–1771*, Cambridge: Cambridge University Press, 1955, pp. cclxxix–clxxxiv.

Joseph Banks at Botany Bay
Transcript: J.C. Beaglehole (ed.), *The Endeavour Journal of Joseph Banks 1768–1771*, Sydney: Angus & Robertson, 1963, pp. 52–6.

James Cook claims New South Wales for the British Crown
Transcript: J.C. Beaglehole (ed.), *The Voyage of the Endeavour 1768–1771*, Cambridge: Cambridge University Press, 1955, pp. 386–9.

Joseph Banks promotes the idea of a settlement in New South Wales
Harold B. Carter, *Sir Joseph Banks 1743–1820*, London: British Museum (Natural History), 1988, p. 165.
Transcript: C.M.H. Clark (ed.), *Select Documents in Australian History 1788–1850*, Sydney: Angus & Robertson, 1977, pp. 26–28.

James Matra's proposal for a settlement
James Cook, *Captain Cook's Journal During the First Voyage Round the World made in H.M. Bark 'Endeavour'*, 1768.
Transcript: *Historical Records of New South Wales*, vol. 1, part 2, Sydney: Charles Potter, 1892, pp. 1–6.

Governor Phillip's first commission
Lord Howe, private correspondence with Lord Sydney.
Transcript: *Historical Records of Australia*, series 1, vol. 1, 1788–1796, Sydney: The Library Committee of the Commonwealth Parliament, 1914, pp. 1–2.

Arthur Phillip on the treatment of convicts in the new colony
George Mackaness, *Admiral Arthur Phillip: Founder of New South Wales*, Sydney: Angus & Robertson, 1937, p. 64.
Transcript: *Historical Records of New South Wales*, vol. 1, part 2, 1788–1792, Sydney: Charles Potter, 1892, pp. 50–55.

Governor Phillip's second commission
Arthur Phillip, *The Voyage of Governor Phillip to Botany Bay*, London: John Stockdale, 1789, p. 64.
Paul G. Fidlon & R.J. Ryan (eds.), *The Journal and Letters of Lt. Ralph Clark 1787–1792*, Sydney: Australian Documents Library, 1981, p. 96.
David Collins, *An Account of the English Colony in New South Wales*, London: T. Cadell & W. Davies, 1798, p. 2
Transcript: *Historical Records of Australia*, series 1, vol. 1, 1788–1796, Sydney: The Library Committee of the Commonwealth Parliament, 1914, pp. 2–8.

Phillip's instructions
Transcript: *Historical Records of Australia*, series 1, vol. 1, 1788–1796, Sydney: The Library Committee of the Commonwealth Parliament, 1914, pp. 9–16.

New South Wales Courts Act
Alex Castles, *An Australian Legal History*, Sydney: The Law Book Company, 1982, p. 46.
David Collins, *An Account of the English Colony in New South Wales*, London: T. Cadell & W. Davies, 1798.
See also David Neal, *The Rule of Law in a Penal Colony*, Cambridge:

Cambridge University Press, 1991, pp. 54–5.
Transcript: <http://www.foundingdocs.gov.au>.

Charter of Justice
David Neal, *The Rule of Law in a Penal Colony*, Cambridge: Cambridge University Press, 1991, pp. 4-6
Transcript: <http://www.foundingdocs.gov.au>.

The arrival of the First Fleet
David Collins, *An Account of the English Colony in New South Wales*, London: T. Cadell & W. Davies, 1798.
Inga Clendinnen, *Dancing with Strangers: Europeans and Australians at First Contact*, Cambridge University Press: London, 2005, p. 52.
Transcript: David Collins, *An Account of the English Colony in New South Wales*, T. Cadell & W. Davies, London, 1798. Australiana Facsimile Edition, no. 76, Adelaide: Libraries Board of South Australia, 1971, pp. xxxviii–4.

A trio of theatre performances in Sydney
David Collins, *An Account of the English Colony in New South Wales*, London: T. Cadell & W. Davies, 1798.
Transcript: Rare Books Collection, National Library of Australia, Canberra (nla aus – vn42002335).

Matthew Flinders writes to Sir Joseph Banks
Lachlan Macquarie, *Historical Records of Australia*, series I, vol. IX. Sydney: National Library of Australia, 1817, p. 747.
Paul Brunton (ed.), *Matthew Flinders: Personal Letters from an Extraordinary Life*, Sydney: Hordern House with the State Library of NSW, 2002, p. 9.
Transcript: Paul Brunton (ed.), *Matthew Flinders: Personal Letters from an Extraordinary Life*, Sydney: Hordern House with the State Library of New South Wales, 2002, pp. 233–5.

First crossing of the Blue Mountains
Lachlan Macquarie, *Tour to the New Discovered Country in April 1815*.
Transcript: Gregory Blaxland, *A Journal of a Tour of Discovery Across the Blue Mountains, New South Wales in the Year 1813*, Sydney: Sydney University Press, 2004, pp. 12–13.

A charter for banking in Australia
R.F. Holder, *Bank of New South Wales: A History*, Sydney: Angus & Robertson, 1970, p. 50
Transcript: Text supplied by Kerrianne George, Manager, Historical Services, Westpac, 6–8 Parramatta Road, Homebush, NSW 2140.

The Bigge Report
J.M. Bennett, 'Bigge, John Thomas (1780–1843)', in Douglas Pike (ed.), *Australian Dictionary of Biography*, Melbourne: Melbourne University Press, 1966, p. 99–100.
Raymond Evans, 'Creating "An Object of Terror": The Tabling of the First Bigge Report', in Martin Crotty & David Andrew Roberts (eds.), *Turning Points in Australian History*, Sydney: UNSW Press, 2009, p 48; p 49.
Henry Bathurst, Royal Commission, 1819.
John Dunmore Lang, *Transportation and colonization: or, The causes of the comparative failure of the transportation system in the Australian colonies: with suggestions for ensuring its future efficiency in subserviency to extensive colonization, 1837*.
Transcript: *Historical Records of Australia*, series 1, vol. 10, January, 1819–December, 1822, Sydney: The Library Committee of the Commonwealth Parliament, 1917, pp. 3–11.

William Charles Wentworth's poem 'Australasia'
Clive Faro with Garry Wotherspoon, *Street Scene: A History of Oxford Street*, Melbourne: Melbourne University Press, 2000, p. 60.
Transcript: W.C. Wentworth, *Australasia: A Poem written for The Chancellor's Medal at the Cambridge Commencement, July 1823*, London: Whittaker & Co., 1873.

Wentworth and Wardell create the *Australian* newspaper
Peter Cochrane, *Colonial Ambition: Foundations of Australian Democracy*, Melbourne: Melbourne University Press, 2006, p. 17.
Wentworth's editorial in the first issue of the *Australian*.
Transcript: *Australian*, 14 October 1824.

Instructions to take possession of Western Australia
Frank Crowley, *Australia's Western Third*, Melbourne: Heinemann, 1960, p. 5.
Transcript: <http://www.foundingdocs.gov.au>.

A declaration of martial law in Van Diemen's Land
The Executive Council Minutes, 1828.
Transcript: Peter Chapman (ed.) *Historical Records of Australia*, series 3, vol. 9, Melbourne: Melbourne University Press, 2006.

An Act for the government of His Majesty's settlements in Western Australia
Transcript: <http://www.foundingdocs.gov.au>.

John Batman's Melbourne deed
A.G.L. Shaw, *A History of the Port Phillip District: Victoria before Separation*, Melbourne: Melbourne University Press, 2003, pp. 45–50.
Transcript: John Batman's Journal (MS13181), Australian Manuscripts Collection, State Library of Victoria, Melbourne.

John Batman and the founding of Melbourne
A.G.L. Shaw, *A History of Port Phillip District: Victoria Before Separation*, Melbourne: Melbourne University Press, 2003, p. 55–7.
Transcript: John Batman's Journal (MS13181), Australian Manuscripts Collection, State Library of Victoria, Melbourne.

Governor Richard Bourke's proclamation
Transcript: <http://www.foundingdocs.gov.au>.

The *Church Act*
Transcript: *The Acts and Ordinances of the Governor and Council of New South Wales*, Sydney: E.H. Statham, 1838.

Proclaiming the province of South Australia
Douglas Pike, *Paradise of Dissent: South Australia, 1829-1857*, Melbourne: Melbourne University Press, 1957, p. 52.
Transcript: <http://www.foundingdocs.gov.au>.

Thomas Mitchell describes the country of Victoria
Transcript: Thomas Livingstone Mitchell, *Three Expeditions into the Interior of Eastern Australia*, London: T. & W. Boone, 1839, pp. 330–3.

Ending the transportation of convicts to New South Wales
Transcript: *Historical Records of Australia*, series 1, vol. 20, February, 1839–September, 1840, Sydney: The Library Committee of the Commonwealth Parliament, 1924, pp. 701–3.

A petition of the free Aborigines of Van Diemen's Land
Henry Reynolds, *Fate of a Free People*, Melbourne: Penguin Books, 2004, p. 7; p. 16; p. 14.
N.J.B. Plomley (ed.), *Weep in Silence: A History of the Flinders Island Aboriginal Settlement*, Hobart: Blubber Head Press, 1987, pp. 148–50.
For a discussion on the right of the Aboriginal people to be treated as equals, see Sally Dammery, *Walter George Arthur: A Free Tasmanian?*, Melbourne: Monash Publications in History: 35, 2001, p. 30
Transcript: N.J.B. Plomley (ed.), *Weep in Silence*, pp. 148–9.

An Act to incorporate and endow the University of Sydney
Carolyn Rassmussen, 'Universities', in Graeme Davison, John Hirst & Stuart Macintyre (eds.), *The Oxford Companion to Australian History*, Melbourne: Oxford University Press, 1998, pp. 657–8.
Transcript: <http://www.foundingdocs.gov.au>.

William Howitt's advice to emigrants and gold seekers
Transcript: Caroline Chisholm, *A Memoir Prepared from Original and Private Sources to which Is Added The Emigrants Guide to the Australian Goldfields ...* London: G.E. Petter, 1853, pp. 78–84.

The Diggers' Ten Commandments
W.B. Withers, *History of Ballarat*, 1870.
Transcript: W.B. Withers, *History of Ballarat*, The Ballarat Star, Ballarat, 1870, pp. 215–16.

The Bendigo Goldfields Petition
Ballarat Reform League Charter, 1854.
Transcript: <http://www.slv.vic.gov.au/collections/treasures/bendigopetition/trans>.

Rules of the Melbourne Football Club
Robert Hess, Matthew Nicholson, Bob Stewart & Gregory De Moore, *A National Game: The History of Australian Rules Football*, Melbourne: Viking, 2008, p. vii; pp 26–8.
Transcript: Robert Hess et al., pp. 26–8.

John McDouall Stuart plants the British flag
Transcript: William Hardman (ed.), *The Journals of John McDouall Stuart During the Years 1868, 1859, 1860, 1861 & 1862 When He Fixed the Centre of the Continent and Successfully Crossed It from sea to sea*, London: Otley & Co., 1865, pp. 164–6.

Robert O'Hara Burke's speech and the last letter of William John Wills
John William Wills, *Successful Exploration Through the Interior of Australia*, 1863.
Tim Bonyhady, *Burke & Wills: from Melbourne to myth*, Sydney: David Ell Press, 1991, p. 79.
Transcript: Sally Warhaft (ed.), *Well May We Say ... The Speeches that made Australia*, Melbourne: Black Inc., 2004, p. 536.

Joining the Overland Telegraph Line between Adelaide and Port Darwin
Peter Taylor, *An End to Silence: The Building of the Overland Telegraph Line from Adelaide to Darwin*, Sydney: Methuen, 1980, p. 10.
Transcript: Peter Taylor, pp. 155–70.

A new anthem: 'Advance Australia Fair'
Transcript: *Advance Australia Fair: Patriotic Song*, Sydney: Reading & Co., n.d.

Ned Kelly's Jerilderie Letter
Australian Dictionary of Biography, 5, Melbourne: Melbourne University Press, 1974, p. 8.
Ian Jones, *Ned Kelly: A Short Life*, Melbourne: Lothian Books, 2002, p. 73
Bill Gammage, 'Edward "Ned" Kelly', in Graeme Davison, John Hirst & Stuart Macintyre (eds.), *The Oxford Companion to Australian History*, Melbourne: Oxford University Press, 1998, pp. 362–3.

Transcript: Justin Corfield, *The Ned Kelly Encyclopedia*, Melbourne: Lothian Books, 2003, pp. 245–6.

The legend of the Ashes
Transcript: Chris Harte, *The Penguin History of Australian Cricket* (rev. edn.), Melbourne: Viking, 2003, pp. 126–7.

A newspaper for women
Olive Lawson, *The First Voice of Australian Feminism: Excerpts from Louisa Lawson's the Dawn, 1888–1895*, Sydney: Simon & Schuster Australia in association with New Endeavour Press, 1990, p 1.
Transcript: *The Dawn: A Journal for Australian Women*, 15 May 1888.

The 9 × 5 Impression Exhibition in Melbourne
Terence Lane, 'The 9 x 5 Impression Exhibition—The Challenge of the Sketch', in Terence Lane (ed.), *Australian Impressionism*, Melbourne: National Gallery of Victoria, 2007, p. 162.
Transcript: Terence Lane (ed.), pp. 156–63.

Sir Henry Parkes addresses the Federation Conference
Transcript: Sally Warhaft (ed.), *Well May We Say ... The Speeches that made Australia*, Melbourne: Black Inc., 2004, pp. 4–11.

Andrew Barton (Banjo) Paterson's 'The Man from Snowy River'
Transcript: Draft version of The Man from Snowy River, 1895, Mitchell Library, State Library of New South Wales.
See also *Treasures from Australia's Great Libraries*, Canberra: National Library of Australia, pp. 128–9.

Bushmen's Official Proclamation
Henry Lawson, *Freedom of the Wallaby*, 1891.
Geoffrey Bolton, 'The 1891 Shearers' Strike Leaders: Railroaded?' in Rick Palmer (ed.), *The Shearers' Strike 1891–1991: A Celebration*, Rockhampton: University of Central Queensland, 1992, pp. 9–19
Transcript: Rick Palmer (ed.), pp. 5–7.

The Monster Petition in Victoria
Adelaide Observer, 2 May 1896.
Transcript: <http://www.parliament.vic.gov.au/womenspetition>.

'Waltzing Matilda'
Christina Macpherson manuscript of 'Waltzing Matilda'.
Transcript: Manuscript Collection (MS9065), National Library of Australia, Canberra.

Female suffrage in South Australia
Transcript: <http://www.foundingdocs.gov.au>.

Creating the Mitchell Library
David Scott Mitchell, quoted in Brian Fletcher, *Magnificent Obsession: The Story of the Mitchell Library, Sydney*, Sydney: Allen & Unwin, 2007, p. 16.
Elizabeth Ellis, 'Ambitious Endeavour', *Upfront*, Library Council of NSW, vol. 15, no. 1, Autumn 2003, pp. 6–7.
Transcript: Mitchell Library, State Library of New South Wales (ML A1461, pp. 195 b–c). See also Microfilm CY 886, frames 331–2.

Commonwealth of Australia Constitution Act
Transcript: Geoffrey Sawer, *The Australian Constitution*, Canberra: Australian Government Publishing Service, 1988.

Instructions for the inauguration of the Commonwealth of Australia
Transcript: National Archives of Australia, NAA: CP8/1.

The office of the Governor-General and Commander-in-Chief of the Commonwealth of Australia
Transcript: <http://www.foundingdocs.gov.au>.

Edmund Barton' speech on a new Australian Commonwealth
Transcript: Papers of Sir Edmund Barton (MS 51, series 5, item 977), National Library of Australia, Canberra.

A national flag for Australia
Commonwealth of Australia Gazette. 29 April, 1901.
Transcript: Carol A. Foley, *The Australian Flag: Colonial Relic or Contemporary Icon?*, Sydney: Federation Press, 1996, pp. 65–6.

Miles Franklin's *My Brilliant Career*
Transcript: Papers of J.F. Archibald, Mitchell Library, State Library of New South Wales (ML MSS 364/7, pp. 1–4).

Immigration Restriction Act
Transcript: *The Acts of The Parliament of the Commonwealth of Australia passed in the session of 1901–2*, Robert S. Brain, Melbourne: Government Printer for the State of Victoria for the Commonwealth of Australia, 1903.

Alfred Felton's bequest
John Poynter, *Mr Felton's Bequests*, Melbourne: The Miegunyah Press, 2008, pp.224–5
Transcript: *The Argus* (Melbourne), 13 January 1904.

The Harvester judgment
Transcript: F.K. Crowley (ed.), *Modern Australia in Documents* (vol. 1), *1901–1939*, Melbourne: Wren Publishing, 1973, pp. 111–13.

Dorothea Mackellar's Australia
Peter Luck, *Dorothea Mackellar's My Country: A Centenary Celebration 1908–2008*, Sydney: Pier 9, 2008, p. 5.
Transcript: Papers of Dorothea Mackellar, Mitchell Library, State Library of New South Wales. See also Peter Luck, p. 6.

An Act to determine the seat of government of the Commonwealth
Graeme Davison, John Hirst & Stuart Macintyre (eds.), *The Oxford Companion to Australian History*, Melbourne: Oxford University Press, 1998, p. 109.
Transcript: *The Acts of The Parliament of the Commonwealth of Australia passed in the session of 1908*, Melbourne: J. Kemp, Government Printer for the State of Victoria for the Commonwealth of Australia, 1909.

Douglas Mawson's ambitions for the Antarctic expedition of 1911–14
Transcript: Papers of Sir Douglas Mawson, Mitchell Library, State Library of New South Wales (ML MSS 171/2 5–6).

The first published account of the ANZAC landing
Sydney Morning Herald, 9 May 1931, p. 17.
Fred & Elizabeth Brenchley, *Myth Maker: Ellis Ashmead-Bartlett The Englishman Who Sparked Australia's Gallipoli Legend*, Milton, Queensland: John Wiley & Sons, 2005.
'Anzac Legend' in Peter Dennis, Jeffrey Grey, Ewan Morris & Robin Prior (eds.), *The Oxford Companion to Australian Military History*, Melbourne: Oxford University Press, p. 38.
Transcript: *Sydney Morning Herald*, 8 May 1915. See also Hobart *Mercury*, 12 May 1915.

Keith Murdoch's letter to Prime Minister Andrew Fisher
C.E.W. Bean, *The Story of Anzac* (vol. VII *The Official History of Australia in the War of 1914–1918*), St Lucia: University of Queensland Press, 1981, p. 782.
Transcript: Papers of Sir Keith Murdoch (MS 2823, Series 2), National Library of Australia, Canberra.

John Monash describes the first Anzac Day
Carl Bridge, 'Anzac Day', in Peter Dennis, Jeffrey Grey, Ewan Morris & Robin Prior (eds.), *The Oxford Companion to Australian Military History*, Melbourne: Oxford University Press, 2008, pp. 34–5.
Transcript: Papers of Sir John Monash (MS 1844/127), National Library of Australia, Canberra.

The Premiers' Plan
Erik Eklund, 'The Premiers' Plan and the Great Depression: High politics and everyday life in an economic crisis', in Martin Crotty & David Andrew Roberts (eds.), *Turning Points in Australian History*, Sydney: UNSW Press, 2009, p. 116.
F.K. Crowley, *Modern Australia in Documents* (vol. 1), *1901–1939*, Melbourne: Wren Publishing, 1973, pp. 502–3.
Transcript: F.K. Crowley, p. 503.

The Bodyline Tests
Ric Sissons & Brian Stodart, *Cricket and Empire: The 1932–33 Bodyline Tour of Australia*, London: George Allen & Unwin, 1984, p. 1.
Transcript: David Frith, *Bodyline Autopsy*, Sydney: ABC Books, 2003.

Australia Day conference of Australian Aboriginal people
Jack Horner & Marcia Langton, 'The Day of Mourning' in Bill Gammage & Peter Spearritt (eds.), *Australians 1938* (Australians: A Historical Library), Sydney: Fairfax, Syme & Weldon, pp. 29–35.
Transcript: *The Australian Abo Call: The Voice of the Aborigines*, no. 1, April 1938, p. 2.

Royal Commission into the Victorian bushfires
Stephen J. Pyne, *Burning Bush: A Fire History of Australia*, Sydney: Allen & Unwin, 1992, p. 309.
Tom Griffiths, *Forests of Ash: An Environmental History*, Cambridge: Cambridge University Press, 2001, p. viii.
Transcript: *Report of the Royal Commission to inquire into The Causes of and Measures Taken to Prevent the Bushfires of January, 1939, and to Protect Life and Property and The Measures to be Taken to Prevent Bush Fires in Victoria and to Protect Life and Property in the Event of Future Bushfires*, 1939, pp. 5–6.

Robert Menzies declares war against Germany
A.W. Martin, *Robert Menzies: A Life*, Melbourne: Melbourne University Press, 1993, p. 284.
Transcript: *Age* (Melbourne), 4 September 1939.

John Curtin declares war against Japan
Transcript: *Sydney Morning Herald*, 9 December 1941.

John Curtin's New Year message
David Day, 'Prime Minister Curtin's New Year Message: Australia "Looks to America"', in Martin Crotty & David Andrew Roberts (eds.), *Turning Points in Australian History*, Sydney: UNSW Press, 2009, p.130.
Transcript: *Herald* (Melbourne), 27 December 1941.

Robert Menzies' appeal to the middle class
Judith Brett, *Robert Menzies' Forgotten People*, Melbourne: Melbourne University Press, 2007, p. 20.

Transcript: R.G. Menzies, *The Forgotten People*, Robertson & Mullens, Melbourne, 1942.

Dame Enid Lyons delivers her maiden speech in federal Parliament
Anne Henderson, *Enid Lyons: Leading Lady to a Nation*, Melbourne: Pluto Press, 2008, p. 282.
Transcript: *Commonwealth Parliamentary Debates* (House of Representatives), 29 September 1943.

Ben Chifley's radio address
Transcript: Paul Hasluck, *The Government and the People 1942–1945*, Canberra: Australian War Memorial, 1970, pp. 595–6.

Ben Chifley's Labor Party address
Transcript: Sally Warhaft (ed.) *Well May We Say ... The Speeches that made Australia*, Melbourne: Black Inc., 2004, pp. 168–9.

The ANZUS Treaty
J. G. Starke, *The ANZUS Treaty Alliance*, Melbourne: Melbourne University Press, 1965, p. 1.
Stuart Macintyre, 'ANZUS Treaty', in Graeme Davison, John Hirst & Stuart Macintyre (eds.), *The Oxford Companion to Australian History*, Melbourne: Oxford University Press, 1998, p. 30.
Transcript: <http://www.dfat.gov.au/geo/new_zealand/anzus.pdf>.

The Miles Franklin Award for Australian literature
Jill Roe, *Stella Miles Franklin*, London: Fourth Estate, 2008, p. 561.
Transcript: Mitchell Library, State Library of New South Wales.

Premier J.J. Cahill plans an opera house for Australia
<http://whc.unesco.org/archive/advisory_body_evaluation/166rev.pdf>.
Philip Drew, *Sydney Opera House*, London: Phaidon Press, 2002, p. 4.
Transcript: *Report of the Proceedings of a Conference convened by the Premier and held in the Lecture Room, Public Library, Sydney, on 30th November 1954, concerning the question of the establishment of an Opera House in Sydney*, Sydney: A.R. Pettifer, Government Printer, 1954.

The Antipodean Manifesto
Bernard Smith, *Australian Painting 1788–2000*, Melbourne: Oxford University Press, 2001, p. 326.
Ann Stephen, Andrew McNamara & Philip Goad (eds.), *Modernism & Australia: Documents on Art, Design and Architecture 1917–1967*, Melbourne: The Miegunyah Press, 2006, p. 697.
Ross Luck, 'Peaceful Co-existence: The Antipodeans', in Ann Stephen, Andrew McNamara & Philip Goad (eds.), pp. 699–700.
Robert Hughes, *The Art of Australia*, Melbourne: Penguin Books, 1970, pp. 246–7.
Bernard Smith, p. 330
Transcript: Ann Stephen, Andrew McNamara & Philip Goad (eds.), pp. 695–7.

The bark petition of the Yolngu people
Julie Fenwick, *'Worrying About our Land': Conceptualising Land Rights 1963–1971*, Melbourne: Monash Publications in History, 2001, p. 38.
Transcript: <http://www.foundingdocs.gov.au/item.asp?dID=104>.

Rupert Murdoch launches the *Australian*
William Shawcross, *Murdoch*, London: Chatto & Windus, 1992, p. 117; p. 115.
William Shawcross, *Murdoch*, New York: Simon & Schuster, 1993, p. 96.
William Shawcross, *Murdoch*, London: Chatto & Windus 1992, p. 96.
Transcript: *Australian*, 15 July 1964.

Australia enters the war in Vietnam
Correspondence between Robert Menzies and Lyndon B Johnson 1965, <http://moadoph.gov.au/learning/national-history-challenge/2007/downloads/Menzies-text.pdf>.
Paul Ham, *Vietnam: The Australian War*, Sydney: HarperCollins, 2008, p. 119; pp 122–3.
Transcript: *Commonwealth Parliamentary Debates* (House of Representatives), 29 April 1965

The case of Ronald Ryan
Mike Richards, *The Hanged Man: The Life and Death of Ronald Ryan*, Melbourne: Scribe Publications, 2002, p. 355.
Bernard & Deirdre Slattery, *The Hanging of Ronald Ryan: Capital Punishment and the Victorian Community*, Melbourne: State Library of Victoria, 1996.
Transcript: Kevin Anderson (ed.), *Victorian Law Reports*, Butterworths for the Council of Law Reporting in Victoria, Melbourne, 1967, pp. 522–5. Used with permission of State Library of Victoria, Howard League for Penal Reform Collection, MS 11553.

The referendum on altering the Australian Constitution
Russell McGregor, 'The 1967 Referendum: an Uncertain Consensus' in Martin Crotty & David Andrew Roberts (eds.), *Turning Points in Australian History*, Sydney: UNSW Press, 2009, p 172.
Bain Attwood & Andrew Markus, *The 1967 Referendum, or When Aborigines Didn't Get the Vote*, Canberra: Australian Institute of Aboriginal and Torres Strait Islander Studies, 1997.
Transcript: *The Acts of the Parliament of the Commonwealth of Australia ... 1967*, Canberra: Commonwealth Government Printing Office, 1969, p. 259.

Gough Whitlam launches the ALP election campaign
Graham Freudenberg, *A Certain Grandeur: Gough Whitlam's Life in Politics*, Melbourne: Viking, 2009, p. 234.
Transcript: Sally Warhaft (ed.), *Well May We Say ... The Speeches that made Australia*, Melbourne: Black Inc., 2004, pp. 178–9.

A letter to the *Age*
Transcript: *Age* (Melbourne), 23 November 1972.

The Australia Council Charter
Transcript: <http://www.mca.org.au/web/fileadmin/user_upload/PDFs/Charters.pdf>.

Gough Whitlam and Vincent Lingiari meet at Daguragu
Gough Whitlam, *The Whitlam Government 1972–1975*, Melbourne: Viking, 1985, p. 466.
Transcript: Sally Warhaft (ed.), *Well May We Say ... The Speeches that made Australia*, Melbourne: Black Inc., 2004, pp. 341–4.

Racial Discrimination Act
Gough Whitlam, *The Whitlam Government 1972–1975*, Melbourne: Viking, 1985, p. 506; p. 499.
Transcript: *The Acts of the Parliament of the Commonwealth of Australia ... 1975*, Canberra: Australian Government Publishing Service, 1978, pp. 349–73.

The dismissal of Gough Whitlam's Labor Government
Paul Kelly, *November 1975: The Inside Story of Australia's Greatest Political Crisis*, Sydney: Allen & Unwin, 1995.
From their different perspectives, Sir John Kerr and Gough Whitlam both provided accounts of the events leading to the dismissal. See John Kerr, *Matters for Judgment: An Autobiography*, Melbourne: Sun Books, 1988 and Gough Whitlam, *The Truth of the Matter*, Melbourne: Melbourne University Press, 2005.
Transcript: John Kerr, *Matters for Judgment: An Autobiography*, Sun Books, Melbourne, 1988.

Lindy Chamberlain pleads for justice
Australian Dictionary of Biography, 13, Melbourne: Melbourne University Press, 1993, p. 396.
Transcript: Papers of Lindy Chamberlain (MS9180), Canberra: National Library of Australia.

Australia Act
Transcript: *The Acts of the Parliament of the Commonwealth of Australia ... 1985*, Canberra: Commonwealth Government Printing Office, 1986, pp. 1816–22.

A charter for the Special Broadcasting Service (SBS)
Special Broadcasting Services 2001–02 Annual Report. <sbs.com.au/sbsmain/2002_annual_report/sbs_intro.pdf>.
'SBS' in Brian Galligan & Winsome Roberts (eds), *The Oxford Companion to Australian Politics*, Melbourne: Oxford University Press, 2007, p. 531.
Transcript: <http://www.sbs.com.au>.

Terra nullius, land rights and *Mabo*
Transcript: 'Mabo and Others v Queensland' 1992 HCA23, <http://www.hcourt.gov.au/>.

Bringing Them Home Report
Peter Read, *The Stolen Generations: The Removal of Aboriginal Children in New South Wales 1883 to 1969*, Sydney: NSW Department of Aboriginal Affairs, 1998.
Tim Rowse, 'Stolen Generations', in Graeme Davison, John Hirst & Stuart Macinytre (eds), *The Oxford Companion to Australian History* (rev. edn.), Melbourne: Oxford University Press, 2001, p. 617.
Transcript: *Bringing Them Home: Report of the National Inquiry into the Separation of Aboriginal and Torres Strait Islander Children from their Families*, Sydney: Human Rights and Equal Opportunity Commission, 1997, <http://www.humanrights.gov.au/social_justice/bth_report/report/index.html>.

John Howard's election policy speech
Transcript: <http://australianpolitics.com/news/2001/01-10-28.shtml>.

A charter of human rights and responsibilities
Alistair Pound & Kylie Evans, *An Annotated Guide to the Victorian Charter of Human Rights and Responsibilities*, Sydney: Lawbook Co., 2008, p. 1.
George Williams, *A Charter of Rights for Australia*, Sydney: UNSW Press, 2007.
Transcript: *A Charter of Human Rights and Responsibilities Act 2006*, <http://www.legislation.vic.gov.au/>.

A national apology to the Stolen Generations
Robert Manne, 'From Tampa to 9/11: Seventeen Days that Changed Australia' in Martin Crotty & David Andrew Roberts (eds), *Turning Points in Australian History*, Sydney: UNSW Press, 2009, p. 246.
Transcript: 'Apology to Australia's Indigenous Peoples' reproduced with permission of the Honorable Kevin Rudd MP, <http://www.pm.gov.au/media/Speech/2008/speech_0073.cfm>.

Note on texts

The documents selected for this collection have been reproduced as they were written or delivered in speech. While most of the texts have been drawn from authoritative printed or published sources, these have not always been presented in the form of the original text. Where it has not been possible to locate the original form of issue or delivery, the most reliable alternative version has been used. In a small number of cases, the text used here is based on original documents held in library collections.

Long documents posed a special problem in compiling this collection. Where long documents were considered to be essential or very desirable inclusions, such as the Australian Constitution or the High Court of Australia's determination in the *Mabo* case, extracts have been chosen to ensure items of special importance were not omitted. In other instances, such as material selected from personal journals or narratives, extracts have been selected to illuminate a moment or occasion of singular significance.

In all cases where abridgements occur, ellipses have been used to indicate editorial excisions from the printed or manuscript original. In some instances, clear errors of punctuation or spelling have been silently corrected where this was needed to ensure clarity and comprehension. Otherwise, each document is published as it was issued or delivered.

A short headnote has been prepared for each document. These short essays are intended to provide contextual and historical information, and to highlight the larger interest, importance or influence of each document. As far as possible, these notes also take account of the varied historical readings or interpretations of material that have been made over time, while also noting, where it is applicable, the most recent or definitive summing up of biographical or historical evidence.

JOHN THOMPSON is a graduate in history from Monash University and the Australian National University. He completed his PhD at the ANU in 2004 with a study of the public career of the distinguished Australian historian Geoffrey Serle. He was Curator of Manuscripts in the State Library of Victoria and subsequently worked in various positions in the National Library of Australia including Director, Australian Collections and Services. He has written and compiled a number of books, among them the National Library's *Faces of Mandurama*, *The Oxford Book of Australian Letters* (co-edited with Brenda Niall) and *The Patrician and the Bloke: Geoffrey Serle and the Making of Australian History*. He has contributed a number of review essays to *Meanjin* and is a frequent reviewer for *Australian Book Review* and *Art Monthly*.

Index

Index of major historical figures and themes

Numbers in *italics* indicate pages with illustrations.

Aboriginal Australians, viii, xii
    apology, xii, 338–49, *338*, *342–3*
    arts, 306
    deaths in custody, 339
    dispossession, viii, 95–6, *97*, 241, 287, 339
    early encounters, 5, 6, 8, 9, 10–12, *19*, 26–44
    as intermediaries, 88
    land rights, 287–8, *289*, 308–10, *309*, 327–9, *329*, 339
    protests, 31, 109–10, *238*, 239–41
    rights, 177, *238*, 239–41, 287–8, *289*, 299–301, *300*, 308, 339
    South Australia, 102, 177
    Stolen Generations, *330*, 331–3, 338–49, *338*, *342–3*
    Tasmanian, 81–4, 109–11, *110*
Aboriginal Day of Mourning, viii, 31, *238*, 239–41
Aborigines Protection Board (NSW), 240
'Advance Australia Fair', x, *140*, 141–2, 173
Antarctica, 218–19
Antipodean Manifesto, 284–6
Anzac Day, ix, 220, 225, 231–2
'Anzac Requiem', ix, x
Anzacs, xii, 220–3, *224*, 225–30, 231–2
ANZUS Treaty, x, 254, *274*, 275–8
Apology, National, xii, 338–49, *338*, *342–3*
Archibald, J.F., viii, 202–3
art, 135, 143, 152, *153*, 154–5, 206–8, 284–6
Arthur, George, 81–4
Arthur, Walter George, 109–11
arts, 306–7
    see also art; film; literature; music; theatre
Ashmead-Bartlett, Ellis, 220–3, 225
Australasia (Wentworth), 70–3
Australia, named, 58–60
Australia Council, 306–7
Australia Day, viii, 31
Australia Felix, 103–5
Australian (Murdoch), *290*, 291–2
Australian (Wentworth), 74–7
Australian Constitutions Act 1850, 85
Australian Labor Party (ALP), 165, 254, 265, 272–3, 275, 302–3, *302*, 304–5, 306, 314–17, *316*, 331
    see also Chifley, Ben; Curtin, John; Keating, Paul; Rudd, Kevin; Whitlam, Gough
Australian Rules football, 128–9, *130–1*

banking, 64–6, *66*
Bank of New South Wales, 64–6, *66*
Banks, Joseph, 5, 9–12, *9*, 15, 17–19, 20, 22, 58
Barton, Edmund, 194–8, *194*, 199
Barwick, Garfield, 314, 317
basic wage, 209–11
Bathurst, Lord, 67
Batman, John, 88–9, *90–1*, 92, *93*, 94
Bean, C.E.W., x, 220, 225
Beazley, Kim (junior), 334
Beazley, Kim (senior), 287
Bigge, John Thomas, 45, 67–9, *68*
Black Friday bushfires, 242–5, *244*
Black power, 299
Blaxland, Gregory, 61–3
Blue Mountains crossing, 61–3
Bodyline cricket, 236–7, *236*
Bolte, Henry, 295
border protection, 334–5
Botany Bay (NSW), 5, 9, 20, 27, 31, 53–5
Bourke, Richard, 95–6, *97*, 98–100
Bradman, Don, 236
Brennan, Gerard, 327–9
Brisbane, Sir Thomas, 64, 74
Britain, links with, 156–9, 195, 196–8, 199, 204–5, 213, 236–7, 246, 254, 321–4, *322*
Bryant, Gordon, 287
Bulletin, viii, 148, 202
Burke, Robert O'Hara, *134*, 135–7, *136*
bushfires, 242–5, *244*

Cahill, J.J., 281–2, *281*, 283
Calwell, Arthur, 293
Canberra, 215–16, *217*
capital punishment, 295–8
Chamberlain, Lindy, 318–20, *319*
Charter of Justice, 47–9, *50*–1

Charter of Human Rights, 182, 336–7
Chifley, Ben, xi, 269–71, *269*, 272–3
Christmas celebrations, 119
Collins, David, 31, 45, *52*, 53–5, 57
Commonwealth of Australia, inauguration, 141, 186–9, *189*, 191, 194, 199
Commonwealth of Australia Constitution Act, ix, 182, *183*, 184–5
communism, 293, 302
Conder, Charles, 152
Constitution, Australian, 182, *183*, 184–5, 191, 299–301, *300*, 339
convicts, viii, 85
    legacy of, 68, 74, 107
    numbers, 85, 107
    end of transportation, 85, *106*, 107–8
Cook, James, viii, 5–8, *5*, 9, 13–16, 17, 20, 55, 60
    treatment of, 27–30, 69
Coombs H.C. 'Nugget', 306
Cooper, William, 239
Copland, Douglas, 233
Corsali, Andrea, xii, 2, 3–4
courts of law, establishment of, 44, 45–6, 47–9, *50*–1
cricket, 148–9, *148*, 236–7, *236*
Curtin, John, xi, 251–3, *251*, 254–7, 265, 269, 272, 302

Darling, Ralph, 79, 98
Dawn, The, 150–1, *150*
Deane, William, 327–9, 331
Democratic Labor Party, 302
Depression, 1930s, 233–5, *235*
diggers, 120–2, *123*
    see also Anzacs

education, 112, 113–15
Eureka flag, xii, 3, 125, 165
Eureka rebellion, 3, *124*, 125–7, *127*
Evans, George W., 61–3
Evans, Ivor, 199
exploration, 61–3, 103–5, *103*, 116, 132–3, *132*, *134*, 135–7, *136*

fascism, 233
Fawkner, John Pascoe, 92

Federation, xii, xiii, 141, 156–9, *156*, 177, 182, *183*, 184–5, 186–9, 191, 194–8, 199, 299
Felton, Alfred, 206–8
Fergusson, James, 138
Field, Barron, 64
film, 158, 202, 220, 318
First Fleet, viii, 27, 31, 45, *52*, 53–5, *54*, 239
First World War, x, xii, 173, 220–3, *224*, 225–30, 231–2, *231*
Fisher, Andrew, 225
Fitzroy, Charles, 107
flag, Australian, xii, 3, 199, *200*, 201
 see also Eureka flag
Flinders, Matthew, 58–60, *58*
Flinders Island, 109–11, *110*
'forgotten people, the', 258–64, 334
Franklin, Miles, x, xiii, 202–3, *202*, 279-80
Fraser, Malcolm, 314, 325
Fremantle, Charles, 79
Friend, Matthew, 110

Gallipoli landing, x, xii, 220–3, *224*, 225–30, 231, 232
Gaudron, Mary, 327–9
Geelong, 88
Gellibrand, Joseph Tice, 88
gold rushes, xii–xiii, 116–19, 120–2, *123*, *124*, 125–7, *127*, 206
Goossens, Eugene, 281
Gorton, John, 306
governor-general, 186, 187–9, *190*, 191–3
Gowrie, Lord, 251
Grassby, Albert Jaime, 311
Gray, Charles, *134*, 135–7, *136*
Grey, Earl, 107
Grimwade, F.S., 206, 207
Gurindji people, 308–10, *309*

Hamilton, Ian, 225, 226–30
Hardy, Frank, 308
Harvester judgment, 209–11
Hawke, Bob, 321, *322*, 325
Higgins, Henry Bournes, 209–11, *209*
High Court of Australia, 186, 194
Hindmarsh, John, 101
Hope, John Adrian Louis (Lord Hopetoun), 191

Howard, John, 258, 275, 334–5
Howitt, Alfred William, 116
Howitt, William, xii, 116–19
Hunter, John, 27, 53, 54

immigration, 116
 see also border controls; gold rushes; multiculturalism; White Australia
independence, Australian, 85, 321–4
 see also Commonwealth of Australia, inauguration; Federation
Indigenous Australians *see* Aboriginal Australians

Jardine, Douglas, 236–7
Jeanneret, Henry, 109–11
Jerilderie Letter, 143–5, *146–7*
Johnson, Lyndon B., 293, 294

Keating, Paul, 272, 327, 331, 339
Kelly, Ned, 143–5, *145*, *146–7*
Kerr, John, 191, 314–17, *316*
King, John, *134*, 135, *136*

labour movement, 165–9, *166*
 see also Australian Labor Party; unions
landscape, Australian, 103–5, 116–19
Latham, Mark, 275
La Trobe, C.J., 125
Lawson, Henry, 150, 165
Lawson, Louisa, 150–1, *150*, *151*
Lawson, William, 61–3
Liberal–Country Party coalition *see* Liberal Party
Liberal Party, 258–64, 302, 305, 306, 308, 334–5
 see also Howard, John; Menzies, Robert
'light on the hill, the', 272–3
Lingiari, Vincent, 308–10, *309*
literature, x, xiii, *52*, 53–5, 116–19, 120–2, *123*, 132–3, 135, 143–5, *146–7*, 165, 180, 202–3, *212*, 213–14, 220–3, 225–30, *225*, 258, 279–80, 308, 318, 331
Lockyer, Edmund, 79
Lyons, Enid, 239, 265–8, *265*
Lyons, Joseph, 239, 265

Mabo, Eddie Koiki, 327–9, *329*
Mabo judgment, 13, 327–9, 339
McCormick, Peter Dodds, *140*, 141–2
McEwen, John, 239
Mackellar, Dorothea, x, *212*, 213–14, *213*
McMahon, William, 302
Macpherson, Christina, 173, *173*, 174–5, 176
Macquarie, Lachlan, 58, 61, 64, 67, 70
'Man from Snowy River, The', 160–4, *160*, *161*
mapping Australia, 58–60
Mason, Anthony, 327–9
Matra, James, 20–4
Mawson, Douglas, 218–19, *218*
media *see* newspapers
Medici, Giuliano de, xii, 3
Melbourne, Batman and, 88–9, *90–1*, 92, *93*, 94
Menzies, R.G., xi, 246–50, *246*, 258–64, 272, 293–4, 334
middle class, 258–64, 262–8
Miles Franklin Award, 279–80
Mitchell, David Scott, 180–1
Mitchell, Thomas, 103–5, *103*
Mitchell Library, 160, 180–1, *212*, 213–14, 279
Molesworth, William, 107
Monash, John, 231–2, *231*
multiculturalism, 311–13, 325–6
 see also White Australia
Munro, James, 171
Munro, Jane, 171
Murdoch, Keith, 225–30
Murdoch, Rupert, *290*, 291–2
Murdoch, William 'Billy' Lloyd, 148–9, *148*
music, *140*, 141–2, 173, *173*, 174–5, 176, 281–2, *281*, *283*, 318
'My Country', x, *212*, 213–14, *213*

national capital, 215–16, *217*
national character, 220, 231, 231–2
 see also Anzacs; multiculturalism; White Australia
National Gallery of Victoria, 206–8
New Holland, 5, 15, 58, 59–60, 79, 80, 85
New South Wales, 215, 239–41
 development of, 67–8, 75, 107–8, 157, 158
 female suffrage, 177
 named, 13
 opera house, 281–2, *281*, *283*

settlement proposed, 17–19, 20–4
newspapers, Australian, 74–7, 120, 150–1, *150, 151*, 154, 165, 220, *290, 291–2*
Newton, Maxwell, *290, 291–2*
New Zealand, 6, 8, 156, 157, 171, 177, 201, 218, 336
    ANZUS Treaty, 274, 275–8
    see also Anzacs
Nolan, Sidney, 135, 143
Northern Territory, 239, 287–8, *289*, 308–10, *309*, 318–20, *319*

Opera House, Sydney, 281–2, *281, 283*, 318
Overland Telegraph Line, x, 132, 138–9, *138*

Parkes, Henry, 156–9, *156,*
parliament, women and, 177, 265–8, *265*
Paterson, A.B. 'Banjo', 160–4, *160, 161*, 173, *173, 174–5*, 176
Patten, J.T., *238*, 239, 240–1
Pearce, George, 225
petitions, 109–11, *124, 125–7, 127,* 170, 171–2, 287–8, *288*
Phillip, Arthur, viii, 25–6, *25,* 27–8, 31–5, 36–44, 57
printing, early, *56,* 57
Proclamation Day (SA), 101, *102*

Queensland, 157, 158, 165–9, *166*
    female suffrage, 177, 218
Queensland Labourers' Union, 165–9
Queensland Shearers' Union, 165–9

racial discrimination, xiii, 194, 204–5, 311–13, 325–6, 338–49, *338, 342–3*
    see also Aboriginal Australians; multiculturalism; White Australia
Read, Peter, 331
reconciliation, viii, xii, 182, 331–3
referendums, 182, 299–301, *300,* 339
religion, 98–100, *101*
republicanism, 125, 182
reserve powers, 191, 314–17
Richardson, Henry Handel, 103
Rights, Charter of Human, 182, 336–7
Roberts, Tom, 152
Rodgers, Don, 254–7

Rudd, Kevin, 336, 338–49, *338, 342–3*
Ryan, Ronald, 295–8

Scullin, James, 233
Second Fleet, 107
Second World War, xi, xii, 254–7, 302, 336
    declaration, 246–50, *246,* 251–3, *251*
    end of, 269–71, 272, 294
Shackleton, Ernest, 218
shearers' strike, 165–9, *166*
Smith, Bernard, 284–6
Smith, James, 154
Solander, Daniel, 5, 9, 15
South Australia, 138–9, 157, 158, 182
    female suffrage, 177–8, *179*
    settlement of, 101–2, *102*
Southern Cross constellation, xii, 2, 3–4, 199, 201
South Pole, 218
sport, 128–9, *130–1,* 148–9, *148,* 236–7, *236*
Starke, John, 295
Stirling, James, 79
Stolen Generations, xii, *330,* 331–3, 338–49, *338, 342–3*
Streeton, Arthur, 152
Stretton, L.E.B. 242–5
strike action, 165–9, *166*
Stuart, John McDouall, 132–3, *132*
Swan River Colony *see* Western Australia

Tampa, MV, 334
Tasman, Abel, 6
Tasmania, 85, 88, 158, 195, 265
    Aboriginal Australians, 81–4, 109–11, *110*
    female suffrage, 177
    martial law, 81–4, *82*
Tench, Watkin, viii
Terra Australis Incognita, 5
terra nullius, 13, 88
    defined, 95–6, *97,* 327–9
    see also Aboriginal Australians
theatre, *56, 57,* 306
Thomson, George Edward, 125
Todd, Charles, 138–9
Torres Strait Islander people, 327–9, *329*
    see also Aboriginal Australians
transit of Venus, 5, 6, 9

transportation *see* convicts

unions, 150, 165–9, *166,* 209
United Australia Party, 265–8
universities, Australian, 113
University of Sydney, *112,* 113–15
US alliance, ix, x, 254–7, 274, 275–8, 293–4, 334
Utzon, Jørn, 281–2

Vancouver, George, 79
Van Diemen's Land *see* Tasmania
Victoria, 157, 158, 215, 262, 284–6
    bushfires, 242–5, *244*
    capital punishment, 295–8
    charter of human rights, 336–7
    female suffrage, *170,* 171–2, 177
    settlement of, 103
    see also Melbourne
Vietnam War, 293–4, *294*

Wakefield, Edward Gibbon, 101–2
'Waltzing Matilda', 141, 173, *173, 174–5,* 176
Wardell, Robert, 74
Wave Hill, 308–10, *309*
Wedge, John Helder, 92
Western Australia, 182, 218, 233
    settlement of, *78,* 79–80, 85–6, *87*
Westpac, 64
Wentworth, William Charles, x, 61–3, 70–73, *70,* 74–7
White, Surgeon General John, 53
White Australia, xiii, 194, 204–5, 311–13
Whitlam, Gough, 191, 293, 302–3, *302,* 304–5, 306, 308–10, *309,* 311, 314–17, *316,* 325
Wills, Thomas Wentworth, 128
Wills, William John, *134,* 135, *136,* 137
Wilson, Ronald, 331–3
Withers, W.B., 120
women, first parliamentarian, 265–8, *265*
    suffrage, *170,* 171–2, 177–8, *179,* 218
    unionism, 150
Woodfull, Bill, *236,* 237
writing about Australia *see* literature
Wylde, John, 64

Yolngu people, 287–8, *289*